WRITING THE LANDSCAPE
EXPOSING NATURE IN FRENCH WOMEN'S FICTION 1789–1815

LEGENDA

LEGENDA is the Modern Humanities Research Association's book imprint for new research in the Humanities. Founded in 1995 by Malcolm Bowie and others within the University of Oxford, Legenda has always been a collaborative publishing enterprise, directly governed by scholars. The Modern Humanities Research Association (MHRA) joined this collaboration in 1998, became half-owner in 2004, in partnership with Maney Publishing and then Routledge, and has since 2016 been sole owner. Titles range from medieval texts to contemporary cinema and form a widely comparative view of the modern humanities, including works on Arabic, Catalan, English, French, German, Greek, Italian, Portuguese, Russian, Spanish, and Yiddish literature. Editorial boards and committees of more than 60 leading academic specialists work in collaboration with bodies such as the Society for French Studies, the British Comparative Literature Association and the Association of Hispanists of Great Britain & Ireland.

The MHRA encourages and promotes advanced study and research in the field of the modern humanities, especially modern European languages and literature, including English, and also cinema. It aims to break down the barriers between scholars working in different disciplines and to maintain the unity of humanistic scholarship. The Association fulfils this purpose through the publication of journals, bibliographies, monographs, critical editions, and the MHRA Style Guide, and by making grants in support of research. Membership is open to all who work in the Humanities, whether independent or in a University post, and the participation of younger colleagues entering the field is especially welcomed.

ALSO PUBLISHED BY THE ASSOCIATION

Critical Texts
Tudor and Stuart Translations • *New Translations* • *European Translations*
MHRA Library of Medieval Welsh Literature

MHRA Bibliographies
Publications of the Modern Humanities Research Association

The Annual Bibliography of English Language & Literature
Austrian Studies
Modern Language Review
Portuguese Studies
The Slavonic and East European Review
Working Papers in the Humanities
The Yearbook of English Studies

www.mhra.org.uk
www.legendabooks.com

Writing the Landscape

Exposing Nature in
French Women's Fiction 1789–1815

❖

CHRISTIE MARGRAVE

l

LEGENDA

Modern Humanities Research Association

2019

Published by Legenda
an imprint of the Modern Humanities Research Association
Salisbury House, Station Road, Cambridge CB1 2LA

ISBN 978-1-78188-704-2 (HB)
ISBN 978-1-78188-435-5 (PB)

First published 2019
Paperback edition 2021

Copy-Editor: Priscilla Sheringham

CONTENTS

❖

ACKNOWLEDGEMENTS

❖

'Thank you' are two very small words, which scarcely do justice to what I wish to express with these acknowledgements. My thanks go to David Culpin and David Evans, the co-supervisors of my doctoral thesis, who were unfailing in their support throughout, and whose thought-provoking discussions helped shape the project. I would also like to thank my thesis examiners, Katherine Astbury and Julia Prest, who provided stimulating discussion and suggestions with regard to the preparation of this manuscript for publication. I am indebted, too, to the publisher's reader, Mary Orr, who saw what the thesis could become and whose invaluable advice helped turn this manuscript into what it is.

I gratefully acknowledge financial support from the University of St Andrews for granting me a University Scholarship over the course of my doctoral research, and from Santander for awarding me a bursary to attend the NeMLA annual convention in 2013. I am also grateful to La Sorbonne, to Bangor, Cardiff and Aberystwyth Universities, and to the Australian National University, who have all given me gainful employment throughout the course of finishing this project. Merci and diolch yn fawr.

I would like to thank the staff of the Bibliothèque nationale de France, the National Library of Scotland, the Taylorian, the Bodleian, and St Andrews University Special Collections who have responded to my queries and helped me to locate the texts I needed. My thanks also go to the Bibliothèque interuniversitaire de santé in Paris for providing the illustrations for the introduction, the Réunion des musées nationaux in Paris for providing the illustrations for Chapter 2, and the U.S. National Library of Medicine for providing the illustration for Chapter 3. I am grateful, too, to Murdo Macdonald for helping me to identify the image of Ossian and Malvina for Chapter 5.

A number of scholars, colleagues and friends have helped me by listening to and discussing my ideas, or by providing support and encouragement over the course of my research. Thank you to Helen Abbott, Stacie Allan, Caroline Aoudia, Nicolas Bourgès, Miriam Buncombe, Kirsty Carpenter, Ellen Carter, Simon Cartwright, Charlotte Cranfield, Jessica Dallender-Jones, Gillian Dow, Ian Fookes, Karen Forbes, Chloe Goodall, Alison Hales, Anna Harbinson, Katie Hawksworth, Marion Heuchert, Stephanie Innes, Rachael Langford, Manon Mathias, Lorna Milne, Graham Nelson, Licínia Pereira, Jennifer Rowe, Anna Saunders, Catriona Seth, Clare Siviter, Richard Wehko, and Margaux Whiskin, who have all, between them, provided hours of stimulating discussion and many reassuring words. Particular thanks go to my copy editor, Cilla Sheringham, and also to Katherine Astbury, Géraldine Crahay, David Culpin, Julie Duran-Gelléri, David Evans,

Aimee Linekar, Marie MacPherson, David McCallam, Ruselle Meade, Helena Miguelez-Carballeira, Mary Orr, Linda Shortt, and Benjamine Toussaint who have read through sections of this monograph at various stages of its development. They are, of course, in no way responsible for any errors or inapt expressions; that responsibility lies with me alone.

Finally, I would like to thank my parents, Elaine and Colin Margrave. They have provided the greatest moral support of all over the years I have worked on this project, and have been its chief financial source. Thanks to Mum, who first inspired in me a love of literature and a feminist spirit, and to Dad, who worked night shifts for forty years so I would never have to.

This book is dedicated to all those suffering from PhD-related mental health struggles. Please approach someone that you trust and talk to them. You can get there. You will get there. This book is the proof.

ABBREVIATIONS,
QUOTATIONS AND TRANSLATIONS

❖

Material from the corpus of primary texts analysed in this monograph will be referenced with the following abbreviations and relevant page numbers in parenthesis immediately following the quotations:

AS *Adèle de Sénange* (Mme de Souza, 1794)
É *Émilie et Alphonse* (Mme de Souza, 1799)
C d'A *Claire d'Albe* (Mme Cottin, 1799)
LMR *Les Mères rivales ou la calomnie* (Mme de Genlis, 1800), hereafter *Les Mères rivales*
M *Malvina* (Mme Cottin, 1800–1801)
D *Delphine* (Mme de Staël, 1802)
AM *Amélie Mansfield* (Mme Cottin, 1802–1803)
V *Valérie* (Mme de Krüdener, 1803)
Mat *Mathilde, ou mémoires tirés de l'histoire des croisades* (Mme Cottin, 1805), hereafter *Mathilde*
C *Corinne, ou l'Italie* (Mme de Staël, 1807), hereafter *Corinne*

The full bibliographical references for each of these novels can be found in the bibliography.

All spellings in quotations taken from eighteenth- and nineteenth-century French texts have been modernized throughout. (This includes the removal of several nominal capitalizations in the letters from Mme de Krüdener to Bernardin de Saint-Pierre.) All translations are my own unless otherwise stated; however, I owe my thanks to Priscilla Sheringham, David Culpin, Benjamin Toussaint, Julie Duran-Gelléri and Géraldine Crahay for their proofreading of them.

In referring to Mme de Genlis, Mme de Krüdener, Mme de Souza and Mme de Staël by surname only, some scholars use 'Genlis', 'Krüdener', 'Souza' and 'Staël' and others 'de Genlis', etc.. The present discussion will employ the former. The sole exceptions to this practice are found when quoting from other scholars who have chosen to employ 'de'; in this case the quotation is not altered.

I have employed capitalized and unitalicized formatting for the term 'Ancien Régime' throughout. The sole exceptions to this practice are found when quoting from other scholars who have employed *ancien régime*, ancien régime, or *Ancien Régime;* in these cases the quotations are not altered. Similarly I have hyphenated the term pre-Romanticism and retained the capital 'R'; however, when quoting from scholars who do not, I have not altered their spellings.

LIST OF ILLUSTRATIONS

❖

INTRODUCTION

❖

A Landscape of One's Own

La nature les avait faites nos esclaves; [...] la femme est notre propriété, nous ne sommes pas la sienne; car elle nous donne des enfants, et l'homme ne lui en donne pas. Elle est donc sa propriété comme l'arbre à fruit est celle du jardinier.

[Nature made them our slaves; [...] woman is our property, we are not hers; for she gives us children, not vice versa. She is therefore a man's property, like the fruit tree is that of the gardener.]

NAPOLÉON BONAPARTE,
Napoléon: Ses opinions et jugements sur les hommes et sur les choses[1]

Le souffle du vent avait un son harmonieux, et répandait dans l'air des accords qui semblaient venir du balancement des fleurs, de l'agitation des arbres, et prêter une voix à la nature.

[The wind breathed melodious harmonies through the air, which all seemed to come from the swaying of the flowers and the rustle of the trees, lending a voice to nature.]

MME DE STAËL, *Corinne*[2]

If she is to make her voice heard amid the male canon, a woman writer must have her own space in which to do so — a room of one's own — argued Virginia Woolf famously in the early twentieth century. A little over one hundred years earlier, French women writers Mme Cottin, Mme de Krüdener, Mme de Genlis, Mme de Souza and Mme de Staël had already identified such a space as a platform for their voices and those of their heroines. This space was not a room or building that they possessed (a part of the domestic sphere), but rather was to be found amid the natural landscapes they created within their fictional works. Their choice to adopt 'a landscape of one's own' is the subject of this book because the androcentric society of the First Republic and First Empire, in which these writers lived, invoked the supposed traditional link between women and nature to subordinate women, not empower them. In order to do so, it drew on both the widely accepted sentiments regarding women and nature in Rousseau's *Émile ou de l'Éducation* (1762)[3] and the scientific writings of eighteenth-century physicians such as Pierre Roussel, Pierre-Jean-Georges Cabanis and Julien Offroy de La Mettrie.[4] Arguments like those made by Napoleon, above, were consequently ubiquitous.[5] Yet, as this book will argue, writers like Cottin, Genlis, Krüdener, Souza and Staël employ images of the natural landscape strategically to re-establish a platform for the female voice — their own, at the same time as that of their literary heroines. In so doing, they expose and confront the social and creative restrictions placed on their sex, challenge the prevalent eighteenth-century argument that a woman's essence defines her existence, and thus carve a vital place for themselves in literary history.

This vital place has not yet been accorded the critical attention it merits for two reasons: firstly, the novels themselves have largely been forgotten, and secondly, even where scholarship has recently begun to recognize the works of women writers of this era, it has overlooked their portrayal of natural landscape. A re-evaluation of the natural settings within the novels of the aforementioned women writers will bring a new dimension to our appreciation of their works and critical stance.

Despite their immense distinction during their lifetimes,[6] Cottin, Krüdener, Souza, and Genlis fell into obscurity after their deaths for over 150 years; Staël alone retained her literary fame. Consequently, as Brigitte Louichon argues, for many decades we have ignored an entire section of French literary history: that which falls between the canonical male names of the early eighteenth century (such as Voltaire and Rousseau) and those of the nineteenth (Hugo, Stendhal, Balzac).[7] Louichon stresses the need to study the female voices who published between the appearance of Rousseau's *Julie ou la Nouvelle Héloïse* and the advent of the nineteenth-century Romantics. In doing so, this monograph will show that far from simply bridging the gap between these two eras, women writers build on and challenge the former, and help pave the way for the latter.

Alison Finch argues that women writers were generally forgotten because of their very status as women.[8] For Joan Hinde Stewart, however, it is more a case of their subject matter:

> The questions that they raise — the passionate nature of women, the economic necessity and indeed the very possibility of marrying and remarrying, the liveability of contemporary marriage, the significance of mothering and domesticity — [...] didn't appear sufficiently important to the literary establishment.[9]

It is true that women tended to favour the sentimental novel: the most acceptable genre in which they might publish. As Margaret Cohen states, '[s]entimentality begins at home', and the home and hearth constituted the permitted domain of women.[10] Women's penchant for sentimental novels has, however, led many critics to take their writing at face value as apolitical and domestic, at odds with France's violent convulsions. Scholarly comments have not only been dismissive but also condescending; Allan H. Pasco, for example, refers to 'Mme Cottin's sentimental drivel'.[11] Building on Claire Jacquier's argument that modern scholars have been particularly dismissive of the sentimental novel in general,[12] Katherine Astbury argues that this attitude is compounded further in studies of the period following the 1789 Revolution 'where such texts carry a double stigma of being sentimental *and* "non-political" at a time when the Nation is reinventing itself'.[13] Women's novels of this era are not apolitical; the Nation's process of reinventing itself included defining the role of women, and female novelists had comments to make in this respect. This was an era in which women were 'factually and legally excluded from the political public sphere',[14] expected to refrain from writing and publishing, restricted to roles as mothers, and 'denied the vote in 1789, prohibited from political mobilization during the Terror, denied civil equality within marriage, and, finally, with the promulgation of the Civil Code in 1804, legally subordinated to the will of their husbands'.[15] Female authors examine the effects of such contemporary socio-political restrictions on their sex: Genlis writes on women's education; Staël, Cottin and Genlis discuss the difficulties confronted by talented women who wish to enter the public sphere; Cottin and Krüdener discuss the notion of the 'ideal woman' and the unrealistic expectations projected on to her; Genlis and Krüdener write about 'ideal motherhood' and the suffering women faced as mothers; and arranged or forbidden marriages feature in novels by all of these women.

Only recently have the female novelists of the Revolutionary period and First Empire been rediscovered and their writings examined in comparison with one another, leading to conclusions that women's writing has its own socio-political role to play.[16] Colette Cazenobe shows how women wrote in order to express unhappiness and argues that the eighteenth-century feminine novel was the precursor to the feminist novel of later centuries. Carla Hesse and Chantal Bertrand-Jennings argue that in leaving out the approach of women writers, we fail to understand a significant portion of the literary movements we study. Hesse talks of an 'Other Enlightenment', addressing women's clear participation in the public sphere of debate despite the increasing restrictions imposed upon them. Similarly, Bertrand-Jennings describes an *autre mal du siècle*, arguing that women's writing of nineteenth-century France addresses a very different ennui and melancholy from the traditional *mal du siècle* generally recognized as a male phenomenon and as a core theme of Romanticism.[17] The subtle power of eighteenth- and early nineteenth-century women's novels has been addressed by Stewart, as well as by Aurora Wolfgang and Kirsty Carpenter.[18] For, if women were to approach a discussion of hot political topics in an era in which they faced controversy over whether they should be writing at all, it was inevitable that their comments often be made subtly. Stewart styles women's fiction a 'covert female rebellion', arguing that 'protest in the novel is masked and mediated'.[19] Similarly, Wolfgang argues that women writers appear to conform to the status quo, whilst nonetheless criticising it,[20] and Carpenter states that Souza uses her novels as 'a way of preserving detachment and at the same time entering into a much more political arena than most women could gain access to'.[21]

The second reason why the vital contribution of women's sentimental novels to the literary field has not been fully explored is that one of the subtle means by which women writers addressed controversial issues remains overlooked. This is the creation of a 'landscape of one's own'. Thus far, scholars have been dismissive of the portrayal of landscape setting in French women's novels of this era, describing it as either unimportant or almost non-existent. Finch argues that women writers 'normally avoided sensuous description of landscape'.[22] Similarly, Cohen states: 'The effacement of description characterizes the sentimental novel [...]. Sentimental novels delineate setting and the material aspect of characters only with a few attributes that are often common place'.[23] According to Machteld de Poortere, 'Genlis avoids long descriptions of nature';[24] Sainte-Beuve argues that 'Mme de Souza d'ordinaire s'arrête peu à décrire la nature' ['Mme de Souza ordinarily has little to say about nature'];[25] Leslie Sykes states that in Cottin's *Malvina* '[l]es descriptions de paysages sont fort rares et toutes conventionnelles' ['descriptions of nature are very rare and all conventional'],[26] in *Amélie Mansfield,* landscape description comprises only clichés,[27] and that *Mathilde*, 'n'est guère plus riche à cet égard' ['is hardly richer in this respect'].[28] So far, only Dana Chase has attempted to begin examining how women's writing 'uses images drawn from nature to address the problems posed by the limitations [...] on women'.[29] Chase addresses issues relating to marriage within Cottin's *Claire d'Albe* and Souza's *Adèle de Sénange,* yet there are many more novels and several other female preoccupations (in addition to a lack of marital freedom) which deserve equal critical attention; moreover, the conclusions to be drawn from extensive analyses of the use of nature across post-revolutionary women's novels can be extended much further.

It seems unlikely that women writers stop to describe nature so rarely in their novels when in fact they often drew inspiration from nature. Yet, conclusions have sometimes been hastily made in this regard, too. As George M. Baker argues, literary critics have repeatedly cited one utterance 'as evidence that the enjoyment of natural scenery was not necessary to Madame de Staël'.[30] According to Sainte-Beuve, Staël is reported to have said:

> Si ce n'était le respect humain, je n'ouvrirais pas ma fenêtre pour voir la baie de Naples pour la première fois, tandis que je ferais cinq cents lieues pour aller causer avec un homme d'esprit que je ne connais pas.

> [Were it not out of respect for what other people think, I would not open my window to see the bay of Naples for the first time, yet I would travel five hundred leagues to talk with a clever man that I did not know].[31]

Baker states that these words 'have since been repeatedly adduced as sufficient proof that she was incapable of either appreciating or interpreting nature';[32] yet he questions assumptions based on this one utterance. Indeed, in a letter to Jean-Baptiste-Antoine Suard in 1805 Staël describes the scenery of the Neapolitan countryside very differently: 'J'ai plus senti la nature ici que je ne l'ai sentie partout ailleurs. Le midi a quelque chose d'actif qui vous parle comme un ami ou vous réveille comme une fête. C'est à Naples que je l'ai senti' [I have appreciated nature here more than anywhere else. There is something active in the South which speaks to you like a friend or awakens you like a celebration. It is in Naples that I have felt this].[33] Similarly, in a letter to the poet Monti, she writes: 'j'ai senti moi-même à Naples cette sorte d'enthousiasme qui tient à l'air, aux parfums, aux merveilles de la nature, et les vers que je vous lirai l'expriment' ['in Naples, I myself have felt that sort of enthusiasm which clings to the air, to the fragrances, to the wonders of nature, and the verses which I will read to you express this'].[34] Staël's *Corinne* echoes, almost exactly, the thoughts on the Neapolitan countryside which appear in her correspondence.

Cottin's correspondence also reveals a strong love of natural landscape, which permeates her novels. In 1803, she wrote to her brother-in-law, André, full of praise for the Bagnères countryside:

> J'ai éprouvé un plaisir si doux et si vif à revoir mes belles montagnes, mes eaux si limpides, mes vertes et fraîches prairies, qu'il me serait impossible de ne pas vous en dire quelque chose; l'effet que produit sur moi la vue de ce pays-ci est bizarre et, quoique toujours le même, il me surprend toujours.

> [I experienced a pleasure so sweet and so lively on seeing once again my beautiful mountains, my crystal clear waters, and my green and fresh meadows, that it would be impossible not to speak to you of it. The effect that the sight of this country has on me is strange and, although it never changes, it constantly surprises me].[35]

Cottin's reading of works by other sentimental novelists also heightened her appreciation of nature. She tells Bernardin de Saint-Pierre: 'Jadis, au milieu des plaisirs de Paris, je regrettais la nature. Elle me plaît davantage depuis que je la vois tous les jours; vos ouvrages m'apprennent à l'aimer mieux encore' [I used to miss nature when I was in the midst of the pleasures of Paris. I appreciate it all the more now I see it every day. Your works are teaching me to love it better still].[36]

Krüdener also wrote to Bernardin about her love of the natural world: 'Non jamais je n'oublierai cette matineé cette émotion attendrissante, si pure si vive, que j'éprouvai au moment du réveil de la nature. C'était comme si je sentais pour la première fois aussi le réveil de mon cœur' ['No, never will I forget this morning and this sweet emotion, so pure, so lively, that I felt at the moment of nature's awakening. It was as if I also felt my own heart's awakening for the first time'].[37] Krüdener's sentiments echo those of Staël and Cottin. It should hardly be surprising, therefore, that these women include frequent, often lengthy, descriptions of nature in their novels, correspondence or journals, or that they should impute an expressive value to it. This is also the case with Souza and Genlis. Genlis's love of nature led her to encourage the teaching of botany to children and to her writing a work entitled *La Botanique historique et littéraire* [*Historical and Literary Botany*], and Souza's husband was the Intendant of the King's Gardens, 'increas[ing] the chances that she may have been privy to court discussions about the recent re-landscaping of Versailles'.[38]

In overlooking the importance of nature to these women writers and particularly the descriptions of natural landscapes within their novels, scholars have left a significant aspect of the burgeoning field of women's writing unexplored. Therefore, when the title of this monograph speaks of 'exposing nature', it is with more than one purpose. In exposing the fact that nature plays a crucial role in the novels' construction, and in exposing the natural landscapes within the novels to close scrutiny and literary analysis, this monograph is able to examine precisely what social and creative restrictions women writers themselves exposed through their creation of a 'landscape of one's own'.

Before examining how natural landscapes are both apt and powerful spaces for critiquing the socio-political status quo, particularly for women, it is first important to note the ways in which the terms 'space', 'place' and 'landscape' will be employed in this study, since continual reference will be made to them throughout. Finding adequate and convergent definitions, particularly of the first two, is challenging.

As Doreen Massey argues, 'the terms space and place have long histories and bear with them a multiplicity of meanings and connotations which reverberate with other debates'.[39] The number of entries allocated to both terms in the *Oxford English Dictionary* is testament to this. Humanist geographers identify 'space' as something abstract and empty, and define 'place' as space imbued with meaning by those who experience and react to it.[40] Their working definitions are largely based on the notion that '[p]lace is specific and location (or space) is general'.[41] However, as Tim Cresswell has made clear, '[a]lthough this basic dualism of space and place runs through much of human geography since the 1970s it is confused somewhat by the idea of social space — or socially produced space — which, in many ways, plays the same role as place'.[42]

The *OED* definitions of space involve, firstly, 'denoting time or duration'.[43] Secondly, they largely comprise entries denoting area sufficient for a certain purpose, or physical expanse of room delimited in some way.[44] This basic definition and the humanist geographers' general, 'empty' definition of 'space', do not take into account the many considerations of space developed over the years by philosophers and literary theorists. Indeed, as Michel Foucault argues, 'Bachelard's monumental work and the descriptions of phenomenologists have taught us that we do not live in an homogeneous and empty space, but on the contrary in a space thoroughly imbued with quantities'.[45] In his seminal work on space,[46] Henri Lefebvre argues 'that space is understood as physical and social landscape which is imbued with meaning in everyday place-bound social practices and emerges through processes that operate over varying spatial and temporal scales'.[47] Massey talks of the 'social relations of space', and space's consequent connections with both gender and class relations.[48] Certainly the domestic ideology of the eighteenth century gendered both social and political space. Gaston Bachelard has made the world aware of the personal, emotional and imaginary connotations attached to space.[49] Foucault's work, aligning space with knowledge and power, has drawn attention to the intellectual dimension of space.[50] Taking into account all these connotations, when the present study refers to the term 'space', it implies not only 'the physical or mental sphere within which a person lives or operates',[51] but also, more deeply, the philosophical sense of being situated somewhere in a social, emotional, or intellectual sphere which is often also profoundly personal and powerful. It may also refer to a duration of time.

John Agnew lists and evaluates the meanings attached by the *OED* to the term 'place':

> Along with its geographic meaning as 'portion of space in which people dwell together' and 'locality', place is also a 'rank' in a list (as 'in the first place'), a temporal ordering (as in something 'took place'), and a 'position' in a social order (as in 'knowing your place'). Notwithstanding this variety, over the greatest span of time it has been the geographic meanings of the term place that have been most important.[52]

For this reason, then, when 'place' is referred to in the present study, it will be taken to mean an actual geographical or historical location, a social position, or an ordinal rank.

The term 'landscape' as it will be employed in this study corresponds largely to that provided by Cresswell: 'a portion of the earth's surface that can be viewed from one spot' [...]. It combine[s] a focus on the material topography of a portion of land (that which can be seen) with the notion of vision (the way it is seen)'.[53] The definition provided by the *OED* corresponds to that of Cresswell: 'A view or prospect of natural inland scenery, such as can be taken in at a glance from one point of view'.[54] It is important to note that these definitions include the notion of vision or point of view, since the landscapes discussed in this study are frequently highly connected with both the personal and the emotional. It is also worth bearing in mind that the Earth's surface is intimately linked with its atmosphere and climate,[55] something noted even in the early-mid eighteenth century by Montesquieu, for whom '[c]limate interacts with landscape'.[56] Staël was also aware of these links as she, too, 'conflates nature and climate as she elaborates her own theory of climates'.[57] Therefore, when the present study refers to 'natural landscapes', it occasionally includes climatic as well as topographical elements of the areas in question. This is particularly the case when discussing desert and mountain landscapes, where the arid heat or the dense fog and cloud appear as much a part of the respective landscapes as do the sand or rock formations.

As consideration of socio-political history forms a large part of the present work, a word must also be added here regarding the use of the term 'post-revolutionary'. Between the outlying dates of the present study, France went from the Absolute Monarchy of the Ancien Régime, to a Constitutional Monarchy (1789–1791), to a Republic (established in 1792), to an Empire (1804–1815). In the Republic the country underwent a constant power struggle, with several political factions seizing control in turn. Whilst it is certain that in many respects writing under the Terror in 1794 was not the same as writing in 1804, the year the *Code Civil* was established, there are nonetheless certain aspects of socio-political history — particularly regarding the subordination of women — which do not change in essentials, though they may change in severity. Therefore, despite the influences of the various political overhauls in France on the lives of women writers, it is not possible to assign a clear agenda (regarding the preoccupations of women) to the woman's novel written in one particular year. Cottin's *Malvina* and Genlis's *Les Mères rivales* were both published in 1800, and both deal with the struggles of a mother whose child is taken from her, yet it is not possible to mark them out as novels specific to the political happenings of 1800, and therefore in that respect different from Krüdener's *Valérie* (1803) which also deals with a mother's struggle upon losing a child. Cottin's *Claire d'Albe* and Souza's *Émilie et Alphonse* were both published in 1799, and though both deal with the drastic consequences faced by a woman when she falls in love with a man forbidden to her, this does not mark these novels out as representative of the final year of the Directory for so doing. Cottin's *Malvina* (1800), *Amélie Mansfield* (1803) and Staël's *Corinne* (1807) also deal with the drastic consequences which arise from succumbing to forbidden love. *Claire d'Albe* and *Corinne* were published eight years apart, one under the Directory and the other under the Empire (three years after the introduction of the *Code Civil*), and yet both deal with the debate faced by many women in late eighteenth- and early nineteenth-century fiction over whether they should lead the dutiful lives expected of them or pursue their own happiness to the detriment of their duty. There are, therefore, literary staples which run across the whole period between the aftermath of the Revolution and the fall of the first Empire, particularly when women writers are addressing the problems faced by their own sex. These general staples involve discussions of marriage, motherhood, madness, death, and authorship. Each new system of government continued the attempt to prevent women from speaking their mind, despite the repeal of the censorship laws in 1789, and women writers (whether living in France, living as *émigrés* under the Terror, or living as exiles under Napoleon) continued to present the consequences of this repression in their novels. Consequently, whilst I will take into account the terms *émigré(e)*, Terror, Directory, Republic and Empire where they are relevant, for the purposes of the present discussion the phrases 'women writers under the First Republic and First Empire' or 'post-revolutionary women writers' will suffice for the majority of cases.

Nature's capacity to provide a space for challenging socio-political conventions is noted by Stephen Bending. In his discussion of 'eighteenth-century women and gardens they created, inhabited, and imagined', Bending argues that 'the shaping of physical space is the shaping also of identity, and that gardens are microcosms, speaking of and reacting to a world beyond themselves'.[58] He argues that a garden was 'designed to look beyond, and to resist domestic containment with its far-reaching views and a vision of large-scale change', and that therefore 'when we turn to accounts of gardening left to us by eighteenth-century women, passive acceptance of gender roles and the cultural narratives that support them is far from universal'.[59] Although Bending's work focuses on English literature, there are nonetheless striking parallels between his arguments and those which can be made regarding French women's writing of the same era, in which we do indeed find literary gardens designed both to promote controversial 'far-reaching views' and to 'resist domestic containment'. Furthermore, when analysing French women's writing from the period 1789–1815, Bending's statement can be expanded to cover not only gardens, but also several other types of natural landscape — including wild mountain scenery, deserts, volcanoes, rivers, parks, forests, and waterfalls — in which there was a particular interest among philosophers, writers, artists and the general public. However, before examining in detail the different landscapes which appear and the pertinence of each to the era, let us first consider why, as Bending argues, women might find nature a useful space of protest.

Nature has long been associated with women, even personified as the female figure Mother Nature. Historians, classicists, philosophers, social scientists, literary scholars and ecocritics have all commented on the woman-nature association.[60] In France, the association certainly pre-dates the eighteenth century. The concept existed in seventeenth-century religious discussion:

> As Pascal said, only some were allowed efficacious grace by God while the rest dwelt in the provenance of concupiscence. This represented a rigorous and unflinching anti-humanist position, while opposing perspectives were also framed as to emphasize the proximity of women to Nature.[61]

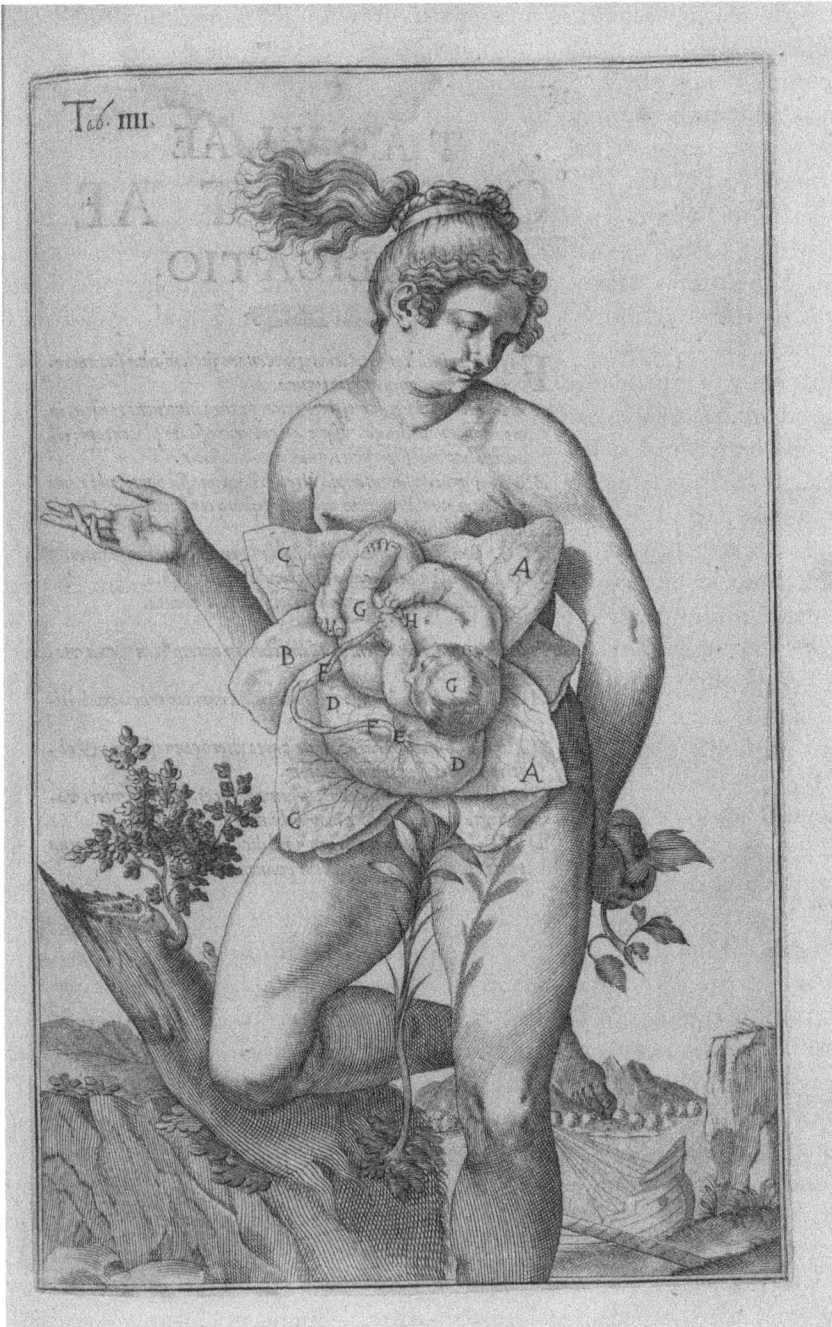

Fig. I.1. *Femme enceinte à l'abdomen ouvert* [*Pregnant Woman with Open Abdomen*], burin engraving in Adriaan Van de Spiegel, *De formato foetu liber singularis, aenis figuris exornatus* (Padua: Patavii, 1626). Image courtesy of: Paris, Bibliothèque interuniversitaire de santé (BIU santé).

Seventeenth-century scientific images also drew on the association, depicting pregnant female bodies surrounded by plants, or portraying the uterus itself as a flower with opening petals (see Figs. I.1 and I.2).

In the eighteenth century, the notion of nature as a feminine entity lies at the heart of the meaning of the word: the 1762 dictionary described nature as 'une bonne mère' ['a good mother'],[62] an image which reappears throughout the work of Rousseau, for whom 'la Nature [...] a tous les attributs de la maternité' ['Nature [...] has all the attributes of motherhood'].[63] Similarly, the *Encyclopédie* states: 'chez les poètes la nature est tantôt mère, tantôt fille, et tantôt compagne de Jupiter' ['for the poets, nature is sometimes mother, sometimes daughter, and sometimes Jupiter's companion'].[64]

Traditionally, a distinction has been drawn between woman's association with nature and man's association with culture.[65] When studying the woman-nature link in the context of the French eighteenth and nineteenth centuries, the theories of Sherry B. Ortner should be considered alongside Colette Capitan's historical analysis of the period, because the arguments of eighteenth-century scientific and philosophic texts fall into the categories outlined by both these scholars. Ortner identifies three levels at which women have been viewed as 'more rooted in, or having more direct connection with, nature': the biological level, the social level and the psychological level.[66] Capitan's analysis of the woman-nature link in the minds of eighteenth-century thinkers reinforces the arguments made regarding the biological and social levels.[67]

Beginning with the biological level, Ortner argues that '[b]ecause of woman's greater bodily involvement with the natural functions surrounding reproduction, she is seen as more a part of nature than men'.[68] A woman's biological role puts her at the heart of nature because '[w]oman creates naturally from within her own being, while men are free to, or forced to, create artificially, that is, through cultural means'.[69] Maurice Bloch and Jean H. Bloch state that in eighteenth-century France in particular, '[t]he traditional view which the philosophers accepted was that woman was closer to nature than man because of her physiological role in sex and motherhood'.[70] Indeed, in medical texts by Cabanis, Roussel and Stahl, 'we find the often noticed association of woman and nature justified by notions of biological maternity and of the female bodily processes'.[71] La Mettrie believed that, during pregnancy in particular, '[l]a femme [...] plus que l'homme est proche de sa nature organique et docile à ses impulsions' ['woman is closer than man to her organic nature and more submissive to its impulsions'].[72] One notable topic discussed by scientists which drew very clear links between woman's biology and nature was the lunar cycle's potential effect on menstruation. Roussel argues that the cycles of certain women were particularly affected by lunar change, and that consequently these women were especially close to nature.[73] Such conclusions were still being drawn in 1861.[74] Furthermore, it was not only scientists who believed in woman's connection with nature at the ontological level. In fact, '[t]out le monde à l'époque [...] pense plus ou moins que les femmes sont dans la Nature, et en particulier tous les philosophes, de Diderot à Grimm en passant par d'Alembert' ['everyone at

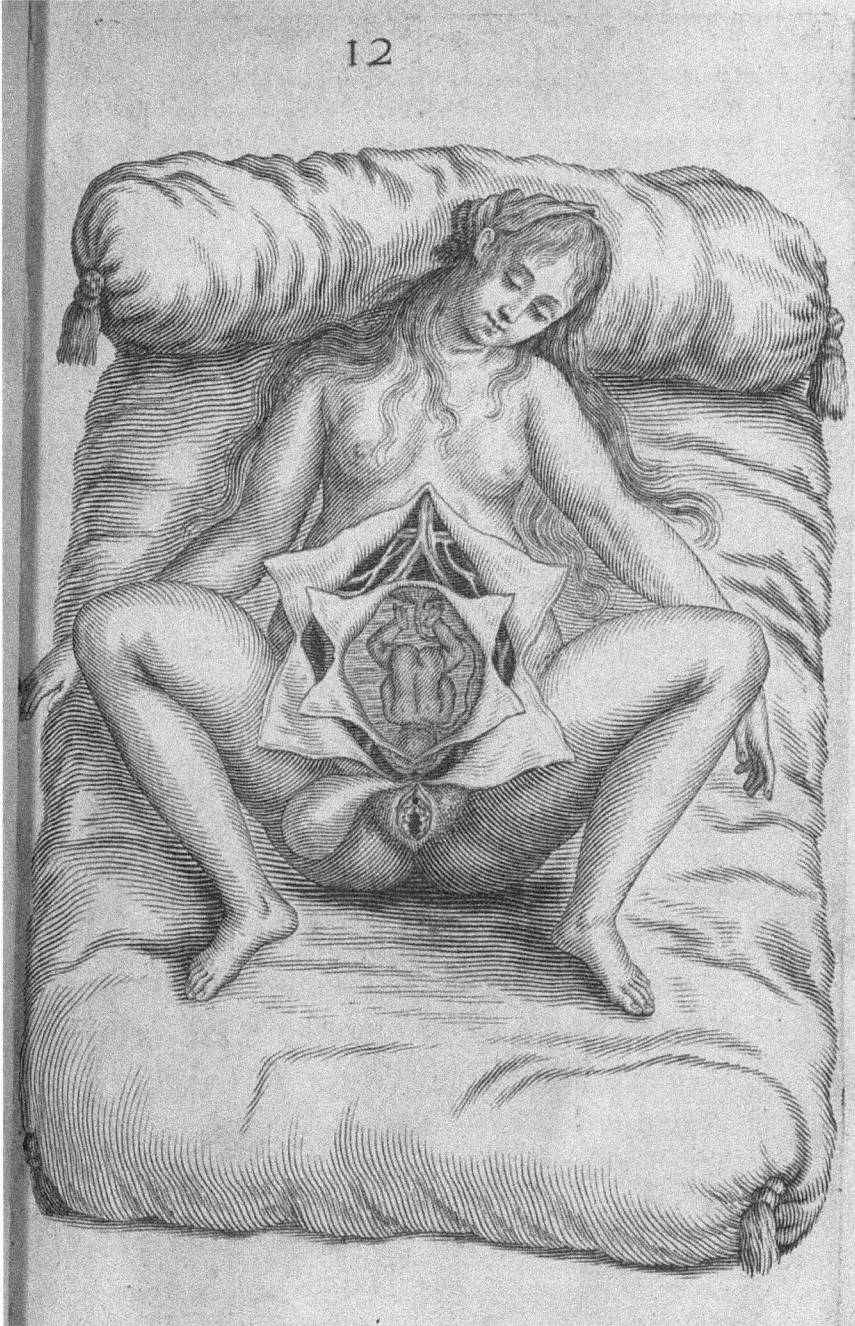

FIG. I.2. *Femme en position pour l'accouchement et représentation de la position de l'enfant dans l'utérus* [*Woman in childbirth position, and representation of the position of the child in the uterus*], burin engraving in Cosme Viardel, *Observations sur la pratique des accouchements* (Paris: Chez l'Autheur, 1674). Image courtesy of: Paris, Bibliothèque interuniversitaire de santé (BIU santé).

the time [...], particularly the *philosophes*, from Diderot to d'Alembert to Grimm, believed more or less that women were in Nature'].[75] For Denis Diderot, a woman's biology also meant her constitution, and this, too, brought her closer to nature than men: 'La femme avec sa constitution plus faible est préservée de ces efforts et, en conséquence, est restée plus proche de l'état de nature' ['Woman, with her weaker constitution, is preserved from these efforts and consequently has remained closer to the state of nature'].[76]

Regarding women's links to nature at the social level, Ortner states:

> [W]oman's physiological functions have tended universally to limit her social movement, and to confine her universally to certain social contexts which *in turn* are seen as closer to nature. [...] I refer [...] to woman's confinement to the domestic family context.[77]

According to Ortner, there are two reasons why this confinement occurs particularly when women become mothers. Firstly, since it is 'in direct relation to a pregnancy with a particular child that the mother's body goes through its lactation processes, the nursing relationship between mother and child is seen as a "natural" bond and all other feeding arrangements as unnatural'.[78] Secondly, the mother must instruct and care for children because they require supervision, since they are 'not yet strong enough to engage in major work, yet are mobile and unruly and not yet capable of understanding various dangers'.[79] Infants themselves are considered closer to a state of nature than adults: 'like animals they do not walk upright, they excrete without control, they do not speak'.[80] Therefore, woman's association with children reinforces the perception of her as closer to nature herself. Ortner's arguments are borne out in an analysis of eighteenth-century scientific and philosophical thought, which contains the recurring idea of nature intending women to undertake a domestic role. Laclos writes: 'Se conserver et se reproduire, voilà donc les lois auxquelles la *nature* a soumis les femmes' ['To preserve and to reproduce: these are the laws to which *nature* has subjected women'].[81] Similarly, '[l]e soin de l'enfance est la destination des femmes; c'est une tâche que la *nature* leur a assignée' ['childcare is the destiny of women; this is a task assigned to them by *nature*'], writes Roussel in 1775.[82] Jacques-André Millot, member of the *Collège et Académie de Chirurgie* [College and Academy of Surgery] in Paris, even quoted Rousseau's arguments regarding women in his work. Millot's 1801 treatise on the moral and physical education of mankind, discusses at length the natural role of women and the importance of breastfeeding, and opens with a dedication *Aux dames françaises* [To French Ladies] stating: 'Jean-Jacques Rousseau a dit: "La première éducation est celle qui importe le plus; parlez donc toujours aux femmes dans vos traités d'éducation"' ['Jean-Jacques Rousseau said: "The earliest education is the most important. Always speak, therefore, to women in your educational treatises"'].[83] Fig. I.3 is taken from Millot's treatise.

The domestic sphere was therefore considered 'a domain of private virtue, free of the corruption of public life, under the reign of women close to Nature',[84] a restrictive domain from which men were freed: 'la société "naturelle" c'est les femmes' ['it is women who are "natural" society'], says Capitan, 'la société civile,

FIG. I.3. *Ô Nature, qu'il est doux de remplir tes devoirs!* [*Oh Nature, how sweet it is to fulfil your duties!*] Engraving in Jacques André Millot, *L'art d'améliorer et de perfectionner les hommes, au moral comme au physique*, 2 vols (Paris: Migneret, 1801), I, p. 130. Image courtesy of: Paris, Bibliothèque interuniversitaire de santé (BIU santé).

émancipée de la Nature [...] les hommes' ['it is men who are [...] civil society, emancipated from Nature'].[85]

Ortner's final argument lies at the psychological level. Ortner is reluctant to stereotype male and female personalities as 'rational' and 'emotional' respectively, preferring to argue that men are seen as 'more objective and category-oriented, women as more subjective or person-oriented'.[86] She defines the feminine personality as 'characterized by personalism and particularism', which 'may have contributed to the universal view of women as somehow less cultural than men'.[87] Eighteenth-century French thinkers did not, however, shy away from gendering the terms 'rational' and 'emotional'. For Jacques-Louis Moreau, 'La femme est un être en qui l'émotion domine sur le raisonnement' ['woman is a being in whom emotion exercises dominion over reason'].[88] Nor did they hesitate to attribute woman's emotion to her biology; Diderot, for example, thought that 'la femme est un être de passions et d'émotions commandé par son utérus' ['woman is a being of passion and emotions controlled by her uterus'].[89] As Wolfgang argues, '[e]ighteenth-century writers in the human sciences articulated new theories of sensibility and sensationalism based on Locke's principles and a medical understanding of the nervous system'.[90] As a result, '[t]he female body, in particular, came to be represented as a "vitally reactive sensible body", responding involuntarily (and hence sincerely) to emotional stimulus'.[91] Emotion was often conflated with the presentation of nature in the work of sentimental novelists and painters alike,[92] where protagonists 'ne savent pas séparer la nature de leurs émotions' ['are unable to separate nature from their emotions'];[93] indeed, nature was often portrayed in literature 'pour mettre dans les âmes les racines tenaces qu'y poussent les émotions puissantes' ['to plant strong roots in the soul, which are encouraged by powerful emotions'].[94] The extremely popular *Julie,* in particular, 'reflète [...] dans la nature les plus ardentes émotions' ['reflects [...] in nature the most intense emotions'].[95] Thus, if women were deemed to be more emotional, then they were considered closer to the natural world. In fact, woman's emotional state, like her social role, was in fact supposedly ordained for her by nature: 'La nature a voulu que la femme régnât par les émotions' ['It was the wish of nature that women should rule by virtue of their emotions'], argued Roussel.[96]

Taking the phrase 'psychological level' to its logical conclusion, the fact that women were believed to be more emotional supposedly increased their susceptibility to hysteria. According to Nancy Rogers, hysteria 'was considered a function of a nervous temperament and the heightened emotions of which only women were capable'.[97] The same organs which connect woman with nature because they cause her to focus on the reproduction of the species are also those which provoke psychological crisis: for eighteenth- and nineteenth-century French doctors, '[w]oman is predisposed toward hysteria by every sex-specific aspect of her physiology. The doctors generally concur that puberty, menstruation, pregnancy, childbirth, lactation, and menopause are particularly risk ridden'.[98] These beliefs, reinforced by the supposed link between women's biology and the natural world in the form of the moon, continued throughout the nineteenth century. Discussing the frequency of psychological crises, Jean-Louis Brachet's *Traité de l'hystérie [Treatise on Hysteria*] argues 'Nous avons surtout remarqué cette périodicité dans les cas où elle était soumise à l'influence de la menstruation. Quelques femmes et même quelques auteurs ont cru, sans doute, alors, lui trouver des rapports avec les phases de la lune' ['We have particularly observed this cyclical recurrence in those cases where it is influenced by menstruation. Consequently, some women and even some authors have no doubt believed that this was due to the influence of the moon'].[99] It is hardly surprising, therefore, that, when women's psychology became manifest in her behaviour, it reminded scientists and thinkers of a life close to nature. La Mettrie 'sees female behaviour as though it were due simply to the closeness of woman to organic nature'.[100] Diderot, who drew many ideas from La Mettrie, wrote that women 'ont conservé [...] l'énergie de nature, et [...] elles sont restées de vraies sauvages en dedans' ['have conserved [...] nature's energy, and [...] their nature remains profoundly untamed'].[101] Similarly, Cabanis argued that during pregnancy and childbirth, women exhibited particularly wild, animalistic tendencies, which expressed the language of nature.[102] Interestingly, as shown in Chapter 3, women often found madness to be, not an inevitable condition of their presumed weakness as a sex, nor a result of their supposed closeness to nature, but rather a means of rebellion against socio-political oppression. In French women's fiction of the early nineteenth century, this is particularly the case when the madwoman re-appropriates the natural setting with which she has been connected.

According to both Sherry Ortner and Simone de Beauvoir, woman's association with nature throughout History has led to her subordination in almost all societies: 'woman is being identified with [...] something that every culture devalues, something that every culture defines as being at a lower order of existence than itself [...], and that is "nature"'.[103] The employment of the woman-nature link as a means of subordination certainly existed in the seventeenth century, though the seventeenth century likened nature to woman in order to rationalize the subordination of nature. Francis Bacon, for example, 'likened the experimental investigation of the secrets of "female" nature to the inquisition of witches on the rack and looked forward to the time when masculine science would shake "female" nature to her very foundations'.[104] His French counterparts presented the self-same image: 'Francis Bacon projected powerful and dangerous "femaleness" onto nature [...] René Descartes declared nature to be feminine and thus totally amenable to manipulation and control by [...] man'.[105] Both Bacon's notion of female nature possessing secrets which should be uncovered and the general impression that nature was improved by male influence penetrate down to the eighteenth century, in which Diderot described nature as 'une femme qui aime à se travestir' ['a woman who likes to disguise herself as a man'].[106] Diderot's work was influenced by the work of Bacon, and perhaps this is one of the reasons why '[b]eaucoup de textes de Diderot autorisent qu'on pense la nature comme femme et comme mère' ['[m]any of Diderot's texts allow us to think of nature as a woman and a mother'].[107] Similarly, the desire to dominate nature was also passed down to the eighteenth century. As far as Cabanis was concerned, for example, masculinity was associated with 'strength, daring, enterprise, hard work and the desire to dominate nature'.[108]

In the eighteenth century, French scientists began to describe the physiological, psychological and emotional distinctions between the sexes, and to decree the distinct roles men and women must play in society because of their differences. As they did so, this time society invoked the feminine connection to nature in order to rationalize subordinating woman herself. Roussel believed that women's bone density, muscle tone and pale skin made them more suited to home-making than to exterior pursuits, and that their internal organs and bone structure rendered them ideally suited to bearing children.[109] Cabanis drew almost identical conclusions.[110] Participating in the 'public' sphere — politics, writing, publishing and business — became the role of men. A woman's role was to take charge of the private sphere: running the household, taking care of her husband, and providing and educating children. She was considered too physically and mentally weak to participate in the public domain. Nature had therefore supposedly intended woman's subordination:

> [C]'est Rousseau qui fait de la Nature le moyen de l'instrumentalisation des femmes, qui fourbit l'arme l'idéologique propre à justifier le statut inférieur qui est le nôtre: les femmes sont dans la Nature, c'est la Nature qui veut qu'elles soient inférieures, il est donc naturel qu'elles soient dominées.
>
> [[I]t is Rousseau who uses Nature as a means of exploiting women, who prepares the ideological weapon suitable for justifying our inferior status: women are in Nature, it is Nature which desires them to be inferior, it is therefore natural that they be dominated].[111]

Other writers agreed. Indeed, 'according to [Antoine Léonard] Thomas it was unthinkable that women could ever be men's equals: their minds were "more pleasing than strong". Such was the will of nature'.[112] Ortner's hypothesis that the woman-nature link has contributed to her subordination is substantiated in the eighteenth-century context, therefore, by the beliefs of pre-eminent thinkers. Woman's biological and psychological essence — in other words, the nature of her being — was granted precedence over her conscious thought and self-identity, and ultimately led to limitations on her socio-political role.

As subordination to man was intended for women by nature itself, it was deemed 'natural'. Rousseau underlines the importance of fulfilling, not turning against, one's natural role: 'L'essentiel est d'être ce que nous fit la nature' ['It is essential to be what nature made us'].[113] This provokes the question: what was considered 'natural' and 'unnatural' in a woman? Firstly, according to Thomas, woman's acceptance of her subjugated role was 'natural': 'celle qui asservie malgré elle aux conventions et aux usages [...] ne perdrait point de vue la nature, et se retournerait encore quelquefois vers elle' ['the woman who conforms to customs and usages in spite of herself [...] would not lose sight of nature and would, from time to time, return to her'].[114] It was also deemed 'natural', in fact biologically natural, for women to display modesty: 'La pudicité est une attitude morale que sanctionne en la femme la nature biologique elle-même' ['Modesty is a moral attitude which is sanctioned by the very biological nature of women'].[115] For Diderot and Rousseau, 'to be a woman in civil society is to be modest, to create but not to have desire. To be otherwise is "unnatural"'.[116] This is perhaps one reason why it was deemed so unnatural for women to quit the private sphere. Did it display a lack of modesty to abandon the role of 'uxorious maternity',[117] and to seek a public name? Certainly, if a woman desired to enter the public sphere by writing and publishing, and, moreover, to use that opportunity to express disagreement with women's attributed societal roles, she was deemed unnatural. Women such as Madame de Staël, Olympe de Gouges, Madame Roland and Mary Wollstonecraft (who dedicated *Vindication of the Rights of Women* to a French bishop), were accused of becoming unemotional mothers, of gaining an '*improper* kind of autonomy, a freedom unbefitting to [their] sex', and were therefore deemed 'unnatural creatures'.[118] Martin Hall argues that, in eighteenth-century France,

> Women are still deemed capable of a significant contribution, but one which is limited by their intellectual and biological inferiority: they are granted the 'feminine' virtues, finesse, sensitivity, spontaneity, but 'male' virtues, strength, imagination, creative capacity, are deemed necessary to create truly 'great' novels.[119]

Thus, if a woman became successful on account of her writing, she was accused of being 'masculine, and therefore unnatural'.[120] This does not mean to say that men were considered unnatural creatures, rather such accusations were intended to insult women writers and politically active women by exaggerating the way in which they were seen to have stepped outside the bounds of their own 'nature'. Genlis, for example, 'was likened to a hermaphrodite — a woman in the bedroom and a man in the salon'.[121]

Since woman's supposed connection with nature contributed to her being pigeonholed into a restrictive role in society in the first place, it is consequently highly relevant that women writers should employ nature to address the issues which they confronted from within the pigeonholes of that social order. However, there is another, equally important, reason for the natural landscape's relevance as a site of socio-political critique. The mid to late eighteenth century saw a radical change in the way in which nature was viewed. This radical change was not accompanied by a corresponding radical change in the way in which women, supposedly connected with nature, were viewed. This leads to a paradox regarding the perception of women and their societal roles, one which women writers are able to exploit.

During the Enlightenment, the definition of nature was an all-encompassing one. The *Encyclopédie* states: 'Nature signifie quelquefois le système du monde, la machine de l'univers, ou l'assemblage de toutes les choses créées' ['Nature sometimes signifies the system of the world, the mechanics of the universe, or the assemblage of all created things'].[122] The 1762 edition of the *Dictionnaire de l'Académie française* describes nature similarly, as: 'Tout l'univers, toutes les choses créées' ['The whole universe, all created things'].[123] The need for universal classification was partially down to a desire to extend scientific knowledge, and partially, indeed largely, down to the aforementioned desire to impose order on nature, demonstrating man's control over it. As Buffon argues: 'la Nature est autant notre ouvrage que le sien; nous avons su la tempérer, la modifier, la plier à nos besoins, à nos désirs; nous avons fondé, cultivé, fécondé la Terre' ['Nature is as much our work as it is her own; we have succeeded in tempering it, modifying it, bending it to our needs and our desires; we have created, cultivated and fertilized the Earth'].[124] The resemblance here to Napoleon's description of women, which opened the present chapter, is striking.

When writing fiction, 'novelists shared with thinkers and artists generally the prevailing eighteenth-century conviction that the "proper study of mankind is man"';[125] indeed, for many, 'outside nature had little place' at all.[126] For this reason, therefore,

> [e]arly French works accord minimal importance to nature description — minimal in the sense both of brevity (usually no more than a line or two) and of infrequency (usually no more than a few descriptive passages in a whole novel). [...] The same use of short, stereotyped nature descriptions — the total absence of any extended or developed depictions of landscape — persists in France down to Rousseau's time.[127]

In most French fiction penned between d'Urfé's *L'Astrée* in the early seventeenth century and Rousseau's *Julie ou la Nouvelle Héloïse* (1761), descriptions of nature did not feature, as Pierre Trahard makes clear.[128]

However, within one generation, nature went from being held in contempt to being elevated on to a pedestal: 'the status of "nature" becomes much higher in this period than it had been in more traditional dialectics, where it was associated with the fall, savages and the failure of education'.[129] This radical about-face was assisted greatly by the writings of Rousseau, who, between *Discours sur l'origine et les fondements de l'inégalité parmi les hommes* [*Discourse on the Origins and Bases of Inequality Among Men*] (1755) and *Les Rêveries du promeneur solitaire* [*Reveries of the Solitary Walker*] (1782), argued that mankind had once known a state of perfection but had been corrupted by civilization.[130] His solution — that a natural state of innocence and virtue could be re-obtained if man returned to live at one with the natural world — became particularly apparent in terms of practical application in his popular novel *Julie ou la nouvelle Héloïse*. As scholarship has long recognized, a new craze for nature took France by storm thanks to the dissemination of Rousseau's concepts: '[n]ature is no longer something to be despised as low; it is rather to be cherished, and, above all, it is the source whereby society, morals, education, even medicine, are to be reformed and purified'.[131] Contemplation of the natural world was now encouraged, and nature itself was no longer to be avoided, but rather actively sought out. Rousseau soon became the major progenitor of a sentimental fiction which included lengthy portrayals of natural landscapes. Furthermore, as Kadish has argued, from the moment these landscapes made 'a striking, visible entry into the pages of one of the most influential novels of the eighteenth century' (*Julie*), literary natural landscapes possessed great power in dramatizing 'multifarious conflicts' including 'social, psychological, political, even metaphysical ones'.[132]

It is at this point that Bloch and Bloch have identified a crucial paradox, which forms the background to the analyses conducted throughout this monograph. Rousseau — like Bacon, Locke, Hobbes and Descartes before him, like his contemporaries Diderot and Thomas, and like the scientists Cabanis, Roussel, Moreau and La Mettrie — continued to expound the belief that nature and women were inextricably linked. Yet, if Rousseau had reversed opinions on nature, extolling it as superior to culture and civilization, then 'surely closeness to nature [...] would, if followed through, imply that woman should offer a guide to the new uninhibited natural man and would be superior to him'.[133] This implication was not followed through. To some extent women did, at least, become the source by which society and morals could be improved: they were the source of moral doctrine in the home. However, in no way were women viewed even as equal to men. The political, economic, legal and social privileges to which men were believed to have an indisputable right were denied to women. In fact the *Code Civil* of 1804 'relegated women "to the status of minors [...] excluding them from the definition of citizenship"',[134] and a woman's role became increasingly restricted to the domestic domain.[135] Previously, therefore, when nature had been held in contempt, 'the association of women-nature-subordination can be said to be 'in harmony'',[136] whilst nonetheless misogynistic. Yet, even after nature became revered, women continued to be viewed as inferiors, and it is 'somewhat surprising that this view of women is maintained not simply by doctors such as Roussel but also by radical French writers who had elsewhere changed the status of nature'.[137]

The writers mentioned here include Rousseau, for, although radical in exhorting new attitudes towards nature, the eminent *philosophe* was particularly conservative in his beliefs about confining women to the domestic sphere. In *Émile, ou de l'éducation*, Émile is to shun society, opting for an education from the natural world. One might expect his perfect match to undergo a similar education. Sophie, however, must conform to all the constraints of the civilization and society which Émile is encouraged to ignore. Therefore, 'in some ways in bringing in Sophie at the last moment Rousseau puts in question the whole edifice he has built, because in introducing woman he reintroduces all the assumptions he elsewhere tried to destroy'.[138] If the perfect society is to be built on the foundation of a return to nature, and natural morals are imparted by the mother, how can the perfect woman, wife and mother be such a social construct, refined and defined by civilization? Moreover, how can the strong association of women and nature continue to be upheld when the latter is regarded so highly and the former so disparagingly? Despite this evident paradox, as Bloch and Bloch make clear, nothing in fact seemed likely to change opinions:

> The acceptance, more or less consciously, of this notion [that of the superiority of nature] by the writers under consideration meant that either they had to negate their valuation of nature in order to accommodate the position of women, or accept the superiority of women, something which they ultimately rejected.[139]

France remained a male-dominated society not only in the late eighteenth century, but also throughout the nineteenth and into the twentieth.

On account of the contradictions and discontinuities in Rousseau's attitudes regarding women 'it is not surprising [...] that his views have given rise to widely divergent interpretations among both his contemporaries and our own'.[140] Even women writers in the mid eighteenth century identified discrepancies in his material. In her *Essai sur l'éducation des demoiselles* [*Essay on the Education of Girls*], Mlle d'Espinassy feels she has something worth saying and has been stimulated to react to that part of *Émile* which specifically targets women. To position herself in relation to Rousseau she seizes on one specific point, that women 'govern' men. She cleverly contrasts this with his apparently contradictory underestimation of women's capabilities and his belief that they should always defer to their husband's judgment.[141]

Such discrepancies open up a possible space for debate which might be exploited by the intellectual writer, and French women writers of the late eighteenth and early nineteenth century took advantage of this. In fact they did so even to the extent of participating in the ambiguity themselves. By their very status as female authors, they contradicted Rousseau's teachings, and yet, simultaneously, they continued to advocate his views. Chase argues:

> Adélaïde de Souza and Sophie Cottin, like many women of the eighteenth century, were inspired by his novels and challenged by his political and social treatises, oftentimes seeing themselves reflected in the characters that filled Rousseau's works. However, both questioned the limited role that he ascribed to women and sought to redefine women's relationship to society and to nature.[142]

Genlis 'rejected Rousseau's limited view of female capabilities and insisted on the liberating force of a solid education for women', yet she remained 'a firm advocate of the Rousseauian ideals of enlightened domesticity and motherhood'.[143] Staël, too, who was notoriously outspoken in public affairs, continued to promote domesticity as the ideal for women. It becomes clear, then, firstly, that women writers realized that where they must criticize, they must do so subtly. An argument which was at once controversial, but also appeared to uphold the popular status quo, allowed the voice of its promoter to be more readily heard. Secondly, it is clear that women writers were not advocating the complete removal of the domestic role from women's lives. It seems they merely sought to encourage the acknowledgment that their sex is capable of filling more than a single role.

With these two points in mind, we must also note that, although Genlis and Staël argue for women's ability to engage in political thought, neither they nor Cottin, Krüdener and Souza attempt to argue that women should be accorded a role of superiority over men, or should join nature on its newly constructed pedestal. Nor is it my intention to prove otherwise. Similarly, given that 'Jean-Jacques Rousseau's views on women have long been the subject of discussion and debate',[144] it is not the aim of the present discussion to reiterate the arguments of others.[145] Rather, this study will address the fact that Cottin, Genlis, Krüdener, Souza and Staël employ nature as a site of socio-political critique in their discussion of a) the issues that women faced because of their relegation to an inferior status and to the domestic sphere, and b) the reactions they exhibit in response to these issues. It is at the point where the changes in the view of nature meet the refusal to change opinions concerning women's societal roles that the answer to why natural description features in women's novels is to be found.

The works of Rousseau, the investigations of medical science, and their joint association of woman with nature were not alone in leading to the subordination of woman and her exclusion from the public sphere. Another reason can be found in the political changes which took place at the end of the eighteenth century, and the consequent transformation and gendering of the public and private spheres themselves.[146] Again, however, we will see that nature — possessing both public and private spatial connotations — becomes a highly appropriate site of socio-political critique from within which women might gain access to both spheres and highlight the issues they face when excluded from one and confined to the other.

As Joan B. Landes argues, '[d]espite the excessively personal and patriarchal character of Old Regime monarchical power, women of the period participated in and influenced political events and public language'.[147] Exclusion from the public sphere was more likely to be conducted on the basis of class than gender. Yet, the influential status that aristocratic women had formerly held in politics and foreign affairs had been, so the revolutionaries believed, responsible for many failures of the former system. Influential noble women

> were held responsible for the supposed 'effeminacy' of the Old Regime and the emasculation of men, who were seen as subject to female whims and political conniving. Female political participation, it followed, was inevitably self-serving and destructive.[148]

In the wake of the Revolution, then, the new society reserved power and public decisions for men, and 'the collapse of the older patriarchy gave way to a more pervasive *gendering* of the public sphere'.[149] Noble women had been able to develop influential public roles during the Ancien Régime with the particular aid of the salons. The salon constituted a space which posited 'aristocratic women at the intersection between public and private concerns'.[150] However, the power of the salons diminished in the years following the Revolution, and, with them, much of the cultural influence of the women who ran them.[151] Alongside the desire to unseat women from positions of public importance, the considerable influence of the press and the distribution of newspapers also contributed to the decline of the salons.[152] So, too, did the growth of the male-dominated *café-cercles* which began to replace them. The decline in women's influential status, both at court and in salons, contributed greatly to the lack of equality that women began to face in the late eighteenth century and would continue to face throughout the nineteenth and into the twentieth. Landes relates the nascence of feminism as we know it 'to the fall of the politically influential women of the absolutist court and salon of Old Regime France'.[153]

The salon, was, as Landes has argued, 'a unique institution',[154] for it constituted a third space, not wholly public and not wholly private, but incorporating elements of both: 'Public and private spheres overlapped in aristocratic salons'.[155] In this respect, the space of the salon echoed Woolf's 'private outlet to the public world which is a room of one's own'.[156] The salon was a space in which women were not marginalized, but rather were permitted intellectual, creative and social freedom. Rather than categorizing men and women according to a set of essential characteristics, the approach of life in the salons was that of a single existential group: 'The salons were controversial because they allowed newcomers to "pass" as noble and also because they were run by women. According to Carolyn C. Lougee, "ladies made gentlemen, then, in an existential sense"'.[157] Once the salon culture declined, it was necessary to find a similar space which incorporated elements of both public and private if women in the post-revolutionary decades were to argue that, as a species, they should not be pigeonholed into one section of society or another based purely on biological essence. Women writers found another example of this type of third space in the natural world, by landscaping gardens (as Bending has argued) or by writing the landscape, as this monograph will show.

Natural landscapes can be found on both private estates and in the public domain, and so belong exclusively to neither. Landscape gardens often provided private retreats for public figures, such as was the case with Marie-Antoinette's *hameau* at Versailles (itself juxtaposed with the palace's extravagant French-style garden, to which Louis XIV himself had written a public guide).[158] Personal gardens might also express elements of public life, as did Josephine's garden at Malmaison, in which she incorporated plants transported from the territories of Napoleon's overseas campaigns.[159] Josephine's personal garden also served a public purpose: firstly, it helped to generate plant life for France's public gardens via the cuttings she sent to parks throughout the country,[160] and secondly her flowers 'were distributed in the name of the emperor as gifts to royal figures and foreign dignitaries', making Josephine's garden 'a living metaphor for the expansion of Napoleon's empire'.[161] Furthermore, those natural spaces which appear on public land — such as spaces of wilderness or landscaped public parks — enable private, personal emotions to be experienced within them and to be expressed to a larger audience. Sophie Le Ménahèze argues, with regard to gardens in particular, that 'l'intimité au jardin repose sur une dialectique du dedans et du dehors' ['intimacy in the garden is the consequence of a dialectic between interior and exterior'];[162] Bending argues, similarly, that

> women who created landscape gardens inevitably engaged with the eighteenth century's understandings of women's place in the world, their relationship with the public sphere, with domestic space [...]. When women gardened, then, they entered a conversation with both men and women, a conversation at once public and private.[163]

Nature's ability to express private emotion in a public way will be seen frequently in the analyses conducted in this study.

The landscaping of real gardens was not the only way in which women were able to use nature to access both public and private spheres. In fiction, female characters' landscaping of gardens also permitted them to transcend binary divisions. To a limited extent, this was even the case in Rousseau's writing: in Julie's Clarens garden, 'women's lives are not radically relegated to the private', because 'while privacy is found, the harsh contrast between public and private is not'.[164] Julie has been allowed some autonomous creativity and independent free-thinking in landscaping her own garden; she is not restricted in the sense that Sophie is. Yet, Cottin, Genlis, Krüdener, Souza and Staël take the notion of feminine autonomy gained through natural landscaping further. Whilst Julie's *Elysée* is 'a miniature walled-off paradise within Wolmar's domain, [...] in itself representative of Julie's enclosure within patriarchy',[165] Émilie, Àdele, Corinne, Malvina, Mathilde, Agnès, Valérie, Rosalba and Amélie inhabit and/or create landscapes which permit them their desired intellectual, creative and emotional freedom often in opposition to the restrictions of oppressive patriarchal society.

Finally, we can take the notion of feminine autonomy gained through natural landscaping to a third level, somewhere between the intra-fictional landscapes of the aforementioned heroines and the real landscapes of Bending's gardeners. For the women writers who wished to engage with eighteenth-century understandings of women's place in the world, the act of *writing* the landscape provides the space necessary to critique their contemporary society's oppression of their sex. Jann Matlock argues that 'women reclaimed public space through the novel [...], gaining a podium to express their values and demands'.[166] This is undeniably true, but often it is the natural space within those novels which becomes that podium. Women writers take a space which has both a public and a private role (and which therefore transcends classification) and they use it as the site within their novels where they craft their arguments regarding woman's own connection to both the public and private spheres, her role in and need to belong to both, and her own inability to be classified or marginalized. Moreover, they take a space connected with woman in the intellectual minds of the era in order to do so. Thus, just as certain protagonists landscape their gardens to empower themselves, women writers craft natural story-worlds to actively reclaim the voice denied to them on the socio-political stage. Like the salon, then, nature echoes Woolf's room of one's own for women writers: 'Woolf's room metaphor not only signifies the declaration of political and cultural space for women, private and public, but the intrusion of women into spaces previously considered the spheres of men'.[167] Writing the landscape allows female authors to penetrate a male-dominated sphere by providing them with the platform from which they might address socio-political issues in the public domain. Therefore, nature again becomes the ideal space for the discussion of women's preoccupations, and a 'room of one's own' quickly becomes a 'landscape of one's own'.

One advantage of landscape writing (over landscape gardening) in order to address women's socio-political issues and roles is that there are no real limitations on the natural space which can be written. Although gardens feature prominently in the novels of women writers, they are by no means the only landscape to provide a podium for the female voice. We might distinguish four general 'umbrella types' of natural landscape which recur throughout this book. They are: tamed nature, nature cultivated to look untamed, wild nature, and natural deathscapes. Each of these types held a particular fascination for the French public in the eighteenth century; the first in the earlier decades of the century, and the latter three in the nascent Romantic mind. As the change in attitude to nature generally led to changes in attitudes towards individual landscapes, certain natural spaces grew in significance in the consciousness of writers, philosophers and the general public. It is these which feature most noticeably in women's writing of the era. As women writers approach each of the preoccupations of their sex, they build on pre-existing ideas or theories developed within the eighteenth century regarding these fashionable landscapes. This is because the prevalent contemporary ideas of and associations with those landscapes assume particular significance for the debate in question, as is outlined briefly below.

In seventeenth- and early eighteenth-century France, as we have seen, 'taming nature' had involved imposing order on it. Since the age of Louis XIV, therefore, the number of *jardins à la française* in the style of those designed by André Le Nôtre at Vaux-le-Vicomte and Versailles had increased. The rigid style of this garden reflects the way nature in the early eighteenth century was generally contemplated: as something to be controlled by mankind, sculpted to suit order and rationality. Later in the century, in accordance with increasing calls for liberty in many other walks of life, it was thought that garden design, too, might incorporate more scope for freedom than previously. Gardens such as the *jardin à l'anglaise* became fashionable. They were cultivated to appear untamed, and rejected straight lines and right angles in favour of mimicking the unordered natural world. The vogue even permeated Versailles, when Marie-Antoinette's *hameau* was created as somewhere 'to escape from the intrigues and formalities of palace life', a space of freedom from order.[168] Marie-Antoinette was not alone. Both the higher and lower echelons of society desired to escape the problems (in particular the pollution and overcrowding) within towns for the idyllic tranquillity and beauty of the countryside, and this led to an increasing fashion for rural idylls and pastoral spaces as well. The public began to seek the 'idealised agricultural scenery'[169] of rustic living, or to meander in country parks. Like the *jardin à l'anglaise,* many of these spaces were cultivated to look untamed. D. G. Charlton discusses the French public's

> sharpened pastoral attitudes — the love for quiet reverie amidst bosky groves and by streams or waterfalls, for tranquil vistas over banked, *disordered* trees, for pleasing walks along *winding* pathways. The aim, as the Marquis de Girardin would put it in his treatise of 1777, was 'a sort of Elysian garden' made for 'peaceful happiness and the true pleasures of the soul.[170]

The use of tamed natural landscapes and landscapes cultivated to look untamed lends several advantages to the works of Cottin, Genlis, Krüdener, Souza and Staël. The rigid, tamed nature in the French-style garden provides an excellent allegory for the dominated, restricted life of the woman in an arranged marriage, while the English-style garden presents an opportune setting in which a woman might discover hitherto unexplored autonomy. The tamed nature of a walled garden presents a highly apt space for portraying the attempts to tame a woman's rebellion against social pressure through madness. Gentle, tranquil parks and gardens create an idyllic, secure space separated off from civilization. These idylls provide the perfect space in which lovers may rendez-vous away from the eyes of disapproving society, or, also, a secluded, peaceful space in which a mother can grieve. A further advantage of employing a tamed natural space as a setting in a novel discussing women's preoccupations (whether intended to appear tamed or not) is that the author can have her female protagonist sculpt the landscape herself. This allows the protagonist to employ the language of plants, flowers and garden design in order to transmit messages that she wishes to convey. Tamed landscapes can therefore be used to create discourse, allowing mothers who have failed to live up to the notion of ideal motherhood, for example, to shape nature physically in order to re-establish communication with a lost child and to communicate their pain to the outside world.

As well as artificially creating landscapes to look untamed, the French became fascinated with truly wild nature, including mountains, stormy oceans, volcanoes and barren deserts. According to Charlton:

> It is one thing to appreciate the gentle pastoral landscape, to feel a sense of harmony with the sunny, contented world of nature represented by the country retreat [...]. It is a more difficult thing to appreciate and feel harmony with nature in its wilder, more threatening expressions — to respond to high, barren mountains, dangerous oceans, savage storms on land or sea, black and perilous night-time. In the eighteenth century, however, for almost the first time in European thinking, a majority achieved these more difficult responses and thereby significantly helped to enlarge men's imaginative and aesthetic reactions to nature.[171]

Mountain scenery became particularly popular. In the seventeenth century 'the dominant tendency in [...] many [...] parts of Europe was to regard mountains as inconvenient, aesthetically repellent, and dangerous not just to one's body but to one's soul'.[172] Similarly depreciatory opinions were also exhibited by Montesquieu in the early eighteenth century on his travels through Italy.[173] However, by the mid eighteenth century '[m]ountains [...] were regarded by the large majority of literate people as among the most beautiful and spiritually uplifting places on the planet'.[174] Louis Ramond de Carbonnières (explorer of the Pyrenees) and Albrecht von Haller (Swiss naturalist and poet) were amongst those who significantly contributed to changing the French perspective on mountain landscapes. Deserts, too, began to captivate attention thanks to the descriptions produced by travel writers who ventured to North Africa and the Middle East.[175] As Nicole Barre states: 'le sentiment de la nature [...] se focalise et s'épanche sur des espaces censément naturels, certes pas inconnus, mais jusqu'alors oubliés, délaissés, guère fréquentés: la mer, la montagne, la forêt sauvage, et, bien entendu le désert' ['the feeling for nature [...] is concentrated on, and is poured out on to spaces that are held to be natural, which were certainly not unknown, but which had hitherto been forgotten, abandoned, scarcely frequented: seas, mountains, wild forests, and, of course, deserts'].[176]

These types of truly wild nature were popular because of their sublimity — the ability, according to Edmund Burke, to thrill and simultaneously to induce terror[177] — and their consequent ability to inspire melancholy. Burke's views on the sublime influenced other European philosophers such as Immanuel Kant, Claude Adrien Helvétius and Denis Diderot. For Kant, 'the sight of a mountain whose snow-covered peak rises above the clouds' and 'the description of a raging storm' could provoke simultaneous awe and fear in the spectator.[178] Nature's sublime power features in the works of several eighteenth- and nineteenth-century French artists and writers, including paintings by Théodore Géricault, Claude Joseph Vernet and Philip James de Loutherbourg, the works of André Chenier and Sylvain Maréchal, Nicolas Chamfort's 1768 'Ode aux volcans',[179] and Gustave

Doré's landscape paintings of the Scottish Highlands, and is employed by several of the writers analysed in this study. Cottin and Staël engage with the wild scenery of northern Britain and the gender egalitarianism of its Ossianic myths in their efforts to contribute to the debate over women's writing. Both authors also incorporate sublime, wild or stormy waterscapes in their discussion of the death of a heroine. The connection of sublime nature with power enables them to highlight how power is restored to women in death. Cottin also engages with the wild scenery of the barren deserts of the Holy Land, and their ability to provide a suitable setting for the rebellion, through madness, of women against their oppression.

Linking the melancholy and Romanticism that are inspired by wild landscapes with the peace encouraged in a garden, a fashion also arose for the natural 'death-scape'. The term 'deathscape' itself was in fact established by cultural geographers in the 1990s, in particular by the work of L. Kong, and that of K. V. Hartig and K. M. Dunn, though the concept is highly applicable to some of the newly fashionable natural spaces in the eighteenth century.[180] Deathscapes include any space associated with death: sites of death itself, cemeteries, sites of mourning, and memorials constructed for a deceased loved one. Two major types of natural deathscape appear in the novels of the women writers studied in this monograph: sites which break down the border between the world of the living and the dead (in order to allow one to die or in order to open up a window on to the afterlife), and memorial gardens, which incorporate a tomb or commemorative stone at the heart of a natural setting. Awareness of the first type of deathscape in the eighteenth century stemmed from traditional, historical and mythological beliefs and theories. The fashion for the second type of deathscape in eighteenth-century France, can be largely attributed to changes in burial practices, the development of more personalized grieving, and the construction of Rousseau's own, celebrated tomb at Ermenonville amid a natural setting. Staël and Cottin engage with common associations with both types as they write a 'deathscape of one's own' which harnesses the powers of nature to announce a woman's oppression, restore her autonomy and voice, and ensure her escape from an untenable situation. In addition, memorial deathscapes feature in Souza's *Adèle de Sénange,* Cottin's *Malvina* and Krüdener's *Valérie*. In these cases, the construction of deathscapes furthers the heroine's ability to communicate her emotions and her arguments, and to convey her future desires.

Within the novels analysed in this study, each of these four 'umbrella' categories may commonly incorporate one natural feature or space more than others. For example, tamed landscapes very often take the form of gardens, but rarely (if ever) include deserts. However, it is important to bear in mind that none of these four categories has a complete monopoly on any particular geographical, topographical or climatic feature, and it is possible to find gardens, parks, mountains, hills, waterfalls, rivers, seashores, deserts, trees, flowers, storms, and several other elements of the natural world in more than one of the aforementioned categories. For this reason it would be both difficult and undesirable to structure this book according to landscape type. Firstly, very different types of natural space often highlight the same debate. This is notable, for example, in the discussion of rebellion through madness, where walled gardens and deserts both serve as replacement madhouses for the insane woman. Dealing with gardens and deserts in separate chapters would, therefore, lead to cumbersome repetition. Secondly, an attempt to construct a chapter dealing solely with one natural feature or one type of landscape would lead to additional problems, since there are several ways in which certain landscapes within women's writing of this period might be understood or classified, not only across the novels, but often also within the same novel. There are, for instance, wild spaces which threaten (*Corinne* and *Mathilde)* as well as wild spaces which liberate (*Malvina* and *Mathilde*). Nowhere is the difficulty to classify and pin down nature more difficult, perhaps, than in the portrayal of gardens. Sometimes a garden undergoes multiple transformations within one novel: Malvina's garden begins as an idyll, becomes a replacement madhouse, and then assumes the features of a deathscape. The gardens which appear in Genlis's *Les Mères rivales,* Krüdener's *Valérie,* Cottin's *Malvina*, Staël's *Corinne* and Cottin's *Amélie Mansfield* are landscaped to include both rigid formalism and autonomous liberalism. In *Les Mères rivales,* Rosalba's garden is landscaped, but whether it is tamed to look untamed or strictly cultivated to appear designed is not so easily ascertained. This is because the garden conforms to neither category in its complete sense: it contains the labyrinth of topiary hedges that may be expected in a French-style garden, but also the Elysian fields of a pastoral idyll; it contains features which evoke Ancient Greece and Rome and yet also hints towards Medieval Myth and seventeenth-century Protestantism. In addition, throughout the novels analysed in this monograph, topographical garden features — such as trees, plants, paths, waterfalls, lakes, rivers and streams — can be viewed differently depending on context. Water can be associated with sublime beauty or else with danger; trees can be associated with identity and personal roots, but also with death; winding paths can be associated with freedom and autonomy, but also with a lack of Christian righteous duty and therefore with evil; flowers and shrubs have different symbolic associations depending on their genus, colour and the reason for planting them.

What can be deduced from the above is that, as well as combining both public and private spatial connotations, nature also expresses multiple images and meanings, and, as a result, it is often difficult to define. Nature possesses an underlying and unchanging essence no more than a woman. Natural landscapes provide examples of middle ground, which is not always possible to discern as one type or another. Rather we have more complex landscapes, which incorporate multiple types of scenery and multiple ideas. This difficulty in classifying a certain natural landscape in one single way makes it a very appropriate podium from which women might make similar arguments about their own existence. Therefore, rather than constructing the chapters of this book in the same manner as Charlton's *New Images of the Natural in France* (with the purpose of analysing a different landscape in each), the chapters of this book will be structured, like those in Cazenobe's *Au Malheur des dames: Le roman féminine au XVIIIe siècle,* according to the debates with which women writers engaged by writing their landscapes. The chapters of this book will show landscapes being used to highlight the plight of women in relation to different socio-political debates: those regarding marriage, motherhood, madness, death or suicide, and authorship.

Given that this book analyses the portrayal of the natural world in fiction, it might at first also seem logical for its methodological approach to be one pertaining to the currently burgeoning field of ecocriticism. However, this is neither the most appropriate nor the most desirable route to take here. To begin with, this is because the principal definition and goals of ecocriticism do not fully fit the purpose and scope of this book. Lawrence Buell's seminal work on ecocriticism defines the latter as 'a study of the relation between literature and environment conducted in a spirit of commitment to environmentalist praxis',[181] and argues that '[h]uman accountability to the environment is part of the texts' ethical orientation'.[182] Similarly, ecocriticism is more than 'simply the study of Nature or natural things in literature; rather it is any theory that is committed to effecting change'.[183] This study aims neither to investigate whether the novels of women writers of the First Republic and First Empire discuss an ethical need for ecological preservation, nor to ascertain how and why they might approach a discussion of changes they would like to see implemented regarding the way in which the environment is treated. Although such investigations as these may indeed prove possible, it is not the focus here, and would be best dealt with in a separate, future academic study.

Similarly, given that this study refers to the traditional distinction which has been drawn between woman's association with nature and man's association with culture, a problem which 'motivates many ecofeminists' (cultural ecofeminists in particular),[184] it may also at first appear as though the field of ecofeminism could provide a methodological lens through which to conduct this study. However, it is no more useful to turn to this as an overarching methodology than it is to turn to ecocriticism in general.[185] Firstly, this is because '[c]ultural ecofeminism is a *response* to the perception that women and nature have been mutually associated and devalued in western culture',[186] not the perception itself, which can be made without a discussion of concerns for the future of the environment. Secondly, and more crucially,

> [t]o cultural ecofeminists the way out of this dilemma is to elevate and liberate women and nature through direct political action. Many cultural feminists celebrate an era in prehistory when nature was symbolized by pregnant female figures, trees, butterflies, and snakes and in which women were held in high esteem as bringers forth of life. An emerging patriarchal culture, however, dethroned the mother goddesses and replaced them with male gods to whom the female deities became subservient.[187]

This is certainly not the message behind post-revolutionary French women's writing, nor is it the message of this volume. As discussed above, women writers' novels do not indicate an intention to place women on a pedestal alongside nature. Finally, for cultural ecofeminists, 'human nature is grounded in human biology. [...] The perceived connection between women and biological reproduction turned upside down becomes the source of women's empowerment and ecological activism'.[188] Such arguments come dangerously close to upholding the essentialist ideas prevalent within the eighteenth century that women writers in fact appear to be challenging. Indeed, 'the use of essentialism by cultural ecofeminists' has been criticized by several scholars.[189]

Ecocritical and ecofeminist theories therefore only go so far in the analysis they permit, and adopting ecocriticism as a methodological lens through which to examine the novels of women writers of this period would not allow for the best way of understanding what those novels achieve in terms of addressing female preoccupations of the period. There are more pertinent, wider-reaching conclusions to be made, including how these women writers re-appropriate nature as a site of socio-political critique and how their portrayal of natural landscape paves the way for later Romantic writing by tapping into the themes which would later become increasingly associated with this movement. For this reason the present study assumes a more historical and socio-political approach to its understanding of the natural descriptions present in women's writing of this period. I root my readings of the novels of Cottin, Genlis, Krüdener, Souza and Staël in an informed context of their writing. Their works will be read through the lens of eighteenth- and early nineteenth-century French theories of the natural spaces which appear within the novels in question, and in light of contemporary socio-political debate around issues which concerned women, rather than through theories regarding environmental concern. Each chapter shows how their engagement with debates regarding natural space enables women writers to make more pointed arguments about debates over women's roles. Blended with this rooting in contemporary context, will be the conducting of close textual analysis of descriptions of natural landscapes within the novels. Given that the appearance of natural landscapes within the works of these writers has thus far been overlooked, it is important that the first study of their descriptions be a detailed one.

Through such detailed analysis, the chapters of this monograph examine how female novelists craft natural landscapes to expose and comment on the problems male-dominant society causes women to experience in France in this period. In addition, they show how these novelists employ the same descriptions of nature to highlight women's responses to the pain and frustration that such social issues provoke for them. The two initial chapters look at the expectations of and restrictions on women in this period, regarding marriage (Chapter 1) and motherhood (Chapter 2). The subsequent chapters investigate the ways in which women writers showed female rebellion against the expectations for and restrictions on a woman's role in life, through madness (Chapter 3), death or suicide (Chapter 4), and writing (Chapter 5). Ultimately, this book shows that the natural landscape was far from being a casually chosen backdrop for Cottin, Genlis, Krüdener, Souza and Staël. Rather, the 'escape into nature' given to their female protagonists was a means to expose and confront the everyday reality and emotional suffering faced by women in the Revolutionary decade and Napoleonic Empire. Furthermore and finally, the corpus of the present study, the approach taken here and the issues that come under discussion in each chapter all work to resituate women's writing in relation to a nascent French Romanticism.

Determining a definite *terminus a quo* and *terminus ad quem* of French Romanticism is problematic. Philippe Van Tieghem identifies the Romantic era in France as the period falling between 1820 and 1850,[190] and Paul Van Tieghem's influential critical work terms the period from 1760–1820 pre-Romanticism,[191] arguing that Rousseau was the prominent pre-Romantic figure from whose ideas many Romantics drew their inspiration. A number of critics argue that Romanticism in fact began with Mme de Staël and Chateaubriand circa 1800,[192] whilst others date the beginnings of Romanticism to Rousseau himself, omitting the term pre-Romanticism altogether.[193] Caroline Warman describes two 'waves' of French Romanticism, and states that in any case: '[m]uch of French Romanticism, in both its first and second waves, was pre-figured in eighteenth-century writing' and particularly that of Rousseau and Diderot.[194] For the purposes of the present work, Susan Noakes' similar delineation of the Romantic time period will be used: 'the "romantic" period [...] extends very roughly through the first half of the nineteenth century but has its roots in the pre-revolutionary period of Rousseau'.[195] However, the most notable problem in the frequent discussions of dates arises from an assumption that very little took place in France between these two periods. We are told that '[i]f romanticism had its first philosophers in Rousseau and Diderot, it did not flourish in France for several decades'.[196] Similarly, Virgil Nemoianu asks: 'Why does French romanticism begin in the eighteenth and again in the nineteenth century?'.[197] In fact, it is not this simple. Rather, as Louichon has argued, in overlooking the most popular works published between these two dominant periods of literary history, we have overlooked the influential early Romantic works of women writers.

Certainly, the compendia on European Romanticism and scholarly works on French Romanticism have, thus far, almost entirely overlooked the influence of French women writers of the First Republic and First Empire. Discussion of women writers is notably absent from *The Oxford Handbook of European Romanticism*,[198] *A Companion to European Romanticism*,[199] *Romantismes européens et Romantisme français*,[200] and *The French Romantics*.[201] The only two French female Romantics to be mentioned are Staël and (the later) George Sand, yet discussions of male writers are prolific. Nicholas Roe's *Romanticism: An Oxford Guide* does include a chapter on feminism, however the only women writers discussed within it are British.[202] Generally representative of scholarly perception of the French Romantic movement is James C. McKusick's statement that '[t]he development of a distinctive French Romantic literature was carried forward by a group of young men associated with the literary journal *La Muse française*, among whom the central figures were Alphonse de Lamartine (1790–1869), Alfred de Vigny (1797–1863), and Victor Hugo (1802–1885)'.[203] Anthologies of Romantic writing display a similar gender bias. In *European Romanticism: A Reader*, the French sections focus on Balzac, Baudelaire, Chateaubriand, Delacroix, Fabre d'Olivet, Gautier, Hugo, Lamartine, Leroux, Michelet, Musset, Nodier, Stendhal, Senancour and Vigny.[204] The only woman referenced is Staël.

However, this monograph resituates the dominant themes of French Romanticism, firstly, as developing earlier than the 1820s and, secondly, as more than a male phenomenon. In exposing their written landscapes, this book argues that the works of the women writers who published between the appearance of Rousseau's *Julie ou la Nouvelle Héloïse* and the advent of the canonical nineteenth-century Romantic writers go further than simply bridging a gap between two Romanticisms, or between a pre-Romanticism and Romanticism. Rather, in engaging with the trends of so-called pre-Romanticism and even challenging some of the ideas expounded by its progenitors, they in fact pave the way for the latter 'waves of Romanticism' and leave their distinctive mark on them.

Whilst it is notoriously difficult to pin down a precise definition for the term Romanticism, and whilst '[i]t is even worse when it comes to French Romanticism' which is 'plural, diverse, contradictory, constantly evolving',[205] there are certain features upon which scholars generally agree. Firstly, Romanticism is a reaction to the reason and rationality of the Enlightenment, the canons of neoclassical aesthetics, and the birth of industrialisation and urbanisation; secondly, the Revolution of 1789 and the socio-political aftermath both of the Revolutionary decade and of the Napoleonic period played a significant role in the development of the movement;[206] and thirdly, there are several core themes or trends which can be commonly identified with Romanticism. Gérard Gengembre argues that:

> Sensibility, a feeling for Nature, melancholy, spleen, nostalgia, generally speaking a world weariness, a number of Rousseauist themes and philosophical ideas [...] compose a complex background upon which romantic writers are free and inspired to imprint their own vision. The lyric sentimentality of the second half of the eighteenth century also paves the way for the expression of the Self.[207]

Alfred Biedermann's compendium counts several major themes of Romanticism: *Le triomphe du 'moi'* [The triumph of the 'self'], *Le mal du siècle* [the sickness of the century], *La nature* [Nature], *L'Amour* [Love], *Les Portes de l'au-dela* [the gates of the beyond], *L'Apocalypse romantique* [The Romantic apocalypse] and *Le Romantisme politique et social* [Political and Social Romanticism].[208] The first three in particular are recurring themes in the works of the women writers under analysis here, and so the present discussion of Romantic themes will focus more closely on these. Nonetheless, the others can be found interspersed with the notions of the self, the *mal du siècle* and nature. It is by intertwining each of these major Romantic themes in their arguments against the oppression of their sex that women writers carve a vital place for themselves in literary history.

The exploration and expression of the self, and especially '[t]he autonomy of the individual, his right to self-determination, to freedom from social constraints and even from cognitive limitations, was to become one of the cardinal tenets of romanticism'.[209] For Rousseau, the habit of self-contemplation — 'looking within himself and examining his heart and soul when he was alone' — was best facilitated by wandering amid nature.[210] The desire for autonomy, freedom and self-identity is seen throughout the chapters of this book as women writers attempt to negotiate a space from which both they and their heroines might make the female voice heard, and, as they both draw on and challenge Rousseau's thinking, it is hardly surprising that they should choose the natural landscape as the site which might express this autonomy, freedom and self-identity.

The *mal du siècle* was 'a contagious disease that appealed dearly to man in his eternal quest for the fulfilment of the self'.[211] Regarding the Romantic writers' desire to express a *mal du siècle*, Charlton argues that they 'were evoking a state of mind that, far from being peculiar to themselves or created by them, was widespread in their own time and had been so from at least the mid eighteenth century'.[212] This state of mind was a melancholic malady, a disillusionment with life and society, 'a long-prevalent mental condition', yet one which had been 'intensified in their own day by the upheavals of the Revolutionary and Napoleonic years and by other social and intellectual factors alike as France moved into the nineteenth century'.[213] The canonical Romantic writers Chateaubriand, Constant, Musset, Vigny and Hugo describe it in such terms.[214] Yet, the promises of the Revolution had failed women even earlier than they had failed the male youth, and in a way which much more severely restricted their freedom and rights: 'republicanism had been even more short-lived for French women, barred from becoming public citizens by the revolutionary government in 1793 and by Napoleon's 1804 civil code'.[215] Bertrand-Jennings describes a separate literary *mal du siècle* for women, one which 'est lié indirectement au recul de leurs droits et à leur statut d'inégalité et d'exclusion' ['is indirectly linked to the decrease in their rights and to their unequal, excluded status'].[216] Charlton also hints towards such an argument when he states, with regard to the *mal du siècle* in the works of two of the better known women writers of the age (Staël and Sand), that '[i]n Delphine the causes are in part society's attitude to women' and '[i]n [...] Indiana it is above all "le rapport mal établi entre les sexes" ["the poorly established relationship between the sexes"] created by society's treatment of women through the constraints of marriage in particular'.[217] The melancholy and depressive situations experienced by the heroines analysed in this book will be shown to originate both from such general societal oppression of their sex, and also from particular restrictions placed on their love and choice of partner.

The space which women — fictional heroines and their creators — re-appropriate in order to express their melancholy, to expose the oppression which causes it, and to establish their autonomy and freedom is nature. It is therefore highly significant that '[o]ne of the defining characteristics of the Romantic movement in Europe is its enduring engagement with the natural world'.[218] The frequency with which the importance of nature to the Romantics and pre-Romantics has been promulgated bears witness to the truth of the notion.[219] Discussion of nature appears particularly in the compendia on European Romanticism. Warman classifies the 'first wave' of Romanticism as 'the rejection of reason and the turn to a mystical inexplicable union (or communion) with nature',[220] and McKusick states that '[t]hroughout the Romantic period, imagery and ideas drawn from nature are omnipresent in the work of poets and novelists, painters and musicians, philosophers and political theorists'.[221] As we have seen, the nascent Romantic period witnessed particular interest in rural and idyllic landscapes, wild and tempestuous natural landscapes, and natural deathscapes (the latter providing a good example of the theme *Les Portes de l'au-delà*). According to McKusick,

> The idea of nature, and indeed the very meaning of the word "nature,"
> underwent a significant transformation over the course of the Romantic
> period. Throughout Europe, writers were rediscovering the simple pleasures
> of a life lived far from urban areas, amid placid rural landscapes. [...] Following
> in the footsteps of Rousseau, young writers all over Europe were seeking out
> wild, scenic, and remote landscapes in which to witness and record the state of
> nature first hand.[222]

Gardens, too, formed part of the Romantic enthusiasm for nature (particularly
the fashion for the newer, English-style garden).[223] The fashion for the Orient, its
exotic deserts and its landscape in general — which fascinated the later, canonical,
male Romantics such as Chateaubriand, Hugo, Nerval, Delacroix and Fromentin
— also appears in the works of women writers of this period, in particular in Mme
Cottin's *Mathilde* (1805) and *La Prise de Jéricho, ou la pécheresse convertie* (1803). Finally,
the entry on nature in the *Dictionnaire du Romantisme* stresses the importance not just
of particular types of landscape but also of the features within those landscapes:

> Le romantisme de la nature évoque immédiatement à l'esprit les paysages
> noyés de brume de Caspar David Friedrich, les forces telluriques que suggèrent
> les peintures de Turner, les descriptions émues ou fastueuses de Rousseau,
> Bernardin de Saint-Pierre ou Chateaubriand, les méditations rêveuses, au
> milieu des bois ou des campagnes, de Lamartine et de Hugo. Mais il ne s'agit
> pas que de paysages. Toute la nature, par ses détails infimes comme dans son
> immensité, semble habitée d'une vie particulière: les fleurs, les insectes, le
> murmure des ruisseaux, la chaleur sèche des déserts.
>
> [The Romanticism of nature immediately brings to mind Caspar David
> Friedrich's landscapes drenched in fog, the telluric forces which Turner's
> paintings evoke, the moving or sumptuous descriptions written by Rousseau,
> Bernardin de Saint-Pierre or Chateaubriand, and the dreamy meditations of
> Lamartine and Hugo in the middle of woods or the countryside. However, it is
> not just about landscapes. The whole of nature, in its minute details as well as
> its immensity, seems inhabited by a particular life: flowers, insects, the murmur
> of streams, the dry heat of the deserts].[224]

For this reason, the present study also attributes as much importance to the
individual features of a landscape as to the landscape as a whole.

Yet, though Cottin, Krüdener, Genlis, Souza and Staël negotiate critical territories alongside those of their male contemporaries such as Bernardin de Saint-
Pierre or Chateaubriand, they also do so differently. French women's novels
employ many natural landscapes — whether a cultivated one, a wild one, or one
incorporating features of both — to achieve three major ends: to create symbolic
depth for their controversial arguments, to enable their heroines to rebel against and/
or escape from oppression, and, perhaps most importantly, to provide a platform
from which the female voice may be heard. This latter aim permits otherwise
impossible discourse to be established between characters, between heroine and
reader, and between author and reader. By re-establishing autonomy, highlighting
self-expression, celebrating the figure of the melancholic wanderer, the social
misfit, the grief-stricken, the mad, the suicidal, and the figure of the writer-poet,

all in the heart of natural landscapes, Cottin, Genlis, Krüdener, Souza and Staël exerted an influence on the literary Romanticism which soon captured the French imagination, at the same time as they challenged the dominant patriarchal discourse and gender dichotomy of their day.

Notes to the Introduction

1. Napoléon Bonaparte, *Napoléon: Ses opinions et jugements sur les hommes et sur les choses*, ed. by M. Damas Hinard (Paris: Duféy, 1838), I, 477–78.
2. Madame de Staël, *Corinne ou l'Italie* (France: Gallimard, 1985), p. 231.
3. 'For Rousseau [...] women's closeness to Nature [...] provided a rationale for the exclusion from citizenship', Genevieve Lloyd, *The Man of Reason. "Male" and "Female" in Western Philosophy* (Minneapolis: University of Minnesota Press, 1984), p. 77.
4. Pierre Roussel, *Système physique et moral de la femme* (Paris: Masson, 1869 [1775]); Pierre J. G. Cabanis, *Rapports du physique et du moral de l'homme* (Paris: Crapart, Caille et Ravier, 1805); J. O. de La Mettrie, *L'Homme-machine* (Paris: Henry, 1865 [1747]).
5. These arguments were not only challenged by the women writers Napoleon deplored (such as the intellectual giant Mme de Staël), but also by those he admired (such as Mme de Souza and Mme de Genlis). Whether or not the women writers in question were speaking out against Napoleon as an individual figure is not the focus of this monograph. Staël unquestioningly did. The focus of this study is rather to analyse the ways in which both Staël and the other women under consideration here subtly challenged the general patriarchal society which imposed social and creative restrictions on their sex.
6. On the popularity of Cottin, see: Charles-Augustin Sainte-Beuve, *Causeries du Lundi* (Paris: Garnier Frères, n.d.), XI, 488; On the popularity of Genlis, see: Heather Belnap Jensen, *Portraitistes à la plume: Women Art Critics in Revolutionary and Napoleonic France* (University of Kansas: ProQuest, 2007), p. 106; On the popularity of Krüdener, see: Chantal Bertrand-Jennings, *Un Autre mal du siècle: Le Romantisme des romancières, 1800–1846* (Toulouse: Presses Universitaires du Mirail, 2005), p. 52; On the popularity of Souza, see: Kirsty Carpenter, *The Novels of Madame de Souza in Social and Political Perspective* (Oxford: Peter Lang, 2007), p. 49; On the popularity of Staël, see: Charles-Augustin Sainte-Beuve, *Portraits de femmes* (Paris: Didier, 1844), p. 64.
7. Brigitte Louichon, *Romancières sentimentales, 1789–1825* (Saint-Denis: Presses Universitaires de Vincennes, 2009).
8. Alison Finch, *Women's Writing in Nineteenth-Century France* (Cambridge: Cambridge University Press, 2000), pp. 2–3.
9. Joan Hinde Stewart, *Gynographs: French Novels by Women of the Late Eighteenth Century* (Lincoln and London: University of Nebraska Press, 1993), pp. 21–22.
10. Margaret Cohen, *The Sentimental Education of the Novel* (Princeton: Princeton University Press, 1999), p. 50.
11. Allan H. Pasco, *Sick Heroes: French Society and Literature in the Romantic Age, 1750–1850* (Exeter: University of Exeter Press, 1997), p. xiii.
12. Claire Jacquier, *L'Erreur des désirs: Romans sensibles au XVIIIe siècle* (Lausanne: Payot, 1998), p. 11.
13. Katherine Astbury, *Narrative Responses to the Trauma of the French Revolution* (London: Legenda, 2012), p. 1. (Original emphasis.)
14. Jürgen Habermas, *The Structural Transformation of the Public Sphere: An Inquiry into a Category of Bourgeois Society,* trans. by Thomas Burger with the assistance of Frederick Lawrence (Cambridge, MA: The MIT Press, 1991), p. 56.
15. Carla Hesse, *The Other Enlightenment: How French Women became Modern* (Princeton: Princeton University Press, 2003), p. 31.
16. See: Hesse; Stewart; Finch; Bertrand-Jennings; Louichon; Cohen, *Sentimental Education*; Colette Cazenobe, *Au Malheur des dames: Le roman féminine au XVIIIe siècle* (Paris: Honoré Champion, 2006).

17. Waller also argues that Staël (and later also Sand) employs *mal du siècle* themes in order to criticize the subordination of women. See: Margaret Waller, *The Male Malady: Fictions of Impotence in the French Romantic Novel* (New Brunswick, NJ: Rutgers University Press, 1993). In addition, Bowman recognizes Cottin's significance as a 'portrayer of the plight of women' in her day. See Bowman's summary of Claire d'Albe in: Frank Paul Bowman, '1799, 10 October: The Ideologists', in *A New History of French Literature,* ed. by Denis Hollier (Cambridge: Harvard University Press, 1989), pp. 596–602 (p. 602).

18. Stewart; Carpenter; Aurora Wolfgang, *Gender and Voice in the French Novel, 1730–1782* (Burlington, VT: Ashgate, 2004).

19. Stewart, pp. 1; 6.

20. Wolfgang, p. 103.

21. Carpenter, pp. 256.

22. Finch, p. 22.

23. Cohen, *Sentimental Education,* p. 48.

24. Machteld de Poortere, *The Philosophical and Literary Ideas of Mme de Staël and of Mme de Genlis,* trans. by John Lavash (New York: Peter Lang, 2007), p. 81.

25. Sainte-Beuve, *Portraits de femmes,* p. 47.

26. Leslie Sykes, *Madame Cottin* (Oxford: Basil Blackwell, 1949), pp. 128–29.

27. Ibid., p. 129.

28. Ibid., p. 129.

29. Dana Chase, *Mother Nature and the Nature of Woman: Rousseau's* Nouvelle Héloïse *and the Novels of Sophie Cottin and Adélaïde de Souza* (Electronically published doctoral thesis, Columbia University, 2001) <http://search.proquest.com/docview/275807092/fulltextPDF?accountid=8312> [accessed 30 November 2012], p. 5.

30. George M. Baker, 'Madame de Staël's Attitude toward Nature', *The Sewanee Review,* 20:1 (1912), 45–64 (p. 45).

31. Sainte-Beuve, *Portraits de femmes,* p. 119.

32. Baker, p. 45.

33. Simone Balayé, *Les Carnets de Voyage de Madame de Staël: Contribution à la genèse de ses œuvres* (Genève: Droz, 1971), p. 116.

34. Ibid., p. 118.

35. Arnelle, *Une Oubliée: Mme Cottin d'après sa correspondance* (Paris: Librairie Plon, Plon-Nourrit et Cie, 1914), p. 150.

36. Ibid., p. 116.

37. Frau [Mrs] Barbara Juliane von Krüdener, baroness von Krüdener, '*Frau [Mrs] Barbara Juliane von Krüdener, baroness von Krüdener to Jacques Henri Bernardin de Saint-Pierre: Tuesday, 7 September 1790 — [letter]*', in *Electronic Enlightenment,* ed. by Robert McNamee et al. <http://www.e-enlightenment.com/item/sainjaVF0031161_1key001cor/> [accessed 5 April 2014]

38. Giulia Pacini, 'A Culture of Trees: The Politics of Pruning and Felling in Late Eighteenth-Century France', *Eighteenth-Century Studies,* 41:1 (2007), 1–15 (p. 11).

39. Doreen Massey, *Space, Place and Gender* (Cambridge: Polity Press, 1994), p. 1.

40. See: Tim Cresswell, *Place: A Short Introduction* (Chichester: Wiley-Blackwell, 2015), pp. 15–17; Eric O. Jacobsen, *The Space Between: A Christian Engagement with the Built Environment* (Grand Rapids, MI: Baker Academic, 2012), p. 55; Yi-Fu Tuan, *Space and Place: The Perspective of Experience* (Minneapolis, MN: University of Minnesota Press, 1977).

41. John Agnew, 'Space and Place', in *Handbook of Geographical Knowledge,* ed. by J. Agnew and D. Livingstone (London: Sage, 2011), pp. 316–30 (p. 318).

42. Cresswell, p. 16–17.

43. *Oxford English Dictionary,* 'space, n.1. I', online <http://www.oed.com> [accessed 11 August 2018].

44. Ibid., 'space, n.1. II'.

45. Michel Foucault, 'Of Other Spaces', trans. by Jay Miskowiec, *Diacritics,* 16:1 (1986), 22–27 (p. 23).

46. H. Lefebvre, *The Production of Space* (Oxford; Cambridge, MA: Blackwell, 1991).

47. Maarja Saar and Hannes Palang, 'The Dimensions of Place Meanings', *Living Reviews in Landscape Research*, 3 (2009), 1–24 (p. 6).
48. Massey, p. 3.
49. Gaston Bachelard, *La poétique de l'espace* (Paris: Presses universitaires de France, 1961).
50. See: Stuart Elden and Jeremy W. Crampton, *Space, Knowledge and Power: Foucault and Geography* (Brookfield: Taylor and Francis, 2016).
51. *Oxford English Dictionary*, 'space, n.1. II.12.c', online <http://www.oed.com> [accessed 11 August 2018].
52. Agnew, p. 316.
53. Cresswell, p. 17.
54. *Oxford English Dictionary*, 'landscape, n. 2.a', online <http://www.oed.com> [accessed 13 August 2018].
55. J. Galewsky et al., 'Climate Over Landscapes', *Eos*, 89:16 (2008), 151 (p. 151).
56. J.S. McClelland, *A History of Western Political Thought* (London; New York: Routledge, 2005), p. 308.
57. Gayle A. Levy, 'A Genius for the Modern Era: Madame De Staël's *Corinne*', *Nineteenth-Century French Studies*, 30:3/4, 2002, 242–53 (p. 249).
58. Stephen Bending, *Green Retreats: Women, gardens and eighteenth-century culture* (Cambridge: Cambridge University Press, 2013), p. 1.
59. Ibid., pp. 4–5. The 'accounts of gardening' to which Bending refers include letters, journals, diaries, fiction and poetry.
60. Amongst others, see: Irène Aghion, *Héros et dieux de l'Antiquité: guide iconographique* (Paris: Flammarion, 1994); Maureen Devine, *Woman and Nature: Literary Reconceptualizations* (Metuchen, NJ: Scarecrow Press, 1992); Paul Hoffmann, *La Femme dans la pensée des Lumières* (Paris: Ophrys, 1977); Hwa Yol Jung, *Transversal Rationality and Intercultural Texts: Essays in Phenomenology and Comparative Philosophy* (Athens, OH: Ohio University Press, 2011); Carolyn Merchant, *Earthcare: Women and the Environment* (New York: Routledge, 1995).
61. Denise Riley, 'Does Sex Have a History? 'Women' and Feminism', *New Formations*, 1 (1987), 35–45 (p. 42).
62. *Dictionnaire de L'Académie française*, 4th Edition (1762), 'Nature, s.f.', p. 198, online <http://portail. atilf.fr/cgi-bin/dico1look.pl?strippedhw=nature&headword=&docyear=ALL&dicoid=ALL&art icletype=1#ACAD1762> [accessed 28 August 2018].
63. Hoffmann, p. 359.
64. *Encyclopédie ou Dictionnaire raisonné des sciences, des arts et des métiers*, 21 vols (Stuttgart; Bad Cannstatt: F. Frommann, 1988 [1751–1772]), XI, p. 41.
65. Sherry B. Ortner, 'Is Female to Male as Nature is to Culture?', *Feminist Studies*, 1:2 (1972), 5–31.
66. Ibid., p. 12.
67. Colette Capitan, *La Nature à l'ordre du jour, 1789–1973* (Paris: Kimé, 1993).
68. Ortner, p. 15.
69. Ibid., p. 16.
70. Maurice Bloch and Jean H. Bloch, 'Women and the Dialectics of Nature in Eighteenth-Century French Thought', in *Nature, Culture, and Gender*, ed. by Carol P. MacCormack and Marilyn Strathern (Cambridge: Cambridge University Press, 1980), pp. 25–41 (p. 32).
71. Ibid., p. 33.
72. Hoffman, p. 112.
73. Roussel, pp. 120–22.
74. Édouard Strohl, *Recherches statistiques sur la relation qui peut exister entre la périodicité de la menstruation et les phases de la lune* (Strasbourg: Silbermann, 1861), p. 6.
75. Capitan, pp. 109–10.
76. Otis Fellows and Diana Guiragossian Carr (eds.), *Diderot Studies XX* (Genève: Droz: 1981), p. 338.
77. Ortner, p. 16 (Original emphasis).
78. Ibid.
79. Ibid.

80. Ibid., p. 17.
81. Choderlos de Laclos, 'Des Femmes et de leur éducation', in Œuvres complètes, ed. by Laurent Versini (Paris: Gallimard, 1979), p. 392. (My emphasis.)
82. Roussel, pp. 219–20. (My emphasis.)
83. Jacques André Millot, L'art d'améliorer et de perfectionner les hommes, au moral comme au physique, 2 vols (Paris: Migneret, 1801), I, p. v.
84. Lloyd, p. 78.
85. Capitan, p. 111.
86. Ortner, p. 21.
87. Ibid., p. 22.
88. Hoffmann, p. 168. See also: Jacques-Louis Moreau, Histoire naturelle de la femme, 3 vols (Paris: Duprat; Letellier, 1803), I, pp. 122–23.
89. Élisabeth Badinter, 'Préface', in A. L. Thomas, Diderot, Madame d'Epinay, Qu'est-ce qu'une femme?, ed. by Élisabeth Badinter (Paris: P.O.L., 1989), pp. 7–47 (pp. 34–35).
90. Wolfgang, p. 18.
91. Ibid., p. 18.
92. Pierre Trahard, Les Maîtres de la sensibilité française au XVIIIe siècle (1715–1789), 4 vols (Paris: Boivin, 1931–33); Daniel Mornet, Le Sentiment de la nature en France de J.-J. Rousseau à Bernardin de Saint-Pierre (Genève: Slatkine, 1980), p. 217, p. 315 and p. 353; Jean Weisgerber, L'Espace romanesque (Lausanne: Editions L'Âge d'Homme, 1978), p. 141. Examples include Rousseau's Julie ou la nouvelle Héloïse, Bernardin de Saint-Pierre's Paul et Virginie, Restif de la Bretonne's Le Paysan perverti and La Paysanne pervertie, Richardson's Pamela, or Virtue Rewarded, Goethe's Die Leiden des jungen Werther, and several of the paintings of Jean-Baptiste Greuze and Hubert Robert.
93. Mornet, p. 197.
94. Ibid., p. 217.
95. Ibid., p.195.
96. Roussel, p. xxxii.
97. Nancy Rogers, 'The Wasting Away of Romantic Heroines', Nineteenth-Century French Studies, 11:3–4 (1983), 246–56 (p. 251).
98. Janet Beizer, Ventriloquized Bodies: Narratives of Hysteria in Nineteenth-Century France (New York: Cornell University Press, 1994), p. 40.
99. Jean-Louis Brachet, Traité de l'hystérie (Paris: J.-B. Baillière, 1847), p. 357.
100. Bloch and Bloch, p. 34.
101. Denis Diderot, Sur les femmes, in Œuvres complètes de Denis Diderot (Paris: Deterville, An VIII [1799–1800]), p. 420.
102. Cabanis, p. 378.
103. Ortner, p. 10. Cf. Jung, p. 6; and Simone de Beauvoir, Le Deuxième Sexe, 2 vols (Paris: Gallimard, 1976 [1949]), I, p. 15.
104. Carolyn Logan, Counterbalance: Gendered Perspectives on Writing and Language (Peterborough, Ontario: Broadview Press, 1997) pp. 148–49.
105. Ibid., p. 148.
106. Denis Diderot, De l'Interpretation de la nature in Textes Choisis, ed. by Jean Varloot, 7 vols (Paris: Éditions sociales, 1953), II, p. 47. The Dictionnaire de l'Académie française of 1798 gives the sense of 'travestir' as: 'Déguiser en faisant prendre l'habit d'un autre sex, ou 'd'une autre condition' ['To dress up in the clothes of the other sex, or of another condition']. Dictionnaire de L'Académie française, 5th Edition (1798), 'Travestir, v.a.', p. 690, online <http://portail.atilf.fr/cgi-bin/dico1look.pl?strippedhw=travestir&dicoid=ACAD1798&headword=&dicoid=ACAD1798> [accessed 28 August 2018].
107. Élisabeth de Fontenay, Diderot ou le matérialisme enchanté (Paris: Grasset, 1981), p. 20.
108. Ludmilla Jordanova, Nature Displayed: Gender, Science and Medicine, 1760–1820 (London; New York, NY: Longman, 1999), p. 169.
109. See: Kathleen Wellman, 'Physicians and Philosophes: Physiology and Sexual Morality in the French Enlightenment', in Eighteenth-Century Studies, 35:2 (2002), 267–77.

110. Cabanis; Anne-Marie Jaton, 'La Définition de la femininité dans 'Les Raports du physique et du moral, de Cabanis et dans *"La Loi naturelle de Volney"*,' ' in *Volney et les idéologues: Actes du colloque d'Angers,* ed. by Jean Roussel (Angers: Presses Universitaires d'Angers, 1988), pp. 183–91.

111. Capitan, p. 111.

112. James F. McMillan, *France and Women 1789–1914: Gender, Society and Politics* (London and New York: Routledge, 2000), p. 8.

113. Jean-Jacques Rousseau, *Émile ou de l'Éducation,* in Jean-Jacques Rousseau, *Œuvres complètes de J. J. Rousseau,* 4 vols (Paris: Furne, 1835), II, p. 563.

114. Antoine Léonard Thomas, *Essai sur le caractère, les mœurs et l'esprit des femmes dans les différents siècles* (Paris: Moutard, 1772), p. 209.

115. Hoffmann, p. 337.

116. Thomas Laqueur, *Making Sex: Body and Gender from the Greeks to Freud* (Cambridge, MA: Harvard University Press, 1990), p. 200.

117. Angelica Goodden, *Madame de Staël: The Dangerous Exile* (Oxford: Oxford University Press, 2008), p. 12.

118. Ibid., p. 11. (Original emphasis).

119. Martin Hall, 'Eighteenth-century women novelists: genre and gender', in *A History of Women's Writing in France,* ed. by Sonya Stephens (Cambridge: Cambridge University Press, 2000), pp. 102–19 (p. 103.)

120. Renee Winegarten, *Mme de Staël* (Leamington Spa: Berg, 1985), p. 11.

121. Anne L. Schroder, 'Going Public Against the Academy in 1784: Mme de Genlis Speaks out on Gender Bias', *Eighteenth-Century Studies,* 32:3 (1999), 376–82 (p. 376).

122. *Encyclopédie,* XI, p. 40.

123. *Dictionnaire de L'Académie française,* 4th Edition (1762), 'Nature, s.f.', p. 198.

124. Georges Louis Leclerc, comte de Buffon, *Les Époques de la nature,* 2 vols (Paris: L'Imprimerie royale, 1780), I, p. 4.

125. Doris Y. Kadish, *The Literature of Images: Narrative Landscape from* Julie *to* Jane Eyre (New Brunswick and London: Rutgers University Press, 1987), p. 2. Kadish quotes from Pope here: 'Know then thyself, presume not God to scan/ The proper study of mankind is man'. See: Alexander Pope, *Essay on Man,* ed. by Mark Pattison (Oxford: Clarendon Press, 1871), Epistle II, p. 89. Pope's verse was a staple of eighteenth-century reading and his opinion commonplace in contemporary thought.

126. D. G. Charlton, *New Images of the Natural in France: A Study in European Cultural History, 1750–1800* (Cambridge: Cambridge University Press, 1984), p. 6.

127. Kadish, p. 17.

128. Trahard, I, p. 15.

129. Bloch and Bloch, p. 27.

130. P. E. Charvet, *A Literary History of France: The Nineteenth Century* (London: Benn, 1967), pp. 3–4; Robin Howells, *Regressive Fictions: Graffigny, Rousseau, Bernardin* (London: Legenda, 2007), pp. 1–7.

131. Bloch and Bloch, p. 31.

132. Kadish, p. 33.

133. Bloch and Bloch, p. 34.

134. Finch, p. 8–9.

135. Geraldine Sheridan has shown how women could become involved in family businesses, doing their husband's accounting or bookkeeping, and thus saving the business money. Léon Abensour has also shown that, in family businesses, 'husband and wife worked side by side as a unit; almost all the legal documents signed by merchants in the archives [...] for Paris and the Île de France, be they leases, contracts or receipts, were countersigned by wives'. See: Geraldine Sheridan, *Louder than Words: Ways of Seeing Women Workers in Eighteenth-Century France* (Lubbock, TX: Texas Tech University Press, 2009), p. 203; Léon Abensour, *La Femme et le féminisme avant la révolution* (Paris: Éditions Ernest Leroux, 1923), p. 168. However, although women could countersign their husband's business dealings, we must not forget that women were forbidden by the *Code civil* from drawing up contracts for themselves alone, solely in their own name. As Geraldine

Sheridan states, 'The legal position was [...] rather bleak for women'. See: Geraldine Sheridan, 'Women in the Book Trade in Eighteenth-Century France', *British Journal for Eighteenth-Century Studies*, 15 (1992), 51–70 (p. 52).

136. Bloch and Bloch, p. 33.

137. Ibid.

138. Ibid., p. 37.

139. Ibid., p. 32.

140. Mary Seidman Trouille, *Sexual Politics in the Enlightnment: Women Writers Read Rousseau* (Albany, NY: State University of New York Press, 1997), pp. 1–2.

141. Jean Bloch, 'The eighteenth century: women writing, women learning' in *A History of Women's Writing in France*, ed. by Sonya Stephens (Cambridge: Cambridge University Press, 2000), pp. 84–101 (pp. 92–93.)

142. Chase, p. 2.

143. Trouille, p. 8.

144. Ibid., p. 1.

145. Amongst others, see: Lloyd; Trouille; Nicole Fermon, *Domesticating Passions: Rousseau, Woman, and Nation* (Hanover, NH: Wesleyan University Press, 1997); Jean-Jacques Rousseau, *On Women, Love, and Family*, ed. by Christopher Kelly and Eve Grace (Hanover, N.H: Dartmouth College Press, 2009); Joel Schwartz, *The Sexual Politics of Jean-Jacques Rousseau* (Chicago: The University of Chicago Press, 1985); John T. Scott, *Jean-Jacques Rousseau: Critical Assessments of Leading Political Philosophers* (London; New York: Routledge, 2006); Penny A. Weiss, 'Rousseau, Antifeminism, and Woman's Nature', *Political Theory* 15:1 (1987), 81–98.

146. A transformation recognized in both Habermas's seminal text *The Structural Transformation of the Public Sphere*, and in Joan B. Landes, *Women and the Public Sphere in the Age of the French Revolution* (Ithaca, NY: Cornell University Press, 1988).

147. Landes, p. 2.

148. Susan K. Foley, *Women in France since 1789: The Meaning of Difference* (Basingstoke: Palgrave Macmillan, 2004), pp. 2–3.

149. Landes, p. 2. (Original emphasis.)

150. Steven Kale, *French Salons: High Society and Political Sociability from the Old Regime to the Revolution of 1848* (Baltimore: The Johns Hopkins University Press, 2004), p. 13.

151. Bertrand-Jennings, p. 14.

152. Jean Larnac, *Histoire de la littérature féminine en France* (Poitiers: Impr. Nicolas, Renault et Cie; Paris, éditions Kra, 1929), p. 163.

153. Landes, p. 1.

154. Ibid., p. 23.

155. Kale, p. 12.

156. A. Snaith, *Virginia Woolf: Public and Private Negotiations* (New York: Palgrave Macmillan, 2003), p. 11.

157. Leora Auslander, *Taste and Power: Furnishing Modern France* (Berkeley: University of California Press, 1996), p. 50. Auslander quotes from Carolyn C. Lougee, *Le Paradis des Femmes: Women, Salons and Social Stratification in Seventeenth-Century France* (Princeton, NJ: Princeton University Press, 1976), p. 54.

158. Louis XIV, *Manière de montrer les jardins de Versailles* (Paris: Catherine Szántó Publication, 2013).

159. Paula Deitz, *Of Gardens: Selected Essays* (Pennsylvania: University of Pennsylvania Press, 2011), p. 115.

160. Andrea Stuart, *Josephine: The Rose of Martinique* (London: Pan Macmillan, 2011), p. 383.

161. Carol Solomon Kiefer, *The Empress Josephine: Art and Royal Identity* (Amherst: Amherst College, 2005), p. 62.

162. Sophie Le Ménahèze, 'Le jardin pittoresque entre ouverture et exclusion: les paradoxes de l'intimité', in *Jardins Et Intimité Dans La Littérature Européenne (1750–1920): Actes Du Colloque Du Centre De Recherches Révolutionnaires Et Romantiques, Université Blaise-Pascal (Clermont-Ferrand, 22–24 Mars 2006)*, ed. by S. Bernard-Griffiths, F. Le Borgne and Daniel Madelénat (Clermont-Ferrand: Presses Universitaires Blaise-Pascal, 2008), pp. 42–53 (p. 42).

163. Bending, *Green Retreats*, p. 7.

164. Mark Sydney Cladis, *Public Vision, Private Lives: Rousseau, Religion, and 21st-century Democracy* (New York: Columbia University Press, 2003), pp. 179–80.

165. Ekaterina R. Alexandrova, ' "This salutary remedy": Female suicide and the novel as *Pharmakon* in Riccoboni's *Histoire de M. Le Marquis de Cressy* and Rousseau's *La Nouvelle Héloïse*' in *Death Representations in Literature: Forms and Theories,* ed. by Adriana Teodorescu (Newcastle: Cambridge Scholars Publishing, 2015), pp. 97–116 (p. 107).

166. Jann Matlock, 'Novels of testimony and the 'invention' of the modern French novel', in *The Cambridge Companion to the French Novel: From 1800 to the Present,* ed. by T. Unwin (Cambridge: Cambridge University Press, 1997), pp. 16–35 (p. 26).

167. Jane Goldman, 'The Feminist Criticism of Virginia Woolf', in *A History of Feminist Literary Criticism,* ed. by Gill Plain and Susan Sellers (Cambridge: Cambridge University Press, 2007), pp. 66–84 (p. 71).

168. Tom Turner, *Garden History: Philosophy and Design 2000 BC–2000 AD* (London and New York: Spon Press, 2005), p. 205.

169. John Dixon Hunt, *The Picturesque Garden in Europe* (London: Thames and Hudson, 2003), p. 127.

170. Charlton, *New Images*, p. 33. (My emphasis.)

171. Ibid., p. 41.

172. William Cronnon, 'Forward', in Marjorie Hope Nicholson, *Mountain Gloom and Mountain Glory, the Development of the Aesthetics of the Infinite* (Cornell: Cornell University Press, 1997), pp. vii–xii (pp. viii–ix).

173. Charles de Secondat, Baron de Montesquieu, *Voyages de Montesquieu,* 2 vols (Bordeaux: G. Gounouilhou, 1894), I, p. 20.

174. Cronnon, pp. viii–ix.

175. These writers included: C-F. Volney, *Voyage en Syrie et en Égypte pendant les années 1783, 1784, et 1785,* 2 vols (Paris: Volland, 1787); François-René de Chateaubriand, *Itinéraire de Paris à Jérusalem* (Paris: Furne et Cie, 1865); Domingo Badía y Leblich (Ali Bey), *Voyages d'Ali Bey el Abbassi en Afrique et en Asie pendant les années 1803, 1804, 1805, 1806 et 1807* (Paris: P. Didot, 1814); Dominique-Vivant Denon, *Voyage dans la basse et la haute-Égypte pendant les campagnes du général Bonaparte* (Paris: P. Didot, 1802).

176. Nicole Barre, *Le Désert et la littérature de voyage européenne du XIXe siècle* (Doctoral Thesis, Università di Bologna, 2014), p. 9.

177. Edmund Burke, *A Philosophical Inquiry into the Origin of Our Ideas of the Sublime and Beautiful; with an Introductory Discourse Concerning Taste* (New York: Harper and Brothers, 1844), p. 168.

178. Immanuel Kant, *Observations on the Feeling of the Beautiful and Sublime,* trans. by John T. Goldthwait (London: University of California Press, 1991), p. 47. The original German edition was first published in 1764.

179. David McCallam, 'The Volcano: From Enlightenment to Revolution', *Nottingham French Studies,* 45:1 (2006), 52–68.

180. L. Kong, 'Cemeteries and Columbaria, Memorials and Mausoleums: Narrative and Interpretation in the Study of Deathscapes in Geography', *Australian Geographical Studies,* 37:1 (1999), 1–10; K.V. Hartig and K.M. Dunn, 'Roadside Memorials: Interpreting New Deathscapes in Newcastle, New South Wales', *Australian Geographical Studies,* 36 (1998) 5–20; Avril Maddrell and James D. Sidaway, *Deathscapes: Spaces for Death, Dying, Mourning and Remembrance* (Surrey, UK; Burlington VT: Ashgate, 2010).

181. Lawrence Buell, *The Environmental Imagination: Thoreau, Nature Writing, and the Formation of American Culture* (Cambridge, MA; London: Belknap Press of Harvard University Press, 1996), p. 430.

182. Ibid., p. 7.

183. Simon C. Estok, 'Shakespeare and Ecocriticism: An Analysis of "Home" and "Power" in King Lear', *Journal of the Australasian Universities Language and Literature Association,* 103 (2005), 13–36 (p. 16).

184. Carolyn Merchant, *Radical Ecology: The Search for a Livable World* (New York: Routledge, 2005), p. 201.

185. This is not to say that certain arguments which echo elements of what critics would later term 'ecofeminism' do not occasionally appear in post-revolutionary French women's writing. Indeed, I have approached some of the texts in the present corpus through this method elsewhere. See: Christie Margrave, 'Early Developments of Ecofeminist Thought in French Women's Early Romantic Fiction', *Essays in French Literature and Culture*, 55 (2018) 43–62.

186. Merchant, *Radical Ecology*, p. 201.

187. Merchant, *Earthcare*, p. 10.

188. Ibid., p. 11.

189. Elizabeth Carlassare, 'Destabilizing the Criticism of Essentialism in Ecofeminist Discourse', *Capitalism Nature Socialism*, 5:3 (1994), 50–66 (p. 50). See also J. Nhanenge, *Ecofeminism: Towards Integrating the Concerns of Women, Poor People, and Nature into Development* (Lanham: University Press of America, 2011), p. 153.

190. Philippe Van Tieghem, *Le Romantisme français* (Paris: Presses Universitaires de France, 1999), p. 5.

191. Paul Van Tieghem, *Le Préromantisme: études d'histoire littéraire européene*, 3 vols (Paris: Felix Alcan, 1924–1947). See also: Virgil Nemoianu, *The Taming of Romanticism: European Literature and the Age of Biedermeier* (Cambridge, MA: Harvard University Press, 1984).

192. Pasco; Émile Faguet, *A Literary History of France* (London: T.F. Unwin, 1907).

193. 'Rousseau n'est pas à l'égard du Romantisme un précurseur. Il est le Romantisme intégral' ['With regard to Romanticism, Rousseau is not a precursor. He is all of Romanticism']. Pierre Lasserre, *Le Romantisme français: essai sur la Révolution dans les sentiments et dans les idées au XIXe siècle* (Genève: Slatkine, 2000), p. 14.

194. Caroline Warman, 'Pre-Romantic French Thought,' in *The Oxford Handbook of European Romanticism*, ed. Paul Hamilton (Oxford: OUP, 2016), pp. 17–32 (p. 17).

195. Susan Noakes, 'The Rhetoric of Travel: The French Romantic Myth of Naples', *Ethnohistory*, 33:2 (1986), 139–48 (p. 139).

196. Maurice Cranston, *The Romantic Movement* (Oxford: Blackwell, 1994).

197. Nemoianu, p. 78.

198. Paul Hamilton (ed.), *The Oxford Handbook of European Romanticism* (Oxford: OUP, 2016).

199. Michael Ferber (ed.), *A Companion to European Romanticism* (Oxford: Blackwell, 2005).

200. Pierre Brunel (ed.), *Romantismes européens et Romantisme français* (Montpellier: Éditions espaces, 2000).

201. D. G. Charlton (ed.), *The French Romantics*, 2 vols (Cambridge: CUP, 1984).

202. Anne K. Mellor, 'Feminism', in *Romanticism: An Oxford Guide*, ed. by Nicholas Roe (Oxford: Oxford University Press, 2005), pp. 182–98.

203. James C. McKusick, 'Nature', in *A Companion to European Romanticism*, ed. by Michael Ferber (Oxford: Blackwell, 2005), pp. 413–32 (427). Although there is a useful chapter on Early French Romanticism in *A Companion to European Romanticism*, the only woman referred to is Staël. The other chapters on French Romanticism do not focus on women at all. Krüdener is alluded to once in the book in passing. Cottin, Souza and Genlis do not appear. Furthermore, whilst there is a chapter discussing nature and Romanticism, this also does not refer to women's writing. Similarly, in Alfred Biedermann (ed.), *Romantisme européen*, 2 vols (Paris: Larousse, 1972), George Sand, Germaine de Staël and Emily Brontë are the only three women mentioned.

204. Stephen Pricket and Simon Haines (eds.), *European Romanticism: A Reader* (London: Continuum, 2010).

205. Gérard Gengembre, 'Introduction to French Romanticism', in *European Romanticism: A Reader*, ed. by Stephen Pricket and Simon Haines (London: Continuum, 2010), pp. 33–37 (p. 33). See also: Stephen Prickett, 'General Introduction', in *European Romanticism: A Reader*, ed. by Stephen Pricket and Simon Haines (London: Continuum, 2010), pp. 1–20 (p. 13). Problems defining the concept were recognized even at the turn of the nineteenth century, when Louis-Sébastien Mercier stated in 1801: 'On sent le Romantique, on ne le définit point' ['One feels Romanticism, one does not define it']. Louis-Sébastien Mercier, *Néologie, ou vocabulaire de mots nouveaux, à renouveler, ou pris dans des acceptions nouvelles*, 2 vols (Paris: Moussard; Maradan, 1801), II, p. 230.

206. Lilian R. Furst, 'Romanticism in Historical Perspective', *Comparative Literature Studies*, 5:2 (1968), 115–43.
207. Gérard Gengembre, 'Introduction to French Romanticism', p. 33.
208. Biedermann.
209. Lilian R. Furst, 'The "Imprisoning Self": Goethe's Werther and Rousseau's Solitary Walker', in *European Romanticism: Literary Cross-Currents, Modes, and Models*, ed. by Gerhart Hoffmeister (Detroit: Wayne State University Press, 1990), pp. 145–61 (p. 146).
210. Prabhu Venkataraman, 'Romanticism, Nature, and Self-Reflection in Rousseau's Reveries of a Solitary Walker', in *Cosmos and History: The Journal of Natural and Social Philosophy*, 11:1 (2015), 327–41 (p. 331).
211. Victor Carrabino, 'The Nouveau Roman and the Neo-Romantic Hero', in *The Comparatist*, 7 (1983), 29–35 (p. 29).
212. D. G. Charlton, 'Prose Fiction', in D. G. Charlton (ed.), *The French Romantics*, 2 vols (Cambridge: CUP, 1984), I, pp. 163–203 (p. 169).
213. Ibid.
214. Ibid., p. 170.
215. Patrick Vincent, 'A Continent of Corinnes: The Romantic Poetess and the Diffusion of Liberal Culture in Europe, 1815–1850', in *A Companion to European Romanticism*, ed. by Michael Ferber (Oxford: Blackwell, 2005), pp. 486–504 (p. 488).
216. Bertrand-Jennings, p.138.
217. Charlton, 'Prose Fiction', p. 171.
218. McKusick, p. 413.
219. See: Mornet; Trahard; Paul Van Tieghem, *Le Sentiment de la nature dans le préromantisme européen* (Paris: A. G. Nizet, 1960); David Williams, *Rousseau: Les Rêveries du Promeneur Solitaire* (London: Grant & Cutler, 1984); Alexander Minski, *Le Préromantisme* (Paris: Armand Colin, 1998); René Goderne 'Les Nouvellistes des Années 1780–1820', in *Préromantisme: Hypothèque ou hypothèse?*, ed. by Paul Viallaneix (Paris: Klincksieck, 1975); Nouchine Behbahani, *Paysages dans La Nouvelle Héloïse* (Oxford: Voltaire Foundation at the Taylor Institution, 1989).
220. Warman, p. 17.
221. McKusick, p. 413.
222. Ibid., p. 431.
223. Raymond Immerwahr, ' "Romantic" and its Cognates in England, Germany, and France before 1790', in *'Romantic' and its Cognates: The European History of a Word*, ed. by Hans Eichner (Manchester: Manchester University Press, 1972), pp. 17–97 (pp. 41–45); Gérard Gengembre, *Le Romantisme* (Paris: Ellipses, 1995), pp. 11–12.
224. Alain Vaillant (ed.), *Dictionnaire du Romantisme* (Paris: CNRS Editions, 2012), Entry on 'Nature', p. 503.

CHAPTER 1

❖

Landscapes of Love and Liberty:
Debates Regarding Marriage

Qui ne frémirait d'horreur en songeant que c'est cependant chez ce peuple,
que l'autorité paternelle dispose, pour sa convenance, du cœur des jeunes gens;
que c'est dans ce pays où le sentiment, qui prépare les longues unions, n'est pas
même consulté. [...] Ce n'est pas un hyménée, c'est un sacrifice.

[Who would not tremble in horror to think that it is amongst our people
that paternal authority disposes of the hearts of young people for its own
convenience, or to think that it is in this country that sentiment, which makes
for long-lasting marriages, is not even consulted. [...] They are not marriages,
they are sacrifices.]

LE COMTE D'ANTRAIGUES, *Observations sur le Divorce.*[1]

Persistent Problems in a Period which Expected Change

During the Ancien Régime, French society was eminently patriarchal, bestowing
on women few, if any, juridical or familial rights:

In the traditional marriage the husband and father exercised both legal and
actual power over the person and property of his wife and children. He
enjoyed management of their property and of the revenue that it produced.
The law permitted him to discipline his wife and children, either by physical
punishment or by confinement in a correctional institution. [...] As his children
matured, he decided whether or not they might marry and, if so, how to
arrange their marriages so as to help them and the family to realize economic
and social goals.[2]

For reasons of finance, inheritance or elevating the family's position within the
social hierarchy, a father arranging a child's marriage was normal. Although not
every enforced marriage was disagreeable, inhibiting an individual's liberty to
choose a partner based on love greatly increased the risk of unhappiness. This was
particularly the case for the female partner, whose dominating father was often
replaced by a dominating husband.

   With the Revolution's calls for liberty and assertion of the rights of mankind
came a new perception of what marriage should entail. The necessity for liberty to
choose a partner based on love was foremost in the minds of would-be reformers,
as was the desire to rail against the constraints of marriage and the impossibility of
divorce. James F. Traer states:

Freedom of choice and affection were to be the basic elements of the modern marriage. Husband and wife were to be equals, and children more nearly equal to parents and sooner freed from the disabilities of legal minority than were their counterparts under the ancien régime. The modern marriage thus became less a means of aiding the spouses' families to attain economic and social goals than an opportunity for the spouses themselves to find self-fulfilment and happiness.[3]

Women also joined the throng of protestors. Genlis desired, in particular, for the *lettre de cachet* to be abolished because of the power it wielded over women. Through the *lettre de cachet*, 'a husband could have his erring wife immured without appeal in a convent for the rest of her days'.[4] Genlis was not alone:

> The cahiers genre of 1789–90 encompassed dozens of grievance pamphlets that claimed female authorship and addressed the National Assembly or the king on behalf of women. [...] [T]he amelioration of women's position within the family and marriage topped the list of demands.[5]

Suzanne Desan continues: 'In sum, in the years between 1789 and 1792, the press, popular societies, women's cahiers, petitioners, satirists, divorce pamphleteers, and lay and clerical moralists increasingly pushed marital reform into the arena of national debate'.[6] Such evident contemporary recognition of the need for reform perhaps gives the impression that the coming decades would herald a change for the better for women. However, this did not prove to be the case.

The issue of divorce seemed resolved when it was legalized in the early days of the Republic, in 1792, yet there were still underlying problems. Firstly, although authorized, divorce was not always approved. Secondly, divorce laws were not equal, it being easier for a man to divorce his wife than for a woman to divorce her husband. By the time of the first Empire, this was so concretized that it appeared in writing.[7] According to Nicholas White, Article 230 of the *Code Civil*, which concerned divorce, 'performed grammatically the dissymmetry of gender in Napoleonic France'.[8] Furthermore, the legalisation of divorce was not accompanied by increased legal rights for those women who remained married. A woman remained inferior to her husband, as article 213 of the *Code Civil* indicates: 'Le mari doit protection à sa femme, la femme obéissance à son mari' [A husband must protect his wife; a wife must obey her husband'].[9] In fact, a married woman had no juridical or political rights whatsoever, as an examination of article 1124 reveals: 'Les incapables de contracter sont les mineurs, les interdits, les femmes mariées, dans les cas exprimés par la loi, et généralement tous ceux auxquels la loi a interdit certains contrats' ['Those unable to draw up contracts are: minors, exiles, married women, in cases outlined by the law, and generally all those to whom the law forbids certain contrats'].[10] The situation regarding arranged marriages also did not improve. Further examination of the 1804 *Code Civil*, in particular the section entitled *De la puissance paternelle* [On Paternal Power], confirms that all family decisions remained with the father. This applied to choices in children's marriage partners as much as anything else. As a result of continued gender inequality, in the wake of the Revolution, '[d]es protestations sporadiques se manifestèrent dès l'application de cette législation "mysogyne" et Fourier, le premier, en 1808, prononça l'expression "émancipation féminine"' ['sporadic protests broke out following the application of this "misogynistic" legislation and Fourier was the first, in 1808, to coin the expression "women's emancipation"'].[11]

Despite the ideals of human rights and increased freedom, the Revolution had disappointed women in this respect. It is under such a regime that Cottin, Genlis, Krüdener, Souza and Staël were living, and such a historical context which informed and influenced their writing. It is perhaps little wonder, then, that in the 1790s and at the turn of the nineteenth century arranged and forbidden marriages still occupied the pen of these female novelists, infiltrating novels including Cottin's *Claire d'Albe* (1799), *Malvina* (1800–1801), *Amélie Mansfield* (1802–1803), *Mathilde* (1805), Krüdener's *Valérie* (1803), Genlis's *Adèle et Théodore* (1782), Souza's *Adèle de Sénange* (1794), *Émilie et Alphonse* (1799) and *Eugénie et Mathilde* (1811), and Staël's *Delphine* (1802) and *Corinne* (1807). This chapter will analyse Cottin's *Malvina*, Souza's *Émilie et Alphonse* and Souza's *Adèle de Sénange* in order to demonstrate how the depiction both of tamed nature and of nature cultivated to look untamed helps to concretize the presentation of issues of arranged and forbidden marriage encountered by female characters. Brief comparison is also made to Cottin's *Claire d'Albe* and Staël's *Delphine*.

The Garden Utopian Idyll in Women's Writing

As the new desire to appreciate nature in its 'more tranquil, immediately attractive forms'[12] overtook the French, a new enthusiasm for 'idealised agricultural scenery',[13] for '"les maisons des champs", "l'idylle champêtre", "plaisirs rustiques", "les jardins", "voyages pittoresques"' ['"houses amongst fields", "the rural idyll", "rustic pleasures", "gardens", "picturesque journeys"'],[14] and for meandering in country parks resulted in nature and rustic living playing a larger role in public social life. As the public sought escape from the horrors of the Revolution and Terror, desire to seek out the tranquillity of rural idylls became more pronounced, an unsurprising phenomenon, as early nineteenth-century observers of landscape taste themselves acknowledged:

> Il semble que la vie de la campagne acquiert un nouveau charme après les grandes révolutions, lorsque les hommes, fatigués des événements, aiment à se reposer quelque temps dans le calme de la retraite. [...] [L]es plaisirs des champs adoucissent leurs maux.

> [It seems that country living aquires a new charm after great revolutions, whose events render men weary, and encourage them to enjoy relaxing for a while in the tranquility of retreat. [...] [T]he pleasures of country fields soothe their sorrows].[15]

All of this, in turn, caused a revival in pastoral literature and fictional utopian idylls, as Astbury has argued with regard to the fiction penned by Bernardin de Saint-Pierre, Jean-Pierre Claris de Florian, Jean-André Perreau, the Baron de Bilderbeck, and other male writers.[16] The works of these writers echoed the rural idylls of

Virgil and Theocritus, and, closer to home, those of Salomon Gessner's *Idyllen*, of which the first translation into French appeared in 1761/2. The *Idyllen* were read by Rousseau upon publication, and they inspired both his own later writings, as well as the Romantic work of Chateaubriand.[17] Astbury asserts that 'Gessner's work clearly touched a chord during the 1760s in particular, feeding into the vogue for sensibility and into the 'return to nature' movement; but there is a surprising revival of interest for his work during the Revolutionary decade'.[18] The era certainly witnessed an interest in reading and writing '"poèmes champêtres", "pastorales", "idylles" and "églogues naïves"' ['"rural poems", "pastoral landscapes", "idylls" and "innocent eclogues"'].[19]

There is also a revival of interest in the utopian idyll at the close of the eighteenth and turn of the nineteenth century in women's writing: some of the garden spaces that we begin to see arise in women's literature of the post-revolutionary period are specifically utopian in nature. Yet the way in which women writers employ utopian idylls at this time has not, thus far, been investigated. This chapter will give a brief, yet significant insight into the ways in which the utopian tradition might be used for the purposes of re-establishing a space for the female voice. Cottin and Souza (and to some extent also Staël) combine images of the garden as a love idyll, a space of erotic encounter, an echo of Eden (including the notion of the Fall), and a space in which the melancholy may wander. In so doing, they highlight both the contemporary desire to seek out natural landscape as a space of romantic emotion and also the oppressive power that society has over women regarding forbidden or arranged marriages.

The women's novels analysed below do not pertain to the classical pastoral tradition. Firstly, they do not involve farming, milkmaids, shepherds, or the rural landscape of antiquity. Secondly, the novels are not backward-looking in the traditional sense: to a mythical golden age. Where the novels do provide nostalgic sentiment or retrospective comment on a paradise lost, it is for an idyll previously experienced by the protagonists themselves early on in the novel, which they lose forever once they have left its boundaries. However, as Astbury states with regard to the pastoral literature of the age in general, the classical model came 'to be replaced by a more general use of the notion of the pastoral which comes to refer to any idyllic countryside setting'.[20] Indeed, she argues that Malcolm Cook's definition of the pastoral as 'a picture of an idyllic world in a real framework'[21] is a more accurate one to portray the pastoral tradition of this period, and it is this definition which will be adhered to within this chapter. Similarly, these novels do not echo the canonical eighteenth-century examples of utopian fiction which describe foreign or imaginary countries, futuristic societies, or states governed by animals.[22] The eighteenth-century definition of utopia quoted by Cook states 'Utopie se dit en général d'un plan de gouvernement imaginaire, où tout est parfaitement réglé pour le bonheur commun, comme dans le pays fabuleux d'Utopie décrit dans un livre de Thomas Morus qui porte ce titre' ['Utopia is generally said to be a design for an imaginary government, where everything is perfectly arranged for common happiness, as it is in the mythical country of Utopia described in the book by

Thomas More which bears the same title'].[23] The novels of Cottin, Souza and Staël do not depict autonomous governments or civilizations, real or imaginary. Nor do their plotlines take place within a fictional exotic paradise in the manner of Bernardin de Saint-Pierre's *Paul et Virginie* or *La Chaumière indienne*, for example. Rather, like Rousseau's *Julie ou la Nouvelle Héloïse* — whose garden at Clarens is often referred to as a utopian setting[24] — these women's novels include the description of a garden which is afforded utopian attributes. Firstly, in these gardens, 'tout est parfaitement réglé pour le bonheur commun' ['everything is perfectly arranged for common happiness'], and therefore the gardens fit the contemporary definition of utopia in this respect. Secondly, the gardens' descriptions highlight their 'clôture spatiale' ['being spatially enclosed'], separating them from external society, deemed a necessary quality for a utopian setting by Jean-Michel Racault.[25] Thirdly, as is argued below, they are presented so that they might be used to critique the problems prevalent within the society inhabited by the authors. Alexandre Cioranescu defines utopia as 'la description littéraire individualisée d'une société imaginaire, organisée sur des bases qui impliquent une critique sous-jacente de la société réelle' ['the individualized literary description of an imaginary society, structured to imply an underlying critique of real society'],[26] and this is precisely what the utopian gardens and parks of post-revolutionary women's writing achieve. These attributes so crucial to utopias will be analysed more closely in conjunction with an application of Mikhail Bakhtin's paradigm of the idyllic chronotope, which in turn will highlight precisely how the physical utopian nature of the gardens is conveyed. However, because Souza and Cottin's novels do not display all the traditional qualities of fictional utopias, in order to avoid confusion between the types of utopian garden featuring in their novels and the traditional utopian society or country with its independent system of idealistic government, I will refer to the gardens in *Émilie et Alphonse* and *Malvina* as 'utopian idylls' or 'utopian gardens' rather than straightforward 'utopias' or 'utopian societies'.

    The choice of a garden setting for a utopian idyll is apt for many reasons. Firstly, it calls to mind the paradise of the Garden of Eden. Secondly, one method of achieving the retreat from urban life so commonly desired on account of the prevailing Rousseauesque Zeitgeist in mid and late eighteenth-century France was by creating a garden to which one could escape: 'In novel after novel, the garden appears as the incarnation of longings running counter to the progressive tide of the time, social norms, urban civilization'.[27] Rousseau himself retreated to the Île Saint-Pierre for several months in 1765, and his heroine, Julie, creates her own utopian garden at Clarens. Julie's 'Élysée' ['Elysium'], comprises 'une verdure animée et vive, des fleurs éparses de tous côtés, un gazouillement d'eau courante et le chant de mille oiseaux' ['lively, animated greenery, flowers scattered on all sides, the babbling of flowing water and the song of a thousand birds'], and provides her with a space of tranquillity, beauty and, more specifically, of safety: the garden 'est tellement caché [...] qu'on ne l'aperçoit de nulle part [...] et il est toujours soigneusement fermé à clé' ['is so hidden [...] that you do not notice it from anywhere [...] and it is always locked with care'].[28] The Clarens garden certainly displays the 'clôture spatiale' necessary for protecting its inhabitant from the rest of vice-ridden society. Other writers, including both those analysed by Astbury and the women writers under consideration here, drew on Rousseau for inspiration as they provided material for the new tastes of the reading public: 'Les jardins entrent en littérature à ce moment à la fois comme cadres [...] mais aussi comme signes de l'appartenance à une nouvelle esthétique' ['Gardens enter into literature at this time not only as settings [...] but also as indications of belonging to a new aesthetic'].[29]

Utopian fiction was not only a means of escape from reality, however, it also provided a means of critiquing the widespread corruption and social and political turmoil in France. Cook states that 'the presentation of a "foreign" reality could, paradoxically, be more persuasive than a critical account of the homeland'.[30] For women writers, the desire to escape and critique French society does not simply involve criticizing the political situation, the wave of libertine *mœurs* sweeping the country, or, in many cases, the violence of the Revolution and Terror. In fact often it may involve very little of this type of criticism. Rather, these writers criticize the oppression of their sex, and the difficulties women faced either within marriage or with regard to choosing a marital partner. Cook's statement still stands, however: often more effective than an outright diatribe against France and its ideas is the presentation of an idyll in which 'tout est parfaitement réglé pour le bonheur commun'. Whilst certain women writers, like their male counterparts, did set their utopian idylls in foreign lands (Cottin sets *Malvina*'s utopian garden in Scotland, and Staël sets *Corinne*'s idylls in Italy), the idyll need not be overseas. In *Émilie et Alphonse,* Souza creates a utopian idyll in France; it is simply 'foreign' in that it is set apart (physically, idealistically, even temporally) from ordinary society and its expectations.

The gently tamed natural countryside retreat or garden utopian idyll works well for addressing issues of love and marriage for several reasons. Firstly it provides the lovers with a hiding place and thus allows a forbidden love to develop secretly. It provides lovers with an escape from those issuing them with orders regarding what they must and must not do apropos of love and marriage. Secondly, the garden permits passion to come to the fore, thus allowing us to witness the emotions engendered in the female protagonist by her forbidden love. The garden idyll is an appropriate scene for encouraging passion because of the early Romantic link between nature and sentimental emotion. With the rise of sentimental novels, new importance became attached to a character's situation within space, their perception of space, and most specifically the emotions which space creates within them. Weisgerber argues:

> La sensibilité de Rousseau [...] se distingue par l'interpénétration des objets et du sujet qui les perçoit. Ainsi, l'espace de *La Nouvelle Héloïse* révèle un double mouvement: projection du 'moi' dans le monde et, inversement, absorption du monde par le 'moi'. [...] [L]e narrateur pénètre résolument dans le tableau qu'il dépeint, imbibant les choses et des sentiments, de ses idées. [...] Le décor s'humanise, les objets sont personnifiés, les émotions se muent en formes visibles.

[Rousseau's *sensibilité* [...] is specific in its interpenetration of objects and the subject which perceives them. Thus, the space in *The New Héloïse* reveals a double movement: the projection of the 'self' in the world and, inversely, the absorption of the world by the 'self'. [...] [T]he narrator penetrates the tableau that he depicts resolutely, imbibing objects and sentiments with his ideas. [...] The decor becomes more human, objects are personified, emotions take on visible shapes].[31]

Moreover, objects in space become viewed for their sentimental value: 'La chose se change en "signe mémoratif", elle n'est pas vue en soi et pour soi, mais renvoie à des sentiments, à des concepts' ['The object becomes a "memorative symbol"; it is not seen in itself and for itself, but rather evokes feelings and concepts'].[32] The natural features of a utopian idyll, therefore, are not simply regarded as objects with no intimate or innate value. When they are gazed upon, it is with the ability to perceive that the garden's nature is capable of eliciting or highlighting an emotional response.

If gazing upon nature supposedly excites emotions, then a garden setting logically provides the necessary opportunity for heightened feelings of love. Indeed, Gail Finney identifies the 'garden as erotic enclave' as the predominant type of garden motif to appear in early nineteenth-century French literature.[33] Finney establishes three possible interpretations of the garden in literature. Alongside the garden as a scene of erotic encounter, she also delineates the 'garden as ethical construct', and the 'garden as a[n] [...] image of Eden'.[34] The present discussion will expand upon the first and third of these types of garden, as both are pertinent to the presentation of utopian idylls in post-revolutionary women's writing.

According to Finney, the garden as erotic enclave

> appears as a natural retreat from the artificiality of urban culture and its conventions. As the only remnant of nature within a domesticized space, the garden serves here as the setting for the recognition of, and frequently the yielding to, sexual desire, for illicit, most often adulterous encounters.[35]

Although, with the notable exception of *Claire d'Albe,* falling in love in Cottin's and Souza's novels does not always entail an extra-marital affair, often one of the protagonists has nonetheless been promised to a third party by parental agreement, thus rendering the amorous encounter with a stranger an illicit liaison by society's standards. Even when no such arranged union has been proposed, the protagonists' love is nevertheless often equally forbidden by society, due to the inappropriate financial or social position of one of the couple, or because their general character is deemed unsuitable. Thus, for the kindling of forbidden love to occur in 'a natural retreat from the artificiality of urban culture and its conventions' (and a consequent retreat from society's contrived obligations) is apt. Furthermore, Finney's statement that the garden is 'the only remnant of nature within a domesticized space' parallels the fact that, for the female protagonist, the garden retreat provides liberty from the restrictions of domestic expectations. Thus, the reaction of a female protagonist who falls in love with a man forbidden to her is to seek out the garden retreat where she can freely both experience and express her emotions.

In Cottin's *Claire d'Albe*, the heroine actually links her new-found, forbidden amorous emotions with nature, writing: 'Que ce sentiment céleste me tienne lieu de tous ceux auxquels j'ai renoncé; qu'il anime la nature; que je le retrouve partout' ['May this heavenly feeling replace all those I have renounced; may it animate nature; may I find it everywhere'] (*C d'A*, p.43) She also consummates her forbidden passion in a natural space at the close of the novel, making love to Frédéric 'au bas de son jardin, sous l'ombre des peupliers qui couvrent l'urne de son père' ['at the bottom of her garden, under the poplar trees which cover her father's urn'] (*C d'A*, p.145). As we have seen, eighteenth-century French physicians and thinkers, such as Roussel and Rousseau, believed that woman was linked with nature because of her greater propensity towards emotion. *Claire d'Albe* engages with this notion, providing an example both of a woman's sentiment bringing nature to life, and of nature providing a space for a female protagonist to display her passionate, erotic emotion.

The notion of being able to identify and express one's emotions freely within a garden is also exhibited in Staël's *Delphine*. The couple pick leaves from the same tree whilst sharing their opinions with one another (*D* I, 148). It is in the garden that Léonce's feelings for Delphine are aroused:

> J'aperçus d'une des hauteurs du jardin, à travers l'ombre des arbres, cette charmante figure que je ne puis méconnaître. [...] Le vent venait de son côté [...]; en respirant cet air je croyais m'enivrer d'elle. (*D* I, 253)

> [From one of the high points in the garden, I noticed, through the shadow of the trees, the charming face that I could not ignore. [...] The wind came from her direction [...]; as I breathed that air in, I felt intoxicated by her.]

Similarly, in her garden at Bellerive, Delphine also contemplates 'l'attendrissement que [lui] causait l'image de Léonce' ['the affection that Léonce's image aroused in her'] (*D* I, 223), stating: 'Je descendis, vers le soir, dans mon jardin, et je méditais pendant quelque temps, avec assez d'austérité, sur la destinée des âmes sensibles au milieu du monde' ['As evening approached, I went down into my garden, and I meditated solemnly for a while, on the destiny of sensitive souls in the midst of the world'] (*D* I, 222). We should note that the garden also permits meditation and reflection. There are clear echoes here both of Rousseau and of European Romantic writers, who also liked to reflect on the self and the world, particularly from within the heart of the natural landscape.

In the case of Souza's *Émilie et Alphonse*, Émilie's mother (the Comtesse de Foix) plans for her to marry the duc de Candale. However, soon after their arrival in Compiègne, where Émilie is to be introduced to the Duke, Émilie ventures into the countryside around the estate, and encounters Alphonse. The description of the countryside setting to which Émilie retreats highlights the idyllic atmosphere around her:

> [J]e me levai hier matin de très bonne heure, pour me promener dans un bois presque contigu à la maison, mais enfermé dans l'enceinte du parc. Un ruisseau de l'eau la plus vive et la plus limpide y serpente; il est bordé par un joli sentier qui conduit à un rocher naturel, d'où la source s'échappe à travers des groupes de saules pleureurs et d'arbres verts: c'est là que je portais mes pas. Le soleil était

depuis fort peu de temps sur l'horizon; la terre, émaillée de fleurs et brillante de la rosée du matin, le silence, la solitude, tout me charmait. Je m'abandonnais à mes rêveries en remontant le ruisseau, et m'arrêtais souvent pour jouir du calme qui m'environnait; je me croyais seule, lorsque j'aperçus aux environs de la source, un jeune homme qui descendait lentement ce même chemin. (É, pp. 6–7)

[[Y]esterday morning I got up at a very early hour in order to take a walk in a wood, which is almost adjacent to the house but is enclosed within the walls of the park. Through the wood, snakes a stream of the brightest, clearest water, alongside which runs a pretty path leading to a natural rock. Here, the source of the stream flows out through groves of weeping willows and green trees. It was here that I wended my way. The sun had only just appeared on the horizon. The earth, adorned with flowers and glistening with morning dew, the silence, the solitude: I was beguiled by everything. I gave myself over to my daydreams as I went up by the stream, and I stopped frequently to enjoy the tranquility which surrounded me. I believed myself to be alone, when, in the vicinity of the spring, I glimpsed a young man who was slowly coming down the same path.]

The 'pretty path' has been arranged to conduct the wanderer to the loveliest parts of the garden: the rocks, willows and source of the stream. Furthermore, as it is 'enfermé dans l'enceinte du parc' ['enclosed within the walls of the park'], it is sufficiently separated from the rest of society for it to be classed as a utopian idyll. The adjectives 'limpide' ['crystal clear'], 'naturel' ['natural'] and 'verts' ['green'] highlight the park's idyllic purity, freshness and verdant health, whilst 'brillante' ['glistening'], 'joli' ['pretty'] and 'émaillée' ['adorned'] underline its beauty and majesty. Coupled with the words 'me charmait' ['I was beguiled'], these adjectives indicate that the space is a joyful one which reflects the heroine's happiness. Émilie does not yet recognize the source of her joy, and therefore struggles to express it in words. The natural landscape, however, is capable of conveying her happiness to the reader through its beauty and brilliance. Positive connotations are abundant, highlighting the positive way in which we are encouraged to view the love born in this space. The dawning of newly awakened feelings in Émilie is mirrored in the dawn of the day: the sun has barely risen, dew lies sparkling on the grass and the world is tranquil. In this space, at the heart of nature, Émilie, like Léonce and Delphine, can reflect on her thoughts.

Inspired by the scene, when she catches sight of Alphonse and perceives his melancholia, Émilie's emotions are aroused. To begin with, she attributes her feelings to compassion, but her description of him reveals to the reader that she finds him physically attractive:

[I]l avançait le regard baissé, absorbé dans une mélancolie profonde. [...] [M]on aimable sœur imaginera de longues paupières noires couvrant de grands yeux qui ne daignaient pas se lever; des traits d'une beauté et d'une régularité parfaites, dont l'expression triste et douce inspire la pitié; une taille élégante et noble, que la lenteur et l'abandon de sa marche empêchaient d'être trop imposante. (É, pp. 7–8)

[[H]e came towards me, his gaze lowered, absorbed in a profound melancholy. [...] [M]y kind sister will picture his large dark eyelids covering his wide eyes, which he did not deign to raise; his perfect, beautiful, symmetrical features,

whose sad and sweet expression inspires pity; his elegant and noble build, which
was made less imposing by his slow, nonchalant gait.]

A handsome stranger has appeared in Émilie's utopian idyll, one whom society will
forbid her from marrying, but who can appear to her in his full glory in this garden
separated from the expectations of the outside world.

Bakhtin's paradigm of the idyllic chronotope distinguishes four types of idyll, one
of which he identifies as 'the love idyll'.[36] He defines this as follows:

> In the love idyll [...] [t]he utterly conventional simplicity of life in the bosom
> of nature is opposed to social conventions, complexity and the disjunctions
> of everyday private life; life here is abstracted into a love that is completely
> sublimated. Beneath the conventional, metaphorical, stylized aspects of such a
> love one can still dimly perceive the immanent unity of time and the ancient
> matrices.[37]

In Souza's novel, the social conventions and complexities of everyday life are indeed
momentarily forgotten as Émilie gazes upon the beautiful setting and the solitary
stranger (who strongly resembles the Romantic-style, melancholic hero) wandering
within it:

> Je m'oubliais depuis longtemps à cette même place, lorsque, me rappelant tout à
> coup qu'il devait être tard, je pensai que ma mère m'avait sans doute demandée,
> et que, pour la première fois peut-être, ce ne serait pas moi qu'elle verrait en
> s'éveillant. (É, p. 9)

> [In this space, I forgot myself for a long time, when suddenly, remembering
> that it must be late, I thought that my mother would certainly have asked for
> me and that, perhaps for the first time, it would not be me that she saw upon
> waking.]

The garden utopia is separated from the outside world temporally as well as spatially.
As Racault states in his definition of utopian idylls, 'la mise à distance spatiale
s'accompagnera presque toujours de la mise en place d'une durée autonome' ['the
spatial distance is almost always accompanied by the setting up of an independent
time span'].[38] Similarly, one of the most significant aspects of Bakhtin's idyllic
chronotope is the 'blurring of all [...] temporal boundaries' which contributes 'to
the creation of the cyclic rhythmicalness of time'.[39] Bakhtin speaks of 'the temporal
boundaries between individual lives and between various phases of one and the
same life' becoming 'less distinct'.[40] This occurs in Souza's novel since, firstly, the
progression of time loses its importance for Émilie when she is within the garden,
and secondly, because the garden permits Émilie to return, figuratively, to life's
origin: it is the *dawn* of a new day, she finds herself at the *source* of a stream. The
scene is, therefore, a perfect love idyll in which Émilie's new-found emotions can
grow while the time and the requirements of external society are forgotten. Within
the idyll, Émilie is protected from society's protests that Alphonse is not a suitable
match. Consequently when Émilie returns to the society external to the idyll, and
we witness these prejudices, they appear all the more striking. As Cook states,
presenting the idyll — a space which lacks the prejudices so frequently seen in real
society — is more effective than simply criticizing French society itself.

Recalled to herself, Émilie is compelled to return home from the utopian idyll. Soon after her encounter with Alphonse, she is introduced to the duc de Candale, and observes the stark contrast between the two men: 'Quelle différence de son maintien à celui de monsieur de Candale!' ['What a difference between his bearing and that of Monsieur de Candale!'] (É, p. 21). Candale strikes her as vain and filled with an arrogant self-importance, embodying all that is wrong with the eighteenth-century French aristocracy. The comtesse desires the union of her daughter with the Duke because he is extremely wealthy and socially superior, yet when Émilie learns of her mother's project, her disgust for Candale is vehemently expressed:

> Monsieur de Candale est l'homme qu'elle a choisi pour gendre, sans savoir si ma préférence justifierait la sienne [...]. Monsieur de Candale, si plein de son mérite, si constamment satisfait! [...] Non, non, jamais, jamais! [...] Mais sûrement ma répugnance pour monsieur de Candale est naturelle, invincible; car jusqu'ici ses manières ne faisaient que me déplaire; à présent que je connais ses projets, il m'est devenu insupportable. (É, pp. 90–91)

> [Monsieur de Candale is the man she has chosen for a son-in-law, without knowing if my preference would bear out her own [...]. Monsieur de Candale, so full of his own worth, so constantly pleased with himself! [...] No, no, never, never! [...] But surely my repugnance for Monsieur de Candale is natural, insurmountable; for, up to now his behaviour only displeased me. And now that I know his designs, he has become unbearable.]

The antithesis of Candale, Alphonse is considerate, reserved and generous. He even saves the lives of Émilie and her mother, when a wooden theatre collapses around them, whilst Candale is too occupied issuing orders to pay attention to his future bride.

Émilie's compassion for Alphonse soon blossoms into love, and as she realizes this, she desires to return to the idyllic natural park in which she first met him:

> Je n'ai pas pu dormir cette nuit; j'avais été trop émue tour à tour de frayeur et de joie. [...] [J]'avoue que j'ai besoin de me retrouver à la place où je l'ai vu pour la première fois; il me semble que là je jouirai mieux, s'il est possible, du bonheur que je lui dois. (É, pp. 43–44)

> [I could not sleep that night. I was too affected by fear and joy in turn [...]. I confess that I need to return to the space in which I saw him for the first time. It seems to me that there I will better enjoy, if it is possible, the happiness that I owe to him.]

If Émilie is truly to open herself to her emotional passion, she recognizes that she must do so in the utopian idyll, the protective garden that gave rise to the ability to perceive these feelings. Yet, Émilie's mother also realizes that her daughter's love for Alphonse was nurtured in the idyllic natural setting. Thus, whilst Émilie wishes to return to the spot in order to allow her love to increase, the Countess believes that Émilie must be removed from the utopian idyll once and for all, to separate her from Alphonse and to facilitate the forced marriage to Candale: 'Je vais quitter Compiègne, ma chère fille; je crains que le bois, la rivière, le sentier ne rappellent trop à votre sœur l'aimable Alphonse' ['I am going to leave Compiègne, my dear daughter; I fear that the wood, the river, the path here remind your sister too much of the amiable Alphonse'] (*É*, p. 54). As Carpenter has argued, *Émilie et Alphonse* is a novel which 'emphasises the damage and destructiveness wrought by society and its norms'.[41] Carpenter, like Wolfgang and Stewart, argues that women writers use subtle methods to critique contemporary reality, and here we have a perfect example — an implicit contrast drawn between a gentle utopian garden in which love grows and flourishes and a cruel society (of which Émilie's mother and Candale are strong representatives) which works to prevent the love from developing further. This contrast ultimately encourages the reader to view the world external to the idyll harshly, and, consequently, to critique the real society upon which it is based.

The utopian idyll does not always constitute the first meeting place of forbidden lovers. Occasionally it provides a space of freedom in which early marital bliss can be enjoyed. In Cottin's *Malvina*, the eponymous heroine and her lover Edmond marry against the wishes of society, and against those of Malvina's benefactress, Mistress Birton, in particular. Birton had previously earmarked Edmond for a family friend, Lady Sumerhill, because the Sumerhill family promised Birton a title should the marriage take place. Furthermore, Malvina had sworn herself to celibacy in order to gain permission to raise Fanny, the daughter of her deceased best friend. Discretion is necessary, therefore, to prevent disapproving society from becoming aware of the marriage until Edmond manages to obtain permission from Fanny's father to adopt the child with Malvina. The couple retreat to a house in the Scottish countryside to gain the freedom and necessary secrecy to enjoy their new life: 'Malvina, après avoir fait [...] mille recommandations de discrétion, monta en voiture avec son époux et sir Charles Weymard, pour se rendre à la campagne que celui-ci leur avait vendue' ['After making a thousand pleas for secrecy, Malvina got into the carriage with her husband and Sir Charles Weymard, in order to go to the country retreat that the latter had sold to them'] (*M* IV, 37–38).

The chapter which immediately follows the relocation, set in the garden of the couple's new home, is entitled 'Bonheur conjugal' ['Conjugal happiness'] and provides a description of the house's situation: 'La maison était petite, mais élégante et commode; elle était située au milieu d'une vaste forêt qui rendait son abord difficile, et entourée d'un enclos considérable bordé de haies vives et de larges fosses' ['The house was small, but elegant and convenient; it was situated in the middle of a vast forest which made it difficult to approach, and was surrounded by a substantial enclosure whose borders comprised hedgerows and wide ditches'] (*M* IV, 38–39). Malvina and Edmond's conjugal countryside home clearly fulfils the utopian requirements of being cut off from society. In fact, the couple go further than simply retreating from urban life, deliberately seeking aspects of nature most capable of concealing them. They situate themselves amid a vast number of trees at the heart of a forest, in a house which is difficult to approach and which is surrounded by tall hedges and wide ditches. Cocooned in this naturally protected environment, they enjoy a few days of marital bliss, their emotions highlighted and encouraged by the perfection of the natural landscape. All nature resounds with their happiness and love:

Malvina se jeta dans les bras de son époux; il la pressa étroitement sur son sein, et tandis que l'amour les unissait si délicieusement, on eût dit que la nature entière cherchait à s'embellir pour eux. Caché dans la feuillée, le rossignol modulait ces cadences touchantes qui semblent partir du cœur et qui vont y mourir; une source d'eau pure, en disputant de murmure avec lui, coulait en filets d'argent sur un tapis d'émeraude; l'astre du jour, en inondant l'occident d'une mer de feu, colorait un ciel d'azur, de nuages d'or et de pourpre; et les premières ombres de la nuit, descendant lentement sur l'univers, luttaient en vain contre les derniers rayons du soleil, tant il semblait que, d'accord avec ces époux, le jour quittât à regret la nature. (*M* IV, 41–42)

[Malvina threw herself into her husband's arms; he pressed her tightly to his chest, and as love united the couple so ecstatically, it seemed as though the whole of nature sought to grow more beautiful for them. Hidden in the foliage, the nightingale modulated its moving cadences, which seemed to come from the heart and return to die there. A spring of pure water, whose murmurings vied with those of the nightingale, ran in silver trickles over an emerald carpet. The sun, the day's star, flooded the west with a sea of fire, and coloured the azure sky with clouds of purple and gold. The first shadows of the night, descending slowly over the world, struggled in vain against the last rays of sunlight, so much so that it seemed as though the day regretted leaving nature behind just as the couple did.]

Nature is steeped in majesty, signalled by the panoply of regal colours — 'silver', 'emerald', 'gold', 'azure' and 'purple' — together with the noun 'star'. The magnificent polychromy of nature is accentuated by the light of the sunset, drawing the reader into a space replete with the happiness that vivid colours and light connote. Beauty abounds in Cottin's natural setting as nature seeks to embellish itself for the lovers. Even the sounds — the song of nightingales and the gentle murmur of a stream — are aptly romantic. In fact, nightingales are not native to Scotland. However, whether the mistake is deliberate or simply a careless oversight does not actually matter here. Either way, the nightingale is present because its romantic overtones complement the image of a utopian love idyll. The waters of this stream, like those in the stream by which Émilie first meets Alphonse, are pure. Nature is embellished with colour, fertility and romance at the very moment the couple's lives, too, become potentially fertile, and filled with romance and vivacity. In this garden, everything is, in the words of the contemporary definition of utopia 'parfaitement réglé pour le bonheur commun' ['perfectly arranged for common happiness'].

Again, echoing Bakhtin's love idyll, temporal boundaries become indistinct. Although night is imminently expected, its attempts to penetrate the scene are in vain, for daylight possesses a will of its own and does not wish to leave this paradise. Through use of pathetic fallacy Cottin ensures that the perfection and happiness provided by the daylight lingers longer than it should, slowing down time, blurring the boundary between day and night, thus underlining the creation of a utopian idyll for her characters' forbidden love.

Despite the suitability of a tamed natural retreat for an amorous encounter, and despite its ability to nurture love within it, such a space rarely endures. According to Finney, 'the escape offered by the garden can only be temporary'.[42] This is the case for Émilie and Malvina. The utopian idyll, like the Garden of Eden, comes to an end and the characters experience a downfall. A happy ending is precluded for them once they have left their Eden. External society ensures that, as punishment for her forbidden love, the heroine either loses any possibility of a union, loses her lover altogether, loses her sanity, or loses her life. Thus Cottin and Souza highlight the oppressive power their own society has over women apropos of love and marriage.

Finney states that the garden as image of Eden is 'the last remnant of nature [...] in an increasingly artificial and mechanized world. In this regard as in others, the garden as image of Eden is informed by Rousseauesque concepts of nature'.[43] In *Émilie et Alphonse* and *Malvina,* the garden in which the protagonists walk together is the last space in which happiness occurs, before the characters (re-)enter dominating society. Edmond and Malvina walk in the garden of their new home, knowing that they must part in order for Edmond to go to Lord Sheridan, Fanny's father. The parting should be temporary, resulting in a happy reunion. However, Mistress Birton discovers that the marriage has taken place, and wreaks her revenge by revealing the truth to Lord Sheridan, before obtaining permission from him to remove the child from Malvina. She tears the child away causing Malvina to lose her mind. When Edmond returns, therefore, there can be no happy ending, as Malvina is insane and dying. On his return, the description of the natural setting around the house reveals a very different atmosphere. The vivid colours, sunlight and beauty with which nature was suffused have all vanished, leaving behind a bleak deathscape to convey Malvina's pain:

> Depuis son départ, les arbres ont perdu leur parure, les fleurs ont disparu, les oiseaux ne chantent plus; un froid piquant a succédé à l'air doux et embaumé qu'on y respirait. Dans son chemin, il aperçoit quelques cyprès religieux, quelques sombres sapins dont les tiges pyramidales conservent un reste de verdure; du haut de leurs sommets le cri du hibou s'est fait entendre; ce son a retenti dans le vaste silence de la nuit, l'écho l'a répété. Edmond frissonne, ses jambes tremblantes se dérobent sous lui; il approche, il est sous les arbres, il heurte une pierre; un rayon de la lune perce le feuillage, et permet à son œil égaré de voir que cette pierre couvre un tombeau; il jette un cri terrible, il tombe; il presse contre son corps cette terre froide et silencieuse. (*M* IV, 156–57)

> [Since his departure, the trees have lost their foliage, the flowers have disappeared, the birds no longer sing. A piercing cold has replaced the sweet, perfumed air . On the path in front of him he perceives several funereal cypress trees and sombre pines whose pyramid-like appearance preserves a vestige of greenery. From their highest treetops, the cries of the owl could be heard, and the sound rang out in the night's vast silence, with the echo repeating it. Edmond shudders; his trembling legs give way beneath him. He comes nearer, he is under the trees and stumbles upon a stone. The moon's rays pierce the foliage and allow his wandering eye to see that this stone covers a tomb. He gives a terrible cry and falls to the ground, pressing his body against the cold and silent ground.]

The garden which once provided safety, happiness and space for the expression of passion has been penetrated by despair. Nature no longer postpones the advent of night, or celebrates love and life. Night has descended, and nature is pervaded by motifs reflecting the iciness and eerie silence of death. Cypresses, representative of death in both ancient mythology and Christian symbolism, are present. Confirming the pertinence of the atmosphere, at the very heart of the garden is a tomb. Malvina is not yet in this tomb, but it awaits her. Nature now reflects the death of the couple's union, and Malvina's literal fate.

The heroine of Cottin's *Claire d'Albe* also feels that nature will reflect her own suffering. The situation is slightly different from that of Malvina, because Claire has not yet succumbed to her desire for Frédéric, however, even the knowledge that she desires an adulterous affair is sufficient for her to feel nature degrade around her:

> J'irai lentement errer dans la campagne; là, choisissant des lieux écartés, j'y cueillerai quelques fleurs sauvages et desséchées comme moi, quelques soucis, emblèmes de ma tristesse: je n'y mêlerai aucun feuillage, la verdure est morte dans la nature, comme l'espérance dans mon cœur. (*C d'A*, p. 130)

> [I will wander slowly in the countryside; there, selecting isolated spots, I will pick some wild flowers which are withered like I am, marigolds, emblems of my sadness. I will not combine any leaves with them; greenery is dead in nature, just as hope is dead in my heart.]

As David Bianciardi states, 'De manière très romantique, le paysage se met en accord avec la situation intérieure du sujet, s'identifiant totalement avec celle-ci' ['In a very Romantic manner, the landscape matches the subject's inner state, identifying completely with it'].[44]

Souza's Émilie leaves her Edenic paradise because she knows her mother is expecting her. Despite her attempts to return to it and to feel her love once again encouraged by nature, she is physically removed from the countryside retreat at Compiègne, and, once married, never permitted to return to it. Instead, the subsequent occasion on which she meets Alphonse, long after her nuptials, is in the wild mountains of the Pyrenees. The couple can never be united, as they well know. Alphonse feels such acute remorse at having let down his dead wife Camille (the reason for his melancholy on his first meeting with Émilie) that it is highly doubtful he would ever seek another union at all; Émilie will not be unfaithful to her husband and will not intrude upon Alphonse's grief for Camille. However, Émilie's love for Alphonse does not disappear. The natural landscape which the two protagonists now find themselves sharing is not the beautiful, tranquil countryside retreat of the beginning of the novel. Instead nature is harsh and unforgiving, filled with 'passages escarpés' ['steep passes'] (*É*, p. 256), a 'sol entièrement aride' ['completely arid soil'] (*É*, p. 377), 'un ciel gris' ['a grey sky'] (*É*, p. 358) and 'petites pluies interminables' ['interminable showers'] (*É*, p. 358). Émilie is even convinced that 'cette grande forêt de pins est remplie de revenants et de sorciers' ['the great pine forest is filled with ghosts and sorcerers'] (*É*, p. 251). Nature has a depressing, dead, even evil aspect to it. Like Émilie's hopes, her utopia has gone, conquered and destroyed by the society forbidding her love. When Émilie first encountered

Alphonse, she perceived his melancholy, but was ignorant of the reasons behind it. His demeanour only made him more attractive to her. However, leaving the utopian idyll of her pre-marriage days has banished all her blissful ignorance, and her attempts to return to Alphonse's side are now accompanied by the harsh realities of his life and hers. She now understands that she can never be with Alphonse, and furthermore, experience has shown her that marriage brings nothing but unhappiness anyway.

The likelihood of the downfall of the utopian paradise is in fact heralded in the first description of the idyll itself, in its similarity to Eden. Reviewing the description of the tranquil nature in which the young couple meet, we notice a play on the image of the serpent: 'Un ruisseau de l'eau la plus vive et la plus limpide y serpente' ['Through the wood, snaked a stream of lively, crystal clear water'] (É, pp. 6–7). Although 'serpente' is employed as a verb to describe the movement of the stream, rather than as a noun to denote the reptile itself, the image is nonetheless present. Like the biblical serpent, harbinger of evil into Genesis' Eden, the expectations and values of external society worm their way into the utopian space, forbidding Émilie's happiness.

At the close of Staël's *Delphine,* the lovers also wish to seek out the landscape which reminds them of their past happiness, hoping that it will bring similar contentment to their future. Léonce suggests:

> Ma Delphine, [...] te souviens-tu de cette maison sur le coteau de Bade dont le site nous rappelait Bellerive? Nous pouvons l'acquérir, nous nous y établirons; quelques légers changements la rendront tout à fait semblable à ce séjour où nous avons passé des moments heureux. (D II, 317)

> [My Delphine, [...] do you remember that house on the hill at Bade whose situation reminded us of Bellerive? We can buy it, we can set ourselves up there. Some small changes will make it exactly like that spot where we spent happy times together].

Yet, as is the case for Émilie and Alphonse, the idyll belongs in the past, and so Léonce and Delphine are, likewise, unable to reobtain it. In further echoes of Souza's *Émilie et Alphonse,* the downfall of Staël's protagonists in *Delphine* is also heralded in the tamed natural space in which the characters fall in love. According to Louichon, 'Bellerive est, dans *Delphine,* cet entre-deux qui semble préserver les amants de la pression sociale' ['In *Delphine,* Bellerive is the 'in-between space' which seems to preserve the lovers from social pressure'],[45] thus making it a utopian idyll for Delphine and Léonce, in which their love can develop. It is worth noting here the use of the phrase 'entre-deux', since the importance of a middle space or 'space between' is a crucial one to the understanding of women's writing the landscape to reclaim their voice and express themselves. The problem in *Delphine* is that '[d]ans ce jardin, déjà en soi lieu de compromis entre art et nature, cette fête durant laquelle Delphine est si heureuse n'est que camouflage et artifice' ['[i]n that garden, already in itself a space of compromise between art and nature, the party during which Delphine is so happy is nothing other than camouflage and artifice'].[46] As Louichon argues, the garden only symbolizes the *illusion* of happiness, and therefore it betrays the couple because of its artificiality. Louichon concludes that 'le jardin, lieu d'artifices, n'est qu'un fugitif lieu de délices, comme le sont, de manière générale, parcs et jardins' ['the garden, a space of artifice, is no more than a fleeting space of pleasure, as parks and gardens generally are'].[47] Perhaps it is unsurprising, therefore, that the garden idyll and park idyll are only temporary, because of the very fact that they are areas of tamed nature, and are, therefore, artificial.

Françoise Le Borgne argues that '[l]e genre pastoral est intrinsèquement lié à la nostalgie' ['[t]he pastoral genre is intrinsically linked to nostalgia'].[48] As with other examples of pastoral literature, then, in *Malvina*, *Claire D'Albe*, *Émilie et Alphonse* and *Delphine*, happiness belongs in the natural idyll, which, in turn belongs in the past. Once the idyll is lost, and the realization that neither it nor the happiness it engendered can be recovered occurs, Malvina, Claire and Delphine perish, and Émilie's happiness is forever destroyed. Mistress Birton, however, survives: she who refuses even to gaze at the countryside, saying '[c]royez-moi, il vaut mieux regarder le beau ciel de France et d'Italie en peinture, que celui d'Ecosse en réalité' ['[b]elieve me, it is better to contemplate paintings of the beautiful skies of France and Italy than it is to look upon the Scottish sky in reality'] (*M* I, 27). Through images of natural perfection and destruction, Cottin and Souza appear to tell their reader that the woman who attempts to defy society, by seeking out a space of freedom to experience and express emotions of love that society forbids, will always be doomed to suffer society's revenge. On the other hand, those who deny nature (Bianciardi even argues that Birton in particular 'figure "l'anti-nature"' ['represents "anti-nature"']),[49] and who accept society for what it is, will survive. Finney's argument supports this hypothesis: 'Characters who cling to the subversive erotic garden realm and what it represents perish [...]; by the same token, characters who reject the escape offered by the garden in favour of social integration and the status quo survive'.[50] One novel which noticeably breaks this trend, however, is Souza's *Adèle de Sénange*.

The *jardin à la française* and the *jardin à l'anglaise* in Souza's *Adèle de Sénange*

Garden spaces which captured the minds of the eighteenth-century French population were not limited to utopian and pastoral idylls. The period also witnessed a metamorphosis in taste regarding garden design, with the *jardin à l'anglaise* — the garden cultivated to look free and untamed — replacing the rigidity of the *jardin à la française*.[51]

André Mollet's treatise *Le Jardin de Plaisir* (1651) indicates clearly what the features of the *jardin à la française*, so popular throughout the seventeenth century, should be:

> [N]ous y ordonnerons les parterres, bosquets, arbres, palissades et allées diverses, de même que des fontaines, grottes, statues, perspectives, et autres ornements sans lesquels ledit jardin de plaisir ne peut être parfait. Néanmoins, il est très évident que toutes ces choses confuses et mal appropriées ne sont pas d'un très bel effet; c'est pourquoi nous essaierons de les disposer chacune en leur lieu, suivant l'ordre que l'expérience nous a appris.

[[I]n it we will arrange flowerbeds, groves, trees, hedges and numerous paths, as well as fountains, grottoes, statues, viewpoints, and other ornaments without which the aforesaid pleasure garden cannot be perfect. Nevertheless, it is very clear that all these things will not create a beautiful effect if they are confused and ill suited. This is why we will try to arrange each in their proper place, according to the order that experience has taught us].[52]

As Alexander Minski informs us, '[l]e principe de ce type de jardin est le parterre, toujours à base de buis' ['[t]he staple of this type of garden is the flowerbed, always featuring box hedges']; he also signals the emphasis given to the importance of geometrical precision in the French-style garden: 'Il est régulier et symétrique, privilégiant la ligne droite et les angles droits' ['It is regular and symmetrical, favouring straight lines and right angles'].[53] In 1747, Antoine-Joseph Dezallier d'Argenville's *Théorie et pratique du jardinage* still prescribes the same features and still insists on the importance of order, geometrical designs, straight lines and predictable shapes: 'Les compartiments et les broderies des parterres sont tirés des figures de géométrie, tant de lignes droites, que circulaires, mixtes, etc. Il entre dans leur composition différents desseins' ['The compartments and arrangements of flowerbeds are drawn from geometrical figures, as many straight lines as circular ones, mixed ones, etc. Their compositions feature different designs'].[54] Theorists described not only what the end product must resemble, but also clarified 'la manière de mettre en exécution ces belles idées' ['the manner of executing these beautiful ideas'].[55] In an era in which nature was generally contemplated as something that must be sculpted to suit order and rationality, and in which 'taming nature' meant imposing order on it, this rigid, geometrical style of garden is perfectly suited to contemporary tastes and philosophies. Furthermore, it proves to be socio-politically allegorical, in that it also perfectly reflects concerns about the rigidity of the Ancien Régime.

Such rigidity eventually engendered a desire for change, and, as has long been noted, '[d]ès le début du XVIIIe siècle en Angleterre, vers 1760 en France, on constate une réaction contre ce type de jardin' ['[f]rom the beginning of the eighteenth century in England, and from around 1760 in France, a reaction against this type of garden becomes noticeable'].[56] As the century advanced, garden design reflected the people's calls for liberation in other spheres, such as the political and the social: 'Every sentimentalist, republican philosopher, or romance writer, rebelling against rigid law and order of any kind, delighted in this so-called return to the freedom of nature'.[57] The new type of garden, modelled on the English fashion, was not 'une construction à partir d'un terrain vierge' ['constructed from virgin soil'],[58] but rather

une adaptation aux éléments de paysage préexistants. C'est l'illusion de la nature qui prime la maîtrise humaine du paysage. Par conséquent, on courbe les lignes droites, on cache les limites du jardin qui doit se fonder dans la campagne environnante.

[adapted to the pre-existing elements of the landscape. The illusion of nature takes precedence over the human mastery of the landscape. Consequently, straight lines become curved, the garden's borders become hidden, in order for it to blend into surrounding countryside].[59]

The landscape architects charged with creating such gardens adapted the environment to express the liberty associated with the English-style garden to its fullest. It was believed that the *jardin à l'anglaise,* which 'consiste à effacer toute trace d'intervention humaine ayant contribué à son ordonnancement' ['involves erasing all traces of the human intervention which contributed to its layout'],[60] should lull visitors into believing they were in the untamed natural countryside, with winding paths and groves of trees scattered with no apparent order. Daniel Mornet argues that the English-style garden was also associated with emotion, another aspect lacking in the French-style garden: '[d]u moment où l'on voulut sentir plutôt que réfléchir, le jardin à la française devait sembler froid et stérile' ['[f]rom the moment when it became desirable to feel rather than to think, the French-style garden must have seemed cold and sterile'].[61] Indeed, in 1808, Alexandre Laborde

> définit l'art des jardins nouveaux comme 'une science morale' en reprenant l'antienne qui fait dire à un autre théoricien des jardins, Christian-Cay-Lorenz Hirschfeld, que 'cet art cesse d'être uniquement l'amusement de sens externes, et devient une source de vrai contentement intérieur pour l'âme, de richesses pour l'imagination, de délicatesse pour le sentiment'.

> [defines the art of the new gardens as 'a moral science', using the very same argument that had led another garden theoretician, Christian-Cay-Lorenz Hirschfeld, to state that 'this art no longer provides pleasure solely for the external senses, but also becomes a true source of inner contentment for the soul, of wealth for the imagination, of finesse for the emotions'].[62]

The change in garden taste was echoed in literature. According to Antoine Nicolas Duchesne, writing in 1775, 'La formation des jardins est devenue un objet également intéressant aux artistes et aux littérateurs' ['The creation of gardens has become something which interests both artists and men of letters'].[63] The desire to replace an ordered *jardin à la française* with a less structured *jardin à l'anglaise* features heavily in Souza's *Adèle de Sénange.* M. de Sénange prizes his Parisian geometric garden and protests dramatically at the suggestion of his young wife and the family friend Lord Sydenham to cut it down and replace it with a modern English-style garden. Sydenham and Adèle are instead granted permission to construct a new *jardin à l'anglaise* on an island on Sénange's Neuilly estate. During their creation of this garden Adèle and Sydenham's love for each other grows. However, more significantly, the garden allows Adèle a sense of independence and self-determination previously denied to her, and, on account of this, also causes a positive transformation in her emotions.

According to Giulia Pacini, specific aspects of garden design were of particular importance when conveying messages in fiction, for example '[i]mages of felled or pruned trees were of especial use to authors who wanted to address various questions of reform'.[64] Pacini addresses the importance of arboreal symbolism to the politics of the eighteenth century, arguing that trees could 'signify both the stability of the ancien régime and the hopes of the new republic'.[65] Expanding on this, she argues that destroying the rigid French-style gardens with their symmetrically arranged trees mirrored the destruction of the rigid old system of government, and replacing these gardens with the liberating English style, with freely growing trees, echoed France's calls for liberty with the installation of a new political system. Pacini cites Souza's work as an example of a literary portrayal of this phenomenon. She states that 'conservative arguments about the importance of respecting (aristocratic) French traditions surfaced in *Adèle de Sénange*', adding:

> Within this text, the author [...] talked in coded fashion about ideal methods of reform. It seems possible that parts of this story were directly inspired by the felling of the trees at Versailles; Souza was closely related to both Marigny and d'Angiviller, the previous and current ministers of the Crown's Building Administration.[66]

This, coupled with the fact that Souza's first husband (the comte de Flahaut) 'administered the king's royal gardens',[67] renders it highly likely that the designing of gardens at Versailles and the designing of gardens in *Adèle de Sénange* are related.

However, it is not only republican freedom which is echoed in the change in garden taste. Chase contends that the passion for the English-style garden also mirrored the desire for freedom in marriage, particularly for women, who continued to experience a lack of freedom both in the choice of whom to marry and within marital life itself:

> The cages, walls and barriers that serve as containment devices for natural elements create tangible images of the limits placed upon women's nature. [...]. Souza uses landscaping and land ownership as a metaphor for women's claim to intellectual creation, and she sees the garden as a representative of a fertile space in which women's creative impulses can find free expression. For Adèle de Sénange, [...] enclosed gardens and gilded birdcages present bittersweet images of bondage: the protected life of the convent or the confinement of a loveless marriage. Through the creation of her own garden on an island separate from her husband's estate, Adèle finds a new way to define herself.[68]

Chase analyses the French-style garden, with particular focus on the image of the birdcage, to highlight how the restrictions of M. de Sénange's rigid *jardin à la française* represent the restrictions of Adèle's married life.

The ensuing discussion revisits and draws together parts of Chase's and Pacini's analyses of *Adèle de Sénange*. However it also builds on these analyses. Whilst Chase and Pacini focus largely on the features of the gardens themselves, I couple this with an analysis of the symbolic horticultural echoes occurring outside the gardens. I also analyse Sénange's *jardin à la française* and Adèle's *jardin à l'anglaise* alongside a third significant garden in Souza's novel: the convent garden. In investigating the ways in which Souza situates these gardens relative to each other, we are able to re-examine the arguments made within the novel regarding liberty, confinement, independence, marriage and socio-historical reform.

At sixteen, Adèle is given in an arranged marriage to seventy-year-old M. de Sénange. Adèle's mother takes on the matchmaking role because Adèle's father is no longer alive to do so. Carpenter elaborates on problematic marital situations for women in Souza's works, stating that Souza dissects the state of matrimony and investigates love. She repeatedly probes what it is that makes a man and a woman happy. This is perhaps why her novels fascinated contemporary readers, who were often the survivors of unhappy marriages themselves.[69]

There is even a glimpse of Souza's own life in Adèle. Like her creator, Adèle is raised in a convent, is not in love with her much older husband, and falls for a young British man. Adèle does not enter into an affair with Sydenham, however; she only becomes involved with him after Sénange's death. Although she is forced into a loveless marriage, Adèle does not disobey society's will, but rather yields to the fate laid out for her. Indeed, her fate is organized by others to such an extent that she is kept completely in the dark regarding any of the marriage contract details. This was in fact very common:

> [Y]oung women were [...] left completely ignorant of the details of their marriage contract. Adèle was told nothing by her mother of the marriage settlement which she knew was signed by the notary. She was present at the reading of the contract but, without any understanding or explanation, it meant little to her.[70]

Adèle de Sénange therefore echoes the fact that arranged and forbidden marriages were frequently more problematic for wives than for husbands.

Adèle's situation is a restrictive one, as the disgusted Sydenham declares shortly after meeting her: 'Que de réflexions ne fis-je pas sur ces mariages d'intérêt, où une malheureuse enfant est livrée par la vanité ou la cupidité de ses parents à un homme dont elle ne connaît ni les qualités, ni les défauts' ['What reflections have I not made on marriages of advantage, where, on acount of the greed and vanity of her parents, a miserable young girl is delivered up to a man whose qualities and faults she knows not at all' (*AS*, p. 18). However, it transpires that the marriage Sydenham so deplores may in fact have been the lesser (and certainly more short-lived) of two evils for Adèle, for the previous years of her life were even more restrictive. She was confined to a convent 'dès l'âge de deux ans' ['since the age of two'] (*AS*, p. 6), by an unfeeling mother, who expressed more interest in Adèle's brothers than in the daughter who would never inherit her family's money or be given a dowry. Sénange discovers, upon questioning Adèle's mother, the ironically named Madame de Joyeuse, that for these reasons Adèle was to be forced to take the veil permanently. He is deeply affected by Adèle's fate, and decides to take action:

> Je fus révolté de voir une mère disposer aussi durement de sa fille, et la livrer au malheur pour sa vie, uniquement parce qu'elle était peu riche. Cette jeune victime, sacrifiée ainsi par ses parents, ne me sortait pas de l'esprit. (*AS*, p. 64)

> [I was revolted to see a mother dispose so harshly of her daughter, and to render her unhappy for the rest of her life, solely because she was not very rich. I could not get this young victim, sacrificed in this way by her parents, out of my mind].

Consequently he suggests to Madame de Joyeuse that he marry the young Adèle, wishing to save her from 'ces vœux terribles' ['these terrible vows'] (*AS*, p. 66) and from being locked within a convent for the rest of her days. He makes clear his concern for Adèle when he states: 'M'étant bien assuré que son cœur n'avait point d'inclination, qu'elle m'aimait comme un père, je me déterminai à la demander en mariage' ['Having assured myself that she had not given her heart to another man, and that she loved me as a daughter would a father, I decided to ask for her hand in marriage'] (*AS*, p. 66). He is aware that Madame de Joyeuse will only rescind her instructions for her daughter to take religious vows if there is the possibility that Adèle will marry a wealthy aristocrat willing to take her without a dowry. He knows too that, although he may perhaps not appear a desirable husband to Adèle (being much older, and in failing health), upon his death his wife will inherit his fortune, and will finally be freed from the restrictions of her family and its expectations, free of the confinement of the cloister, and able to make her own decisions regarding her future: 'je me persuaderais encore qu'un lien qui, naturellement, ne doit pas être long, vaut toujours mieux que le voile et les vœux éternels qui étaient son partage' ['I would persuade myself again that a relationship which, naturally, would not last long, is always better than her taking the veil and the eternal vows which would be her lot'] (*AS*, p. 67).

Madame de Joyeuse agrees to the marriage, and Adèle passes from one restrictive space (the cloister) into another (the domestic home). However, rather than arguing that both the garden of the convent cloister and Sénange's *jardin à la française* — a key feature of Adèle's new domestic home — represent equal restrictions placed upon Adèle, the present discussion will identify these gardens as separate points along a progressive axis, demonstrating how Adèle's independence is somewhat improved with her change in space.

Examining the space Adèle leaves behind — the convent and its garden — before she encounters the French and English gardens during her marriage helps the reader to understand Adèle's first steps to freedom. When first introduced to Adèle, we are told that she has been walled up and separated from the world throughout her life (*AS*, p. 7). In a later episode, after her marriage, Adèle describes Sénange's visits to the convent whilst she lived there. Sénange brings baskets of fruit and places them 'sur une table près de la grille' ['on a table near the bars'] (*AS*, p. 98). When Adèle requests that her fellow nuns be permitted to share the present, the imagery in Souza's description begins to echo that of a gaol:

> [L]a vue des paniers fit bientôt disparaître cet air cérémonieux. Comme il était impossible de les faire entrer par la grille, chacune d'elles passait sa main à travers les barreaux, et prenait, comme elle pouvait, les fruits dont elle avait envie. (*AS*, p. 98)

> [[The] sight of the baskets soon dispelled the ceremonious air. As it was impossible to pass them through the railings, each nun put her hand through the bars and took, as best she could, the fruit she desired].

The nuns stretch their hands through prison-like bars in order to obtain the natural delights of the world beyond.

This imagery is heightened when Sydenham receives a letter from one of the nuns still at the convent. Orphaned and brought up by the nuns, Eugénie finds the prospect of spending the rest of her life in the convent terrifying: 'Le soir en rentrant dans ma cellule, je pensais avec terreur que je n'en sortirais que pour mourir. [...] [L]es vœux éternels que je venais de prononcer me firent frémir' ['As I went back to my cell in the evening, the terrifying thought occurred to me that I would only leave it when I died. [...] [T]he eternal vows that I had just taken made me tremble'] (*AS*, pp. 116–17). However, soon a gap appears in the convent garden wall, and Eugénie begins to visit the garden regularly to gaze out at the nature of the vast world beyond. At this point, the reader witnesses the desperate desire to escape the restricted, prison-like convent from a nun's own perspective:

> [T]out un pan du mur du jardin était tombé. [...] [L]a brèche était considérable; et je ne saurais vous rendre le sentiment de joie que j'éprouvai, en revoyant le monde une seconde fois. A cet instant, je ne me sentis plus; je riais, je pleurais tout ensemble. (*AS*, p. 119)

> [[O]ne whole section of the garden wall had fallen down. [...] [T]he hole was considerable, and I don't know how to describe the feeling of joy that I experienced, seeing the world for a second time. At that moment, I was beside myself with emotion; I laughed and cried all at the same time].

Considering the semantic structure of the episode of the convent garden, we are able to understand more about the position of the nuns in relation to their space. The construction of the sentence focuses more on the nun's emotions than on physical description of the space itself, and consequently the reader is permitted a clear view of the effect the space has upon the figures located within it. The triple semantic techniques of replacing description of space with description of emotional reaction to the space, the swift build up of verbs expressing this emotion, and the separating of the verbs with frequent punctuation all serve to give the impression of overwhelming catharsis, bringing Eugénie's previous depression into stark relief.

She feels the need to return to the garden as soon as possible, to gaze through the wall at the nature beyond:

> Le lendemain, dès cinq heures du matin, j'étais dans le jardin; cette brèche donnait dans les champs, et me laissait apercevoir un vaste horizon. Je contemplai le lever du soleil avec ravissement. La petitesse de notre jardin, la hauteur de ses murs, nous empêchent de jouir de ce beau spectacle. (*AS*, p. 119)

> [The next day, I was in the garden as early as five o'clock in the morning. The hole looked on to the fields and allowed me to glimpse a vast horizon. I gazed upon the sunrise with rapture. The small size of the garden and the height of its walls usually prevent us from enjoying this beautiful sight.]

This time, Eugénie is situated within a much wider spatial ground, incorporating not only the convent garden, but also the natural world beyond it. Contemplating the nature outside the convent garden as well as that inside it provides hope for Eugénie. The large fields extending to a vast horizon contrast sharply with the small garden surrounded by high walls to which she is accustomed, and allow her, temporarily, to feel the freedom of spirit granted by such a vast expanse of open space — a feeling which will also be experienced by Adèle in her *jardin à l'anglaise*. The dawn, with its beautiful sunrise, echoes the awakening of this new-found spiritual freedom within Eugénie. Nature reminds her of what she lacks, and provides an outlet for her emotion.

Nonetheless, only Eugénie's gaze is permitted to wander beyond the garden wall; she herself is still physically bound by the restrictions of her prison, and although she decides to 'ne plus quitter le jardin' ['no longer leave the garden'] (*AS*, p. 120) in order to continue to view the world beyond, it is 'sans oser franchir la ligne où le mur avait marqué la clôture' ['without daring to cross the line where the wall had demarcated the enclosure'] (*AS*, p. 120). Spiritually and emotionally, the nun has gained access to a much wider spatial field, but, physically, she remains fixed within the garden. Before the wall can be rebuilt, more bricks must be removed, and, as the hole is widened, gazing upon an increasing expanse of nature suffices to help her overcome her depression. However, when repair work commences, and the wall begins to close in again, the nun's fear and depression return with such violence that she writes:

> [J]'aperçus qu'il y avait une pierre de plus que la veille: on commençait à rebâtir!... Je jetai un cri d'effroi, et cachant ma tête dans mes mains, je courus vers ma cellule, comme si la mort m'eût poursuivie: j'y restai jusqu'au soir, anéantie par la douleur [...]. Arrachez-moi d'ici, milord, arrachez-moi d'ici. (*AS*, pp. 120–21)

> [I noticed that there was one more stone there than there had been the previous day: they had started to rebuild the wall!... I gave a cry of fright, and, hiding my head in my hands, I ran towards my cell, as though death itself pursued me. I stayed there until the evening, devastated by grief [...]. Tear me away from here, my lord, tear me away from here.]

Analysing Eugénie's use of verbs, here, makes her ultimate goal abundantly clear. The repeated imperative 'arrachez-moi' ['tear me away'] signals her violent desperation to be physically ripped from her prison and her torment, whilst simultaneously reminding the reader of her powerlessness: Eugénie (represented by the disjunctive pronoun 'moi') is a direct object here, not the subject of the verb. She is not in control of her movement from one space to another, rather she is entirely dependent on the assistance of others as to how, and even whether, she moves to a new space. It seems that a view of nature and the freedom it affords is required for Eugénie finally to act to escape her prison. Adèle, however, has already been rescued by M. de Sénange, and so, unlike Eugénie, at the point of her release from the convent she does not yet realize the power of nature to liberate the mind. This is what she will learn in her encounters with the *jardin à la française* and the *jardin à l'anglaise*.

What, then, are the restrictions of the *jardin à la française* and how are they reflected in Adèle's life outside the garden? Sydenham describes the garden on Sénange's Paris estate thus:

> [C]'est l'ancien genre français dans toute son aridité; du buis, du sable et des arbres taillés. La maison est superbe; mais on la voit toute entière. Elle ressemble à un grand château renfermé entre quatre petites murailles; et ce jardin, qui est immense pour Paris, paraissait horriblement petit pour la maison. (*AS*, p. 31)

> [[I]t is the old French style in all its dryness: box hedges, sand and pruned

trees. The house is superb, but you can see all of it. It resembles a large château enclosed within four small walls, and this garden, which is enormous for Paris, appeared horribly small for the house.]

This garden is a clear example of a space of rigidly tamed nature. It echoes Mollet's, Minski's and d'Argenville's description of the *jardin à la française* and its traditional features of box trees, sand-covered pathways and perfectly pruned trees. Even the château dominating the scene reminds us of the descriptions of the real *jardins à la française* that existed at this time, which often appeared 'en contrebas du château' ['below the house'].[71] The aridity and restrictions prevalent within the French-style garden infringe upon the liberty of those within it. Nowhere is this more apparent than in the description of the gilded birdcage: 'Adèle voulut savoir si je trouvais sa volière jolie. Je lui répondis qu'elle allait bien avec le reste du jardin. Ce n'était pas en faire un grand éloge, car il est affreux' ['Adèle wanted to know if I found her aviary pretty. I replied that it went well with the rest of the garden. This was not great praise, because it is awful'] (*AS*, p. 31). Sydenham adds that in his own *jardin à l'anglaise*, although he also has many birds, 'les miens seraient malheureux s'ils n'étaient pas en liberté' ['mine would be unhappy if they were not free'] (*AS*, p. 32). Chase argues that the aviary

> acts as a metaphor for Adèle's role in marriage. [...] In *Adèle de Sénange*, the limitations of marriage visibly constrict the female protagonist. Traditionally a golden birdcage represents a forced marriage, and for Adèle there is little attempt to cover up the restrictions her marriage places upon her under the guise of natural happiness. [...] On her marriage day she emerges from the church as elegantly decorated as a gilded birdcage.[72]

Undoubtedly Adèle's life is as regulated for her as a French garden is geometrically regulated. However, this is not the only occasion when Adèle's finery is appropriate for a French-style garden. If we examine the *jardin à la française* again we can see more clearly how descriptions of Adèle after her marriage to Sénange fit with those of a garden in the style of André Le Nôtre. The most famous of the French-style gardens was indeed at Versailles, but Le Nôtre designed the King's garden on the strength of his previous work at Vaux-le-Vicomte, described thus by an eighteenth-century vistor: 'C'était une confusion de si belles choses qu'on ne peut l'exprimer. Ces eaux jaillissantes, ces canaux, ces cascades, ces allées remplies de dames et de courtisans chargés de rubans et de plumes' ['It was a chaotic mix of such beautiful things that it is hard to describe. The spouting water fountains, the canals, the waterfalls, the paths filled with ladies and courtiers laden with ribbons and feathers'].[73] The women adorned with ribbons and feathers, signs of riches and luxuriance, who paraded along the pathways were as much a part of the appeal of this style of garden as were the water features, topiary and paths themselves. As Tom Turner argues, 'Vaux-le-Vicomte is theatrical: a magnificent spectacle to be viewed from the house'.[74] The French-style garden provides the theatrical stage on which the horticultural features (stage props) and the ornamental parading visitors (the actors) can be found. It is this description which must be borne in mind when Sydenham meets Adèle at the opera, a similar theatrical spectacle, and declares:

> Je n'ai jamais vu tant de diamants, de fleurs, de plumes, entassées sur la même personne. [...] 'Voilà', disais-je, 'de bien belles plumes! Vos diamants sont d'une bien belle eau!' [...] Je lui parlai de sa robe, de ses rubans! (*AS*, pp. 20–22)

> [I have never seen so many diamonds, flowers, and feathers heaped on the same person. [...] 'Those', I said, 'are very attractive feathers! Your diamonds are beautifully transparent!' [...] I spoke to her of her dress and of her ribbons!]

Adèle is adorned with decorations — ribbons and feathers — identical to those which were customarily on view in the *jardin à la française* according to the guest at Vaux-le-Vicomte. She is even decorated with flowers, as though part of a garden. Moreover, the feathers and flowers are heaped upon her, evoking the image of a bejewelled flowerbed rather than that of a woman. The restrictions of the French-style garden therefore accompany Adèle wherever she goes, and, wherever she happens to be, she is on display, 'enchantée de voir et d'être vue' ['enchanted to see and to be seen'] (*AS*, p. 21), just as the *jardin à la française* was intended to be ostentatiously flaunted. Sydenham even remarks that '[t]oute la magnificence qui entourait Adèle me semblait le prix de son consentement' ['[a]ll the magnificence which surrounded Adèle seemed to be the price of her consent'] (*AS*, p. 22). Agreeing to the arranged marriage has its cost: empty ornaments, the chains tying her to a restricted life and space. Finally, just as Sydenham described the French-style garden as 'affreux' ['awful'], he is similarly struck by Adèle's finery, referring to it as 'l'odieux éclat qui l'environnait' ['the ghastly brilliance which surrounded her'] (*AS*, p. 22). The adornment of Adèle in bad taste, as though she were a feature of the *jardin à la française,* echoes Rose Standish Nichols' statement that '[i]t seemed as though the proprietor was principally desirous of showing the extent of his property, and the gardener his knowledge of geometry, while neither displayed a ray of originality'.[75]

On other occasions within the novel, echoes of the regular geometric shapes common to French-style gardens appear in descriptions of Adèle. When Sydenham sees Adèle with her mother, he notes: '*la régularité* de leurs traits les feraient distinguer parmi toutes les femmes' ['*the regularity* of their features make them stand out amongst all women'] (*AS*, p. 17).[76] When Adèle dances at the ball held in honour of her husband, she appears at the centre of a geometric shape: 'On fit un cercle autour d'eux pour les voir et les applaudir' ['They made a circle around them in order to see and applaud them'] (*AS*, p. 107). Another circular image appears whilst Adèle is in the *jardin à la française.* According to David Herman, the research of several cognitive linguists, including that of Gillian Brown, Barbara Landau and Ray Jackendoff has given rise to the understanding that 'motion verbs contribute crucial semantic information concerning the participants' *emerging* whereabouts in space — their spatial trajectories over the duration of the event sequence being narrated'.[77] In the *jardin à la française,* we see Adèle's spatial trajectory clearly as she moves in circles, trying to care for and to please her birds, her husband and her guest:

> Pour Adèle, elle fut voir ses oiseaux, leur parler, regarder s'ils avaient à manger; et continuellement, allant à eux, revenant à nous, ne se fixant jamais, elle s'amusa sans cesse de s'occuper de son mari, et même de moi. (*AS*, p. 31)

[As for Adèle, she went to see her birds, to talk to them, to see if they had something to eat; and, continually going back and forth between them and us, never settling down, she amused herself while still looking after her husband and even looking after me.]

The word 'continuellement' ['continually'], in addition to the motion verbs 'allant' ['going'] and 'revenant' ['coming back'], and the expression 'ne se fixant jamais' ['never settling down'], all of which occur in immediate succession in the sentence, create the impression of a constant circle; Adèle's motion has neither end nor pause. She is tamed here to cater to the desires of others.

Yet, Adèle caters to Sénange because she realizes that, although the arranged marriage has its restrictions, the very fact of it taking place has saved her from an even more restrictive life: 'Si vous saviez [...] combien il est bon; tout ce que je lui dois!' ['If you knew [...] how good he is, and everything that I owe him!'] (AS, p. 58). Thus, it is in her attentions to Sénange that we begin to see evidence of her emerging autonomy. Sydenham observes:

> Si vous saviez avec quelle attention elle soigne monsieur de Sénange! Comme elle devine toujours ce qui peut le soulager ou lui plaire! Elle est redevenue cette sensible Adèle [...]. Ce n'est plus madame de Sénange vive, étourdie, magnifique; c'est Adèle, jeune sans être enfant, naïve sans légèreté, généreuse sans ostentation (AS, p. 60).

> [If you knew with what attention she cares for M. de Sénange! How she always is able to guess what might comfort or delight him! She has become that sensitive Adèle again [...]. She is no longer Mme. de Sénange, lively, giddy, magnificent; she is Adèle, young without being a child, naïve without frivolity, generous without ostentation.]

When she realizes that her marriage has moved her forwards, we see her identified as a woman in her own right (Adèle) rather than by her status as a married woman (Mme de Sénange) as we might expect. The empty ornaments have also been removed. The fact that the spatial imagery has progressed — from imprisoning walls and bars which promote a one-dimensional, sedentary life to a garden in which a certain amount of two-dimensional movement (albeit still within regulated, geometric space) is permitted — highlights the forward momentum of Adèle's situation.

Furthermore, Sénange also provides the ultimate space in which Adèle might experience autonomy: the *jardin à l'anglaise*. The presentation of this final space forms a stark contrast to the horticultural images previously encountered. When Sydenham informs Adèle of his own English-style garden, she is enchanted by the idea of such a space:

> J'essayai de lui peindre ce parc si sauvage que j'ai dans le pays de Galles: cela nous conduisit à parler de la composition des jardins. Elle m'entendit, et pria son mari de tout changer dans le leur, et d'en planter un autre sur mes dessins. [...] [D]ès que je lui eus rappelé les campagnes qu'il avait vues en Angleterre, [...] il finit par désirer aussi que toutes ces allées sablées fussent changées en gazons. (AS, p. 32).

[I tried to describe for her the wild park I have in Wales: this led us to talking about the arrangement of gardens. She listened to me and begged her husband to change everything in their own garden, and to plan another in its stead according to my designs. [...] [A]s soon as I had reminded him of the countryside he had seen in England, [...] he ended up also wanting all the sand-covered paths to be turned into lawns].

The apparent wildness of Sydenham's *jardin à l'anglaise* holds many attractions for Adèle, principally because of the sense of liberty that it expresses. Her husband agrees to her request to replace their arid, geometrically regulated garden with a freer one, but when he later sees the plans to tear down his trees, he changes his mind:

Ces arbres, plus vieux que moi encore, et qu'intérieurement je vous sacrifiais avec un peu de peine, l'été, me garantiront du soleil, l'hiver, me préserveront du froid; car à mon âge tout fait mal. Peut-être aussi la nature veut-elle que nos besoins et nos goûts nous rapprochent toujours des objets avec lesquels nous avons vieilli. Ces arbres, mes anciens amis, vous les couperiez! ils me sont nécessaires. (*AS*, pp. 33–34)

[These trees, older even than I am, and that inwardly I would sacrifice to you with some chagrin, safeguard me from the sun in the summer and preserve me from the cold in winter; for at my age everything hurts. Maybe nature also wants our needs and tastes to bring us ever closer to the objects with which we have grown old., You would cut down these trees which are my old friends! They are essential to me.]

Like Sénange, the trees belong to a bygone age, and he feels that, if they are cut down, he will also be destroyed. Adèle's heart, however, is set on having an English-style garden because of the freedom that it will bring, and Sénange is not cruel. His wife respects his needs by nursing him and remaining loyal to him, and he respects her need for creative and intellectual freedom and self-determination. He therefore agrees that, rather than uprooting the trees in his Parisian garden, she might create a new garden on the island on his country estate at Neuilly: '[I]l y a une île de quarante arpents' ['[T]here is an island of forty acres'], he informs her, 'je vous la donne. Vous y changerez, bâtirez, abattrez tant qu'il vous plaira; tandis que moi je garderai cette maison-ci telle qu'elle est' ['I will give it to you. You can change or construct things there, cut things down to your heart's content; but I will keep this house here exactly as it is'] (*AS*, p. 33). Adèle is delighted to have an island of her own, and cannot wait to commence her alterations: 'Adèle sautait de joie en pensant à son île. "Il y aura", disait-elle, "des jardins superbes, des grottes fraîches, des arbres épais"' ['Adèle jumped for joy thinking about her island. "There will be", she said "superb gardens, cool grottoes, and thick trees"'] (*AS*, p. 34).

Adèle and Sydenham do become closer on Adèle's island; however, ultimately, it is much more than a space permitting her to be with the man she loves. It does not become a garden of erotic encounter, nor is it even a space in which Adèle expresses her passion for the man of her dreams, as was the case for Malvina, Émilie, Claire and Delphine in their tamed idylls. Upon arriving on her island, Adèle is, in fact, consumed with a different emotion. For the first time in her life she feels a sense of liberation and autonomy; the island garden 'metaphorically depicts separation from others by giving the female protagonist an opportunity for self-expression and independence'.[78] Therefore, when Adèle arrives on the island, we are not presented with a vocabulary of eroticism or love, but with one which concretizes Adèle's autonomy and control of her own space: 'Enfin, *elle* a pris possession de son île' [Finally *she* has taken possession of her island'] (*AS*, p. 38).[79] The italicization of the personal pronoun emphasizes that Adèle has never before possessed such a space of her own; indeed, eighteenth-century women in general rarely did. The description of Adèle on her island highlights her new-found liberty:

> [E]lle nous quitta, et se mit à courir, sans que ni la voix de son mari, ni la mienne, pussent la faire revenir. Je la voyais à travers les arbres, tantôt se rapprochant du rivage, tantôt rentrant dans les jardins; mais en quelque lieu qu'elle s'arrêtât, c'était toujours pour en chercher un plus loin. (*AS*, p. 39)

> [[S]he left us and began to run, and neither her husband's voice nor mine could get her to come back. I saw her through the trees, sometimes approaching the bank, sometimes going back into the gardens; but wherever she stopped, it was always to look for somewhere further away].

The *jardin à la française* permitted Adèle a certain amount of movement after being held stationary behind prison walls. Nonetheless, she was still somewhat restricted, running in geometric circles between her husband and Sydenham. Now, here in the *jardin à l'anglaise,* Adèle is pictured running away from both men, with neither able to rein her in. She is now in control both of herself and of her space. Adèle, like the *jardin à l'anglaise* which she will construct on this island, is not subject to rigidity or geometry, but, rather, is free to go wherever she desires. Her freedom is reflected in the verbs which characterize her movement: 'Pour Adèle, elle y alla toujours sautant, courant, car sa jeunesse et sa joie ne lui permettaient pas de marcher' ['As for Adèle, she was still jumping and running as she went, for neither her youth nor her joy permitted her to walk'] (*AS*, p. 39). We no longer witness her simply 'aller' ['go'] and 'revenir' ['come back'] as in the *jardin à la française*. Now the verbs are much more energetic. Her movement is therefore more three-dimensional, multidirectional, and often so unregulated that it is difficult to keep track of, as becomes clear from the repetition of 'tantôt' ['sometimes']. She is able to experience physically the freedom that Eugénie (and indeed Adèle herself while still in the convent) could experience only visually, and this is the reason for such haphazard verbs of motion. It is little wonder that 'la joie brillait dans les yeux d'Adèle' ['Adèle's eyes shone with joy'] (*AS*, p. 38). Free nature provides her with the liberty she has never known, and the further it removes her from her responsibilities, the happier she becomes. She recognizes the difference herself, when she replies to Sénange's offer of the Neuilly island with the words: 'je serai heureuse' ['I will be happy'] (*AS*, p. 36). Souza makes clear that the change in space provokes the upswing in Adèle's emotions when she informs us that setting foot on the island is all that is needed to lift Adèle's spirits: 'dès qu'elle fut descendue dans son île, sa gaieté revint' ['as soon as she stepped on to her island, her gaiety returned'] (*AS*, p. 97). In her novel, Souza therefore highlights the English-style garden's believed ability to reflect and heighten emotion, and uses it to create for her heroine a 'landscape of one's own' in which she might experience hitherto undiscovered autonomy.

Considering the three gardens simultaneously, in relation to each other, helps to concretize our understanding of the change wrought in Adèle by her movement through space. During the course of Adèle's story, her current spatial situation is always relative to her past situation in other spaces. That is, she is more restricted in the convent and its garden than she is later in the rigidly tamed *jardin à la française*, and when she begins to design her *jardin à l'anglaise*, eradicating any impression of tamed nature, she attains her greatest freedom. Her spatial vicissitudes proceed along a horizontal axis, and, as she moves along this axis, her emotions change radically. Adèle's current spatial situation must, therefore, always be viewed in relation to the other fixed points on her spatial axis. Souza expands upon the simple French-versus English-style garden dichotomy by placing complete confinement and complete freedom on a sliding scale. As she does so, we begin to see the necessity to expand on the way in which French- and English-style gardens in eighteenth-century France were often perceived. The French had such a strong tradition of formalism to counteract that it influenced the design and appearance of the English-style gardens. As Martin Calder indicates:

> Eighteenth-century French treatises on landscape garden design were not content just to describe how a garden should be, but frequently emphasised what it should not be: it should not be formal, nor symmetrical; it should not be tedious; in short, it should not be like Versailles. Early full-scale landscape gardens constructed in France in the 1760s and 1770s were described as 'anti-Versailles'.[80]

Thus, when the French created English-style gardens, their attitudes often encouraged the image of two contrasting extremes — rigidly tamed, or tamed to look untamed — to arise. Such practice implies a garden-design binary which is rigid in itself, for it does not allow for wider possibilities. It is also unrepresentative of reality. Charlton explains that '[b]etween the two extremes of that contrast lies [...] the whole, well-documented evolution from formal to increasingly informal'.[81] In this way, the apparent garden-design binary is not dissimilar to the spatial binary created around the expectations regarding gender roles in eighteenth-century France. Associating men with culture and access to the public sphere whilst denying women creative and intellectual freedom in an attempt both to confine them to the private sphere and to restrict their rights creates a system too rigid to allow full consideration of an individual's desires and potential capabilities. In other words, it does not account for the reality of the multitude of people who do not fit into — or do not wish to be forced into — one extreme or the other. We begin to see, therefore, how positioning the *jardin à la française* and the *jardin à l'anglaise* on a sliding scale of gardens allows for subtle critique of gender pigeonholing. Neither nature nor women can be confined merely to one half of a binary system, rather they incorporate many, varied features.

Adèle de Sénange is original in several respects. Unlike Cottin in *Claire d'Albe*, *Amélie Mansfield* and *Malvina*, unlike Staël in *Corinne* and *Delphine,* and unlike Souza herself in her own later novel *Émilie et Alphonse,* Souza shows the reader in *Adèle de Sénange* that the secret desire of the heart of the eighteenth-century woman forced into an arranged marriage is not necessarily the 'mariage contrarié' ['thwarted marriage'] or the extra-marital affair with a more desirable man. Her secret desire is for the freedom to choose her own destiny, whatever that may be. *Adèle de Sénange* is also unusual because it is one of the few sentimental novels by women writers of this period with a happy ending. The focus on a desire for liberty and the joyful emotions that this grants, as opposed to a desire for forbidden erotic pleasure, is partly responsible for this happy end. Souza argues that we must not focus on radical revolt against the oppressive situation in which we find ourselves, but rather we must focus on the more fundamental rights to which we are all entitled. As a result, unlike Émilie, Malvina, Claire d'Albe and Delphine, Adèle is successful both in accepting society uncomplainingly for what it is and in seeking out a space of freedom (which she will be able to keep forever) to express her emotions and her self. In accepting her arranged marriage, and refusing to rebel against it through an adulterous affair, Adèle retains the good opinion of her husband and of society. She is therefore rewarded for her patience: she is not cast out of society like Émilie, Malvina, Amélie, Claire and Corinne. Nor does society wreak its revenge on her for her eventual marriage to Sydenham, as it destroys Malvina for marrying Edmond, Claire for conducting an affair with Frédéric, Amélie for eloping with M. Mansfield, Delphine for loving Léonce, and Corinne for loving Oswald. Rather, on Sénange's death, Adèle receives both his inheritance and his blessing for her future marriage, and so the rest of society must accept her marriage to Sydenham too.

Finally, the sliding scale of more to less restrictive space created by Souza allows us to unpick her message regarding how marriage reform might be successfully instigated; for, Sénange's death is not cause for a celebratory end of the old system or of the *jardin à la française.* On the contrary, Souza continues to remind us of the importance of the old and the new working together towards reform and a better world. On one of the occasions when Adèle and Sydenham take Sénange with them to Adèle's island, the old man states that he would like his tomb to be erected there:

> Hier nous avons été à la pointe de l'île; elle est terminée par une centaine de peupliers, très-rapprochés les uns des autres, et si élevés, qu'ils semblent toucher au ciel. Le jour y pénètre à peine; le gazon est d'un vert sombre; la rivière ne s'aperçoit qu'à travers les arbres. Dans cet endroit sauvage on se croit au bout du monde, et il inspire, malgré soi, une tristesse dont monsieur de Sénange ne ressenti que trop l'effet, car il dit à Adèle: 'Vous devriez ériger ici un tombeau; bientôt il vous ferait souvenir de moi'. (*AS*, p. 57)

> [Yesterday we went to the tip of the island; its furthest edge is covered with a hundred or so poplar trees, very close together, and so tall that they seem to touch the sky. Daylight can hardly penetrate the dense foliage; the lawn is a dark green; the river can only be glimpsed through the trees. In this wild space you think that you are at the edge of the world, and, in spite of oneself, it inspires a sadness whose effect Sénange perceived greatly, for he said to Adèle: 'You should erect a tomb here; soon it will remind you of me'].

Adèle later does erect her husband's tomb, complete with memorial obelisk, in this spot. It is fitting that Sénange's memorial be in the *jardin à l'anglaise* rather than in his *jardin à la française* amongst his beloved trees, because it serves as a constant reminder of his role in liberating his young wife. Engraved on Sénange's tomb are the words: 'Il ne me répond pas, mais peut-être il m'entend' ['He does not reply to me, but perhaps he can hear me'] (*AS*, p. 175). Adèle hopes that Sénange will hear and understand her thanks and her will to honour both his memory and his kindness. The addition of the old aristocrat's tomb permits the garden to combine elements of the deathscape with a topography cultivated to look untamed, and also permits this mixed space to conflate past, present and future. The characters stand, in the present, gazing down at the reminder of the past generation whilst contemplating the future that Sénange has permitted them. This thus underscores the argument that past and present, old and new, male and female must stand together if a happy future is to be found.

This argument is mirrored in the very fact that the novel does not permit the wilful destruction of the old garden. Souza engages with common practice regarding the construction of the new style gardens in eighteenth-century France; as Mornet reminds us: 'le passé n'est pas brusquement submergé par le présent. Jusqu'à la fin du XVIIIe siècle, il y eut des gens pour aimer et même préférer le jardin français' ['the past is not suddenly submerged by the present. Until the end of the eighteenth century, there were people who loved and even prefered the French-style garden'].[82] Whilst '[i]n England, many formal gardens were destroyed during the eighteenth century, as the parkland was brought right up to the house [...] [i]n France, it was often the case that the old formal garden near the house was retained, while the newer landscape garden was built beyond it'.[83] By engaging with such common contemporary practice — famously seen at Versailles, Chantilly, Fontainebleau and in the Jardin du Luxembourg[84] — Souza creates a positive image of coexistence and respect, upon which she draws in order to make her subtle arguments about how reform might be instigated successfully. According to *Adèle de Sénange* the answer to a problem is never the destruction of one system, or indeed garden, for the foundation of another, but rather gradual change:

> [T]he novel underscores the violence with which the young architects would have superimposed an English style onto a French garden. Souza stresses the fact that, although alterations may be desirable, they need not be so drastic, nor be implemented so quickly.[85]

Ultimately if a happy ending is to be found and joyful emotion celebrated, we must not attempt to seek it through violent passion, reckless abandon, or adamant defiance of the system already in place. Rather, we should go about it gently and respectfully, for change is to be ushered in slowly if it is to succeed.

Conclusion

In 1777 Restif de la Bretonne argued in his essay *Les Gynographes,* subtitled 'Pour mettre les femmes à leur place' ['To put women in their place'], that a woman should always be the subordinate of her husband:

> Les femmes obéiront en tout à leurs maris, ne prendront jamais que la seconde place et seront sous leur puissance comme un de leurs enfants; toute l'idée d'égalité sera absolument abolie; le père ou le chef sera le souverain de la maison; de sa volonté seule [...] dépendra le mariage de ses filles et de ses garçons.

> [Women will obey their husbands in everything, will only ever take second place, and will be subject to their power like one of their children. The whole idea of equality will be abolished absolutely. The father or the man in charge will be the sovereign of the household; on his wishes alone [...] will depend the marriage of his sons and daughters].[86]

Throughout the Republic and Empire, despite calls for change generated with the Revolution, women continued to experience this lack of freedom both with regard to choosing a marital partner, and within marriage itself. Writing in an age in which an argument such as Restif's was far from exceptional, Cottin, Souza and Staël address precisely these feminine issues in their novels, and in order to do so, they employ images of natural landscapes, including rigidly tamed landscapes, gently tamed landscapes, landscapes designed to be as untamed as possible, and even deathscapes. Nature — to which their sex has long been linked — becomes the mouthpiece for women writers to critique the marital oppression their sex faced within their own lifetimes. Utopian garden idylls are used to illustrate the problem of forbidden marriages. French- and English-style gardens, juxtaposed with the convent garden, are used to engage with the debate over arranged marriages.

Cottin, Staël and Souza depict natural landscapes for which there was a particular vogue or interest at the time they were writing. Presenting a space with which the reader is familiar and whose attributes the reader will understand without explanation, allows the author to enter into a subtle dialogue with the reader, who understands the meanings encoded within that space. In drawing upon the contemporary vogue for utopia and the pastoral, Cottin, Souza and Staël achieve the same end as writers such as Louis-Sébastien Mercier or Bernardin de Saint-Pierre: they critique French society. In the case of Cottin, Souza and Staël, they draw our attention to the oppression of women that was prevalent within their contemporary society and to the consequent melancholy of their sex, both of which are seen starkly in contrast to the freedom and happiness of the utopian idyll. As Racault states, no utopia can stand alone. It always stands in opposition to the society which it opposes. 'Il faut signaler enfin' ['Finally, it must be pointed out'] continues Racault 'que le texte utopique, loin de trouver sa finalité dans le tableau de la société imaginaire qu'il décrit, a pour vocation de faire retour au réel dans un mouvement de confrontation qui lui donne son sens' ['that the utopian text, far from being limited to the picture of the imaginary society it describes, aims to return to reality in a confrontational movement which imbues it with meaning'].[87] However, Cottin, Souza and Staël not only return their characters to the society external to the utopian idyll so that we might be able to compare the two spaces better, they also actively use the values and expectations of the non-utopian space to destroy the very foundations of the utopian idyll itself. In so doing, they move from merely highlighting to actually dramatizing the oppressive and destructive power society has over love-struck women when their love is forbidden. The fact that the utopian idylls they employ to present their arguments are areas of tamed nature is also apt: the female protagonists who discover their love in an area of tamed nature will find that they themselves are ultimately 'tamed' and bent to the will of society. Ultimately, these women writers rework the genre in order to suit the aspects of French society that they particularly wish to critique. Astbury argues, with regard to pastoral fiction published at the time of the Revolution, that 'authors are not simply continuing within an existing highly conventional and artificial tradition but reworking it for a new sociology-literary context'.[88] This is also true of women writers in post-revolutionary French society; utopian and pastoral idyllic landscapes are written to provide apt podia from which the protest against the situation for women might be heard.

What can a woman do in the face of a restrictive society, if defying it and seeking a space in which she can express her forbidden love will result in her destruction? Souza's earlier novel, *Adèle de Sénange* provides an answer. Drawing on the contemporary opinions of French and English-style gardens, Souza is able to present both a critique of the restrictions of arranged marriages and the hoped-for freedom that the calls for marriage reform might bring. Simultaneously, Souza's sliding scale of restrictive garden space enables us to see how old and new ideas must work together to create a better future in which women may have more choice in marrying for love. Just as Cottin, Staël and Souza herself (in her later novel) appear to rework the utopian, pastoral tradition, building on it to the advantage of their arguments, so too does Souza build on expectations regarding the presentation of the French- and English-style gardens in *Adèle de Sénange*. She does not simply engage with the established garden binary, she expands upon it, and in so doing uses it to expand our perception of how the gender binary (and its consequent limitations on women) that she is critiquing might be reformed. She therefore reworks the way in which the *jardin à l'anglaise* and the *jardin à la française* are presented in order to suit a new socio-literary context.

Souza leaves her reader with one final thought. Ironically, through its subtlety, *Adèle de Sénange* defies Restif even more greatly than *Émilie et Alphonse, Claire d'Albe, Delphine* and *Malvina* in many ways. According to Stewart, 'In *Les gynographes*, Restif features marriage and motherhood as the biological and moral destiny of every woman [...]. In his version of utopia, good girls are rewarded with husbands and bad girls denied them'.[89] Souza, on the other hand, crafts natural spaces within her novel to argue that a woman's search for autonomy, freedom and individual rights is more important and more rewarding than any marriage, happy or unhappy.

Notes to Chapter 1

1. Le Comte d'Antraigues, *Observations sur le Divorce* (Paris: Imprimerie nationale, 1789), pp. 11–12.
2. James F. Traer, *Marriage and the Family in Eighteenth-Century France* (Ithaca; London: Cornell University Press, 1980), p. 15.
3. Ibid., p. 16.
4. Renee Winegarten, *Accursed Politics: Some French Women Writers and Political Life, 1715–1850* (Chicago: Ivan R. Dee, 2003), p. 136.
5. Suzanne Desan, *The Family on Trial in Revolutionary France* (California: University of California Press, 2006), p. 21.
6. Ibid., p. 25.
7. Inequality was particularly clear in the case of divorce proceedings arising from adultery, and also with regard to the possessions to which a spouse would be entitled once a divorce had been concluded. See Articles 229, 230 and 1492 of: *Code civil des Français* (Paris: Imp. de la République, an XII [1804]).
8. Nicholas White, *French Divorce Fiction from the Revolution to the First World War* (Oxford: Legenda, 2013), p. 29.
9. *Code civil des Français*, Article 213.
10. Ibid, Article 1124.
11. Catherine Toubin–Malinas, *Heurs et malheurs de la femme au XIXe siècle: 'Fécondité' D'Émile Zola* (Paris: Méridiens Klincksieck, 1986), p. 83.
12. Charlton, *New Images*, p. 18.
13. Hunt, p. 127.
14. Charlton, *New Images*, p. 18.
15. Alexandre de Laborde, *Description des nouveaux jardins de la France et de ses anciens châteaux, mêlée d'observations sur la vie de la campagne et la composition des jardins* (Paris: Delance, 1808), p. 1.
16. Astbury, pp. 17–40.
17. Fabienne Moore, 'Early French Romanticism', in *A Companion to European Romanticism*, ed. by Michael Ferber (Oxford: Blackwell, 2005), pp. 172–91 (p. 184).
18. Astbury, p. 18.
19. Charlton, *New Images*, p. 18.
20. Astbury, p. 18.
21. Malcolm Cook, 'Politics in the Fiction of the French Revolution, 1789–1794', *Studies on Voltaire and the Eighteenth Century*, 201 (1982), 233–340 (p. 290).
22. Malcolm Cook, 'Utopian Fiction of the French Revolution', *Nottingham French Studies*, 45 (2006), 104–13.
23. *Dictionnaire de l'Académie française*, 5e édition, 2 vols (Paris: J.J. Smits, L'An VI de la République [1798]).
24. James Fleming Jones, *La Nouvelle Héloïse: Rousseau and Utopia* (Genève: Droz, 1977).
25. Jean-Michel Racault, *L'Utopie narrative en France et en Angleterre 1675–1761* (Oxford: Voltaire Foundation, 1991), p. 21.
26. Alexandre Cioranescu, *L'Avenir du passé: utopie et littérature* (Paris: Gallimard, 1972), p. 22.
27. Gail Finney, 'Garden Paradigms in Nineteenth-Century Fiction', *Comparative Literature*, 36:1 (1984), 20–33 (p. 21).
28. Jean-Jacques Rousseau, *Julie ou La Nouvelle Héloïse* (Paris: Garnier Flammarion, 1967), p. 353.
29. Minski, p. 92.
30. Cook, 'Utopian Fiction', p. 104.
31. Weisgerber, p. 141.
32. Ibid., p. 142.
33. Finney, pp. 20–33.
34. Ibid.
35. Ibid., p. 22.
36. Bakhtin also identifies the idyll of agricultural labour, the idyll of craft-work and the family idyll. Mikhail Bakhtin, *The Dialogic Imagination: Four Essays,* ed. by Michael Holquist, trans. by Caryl Emerson and Michael Holquist (Austin, University of Texas Press, 1981), pp. 224–42.

37. Ibid., p. 226.

38. Racault, p. 182.

39. Bakhtin, p. 225.

40. Ibid., p. 225.

41. Carpenter, p. 49.

42. Finney, p. 27.

43. Ibid., p. 30.

44. David Bianciardi, *Sophie Cottin, une romancière oubliée à l'orée du romantisme (contribution à l'étude de la réception)* (Doctoral Thesis, Université de Metz, 1995), p. 583.

45. Louichon, p. 85.

46. Ibid.

47. Ibid.

48. Françoise Le Borgne, 'Idylle et intimité dans *Les Jardins* de Delille' in *Jardins Et Intimité Dans La Littérature Européenne (1750–1920): Actes Du Colloque Du Centre De Recherches Révolutionnaires Et Romantiques, Université Blaise-Pascal (Clermont-Ferrand, 22–24 Mars 2006)*, ed. by S. Bernard-Griffiths, F. Le Borgne and Daniel Madelénat (Clermont-Ferrand: Presses universitaires Blaise-Pascal, 2008), pp. 67–79 (75).

49. Bianciardi, p. 693.

50. Finney, p. 22.

51. See: Minski; Turner; Charlton, *New Images*; Michel Baridon, 'Understanding nature and the aesthetics of the landscape garden', in *Experiencing the Gardens in the Eighteenth Century*, ed. by Martin Calder (Oxford: Peter Lang, 2006), pp. 65–85; Martin Calder, 'The Experience of Space in the Eighteenth-Century French Garden: From Axis to Circuit to Closed Circuit', in *Space: New Dimensions in French Studies,* ed. by Emma Gilby and Katja Hautsein (Oxford: Peter Lang, 2005), pp. 41–58; Rose Standish Nichols, *English Pleasure Gardens* (Jaffrey, N.H.: David R. Godine, 2003).

52. André Mollet, *Le Jardin de Plaisir* (Moniteur: Paris, 1981 [1651]), p. 31.

53. Minski, p. 92.

54. Antoine-Joseph Dezallier d'Argenville, *Théorie et pratique du jardinage* (Paris: Mariette, 1747), p. 44.

55. Ibid., p. 103.

56. Minski, p. 92.

57. Nichols, p. 220.

58. Minski, p. 93.

59. Ibid.

60. Ibid.

61. Mornet, p. 219.

62. Le Ménahèze, p. 43.

63. Antoine Nicolas Duchesne, *Sur la formation des jardins* (Paris: Pissot, 1779), p. v.

64. Pacini, p. 4.

65. Ibid., p. 1.

66. Ibid., p. 10. (Original parenthesis.)

67. Chase, p. 80.

68. Ibid., pp. 7–8.

69. Carpenter, p. 35.

70. Ibid., p. 33.

71. Minski, p. 92.

72. Chase, pp. 85–86.

73. Ehrenfried Kluckert, *Parcs et jardins en Europe de l'antiquité à nos jours* (Potsdam: h.f.ullmann, 2005), p. 189.

74. Turner, p. 170.

75. Nichols, p. 221.

76. My emphasis.

77. David Herman, *Story Logic: Problems and Possibilities of Narrative* (Lincoln; London: University of Nebraska Press, 2002), p. 283. (Original emphasis.)

78. Chase, p. 95.
79. Original emphasis.
80. Martin Calder, 'Foreward' to *Experiencing the Gardens in the Eighteenth Century*, ed. by Martin Calder (Oxford: Peter Lang, 2006), pp. 7–11 (9).
81. Charlton, *New Images*, p. 31.
82. Mornet, p. 219.
83. Calder, 'Foreward', p. 10.
84. Charlton, *New Images*, p. 33.
85. Pacini, p. 12.
86. Restif de la Bretonne, *Les Gynographes, ou idées de deux honnêtes-femmes sur un projet de règlement proposé à toute l'Europe: pour mettre les femmes à leur place, et opérer le Bonheur des deux sexes; avec des notes historiques et justificatives, suivies des noms des femmes célèbres* (Paris: Gosse & Pinet; Humblot, 1777), p. 92.
87. Racault, p. 22.
88. Astbury, p. 37.
89. Stewart, p. 11.

❖

CHAPTER 2

Landscapes of Loss: Communicating Maternal Grief and Guilt

C'est à toi que je m'adresse, tendre et prévoyante mère, qui sus t'écarter de la grande route, et garantir l'arbrisseau naissant du choc des opinions humaines! Cultive, arrose la jeune plante avant qu'elle meure; ses fruits feront un jour tes délices. Forme de bonne heure une enceinte autour de l'âme de ton enfant; un autre en peut marquer le circuit, mais toi seule y dois poser la barrière.

[It is you I address, tender and provident mother, you who knew how to distance yourself from the highway, and to protect the budding shrub from the impact of human opinions. Cultivate and water the young plant before it dies. Its fruit will one day be your delights. Build an enclosure around your child's soul early on. Someone else can mark out its circumference, but only you must build its border].

ROUSSEAU, *Émile ou de l'Education*.[1]

Motherhood and Mother Nature

The analyses conducted within this chapter also have as their focus the tamed nature of gardens. Whilst these gardens may incorporate some of the physical natural features seen in the previous chapter, nonetheless, their design is for a very different purpose. This chapter analyses novels by Krüdener and Genlis in order to understand how these authors portray the problems of infant mortality and child abandonment. It also shows how the mothers in these women's novels who fall short of the expected motherhood ideal attempt to convey their intense emotional turmoil through moulding and taming the natural world.

Prior to the late eighteenth century in France, certainly amongst the higher echelons of society, mothers had exhibited indifference and negligence towards their children, for motherhood was not the primary concern of an upper-class woman.[2] The figure of the child had been denigrated in early eighteenth-century sermons, which presented children as self-centred and immoral, thus provoking one principal reason for parental indifference.[3] The church's view of children's depravity derived from the notion that infants were 'born steeped in original sin', and that as a consequence, 'their tendency to greedy self-indulgence and outright iniquity had to be corrected by parents and educators who would force them to conform to proper (and adult) ways of behaving'.[4] Furthermore, a child was also often seen by parents '"comme un embarras et une charge", par l'attention continuelle qu'il demande'

[' "as a cumbersome burden", because of the constant attention that it demands'].[5] It therefore became the norm for infants to be sent to wet nurses for the first years of their lives.[6] The statistics were in fact overwhelming; even in 1780, the *lieutenant de police,* Jean Charles Pierre Lenoir, remarked that only about one thousand in every twenty-one thousand children born in Paris every year were nursed by their mothers.[7]

Towards the second half of the century, however, as has previously been noted by scholars such as Jennifer J. Popiel, Margaret H. Darrow, Élisabeth Badinter and Maria Mann, certain catalysts began to revise the way motherhood was perceived, and, consequently, the attitudes of mothers themselves.[8] As Badinter states: 'C'est Rousseau, avec la publication de l'*Émile* en 1762, qui cristallise les idées nouvelles et donne le véritable coup d'envoi à la famille moderne, c'est-à-dire à la famille fondée sur l'amour maternel' ['It is Rousseau, who, with the publication of *Émile* in 1762, crystallizes the new ideas and really launches the modern family: the family based around maternal love'].[9] Rousseau argued that 'children were not by nature beastly but instead were capable of rational thought and good actions if they were removed from the constraints placed upon them by society and nurtured by a domestic mother',[10] who was to be the first point of education for all children. It was at her knee that they should learn morals, self-control and how to live according to nature. In *Émile ou de l'éducation* Rousseau outlined guidelines for mothering, arguing that mothers must breastfeed their own children, cease to place children in the care of nurses, and allow freedom for children to move and play. Breastfeeding children and keeping them at home promoted the creation of a bond of love and trust between mother and child. This bond would encourage a mother to educate her child, and the child to heed its mother's words. According to Rousseau, from the first moment of breastfeeding, society would change for the better.[11]

The situation did not change overnight. According to Darrow:

> Although Rousseau's ideas about motherhood and breastfeeding achieved a certain vogue among noblewomen at the end of the *ancien régime*, in practice their experiments rarely went deeper than play acting à la Marie-Antoinette's rustic *hameau*. The adoption of domesticity by noblewomen was not the result of a gradual drift throughout the eighteenth and nineteenth centuries but was accomplished within one generation, during the French Revolution.[12]

It took the desire to create a new regime to concretize the alterations which Rousseau had advocated. A peaceful, ordered society in which both genders had their place, and in which self-control, morals and sensibility were taught early on, seemed to form the perfect contrast to the turmoil of the Revolution and the inequalities of the Ancien Régime. The late eighteenth-century reader of Rousseau saw the latter's analysis of a woman's role 'as an integral part of his emphasis on the need for virtuous action and the creation of individuals for a new society'.[13] When both self-control and sensibility finally became imperative, as opposed to simply desirable, then the concept of the mother as primary educator was finally put into practice. Mothers took on this important role wholeheartedly, viewing it as one to be performed with great love and care.

Literature frequently echoed the attitudes of society. The mothers who appeared in early eighteenth-century fiction reflected the indifference exhibited in society itself.[14] Literary descriptions of doting mothers were lacking; there was no desire on the part of fictional women, just like their extra-fictional counterparts, to breastfeed their children; there was little or no analysis of mother-child relationships, or of the personal significance of being a mother. In fact, the mother figure was rarely present at all.[15] Often, when a mother was absent from literature, it was due to death in childbirth. Thus, in fairy tales, novels and drama alike, literary matriarchs were often stepmothers, and they were usually cruel and uncaring. However, as the century wore on,

> [t]he promotion of these new ideas — the idea of childhood as a unique phase of human growth and that of the family as an intimate and harmonious social unit — became a major activity, a veritable cause, of Enlightenment writers. In novels, on the stage and in educational, medical and philosophical treatises, the new ideals of the happy and healthy family were dramatized and explained.[16]

Thus, from the 1760s onwards we see a growing body of fiction in which the mother not only appears, but in which she plays a vital role. Primary amongst these works were sentimental novels, typified by Rousseau's *Julie, ou la Nouvelle Héloïse*, whose eponymous heroine is depicted as the perfect mother. Surrounded by nature in an Elysian garden, Julie nurses and educates her children, lavishing them with maternal affection. Towards the end of the century, as mothers' attitudes changed, motherhood was portrayed even more frequently in fiction, and '[b]y 1789 the theme of "Republican motherhood" had become a literary staple'.[17] Inspired by Rousseau, many female novelists displayed the image of the new motherhood ideal in their work. Several women writers composed novels, plays, short stories and treatises about what a good mother should be, advising their contemporaries, as well as future generations, on how to raise children.[18] Chief amongst these women writers was Genlis, whose novels often deal with the themes of motherhood and education.

The natural setting for Rousseau's *Julie* is significant, because for eighteenth-century thinkers, '[t]he relations between mother and child were especially interesting, since they seemed of all kin relations the most deeply embedded in nature'.[19] In fact, the link between mothers and Mother Nature became central to the new motherhood ideal, thus reinforcing the belief in a woman-nature connection. Rousseau established clear links between motherhood and nature throughout his works. This is evident in the epigraph to this chapter, in which Rousseau employs horticultural vocabulary, arguing that a mother should both 'cultiver' ['cultivate'] and 'arroser' ['water'] her children, to allow them to blossom. In so doing, he creates a metaphor in which the mother appears either as a gardener asked to fashion the natural landscape represented by the child, or as Mother Nature herself, cultivating the shrubs which grow from her. In the twelfth book of *Les Confessions*, Rousseau again conjoins the figure of nature and that of the mother: 'O nature! ô ma mère! me voici sous ta seule garde; il n'y a point ici d'homme adroit et fourbe qui s'interpose entre toi et moi' ['Oh nature! Oh my mother! I am

FIG. 2.1. Constance Mayer, *L'Heureuse mère* [*The Fortunate Mother*], 1810. Reproduced here with permission from the Réunion des musées nationaux in Paris.

here under your sole guardianship. There is no clever and deceitful man here who might come between us'].[20] When the public turned their attention to Rousseau's work and his promotion of the new maternal ideal, therefore, the bond between the mother figure and nature would permeate strongly into their consciousness.

It became common for mothers to be painted with their children in a natural setting. Moreau le Jeune's *Les Délices de la maternité* [*The Delights of Maternity*] (1777), for example, depicts a mother and father sitting in a verdant park, surrounded by their children. Jean-Honoré Fragonard's similarly titled *Les Délices maternelles* [*Maternal delights*] portrays a mother surrounded by blossoming nature, pushing her infant amid the plants of a rustic setting. These types of depictions became popular, indeed '[y]oung rustic mothers, their nursing breasts virtuously exposed, became a staple of the printseller'.[21] Constance Mayer's 1810 painting *L'Heureuse mère* [*The Fortunate Mother*] (Fig. 2.1) shows this very image: a young mother happily cradling a sleeping baby, her 'breasts virtuously exposed', in a woodland setting; trees tower above the young woman who sits on a grassy mound amid wild flowers.

We see similar images of mothers and nature in French women's literary fiction of the period. In the 1780s, 1790s and early 1800s, Genlis, Krüdener, and Cottin imitate Rousseau in displaying the new, loving mother in their novels and coupling this notion with aspects of the natural world.[22] Much has been written on how the novels of women writers at this time portray loving mothers who breastfeed their children, and how these novels advise women to be good mothers.[23] However, there is little critical literature on the relationship between the description of nature and motherhood in these novels. This is somewhat surprising, given that scholars have discussed images of nature and motherhood in Rousseau's *Julie* and Bernardin's *Paul et Virginie*.[24]

In particular, however, there exists almost no critical analysis of the ways in which nature can be used to discuss the problems that women now faced in their roles as doting mothers. The very creation of a new ideal of motherhood raises the question of what happened to those women who were unable to fulfil this role as expected, either because their child died or because they were forced to give up the child on account of its being born out of wedlock. The ensuing sections of this chapter will examine the image so prevalent in its epigraph: that of the mother as fashioner and cultivator of natural landscape. The chapter will explore certain aspects of 'garden language', as outlined by McIntosh:

> First, there is the form of the garden as a whole. This includes the lines traced by the perimeter and internal divisions. [...] The second basic ingredient of the language consists of the objects that are created or placed in the garden or the existing landscape features to which specific meanings are attached. These might be natural or man-made hills, rivers, ponds, caves [...]. Such features might also include fountains, statues, reliefs, topiary hedges, labyrinths, pavilions and gazebos. The third ingredient of the language relates to the plants in the garden and the meanings they are given. A plant has of course a large number of different meanings and associations depending on the region and culture. Its meaning can be shaped by physical characteristics, such as colour, shape or chemical properties.[25]

The ways in which these elements of garden language function in *Valérie* and *Les Mères rivales* will be analysed, as will the ways in which Krüdener and Genlis engage with contemporary vogue for (and consequent common associations with) features of garden landscapes and particular types of garden: respectively, the memorial garden deathscape and the notion of a garden designed to convey an invitation to moral reflection. It will be argued that in *Valérie* and *Les Mères rivales,* mothers who have lost or abandoned children are depicted as landscape gardeners who tame and mould nature in order to use garden language to re-establish communication with their lost child and to convey to the outside world linguistically inexpressible emotions of loss and/or guilt. Ultimately, by not only writing the landscape itself, but by also writing their heroines' act of landscaping, Krüdener and Genlis are, themselves, able to communicate to their reader the problematic consequences of the new ideal of motherhood.

The Grieving Mother as Landscape Gardener in Krüdener's *Valérie*

Constance Mayer also painted a picture entitled *La Mère infortunée* [*The Unfortunate Mother*] (Fig. 2.2), which was intended to be displayed alongside *L'Heureuse mère* at the Salon of 1810. The two paintings illustrate two very opposite maternal emotions. Where *L'Heureuse mère* depicts the happiness of a mother holding and nursing a sleeping infant, the child of *La Mère infortunée* is sleeping in a very different sense. In both paintings mother and child are surrounded by nature in a shadowy woodland setting. In *La Mère infortunée*, however, the mother's gaze is fixed on a tomb in which the infant is interred. The tomb is marked by a crucifix and surrounded by nature. What this second painting suggests, in its title as well as its composition, is not that the *mère infortunée* is a bad or indifferent mother, but rather that she would have conformed to the new ideal had her child not died. She experiences emotional tenderness towards her child, but her ability to convey this directly to the infant has been removed.

The death of young children was an ever-present issue in eighteenth- and nineteenth-century France, despite attempts to curb the infant mortality rate. According to Yves Blayo's demographic research: 'La moitié des enfants mouraient avant 10,5 ans dans les décennies précédent la Révolution' ['Half of all children died before they reached ten and a half years old in the decades leading up to the Revolution'].[26] Geneviève Masuy-Stroobant and Michel Poulain inform us that:

La perte d'un enfant, jadis considérée comme 'normale' devient progressivement inacceptable, du moins dans les classes sociales les plus favorisées. Néanmoins, faute de moyens de lutte appropriés, le risque de mortalité infantile reste élevé: pour l'ensemble de la France, il s'élève à 297% pour la décennie 1740–1749 et à 278% entre 1780 et 1789.

[The loss of a child, previously considered to be 'normal', became more and more unacceptable, at least among the more privileged social classes. Nevertheless, for want of appropriate means to combat it, the risk of infant mortality remained high. For the whole of France, it amounted to 297% for the decade between 1740 and 1749 and 278% between 1780 and 1789].[27]

Fig. 2.2. Constance Mayer, *La Mère infortunée* [*The Unfortunate Mother*], 1810. Reproduced here with permission from the Réunion des musées nationaux in Paris. Note the cross in the shadows at the bottom right of the picture, towards which the unfortunate mother's gaze is directed.

Although the number of deaths fell in the early nineteenth century, in the 1820s there nonetheless remained a 36.1% likelihood that a child would not survive to its first birthday.[28] In 1803, when Krüdener's *Valérie* was published, under the first Empire, there was a striking 41.8% likelihood of losing a baby.[29] However, mothers were no longer distanced emotionally from their child, and so it is unsurprising to see a sense of intense maternal grief portrayed both in paintings such as Mayer's and in literature.

In fact, it is further unsurprising to see an increase in the portrayal of maternal grief given that mourning and contemplation of death in general became more customary in the mid-to-late eighteenth century than they had previously been. Voltaire was well aware of the aversion to contemplating death in the early eighteenth century, and comments scornfully thereupon in his *Lettres philosophiques* [*Philosophical Letters*], arguing that '[o]n ne peut pas dire qu'un homme supporte la mort aisément ou malaisément, quand il n'y pense point du tout' ['[y]ou cannot say that a man accepts death easily or not when he does not think about it at all'].[30] Death may have been inevitable, but that did not mean that it must be dwelt upon. Yet, as the Enlightenment's counter-current of *sensibilité* emerged, concerned with experiencing and displaying emotions, the public's views on mortality altered:

> Sorrow was found to have a hypnotic attraction, and there were sophisticated delights to be discovered in melancholy [...] [and] the nuances of emotion which we feel at the thought of death and its exigencies, at the sight of its ceremonies and monuments.[31]

The eighteenth century in France became an age in which death was 'more personalized than previously, even more deeply felt', and in which 'grieving seems to have become even more intense than earlier'.[32]

Krüdener's *Valérie* provides an abundantly clear example of a mother's grief at the loss of a child. The eponymous protagonist is the image of the ideal, loving mother advocated during the final decades of the eighteenth century:

> [J]'ai vu la sensible Valérie, mille fois plus belle, plus touchante que jamais, répandre sur son fils les plus douces larmes, me le montrer éveillé, endormi, me demander si j'avais remarqué tous ses traits, pressentir qu'il aurait le sourire de son père, et ne jamais se lasser de l'admirer et de le caresser. (*V*, p. 90)

> [I saw the sensitive Valérie, a thousand times more beautiful, more touching than ever, weep the sweetest tears over her son, show him to me awake and asleep, ask me if I had noticed all his features, predict that he would have his father's smile, and never tire of admiring or caressing him.]

Yet Valérie's son, Adolphe, dies shortly after his birth, leaving his mother broken-hearted:

> Hélas! quelque temps après, ces mêmes yeux ont répandu les larmes de deuil et de la douleur la plus amère: le jeune Adolphe n'a vécu que quelques instants, et sa mère le pleure tous les jours. (*V*, p. 90)

> [Alas! A short time afterwards, these same eyes shed tears of grief and the bitterest sorrow: little Adolphe lived only a few moments, and his mother mourns him every day.]

As the child was born while the family was travelling in Venice, Valérie is unable to take him home for burial. She therefore buries him on the island of Lido, in grounds belonging to a convent.

As the mother-child relationship has been cut short by death, the distraught mother constructs — according to her specific design — a small private garden around the child's tomb on the island, which she visits as often as she can while the family is in Venice. She elects to bury Adolphe in an area set aside from the urban life of the city, an area of natural beauty. In writing such a landscape of loss, Krüdener certainly maintains the connection between mother, child and nature established during the period; however, she also provides echoes within her novel of the changes both in burial practice and in the grieving process which occurred during the late eighteenth and early nineteenth centuries in France. Previously, the custom had been to put most bodies 'in the *fosse commune*, the burial pit, and this stayed open — with just an inch or two of earth thrown over each new arrival — until the quota of corpses was complete'.[33] The later decades of the eighteenth century saw a move away from 'the age-long practice within Christendom [...] of burying the dead in or close to the church [...] and towards creating cemeteries out of the town', and in the countryside.[34] One significant reason for this was the increasing health issue originating from the presence of many communal graves and overcrowded cemeteries within towns. However, as Charlton argues, 'the quite rapid acceptance of the new locations surely suggests also that even amongst the public at large there was perhaps a growing sense that "returning to nature" was an apt conclusion to one's life'.[35] As a result of the shift in burial practice, family plots and communal graves were replaced with an increasing number of personal graves, allowing the new practice to accord 'with a growth of a more personalised grieving'.[36] The process of experiencing personalised grieving, like the situation of the graves themselves, was felt to be apt amid a natural landscape:

> To mourn for someone deeply loved and forever lost, to mourn in solitude, far from the busy world which does not understand the secret magic of a unique love, [...] to mourn and be in love with mourning — the concept, a stage in the development of human affection and individuality, was formed, but it required an appropriate setting. Where else should this be found but against the tremendous backdrop of Nature? — Scenery changing from light to darkness and from colour to greyness as the days and the seasons revolve, ever beautiful to recall us to our memories of departed beauty, but with sombre moods conveying the charm of melancholy to purify and sustain our grief.[37]

Personal tombs were not only to be found in countryside cemeteries. There was also a desire for images of death and experiences of mourning to permeate private gardens. As MacArthur affirms, '[v]irtually all gardens of the final third of the eighteenth century in France were influenced by Rousseau's writings [...] and then [...] by the site of his tomb at Ermenonville'.[38] France had witnessed Rousseau's advocacy of a return to nature in his novels and treatises, and the public's taste for nature increased dramatically following their publication. Consequently, when Rousseau died, and was entombed in a natural landscape, this spoke directly to the heart of the nation's sentimentality. Ermenonville was 'the generation's ideal sepulchre — the trees, the clear water, the silence, a resting-place for one who had been Nature's closest friend'.[39] As well as Ermenonville, there were other famously visited gardens of mourning and remembrance. Charlton states that '[m]any of the upper classes expressed the new attitudes similarly, siting tombs and monuments in their informal gardens — as at Bagatelle in the Bois de Boulogne, Méréville (with a memorial to Captain Cook included), and numerous other places'.[40] Thus, the natural landscape became a fitting setting 'for memorials to the dead as well as for their graves'.[41] The image of a resting place and memorial site at the heart of nature is precisely what we see in the garden of mourning constructed by Krüdener in *Valérie*. In fact, Krüdener's landscape echoes Ermenonville itself even further. Rousseau's tomb at Ermenonville was famously placed on a small island within the park, and Krüdener has Valérie not only incorporate Adolphe's gravesite in a natural setting, but actually has her bury the child on a small island. Krüdener draws on the advantages that such contemporarily recognizable spaces afford for the purposes of making her argument about maternal grief. The established connections that natural and island gravesites have with emotion, melancholy, idylls, retreat and personalized grieving are highly appropriate and useful. Furthermore the physical features of the natural landscape and the physical characteristics of the island permit messages and emotions to be transmitted which cannot be conveyed linguistically.

Valérie has the garden constructed in such a way that particular aspects of nature are employed to convey both her love for the child and her sense of loss. Following Valérie's design, the family friend Gustave plants foliage symbolically connected to the rituals of funerals, death or grief: 'j'ai planté des saules d'Amérique et des roses blanches auprès du tombeau d'Adolphe' ['I planted American willows and white roses near Adolphe's tomb'] (*V*, p. 93). McIntosh argues that '[t]he third ingredient of [garden] language relates to the plants in the garden and the meanings they are given'.[42] The planting of willows and white roses are significant, because their symbolic meanings allow Valérie to communicate to her child, through natural language, her love and grief for him. The willow, according to botanical symbolism, is traditionally associated with resonance and harmony.[43] As a loving mother, Valérie desires her son to be buried in a space which will allow him to repose in peace. Furthermore, according to Hageneder, the biblical reference to willow trees in Psalm 137 'caused generations of European poets to interpret the willow as a symbol of mourning and despair'.[44] The psalmist writes 'By the rivers of Babylon, there we sat down, yea, we wept, when we remembered Zion. We hanged our harps upon the willows in the midst thereof'.[45] The willow in this psalm is associated with the grief and suffering of the Jewish people at the loss of Jerusalem to the Babylonians. In later Western literature, therefore, it makes frequent appearances in cemeteries, or in gardens of mourning such as that which Valérie has constructed for her dead son. The weeping willow cries for the dead, as the mother for her child, and as the Jewish people for their home. Valérie concretizes the image of weeping in our mind, drawing explicit links between grief and the willow tree as she describes 'ce saule si triste, inclinant sa tête, comme s'il sentait ma douleur' ['that very sad willow tree, bending its head as though it felt my grief'] (*V*, p. 106). The willow in the garden designed by Valérie is planted for its ability to sympathize with her grief, and thus to communicate to others who neither share nor understand her pain the emotions that she finds impossible to explain in words. The connection between the willow and sadness was well known in the early nineteenth century. As McManners argues, 'Nature itself must be in sympathy with human grief, and thus the drooping willow came to be considered a more appropriate symbol than the formal cypress or evergreen'.[46] In 1819 Charlotte de La Tour published her *Le Langage des fleurs* [*The Language of Flowers*], which includes a glossary of a large number of plant meanings. The 'Saule de Babylone (ou pleureur)' ['Babylon (or Weeping) Willow'] signifies melancholia, according to de La Tour.[47] Even in the pagan religion of antiquity, the willow held associations with the world of the dead:

> Belili, the Sumerian goddess of love, the mood and the underworld, resided in willow trees, springs and wells. In ancient Greece, Persephone had a grove of aged willows, and the priestess Circe guarded a willow grove dedicated to Hecate, the goddess of death and transition.[48]

Belili, Persephone and Hecate were all pagan female divinities associated with the underworld, and each had links to the willow tree, making it a very clear symbol of death and the afterlife. As a triple representative of death, of transition to the afterlife, and of the grief of those left behind, it is a highly appropriate natural image for Valérie to plant by the side of her child's grave.

The white rose traditionally signifies innocence and purity, and Valérie certainly associates her child very starkly with innocence, and not with the original sin with which it was believed, during the Ancien Régime, that children were tainted. She reiterates the image of innocence when she has carved on Adolphe's tombstone the words: 'Ici dort Adolphe de M..., du double sommeil de l'innocence et de la mort' ['Here lies Adolphe de M..., sleeping the sleep of innocence and death'] (V, p. 107). In addition, the rose is traditionally associated with love, which Valérie wishes to communicate to Adolphe, and also with rebirth, 'because of the semantic kinship between the Latin words *rosa* (rose) and *ros*, meaning "dew" or "rain"'.[49] The third desire that Valérie wishes to communicate with the rose, then, is that her son be reborn to eternal life. Jean Chevalier and Alain Gheerbrant explain that '[i]t was because they were a symbol of regeneration that, in Classical antiquity, the custom was established of placing roses upon graves'.[50] Genlis, who, in her *La Botanique historique et littéraire* [*Historical and Literary Botany*], describes various appearances of the rose as a symbol in mythology and history, writes of roses being placed specifically on the coffins of children: 'En Pologne, on couvre de roses le cercueil d'un enfant; et quand son convoi passe dans les rues, on jette des fenêtres une multitude de roses' ['In Poland, they cover a child's coffin with roses; and when the cortège passes by in the streets, people throw a multitude of roses from the windows'].[51]

The willow and roses permit both a continuing relationship between Valérie and Adolphe, and also the communication of intense maternal grief. However, not only do objects in the natural world play an important part with regard to symbolism of death and grief, the seasons of the natural world also come into play, showing how nature's time, as well as space, communicate Valérie's emotions. Valérie knows that the roses will only be visible for a small portion of the year, and does not wish her son's grave to be unadorned in the winter months. She therefore asks Gustave to plant another type of shrub in addition, to ensure the perpetual presence of flowers on the grave:

> Je vous envoie aussi de jeunes arbustes que j'ai trouvés dans la Villa-Médicis, qui viennent des îles du sud, et fleurissent plus tard que ceux que nous avons déjà: en les couvrant avec précaution l'hiver, ils ne périront pas, et nous aurons encore des fleurs quand les autres seront tombées. (*V*, p. 107)

> [I am also sending you some young shrubs that I found at the Villa Medici and which come from the islands in the South. They bloom later than those which we already have. If we cover them carefully in the winter, they will not die, and we will still have flowers when the others have fallen.]

Although Valérie is happy for the natural world to be associated with the afterlife, she is not willing for nature to present a physical image of decay to the spectator, thereby reflecting the decaying corpse beneath it. By ensuring the presence of flowers even in winter months, Valérie prevents harsh winter from becoming the harbinger of yet more death to the island. Taming the landscape in this way permits the natural time in the garden of the dead son to be transcended, even cheated. There is a further example of this cheating of time. The visits to the graveside take place in October, an apt time to visit, since nature itself begins to die in autumn, the season associated with the 'Mythos of Tragedy', according to Northrop Frye.[52] However, unusually, the time, season and climate are confused:

> La journée était encore fort chaude, quoique nous fussions déjà à la fin d'octobre. [...] Nous écartâmes des branches touffues d'ébéniers qui avaient fleuri encore une fois dans cette automne [sic], et quelques branches de saule et d'acacia. (*V*, pp. 93–94)

> [The day was still extremely hot, even though it was already late October. [...] We removed dense ebony branches which had blossomed once again this autumn, and also a few willow and acacia branches.]

Late October is as hot as mid-summer, so much so that when Valérie and Gustave reach the site of the infant's burial, the heat has caused autumn to slow down, staving off the death of nature, and allowing one final floral blossom. The gravesite of the child is almost idyllic in its ability to 'cheat' the death of nature. Indeed, as Le Borgne remarks, 'si l'univers idyllique est avant tout celui de l'innocence et des doux plaisirs de l'âge d'or, il est également, dès l'origine, marqué du sceau de la perte et du deuil' ['if the idyllic universe is above all one of innocence and the sweet pleasures of the golden age, it is equally, from the beginning, stamped with the seal of loss and grief'].[53] Bakhtin models the interdependent relationship between time and space as follows:

> We will give the name *chronotope* (literally 'time-space') to the intrinsic connectedness of temporal and spatial relationships that are artistically expressed in literature. [...] In the literary artistic chronotope, spatial and temporal indicators are fused into one carefully thought-out, concrete whole.

> Time, as it were, thickens, takes on flesh, becomes artistically visible; likewise, space becomes charged and responsive to the movements of time, plot, and history.[54]

As noted in Chapter 1, in his discussion of the chronotope as it appears in fictive utopias, Bakhtin highlights the 'special relationship that time has to space in the idyll'.[55] Idyllic settings permit the time-space barrier to be broken down. In the case of the idyll of grief in *Valérie*, natural spatial features are employed to transcend time gaps to the point where they no longer exist. This involves what Bakhtin terms a 'unity of place'.[56] In his paradigm this spatial unity refers to the enduring of one idyllic space over generations, allowing no change to take place during the passing of time. No change in nature seems to occur in the immediate vicinity of the child's grave. No matter what the season of the year, whether it be the season of birth (spring), life (summer), dying (autumn) or death (winter), the child's tomb is never without blossoming flora. Therefore we have a further example of a tomb at the heart of nature which allows time to be transcended. Here, the transcendence permits Valérie to create an eternal idyll for the child to rest in, to replace the idyll she would have given him in life. Thus the mother-child bond is strengthened thanks to the natural features of the gravesite, as is the mother's ability to communicate her feelings to the child.

The fact that Valérie constructs her son's grave and memorial garden on an island must also be considered, for the plant life is not the only aspect of the garden able to convey meaning. In his discussion of garden language, Christopher McIntosh states that the first element thereof 'is the form of the garden as a whole. This includes the lines traced by the perimeter and internal divisions'.[57] The physical situation and delimitations of Valérie's garden are highly significant factors in the successful communication of several ideas. Firstly, because the island is apart from the rest of the world it becomes easier to believe in its existence as an idyll, thus facilitating Valérie's communication of the messages discussed above. Secondly, the isolated situation of the space also ensures that Valérie can literally cut herself off from the rest of society when she visits the grave. The sea surrounding the island forms a perfect natural barrier, discouraging entry, and the gravesite itself is situated in the walled 'enceinte' ['enclosure'] of a convent, whose gate is locked and which is only accessible to those who possess a key. The island physically embodies the grieving mother's feeling of emotional distance from those who neither share nor understand her pain, thereby simultaneously both allowing her the necessary private time and space to come to terms with the death of her son, and imparting this deep-seated need to her entourage. The island is thus able to convey Valérie's most intimate emotions because, as Carlota Vicens-Pujol argues, '[c]ercle dans le cercle, le jardin à l'intérieur de l'île symbolise donc ce qu'il y a de plus caché dans l'homme' ['[a] circle within a circle, the garden on an island thus symbolizes that which man keeps most hidden'].[58]

In turn, the island setting is useful to Krüdener herself. By echoing the image of the famous garden-island gravesite at Ermenonville, Krüdener has created for her reader a burial space that is well-recognized as both an isolated and an idyllic retreat. This facilitates the communication of maternal grief — which, as we have seen, relies on the dual image of isolation and idyllic nature — to the extra-fictional audience. Krüdener's evocation of Girardin's garden-tribute to Rousseau also enables her to bring a trace of the celebrated philosopher himself into the text, thereby allowing his arguments regarding nature, women and motherhood to resonate within the island space. By doing so, Krüdener encourages the reader to view Valérie's efforts in the light of the maternal ideal propounded by Rousseau. Once the reader does this, (s)he is made forcibly aware of Valérie's strong resemblance to the ideal mother figure: she loves, cares, nurtures, and provides. However, the irony of this comparison also becomes abundantly clear: Valérie cannot embody the ideal of motherhood as Rousseau intended it, because her child has died. Krüdener's implicit echoes of Rousseau therefore appear less a homage than a reminder that his exhortation to a new style of motherhood failed to take into account motherhood's potentially painful consequences. In the final analysis, then, the choice of an island setting turns Valérie's garden of mourning into both a public and a private landscape of one's own. It is a space which creates a sense of personal isolation and permits private dialogue between mother and dead child; yet it also conveys private emotions to a wider intra-fictional audience and speaks loudly to the reading public about the more problematic consequences of this new ideal of motherhood.

Valérie wishes to visit the gravesite as often as possible while still in Venice, and so informs one of the nuns: 'Ma sœur, vous devriez remettre une clef à un de mes gondoliers; je vous donnerai trop souvent la peine d'ouvrir cette porte' ['Sister, you should give a key to one of my gondoliers, because otherwise I will trouble you too often to open this door'] (V, p. 93). Therefore, whilst Valérie feels separated from the rest of the world, she clearly exhibits a need for closeness to the child itself. Although literally regaining contact is impossible, maintaining a sense of attachment with the deceased child allows Valérie to adapt to his death. She is permitted to process the loss and to begin to move on with life, whilst recognizing that the child must be integrated into her life in a new way. Valérie tries to be as physically and emotionally close to her child in his death as she was, if only momentarily, while he lived. Her presence at the gravesite ensures physical proximity, as does the direction of her gaze: 'Valérie fixa ses regards sur la tombe d'Adolphe' ['Valérie fixed her gaze upon Adolphe's tomb'] (V, p. 95). The image of Valérie gazing mournfully upon the tomb of her child surrounded by nature resembles Mayer's picture of La Mère infortunée, who stands gazing upon a similar tomb, in a similar setting, in similar circumstances. Valérie gains emotional proximity through designing the landscape garden herself, which permits her to go through the nesting process that could not be completed during the child's life. She constructs a space in which the mother-child bond is strong. Instead of making the nursery ready for a living child, Valérie prepares the garden and tomb for her deceased child, using nature itself to create a gift, and thus to communicate love to her son.

Although the garden allows proximity on both a physical and a metaphysical level, Valérie does not live permanently in Venice. Consequently, when the family leaves, she must find another way to maintain these attachments with Adolphe. Valérie decides to capitalize on her husband's decision to commission a portrait of her, and requests that the painting be of herself in the graveside garden. She writes to Gustave:

> Mon mari désirait longtemps avoir mon portrait [...] et j'ai pensé qu'un tableau tel que j'en avais l'idée pouvait réunir nos deux projets. Ma pensée a merveilleusement réussi; jugez-en vous-même. N'est-ce pas Valérie, telle qu'elle était assise si souvent à Lido, la mer se brisant dans le lointain, comme sur la côte où je jouais mon enfance; le ciel vaporeux; les nuages roses du soir, dans lesquels je croyais voir la jeune âme de mon fils; cette pierre qui couvre ses formes charmantes, maintenant, hélas! décomposées; et ce saule si triste, inclinant sa tête, comme s'il sentait ma douleur; et ces grappes de cytise, qui caressent en tombant la pierre de la mort. (V, p. 106)

> [My husband has long desired to have a portrait of me [...] and I thought that the picture I had in mind would unite both our aims. My idea succeeded marvellously; judge for yourself. Is this not Valérie, as she so often sat at Lido, with the waves breaking in the distance, as they did on the coast where I spent my childhood; the hazy sky; the pink evening clouds, among which I thought I could see my son's young soul; the tombstone which covers his beautiful features, alas now decomposed; and that sorrowful willow tree, bending its head as though it felt my grief; and the bunches of cascading laburnum flowers which caress the stone of death.]

Krüdener's heroine is now not only similar to the figure in Constance Mayer's painting *La Mère infortunée*, she could easily have been that mother. Valérie's commissioned painting provides her, firstly, with the chance to re-establish the sense of physical and emotional attachment between herself and her son, and, secondly, with an outlet for her grief which mirrors (quite literally) that provided by the garden.

The sense of physical attachment is maintained partially by the painting's distinct advantage over the gravesite: it is portable. It can be removed from the wall and taken wherever Valérie travels, giving her a permanent, tangible link to her son. However, the painting also has one distinct disadvantage: it is two levels removed from the child, and thus risks hindering the sense of physical attachment. Valérie cannot hold her son because he is dead; she can no longer visit the island on which the child is buried because she has left Venice; she must now content herself with an image of the garden, as she does not even possess an image of her son himself. Valérie surmounts this disadvantage by having her own image inserted into the painting of the garden. Instead of allowing her husband to commission an ordinary portrait of her, and privately asking the painter also to create a picture of the gravesite of her child, Valérie fuses the two images together. In ensuring that the painting contains a visual juxtaposition of herself and Adolphe, she establishes it as a locus for continued contact between them — a psychological meeting place — which permits the distance between the worlds of the living and the dead to be transcended.

Notably, Valérie also ensures that the painting captures the natural features of the garden that she worked so hard to pour meaning into, thus enabling the continued communication of her emotions. Just as in the real garden itself, willows appear in the painting, a symbol to convey Valérie's sorrow at the child's loss. She even allows Mother Nature to assume the roles she herself could not fulfil. The laburnum tree and its flowers literally caress the grave, as the mother herself would wish to caress the living child. Furthermore, Valérie imagines she sees the image of her son's soul in the clouds, echoing her hopes that her child has attained everlasting life in Heaven. Again, this shows aspects of nature providing a home for Adolphe in a way that his mother cannot. Mother Nature and the mother figure are thus merged in Valérie's portable keepsake.

In nineteenth-century France 'the twin themes of birth and death open onto a variety of issues', write Nigel Harkness, Lisa Downing, Sonya Stephens and Timothy Unwin, not least because the culture of the age is 'caught between an obsession with the new and innovative and a paranoid sense of its own encroaching decay', and because this was an age which 'glorified maternity and constructed motherhood as the basis of women's social role' and which simultaneously 'sees the growth of a cult of tombs'.[59] These bookends of life are strongly connected to nature in the minds of the day: the mother figure is frequently portrayed in a natural setting and told that her role as a nurturing mother is expected by nature; contemporary fashions to bury the dead at the heart of nature or to experience grief within specifically created memorial gardens were ubiquitous. It is highly appropriate, then, that the most obvious space in which birth and death intersect — the issue of infant mortality — should also appear so strongly connected with nature. Indeed, Krüdener takes advantage of this fact. She shows garden design playing an important part in the expression of maternal grief. Physically moulding the landscape and speaking through the language of gardens enable communication both from mother to child and from the mother to those in the outside world who do not understand her grief. Communication takes place within nature in a way that it could not elsewhere, and communication takes place via nature when words alone do not suffice. Furthermore, when the purposefully designed garden cannot be visited, an image of it must be reproduced, thus underlining the importance that this landscape holds for the grieving mother. Valérie's moulding of nature in both garden and painting helps us to understand her psychological state and her consequent attempts to maintain contact with her child.

Nature and the Abandoned Child in Genlis's *Les Mères rivales*

A further example of an interrupted mother-child relationship exists in cases of child abandonment. This, like infant mortality, was another persistent problem in the late eighteenth century. Roger Mercier states:

> Le nombre des enfants trouvés recueillis dans les hôpitaux est considérable [...] et ne cesse d'augmenter au cours de tout le XVIIIᵉ siècle. À Paris, les registres de la Maison de la Couche donnent des chiffres en progression constante.

> [The number of foundlings taken into hospitals is considerable [...] and continues to grow larger throughout the eighteenth century. In Paris, the registers of the Maison de la Couche reveal constantly increasing numbers].[60]

Mercier provides statistics regarding the number of children abandoned in Paris from 1680 up to the Revolution. The number drops slightly after the peak of 7,676 abandonments out of 18,713 births in 1772; nonetheless, the number of foundlings still reached 5,842 in 1790,[61] and, according to Claude Delasselle, 4,230 foundlings were recorded in 1793.[62] Although child abandonment later began to fall steadily throughout the nineteenth century, during the early decades of the 1800s, the number of foundlings was strikingly high: 'Dans la première moitié du XIXe siècle, il semble que 4 ou 5 enfants naturels sur 10 sont abandonnés' ['In the first half of the nineteenth century, it appears that 4 or 5 out of every 10 children born out of wedlock were abandoned'].[63] Such statistics at first seem surprising, as they do not correspond with the image of the new, loving mother; however, there are at least three likely reasons why foundlings remained so numerous in the latter decade of the eighteenth century and into the nineteenth. Firstly, it is possible that a child's family may have been killed during the Terror. Secondly, many families were still poor, and may have found it necessary to hand a child to the foundlings' hospices to ensure its survival. Thirdly, if a baby were born illegitimately, often a mother suffered pressure to renounce the child for the sake of family honour.

However, given that women were now encouraged to love their children, and that most women took up this new role enthusiastically, it is unsurprising to see that when a mother was forced to give up her child, then she, like the grieving mother, would suffer. As literature began to show images of the loving mother grieving for the loss of her dead child, so too did it show images of sorrow and guilt on the part of women who had to give up their children. Genlis's *Les Mères rivales* is one example of such a novel. Rosalba, the comtesse de Rosmond, gives birth out of wedlock and, following family pressure, hands over her child to be raised by Pauline, the marquise d'Erneville. Throughout the rest of her life, Rosalba attempts to atone in several ways for having abandoned her motherly duties. Firstly, she vows never to marry, instead deciding to take into her home another woman, Agnès, who is in a similar situation but who lacks money to support herself. This act provides Rosalba with an ally, but does little to assuage her sorrow and remorse. Rosalba therefore decides to create an allegorical garden which will both offer the visitor an insight into Rosalba's personal painful emotions, and provide sage counsel and show the path to moral virtue, salvation and happiness (all of which Rosalba believes she herself has failed to achieve). The creation of the garden helps, but does not entirely resolve her problems. Rosalba therefore seeks to reinsert herself into the life of her daughter, Léocadie, to communicate with her, and to become the mother that she has never been. She employs elements of nature in order to make this connection possible. Her attempt is somewhat successful, in that it grants her brief maternal happiness. However, she is forever aware that Léocadie loves Pauline as a mother equally, if not more. Consequently, Rosalba's feelings of guilt and sorrow persist. Her final attempt at retribution involves taking the veil. She hopes that dedicating her life to God will atone for her mistakes, and for the problems and emotional turmoil she has caused others. Each of Rosalba's endeavours to atone exhibits one of the Christian virtues of faith, hope and charity. She is charitable in providing Agnès with a home; faith is exhibited upon her ultimate decision to take the veil; and hope is experienced in both the creation of the garden and the attempts to communicate with Léocadie. The present discussion will demonstrate how Rosalba moulds the natural landscape to attempt to renew contact with Léocadie, to deal with her own emotions of sorrow and guilt, to atone for the abandonment, and to warn others of the pain and damage that child abandonment causes a mother.

Rosalba's garden, like Valérie's, also involves taming nature: she arranges and plants certain types of flora to convey meaning. '[A] garden', we are told by McIntosh, 'can convey meaning in the same way that a building can',[64] but how does Rosalba create meaning in her allegorical garden? Monique Mosser and Georges Teyssot argue that 'the garden always has two roles, and it is as inseparable from its utilitarian function as it is from its aesthetic or ideal function'.[65] Rosalba's personal emotions are coupled with doctrines of Christian virtue as they pervade both the visually aesthetic features of the garden — such as the flowers, trees, and picturesque view — and the utilitarian aspects within the garden, for example the paths and signposts. Most often personal emotions are exhibited in the horticultural aesthetic features, whilst doctrines of Christian virtue are exhibited through the paths and signposts.

Upon a visit to Rosalba's estate, the vicomte de St. Méran is given a tour of the garden by the hostess. In permitting tours of her garden, Rosalba allows the private and personal emotions she expresses through the landscaping of it to be exposed to a wider, more public audience. St. Méran subsequently describes the garden in a letter to his and Pauline's friend M. du Resnel, so that the latter will be able to acquaint Pauline with a marvellous horticultural allegory of virtue. In his lengthy description, which continues over nine pages of the novel, he takes the reader on the same tour of the garden that he himself experiences.

Rosalba designs her allegorical garden to represent 'La Vie humaine' ['Human Life']. Consequently, the first feature encountered is a representation of childhood. The *pavillon de l'Enfance* [*pavilion of Childhood*] contains frescos and statues of happy children playing, and immediately outside it we encounter natural greenery intended to symbolize the innocence of infancy. We are shown 'une longue allée, tapissée d'un gazon émaillé de fleurs; de superbes vases d'albâtre posés au pied de tous les arbres, ne contiennent que des lys, symboles de l'innocence' ['a long path, carpeted with grass spangled with flowers, as well as superb alabaster vases placed at the foot of every tree and containing only lilies, symbols of innocence'] (*LMR* II, 311). Rosalba intends for the innocence and virtue innate in the young to be fixed in her visitors' minds when they arrive at the later parts of the garden and discover that this virtue and innocence can either be upheld or ruined on entering adulthood. The frescoes of happy children playing are also a painful reminder of the aspects of Léocadie's life that Rosalba has missed.

Rosalba's Christian name represents another floral metaphor for innocence: from the Latin 'rosa', meaning 'rose' and 'alba', signifying 'white'. Before inheriting her title, the *comtesse* was known only as Rosalba or Rose, signifying that as a child she was pure and innocent, qualities symbolized by the white rose. It was only later in life that she began avidly reading libertine novels, and became involved with friends who led her astray, both of which are believed to have been the root cause of her loss of innocence. At roughly the same time as she begins to keep the company of people of whom her family do not approve, her grandmother, unaware of Rosalba's conduct or of her later affair and pregnancy, decides that her Christian name should be altered:

> Ma grand-mère trouvant que le nom de *Rose*, mon nom de baptême, manquait de noblesse et d'élégance, me donna celui d'*Uranie*, ce qui ne me parut qu'une idée bien simple, car depuis longtemps les flatteurs qui entouraient la duchesse, me comparaient aux Muses. (*LMR* IV, 174).

> [My grandmother found that Rose, the name I was given at my baptism, lacked nobility and elegance, and so gave me the name Uranie. This seemed to me to be only too straightforward an idea, as the admirers who surrounded the Duchess had long compared me to the Muses.]

At the very point in her life when her virtue begins to dissipate, Rosalba's family replaces the name signifying innocence with one suited to the fact that she draws attention from men flattering and flirting with her.

The visitor to the garden arrives next at a fork in the path marked by 'une statue de la Vérité' ['a statue of Truth'] (*LMR* II, 311), upon which is engraved a warning which informs the visitor that they must select which path to take. We are advised to choose carefully, for '[l]'un est celui de la sagesse, et l'autre est celui de l'erreur' ['[o]ne is that of wisdom, and the other that of error'] (*LMR* II, 312). By means of the engraving on the statue, the *comtesse* advises the visitor to heed the warning she herself ignored, and not to select the path she followed. The tour takes us briefly down *la route de l'Erreur* [the route of Error] to see what features the garden displays there, before forcing us to retrace our steps and pursue the virtuous path:

> L'entrée de *la route d'Erreur* est décorée d'un élégant portique en treillage, recouvert de chèvrefeuille. Cette route est tortueuse, mais unie et facile; on y voit des deux côtés des caisses remplies de fleurs, qui ne cachent qu'à moitié des buissons *d'épines*, des orties et des plantes véritables productions du terrein [sic]. (*LMR* II, 312)

> [The entrance to the *route of Error* is decorated with an elegant portico trellis, covered with honeysuckle. This path is winding, but smooth and easy; on both sides you can see pots filled with flowers, which only half conceal *thorny* bushes, nettles, and the true plants produced by this terrain].[66]

The pleasant yet deceitful cursory first impression of the *route de l'Erreur* is highly reminiscent of biblical scripture, which also warns of following paths that seem pleasant but that are dangerous and painful in reality. The arrangement of natural features in Rosalba's garden therefore has deliberate religious undertones.

At the end of this path lies a labyrinth, a particularly appropriate image for Rosalba's garden. Vicens-Pujol writes: 'trop souvent, des personnages vulnérables, fragiles, sombrent dans les eaux marécageuses de la mélancolie et de la faute. C'est alors l'image du labyrinthe qui s'impose' ['too often, vulnerable, fragile people founder in the marshy waters of melancholy and wrongdoing. In these cases it is the image of the labyrinth which imposes itself'].[67] This is clearly the case for Rosalba, who has become mired in sorrow and guilt over the fault she committed: the abandonment of her daughter. Vicens-Pujol also argues that 'tout labyrinthe est une écriture secrète' ['every labyrinth is a secret script'],[68] and Rosalba's labyrinth has certainly been arranged in order to communicate a clear and powerful message in Genlis's novel, even without the need of an explicit engraving such as that which appears on the *statue de la Vérité*. According to Paolo Santarcangeli's *Le Livre des labyrinthes* [*The Book of Labyrinths*], the most important concepts behind the labyrinth image are: losing one's way, doing so very easily, and, in doing so, risking being unable to rectify your mistake.[69] This garden feature thereby becomes a useful allegorical means to discuss righteous and unrighteous pathways and the loss of one's way in terms of virtue and morals. Bending argues that it is on account of 'their visual intricacy' and 'the etymological link between error and wandering' that labyrinths have a long-established connection with moral error.[70] Accompanying this is, of course, 'the mythos of error that accompanies gardens historically'.[71] However, Bending also argues that mazes 'speak to the biblical promise that, when tempted, the elect will find a way of escape', for '[i]n the biblical scheme, error not only signifies wandering, but also [...] failure and recompense'.[72] The labyrinth is therefore a very useful garden feature by which Rosalba might introduce into her tour further discussion of Christian conceptions of error and redemption. At the centre of Rosalba's labyrinth stands the cypress, long associated with cemeteries. The meaning she conveys to her visitors could not be plainer: if you stray down the path of Error, you will lose your way in the labyrinth, where you will meet death; however, if you turn back and follow *la route de la Vertu* [the route of Virtue], there is hope for your salvation. The long-established tradition of a labyrinth which is both physical and allegorical had also permeated earlier eighteenth-century literary descriptions of famous gardens: in Linguet's mid eighteenth-century short story *Voyage au labyrinthe du jardin du roi* [*Journey Through the Labyrinth in the King's Garden*], for example, the physical labyrinth of the story becomes a space in which to discuss choices of moral direction. The narrator informs the reader: 'Après m'être reposé quelque temps, nous nous engageâmes dans les routes du labyrinthe, où nous nous égarions à l'envi' ['After resting a little while, we entered the labyrinth's pathways, where we lost our way again and again'].[73] While they are lost, the narrator's companion composes a verse, which informs him:

> C'est ainsi, mon cher, qu'on s'égare,
> En courant après le bonheur.
> Le sentier qu'on croit le meilleur
> Est celui qui nous en sépare:
> Une seule route y conduit;
> A nos yeux s'en présentent mille,
> Nous choisissons la plus facile,
> L'apparence ainsi nous séduit.
> Ainsi nous errons dans ce monde
> Entourés d'une nuit profonde
> Pour suivre une ombre qui nous fuit.

[This, my dear, is how we lose our way,
Chasing after happiness.
The path that we believe to be the best
Is the one which leads us away from it:
Only one route leads there;
Yet a thousand present themselves to our eyes,
We choose the easiest,
Seduced as we are by appearance.
Thus we err in the world
Surrounded by profound darkness
In order to follow a shadow which flees from us].[74]

The message is strikingly similar to that conveyed in Genlis's *Les Mères rivales*, when Rosalba conducts her visitors along the *route de l'Erreur* towards the labyrinth.[75] In engaging with well-established natural allegories, Genlis partakes in a tradition of garden language in order to convey her heroine's moral message both to the fictional garden's visitor and to her own reader.

Genlis was well known for writing tales of morality, and for combining them with images of nature. Describing Genlis's earlier work *Les Veillées du château* [*Tales of the Castle*] (1782), Gillian Dow writes that, for the characters, '[t]he days are spent taking long walks in the countryside, cultivating the garden and educating the local peasantry. Each evening either the grandmother or Mme de Clémire tells the children stories. All of these tales are of a moral nature'.[76] Morality and interacting with the natural world therefore seem to go hand in hand for Genlis. Even more telling is Genlis's set of moral tales, entitled *L'Herbier moral* [*The Moral Herbarium*], published in 1799, in which plants themselves become characters and, through exhibiting individual characteristics, permit moral messages to be conveyed. In the *Épître dédicatoire* [*Dedicatory Letter*] which precedes the *Herbier moral*, Genlis writes:

> Les plantes ont plusieurs caractères distinctifs, outre ceux qui résultent de leurs propriétés. Leur genre d'utilité ou de beauté, leur aspect, leur port, les lieux où elles paraissent se plaire, les fictions consacrées par la poésie, les vertus dont elles sont les symboles, leur ont fait attribuer une multitude dont il n'est pas permis de les dépouiller. Par exemple il serait absurde de faire parler avec arrogance *l'humble violette*, de donner le caractère de l'effronterie et de l'audace à la craintive et chaste sensitive. Le cèdre majestueux ne doit pas avoir le langage du champêtre et simple noisetier, etc. J'ai tâché dans cet essai de faire parler mes plantes conformément à leur nature réelle, ou *poétique*.

> [Plants have several distinctive characteristics, in addition to those which result from their properties. Their type of use or beauty, their appearance, their bearing, the areas in which they appear to thrive, the tales established in poetry, the virtues that they symbolize, all these things have attributed to them a multitude of characteristics of which it is impossible to strip them. For example, it would be absurd to make the *humble violet* speak with arrogance, to give an impudent and bold character to the timid and innocent sensitive plant. The majestic cedar tree must not speak the language of the simple, rustic hazel tree, etc. In this essay, I have tried to make my plants speak in compliance with their real or *poetic* nature].[77]

It becomes immediately obvious upon reading this work that Genlis was well aware both of the pre-established symbolic meanings attached to flowers and plants and of the moral virtues which those meanings might permit to be conveyed. Therefore, when the plants and features of the garden in *Les Mères rivales*, published the following year, imply the communication of didactic moral messages, it is undoubtedly intentional.

Genlis was not alone in tying garden design to a didactic of ethics. As Bending argues, 'there is a long poetic tradition which offers exactly this invitation to moral reflection, which links the country with the natural, the natural with the moral, and which sets both against the misguided but nevertheless pleasurable world of the city'.[78] Even late eighteenth- and early nineteenth-century garden design theorists wrote of the garden's link to morality in addition to its association with the experiencing and expression of emotions. Alexandre de Laborde, for example, writes:

> L'art des jardins, dont le but consiste à imiter la nature, à la transporter sous nos yeux, devient alors, si on le considère philosophiquement, une science morale qui tient autant au sentiment qu'à l'imagination, et qui peut contribuer beaucoup à détruire ou à conserver les impressions que l'on éprouve.

> [The art of gardens, the aim of which consists of imitating nature and placing it in front of our eyes, therefore becomes, if we consider the matter philosophically, a moral science that is as much about emotion as it is about imagination, and which can do much to destroy or preserve the feelings one experiences].[79]

The garden, it seems, was a useful space in which women in particular might be advised on their moral behaviour in the eighteenth century:

> The exemplary woman gardener, with her careful (and natural) attention to detail and her self-cultivated moral vigour is a trope which would find itself repeated throughout the century, and it is the flower garden, perhaps more than any other kind, to which writers would repeatedly return as a fit place, and convenient metaphor, for female domesticity and moral worth.[80]

Indeed, Bending cites examples in late eighteenth-century British literature of garden features being employed to just such an end. He refers specifically to *Letters to Honoria and Marianne* (1784), whose eponymous heroines are told:

> A bed of tulips, a border of pinks, the jessamine and woodbine, not only regale my sense, but, by a secret finger, seem to point to the power who made them. Lessons of the finest morality may be conveyed by such lovely monitors. For my part, I know not a single flower that is less abounding in moral instruction, than in beauty and sweetness.[81]

According to Bending:

> Honoria and Marianne are finally advised, "There is, undoubtedly, the closest affinity between a proper cultivation of a flower-garden, and the right discipline of the human mind". [...] The power of this image, of cultivation at once physical and moral, becomes even more apparent when we turn from inevitably moralising conduct books to women's private letters. For here, too,

that merging of physical and moral weeds comes naturally to mind. [...] Indeed — as *Honoria and Marianne* suggests — the *idea* of the flower garden as a moral site becomes hard to disentangle from the physical flower garden in the social world: one is always, it seems, in both.[82]

Genlis's novel exhibits this concept too, though on a scale far larger than that of a small flower garden. Rosalba attempts to atone for her previous faults through designing her own landscape garden (which covers much of the land attached to her château) as a warning to others and as a means of conveying the regret she feels as a consequence of her actions. The very cultivation of the garden becomes a moral undertaking for Rosalba, and a consequent part of the moral message that her creator, Genlis, imparts to the reading public.

As we have seen in the previous chapter, Finney establishes three possible interpretations of the garden in literature: the garden as a scene of erotic encounter, the garden as ethical construct, and the garden as an image of Eden. In Genlis's *Les Mères rivales,* we see the garden's association with ethical and religious images combined, for the doctrine of ethics imparted by the garden in Genlis's work is undoubtedly specifically Christian. Bending argues that garden spaces lend themselves particularly well to conveying Biblical ideas since '[g]ardens [...] occupy the domains of the natural and the symbolic', and 'the natural [...] provides a potential hermeneutic, as John Bunyan illustrates in *Pilgrim's Progress*: in the *tableaux vivants* in the House of the Interpreter, allegory converts things into signs'.[83] The hermeneutic assistance of the paths and signposts in Rosalba's garden clearly appears to uphold such a claim. Indeed, even the reference to Bunyan's seventeenth-century text is highly relevant to an analysis of Genlis's novel, for, from the moment that the visitor to Rosalba's garden is presented with the choice of paths, the description of the allegorical garden and our tour through it in fact bear striking resemblances to Bunyan's similarly allegorical *The Pilgrim's Progress*.[84] Seeking redemption from his burden of sin, Bunyan's protagonist, Christian, journeys from his home in 'the City of Destruction' to the 'Celestial City', Mount Zion. Similarly, after being shown the *route de l'Erreur,* both Rosalba and the visitor to her garden must undertake a journey from the point of error to the pinnacle of virtue and paradise which is to be found at the end of the garden: *l'autel de la Vertu* [The Altar of Virtue], *le temple de la Paix* [The Temple of Peace] and *l'Elysée* [Elysium]. Following the *route de la Vertu,* we notice that, in contrast to the path of Error, this road appears hard but has its rewards: 'On entre d'abord dans une allée droite, mais étroite et raboteuse; on voit devant soi un chemin très escarpé... mais à mesure qu'on avance, la route s'embellit. On arrive dans une plaine riante, entrecoupée de ruisseaux' ['You first enter a path which is straight, but narrow and uneven. You see a very steep pathway in front of you... but, as you proceed, the road becomes more beautiful. You come to pleasant plains, interspersed with streams'] (*LMR* II, 314).[85] The adjectives 'droite' ['straight'] and 'étroite' ['narrow'] emphazise the moral nature of the path as well as its physical appearance. These predicates contrast sharply with the 'route tortueuse' ['winding path'] which constitutes the *route of Error,* and the winding labyrinth which appears at its end. In Bunyan's tale, when Christian asks of Good Will,

'Is there no turnings nor windings, by which a stranger may lose the way?', he receives the reply, 'Yes, there are many ways [...] and they are crooked, and wide; but thus thou may'st distinguish the right from the wrong, that only being the straight and narrow'.[86] In the 1772 translation of the text, this response was rendered in French as follows: 'Oui, il y en a plusieurs [...] mais ils sont tortueux et larges; ce qui vous fera distinguer le bon du mauvais, c'est que le bon est le seul qui soit *étroit*, et en *droite* ligne'.[87] Genlis's description of Rosalba's allegorical garden echoes Bunyan's text very firmly, therefore. The echoes appear even stronger since the turnings and 'windings by which a stranger might lose the way' in Rosalba's garden are many, as they are in Bunyan's text: 'la longue route de la vertu est toujours coupée par de petits sentiers tortueux de traverse, qui tous conduisent *au chemin de l'Erreur'* ['little, winding, crooked paths, which direct you towards the *path of Error*, cut across the whole of the long road of virtue'] (*LMR* II, 317). The straight and narrow road, which, as Bunyan constantly reminds us, leads to the rewards of everlasting life in paradise, is the road that Rosalba wishes she had pursued from the beginning, and which she has since been trying to rediscover. The paths, therefore — utilitarian and practical features of the garden (in that they allow the reader to follow a course through it) — are associated with the doctrines of Christian moral virtue, just like the signposts.

When referring to concepts such as virtue and morality, Rosalba has particular issues in mind. In designing the utilitarian aspects of her garden, she specifically attempts to dissuade her visitors from making her own mistakes. Her advice appears in the form of verses on the plinths of statues. The statue of Truth near the cypress in the labyrinth, for example, bears the inscription:

> Tu peux encore retourner en arrière!
> Tu peux encore poursuivre une heureuse carrière
> [...]
> On passe de l'erreur au crime
> En osant le franchir; dans un affreux abîme
> Un pas de plus va te précipiter.
> Là, tu me reverras, mais pour t'épouvanter. (*LMR* II, 313)

> [You can still turn back!
> You can still pursue a happy course
> [...]
> You pass from error to crime
> In daring to cross; one more step
> Will cast you into a dreadful abyss.
> There, you will see me again, but only to terrify you.]

The opening two lines act as a physical signpost offering directions to the wanderer; thus, again, a pragmatic feature within the garden communicates a moral message. The anaphora in these two lines reminds the visitor, however, that in real life such signposts can only offer counsel, and cannot force us down the righteous route. The expression 'on passe de l'erreur au crime' ['You pass from error to crime'] implicitly refers to Rosalba's history, stating that whilst she committed a grave error in succumbing to her adolescent passions and enjoying extra-marital sexual relations with a married man, this was not her most guilty sin. The crime that she moved on to in the wake of the error — the abandonment of her child — was her true sin and the true cause of her remorse. Rosalba thus moulds the landscape to suit the tale she wishes to tell. If we are in any doubt as to whether the moral crimes mentioned within the garden are intended to be those of Rosalba, the comtesse de Rosmond, our doubts are assuaged at the end of the tour, when the gardens on the Erneville and Rosmond estates are aligned with their respective mistresses. The vicomte de St. Méran describes Rosalba's garden as 'le jardin allégorique, qu'on ne peut comparer [...] qu'à celui d'Erneville, comme on ne peut comparer que *deux femmes*, quand on a pu les connaître l'une et l'autre: *Pauline et la comtesse de Rosmond!*' ['the allegorical garden, that can only be compared [...] to that at Erneville, just as you can only compare *two women* when you have been able to get to know both of them: *Pauline and the Countess of Rosmond!*] (*LMR* II, 318).[88] This is one of many occasions in the novel which prompts a comparison of the two mother figures, praising the mothering instincts and virtue of Pauline, the marquise d'Erneville, and counselling against Rosalba's course of action. Indeed, the very title of the novel prompts comparison between the two.

The journey continues, and the visitor is encouraged to ascend

> une haute montagne qui paraît couverte de rochers et de ronces!... Fortifié par *l'Espérance,* on se décide courageusement à la gravir: on n'y trouve d'abord aucun sentier battu; il faut marcher péniblement, à travers les épines, sur les roches glissantes... mais bientôt les rochers disparaissent, la montagne s'aplanit, la verdure et les fleurs se reproduisent, et la perspective surtout s'embellit... On monte, on s'élève toujours, par un chemin doux, agréable, qui n'a rien de fatiguant... on aperçoit dans le lointain une foule d'objets ravissants!... Enfin on parvient au sommet de cette longue montagne. (*LMR* II, 314–15)

> [a high mountain which seems to be covered with rocks and brambles!... Fortified by *Hope*, you courageously decide to climb it: firstly, there is no well-trodden path to be found. You must make your way with difficulty, through thorns, across slippery rocks... but the rocks soon vanish, the mountain levels out, the greenery and the flowers return, and, above all, the view grows more beautiful... You climb, still ascending by a sweet and pleasant path, which is not laborious... in the distance you see a host of delightful things!... Finally, you reach the top of this high mountain].[89]

The path up Rosalba's hill is steep and difficult, reminiscent of the 'Hill of Difficulty' which must be climbed by Bunyan's Christian on his path to salvation.[90] The garden's path of virtue, like its real counterpart, is not smooth; the visitor must undergo severe toil before the path begins to show rewards. However, the path ends atop a mountain where rest is granted to the visitor upon another statue-signpost, which states: 'Après les travaux le repos' ['after work, rest'] (*LMR* II, 315). The mountain also offers an impressive vantage point upon the course taken to arrive there: 'On découvre de là des cascades, des fleurs, des buissons de lauriers qui étaient masqués de l'autre côté par des roches effrayantes!' ['From there, you discover waterfalls, flowers, and laurel bushes which were obscured from the other side by terrifying rocks!'] (*LMR* II, 315–16). Again, a parallel can be drawn with

Bunyan. The image of a mountain top as a vantage and rest point in Rosalba's garden is akin to the image of the summit of the 'Delectable Mountains': '[S]o they went up the mountains to behold the gardens, and orchards, the vineyards, and fountains of water, where they also drank, and washed themselves, and did freely eat of the vineyards'.[91] However, although the visitor rests on the mountain, it is not Mount Zion. We have not yet reached the end of the journey and the Heaven which awaits if we continue along the route of virtue.

The final stop on Rosalba's tour is paradise itself — the Zion of Bunyan's tale, or the Elysium of antiquity — which can only be seen after passing through the Cave of Sleep. We are told: 'Par-delà cette île, tout le reste du jardin offre un véritable *Elysée*, où le goût, l'art et la nature ont rassemblé tout ce qu'on peut imaginer de plus charmant et de plus varié' ['Beyond this island, the whole of the rest of the garden offers a veritable *Elysium*, where taste, art, and nature have brought together the most charming and varied things you can imagine'] (*LMR* II, 317).[92] Arriving at the *Elysée* brings the visitor full circle in the allegorical garden, but (s)he is only permitted eternal life on two conditions. Firstly, the visitor can only physically reach the *Elysée* by following the path of moral virtue. Secondly, mindful that Rosalba has designed her garden to mirror *La Vie humaine,* in order to arrive in allegorical paradise, the reader must pass through allegorical death, just as Bunyan's protagonist walks through the 'Valley of the Shadow of Death', before arriving at Mount Zion. The final spaces encountered in the garden bring us full circle, from birth and the *pavillon de l'Enfance,* through to death and eternal awakening. Therefore the penultimate space in the garden presents a visual representation of eternal repose and slumber. For this representation, Rosalba chooses the Cave of Sleep from Ovid's *Metamorphoses.*[93] Genlis's Cave of Sleep is alike in almost every particular to that of Ovid. Yet, unlike the references to *The Pilgrim's Progress*, the Ovidian references highlight not a call to Christian virtue as a means of expiating the sins of the past, but rather an attempt to deal with the private emotion felt at having lost a child through one's own actions. As such, these Ovidian intertextual references become less associated with utilitarian features in the garden and more with the aesthetic. Indeed, the classical intertext perhaps appeals more to Rosalba's poetic nature than to her religious one. She did, after all, first seduce the Marquis d'Erneville whilst dressed as the hunting goddess Diana, firing arrows to which she had attached messages.

The garden's cave, named *l'antre de Morphée,* is described thus:

> Cette grotte charmante, entourée de pavots et de roses, est située dans une île ravissante par la beauté des ombrages et des eaux; après avoir passé sur un pont d'une légèreté et d'une élégance remarquables, on découvre la grotte; l'intérieur en est tapissé de mousse, elle est remplie de plantes odoriférantes qui exhalent les plus doux parfums; un ruisseau qui la traverse tombant mollement sur du gazon, semble, par son agréable murmure, inviter au repos. (*LMR* II, 316)

> [This charming grotto, surrounded by poppies and roses, is situated on a beautiful island embellished by shade and waters. After passing over a remarkably light and elegant bridge, you discover the grotto. It is carpeted with moss inside, and is filled with fragrant plants which give off the sweetest scents.

> A stream, which penetrates the grotto and tumbles gently onto the grass, seems to invite rest on account of its pleasant babbling.]

The murmuring of the stream, conveyed via the alliteration on the letters 'm' and 'l' coupled with the sibilant 's' sounds, echoes precisely the same onomatopoeia in Ovid's Latin description of the same stream, in front of the same cave. In both cases, the effect created is lulling and soporific:

> muta quies habitat; saxo tamen exit ab imo
> rivus aquae Lethes, per quem cum murmure labens
> invitat somnum crepitantibus unda lapillis.

> [Hushed rest dwells there; however, from the bottom of the rock
> the stream of Lethe's water pours forth; through which the gliding wave
> invites sleep with the murmuring of its rustling pebbles].[94]

Lulling a child to sleep is a maternal action Rosalba never achieved. She now wishes that she herself might sleep, in order to forget. The stream appearing in both texts is Lethe, river of forgetfulness, and Rosalba hopes that as she crosses it, she will forget her pain and leave behind all memories of her sorrowful crime. The poppies surrounding the cave in Rosalba's garden also feature in the Ovidian text, and recall the sedative effects of opium:

> ante fores antri fecunda papavera florent
> innumeraeque herbae, quarum de lacte soporem
> Nox legit et spargit per opacas umida terras.

> [Before the mouth of the cave, fertile poppies bloom,
> and innumerable herbs, from whose juice
> damp Night gathers and sprinkles sleep through the dark world].[95]

This, too, is an attempt on Rosalba's part to deal with her emotional turmoil by dulling her senses. She hints, through the mouthpiece of her garden, that only in the eternal slumber of death will she be able to find the peace and self-forgiveness that she desires after committing the crime of giving up a child.

The garden is specifically landscaped by Rosalba to juxtapose an expression of personal emotion with the communication of Christian moral teaching that we have already seen, and, as it does so, it combines elements of the aesthetic with the pragmatic. Describing the intentions and achievements of garden design throughout history, Mosser and Teyssot state:

> The garden is [...] intended to fulfil private needs for peace and seclusion and at the same time to provide for the common good. [...] The garden is an external expression of an interior world, a setting for meditation under an open sky and for the revelation of secrets to those worthy of hearing them.[96]

Rosalba's garden achieves precisely this marriage of providing for the common good (which we might associate with the public sphere) and expressing an interior world (which we can associate with the private sphere). Regarding the first of these provisions, Mosser and Teyssot's remark refers to constructing public gardens to allow the common (wo)man to experience the bounty provided by the natural world. However, Rosalba takes this further, and provides for the common good in the sense that she attempts to improve the morals of society through the garden's construction. Yet, the garden is intended to heal as well as to teach. Therefore, it also provides space for peace and seclusion from the outside world, as well as space in which she can reflect upon her personal emotions, attempt to deal with them, and express her interior world to others via nature where words alone will not suffice.

The garden provides hope for Rosalba, because, in designing it, she is eventually able to communicate with her daughter. After St. Méran describes the allegorical garden to Resnel and Pauline, Pauline is so struck by the description that she, in turn, informs Léocadie of it. Léocadie, unaware that the garden's creator is in fact her biological mother, is enraptured at the thought of such a garden, and asks for a detailed plan of it so that she may construct a model. Thus, unintentionally, the manipulation of the landscape to create a garden which would help Rosalba deal with her emotions at having abandoned her child, in fact permits communication from mother to daughter. Unfortunately for Rosalba, however, the discourse permitted is one-way: Léocadie receives the plan for the garden, but does not send a missive in return. Rosalba, therefore, employs a new method of communicating through nature to open a two-way discourse.

On several occasions she picks a rose and sends it to Léocadie after attaching a message to it. The first time Rosalba does this, Léocadie is walking in the countryside, and stops by a river bank:

> Au bout de quelques minutes, jetant les yeux sur la rivière qui coulait à mes pieds, j'aperçus la plus jolie chose du monde; c'était la plus belle rose que j'aie vue, qui flottait sur la surface de l'eau, et qui, entraînée par le courant, se dirigeait doucement vers moi. [...] Quelle fut ma surprise en voyant sur la grosse branche un petit morceau de vélin attaché avec une soie, et sur lequel ces mots étaient écrits: *A Léocadie!* J'examinai la fleur d'une beauté toute nouvelle pour moi: c'était une rose mousseuse. (*LMR* III, 267)

> [After a few minutes, glancing at the river which flowed at my feet, I noticed the loveliest thing in the world: the most beautiful rose I had ever seen, floating on the surface of the water and gently heading towards me, carried along by the current. [...] How great was my surprise upon seeing that a little piece of velum had been attached to the stem with a silk thread, and that on it had been written the words: *To Léocadie!* I examined this flower, which had a beauty I had never seen before. It was a moss rose].[97]

The moss rose, developed by breeders between the seventeenth and nineteenth centuries, was believed to convey love in the language of flowers, according to La Tour.[98] Indeed, the rose in general had been connected with love even in the Middle Ages, when *Le Roman de la rose* described and discussed the Art of Love. The rose's traditional connection with love was well known to Genlis, who, as we have seen, was a keen scholar of the symbolic significances attached to flowers. It is fitting, therefore, that this flower be employed as a missive by the mother wishing to communicate love to her daughter. Moreover, as we have seen, the rose is tied to Rosalba through her Christian name, and is consequently the perfect aspect of nature to communicate her voice. Léocadie does sense something maternal about the rose, perhaps because of its long-standing representation of love, but she attributes the gift to Pauline rather than to her biological mother (*LMR* III, 268). The rose also represents, as noted earlier, regeneration and rebirth, as if Rosalba wishes her daughter to be 'reborn' in order that she might have a second chance to fulfil her maternal role.

The following day, Léocadie returns to the river and again finds a rose floating towards her. 'Cette rose éclatante' ['This dazzling rose'], she says 'était plus épanouie, plus fraîche, plus belle encore que celle de la veille' ['was even fresher, even more radiant, and even more beautiful than that of the previous day'] (*LMR* III, 268). The rose's ability to grow in beauty and magnificence indicates the build towards the climax which will occur when mother and daughter eventually meet. On the third occasion Léocadie ventures towards the river, a messenger offers her 'une superbe branche de *roses mousseuses*' ['a superb branch of *moss roses*'] (*LMR* III, 270).[99] Again, we see the natural imagery amplifying — this time in number — as we near the climax. Léocadie inquires as to whether the roses have been sent by her mother, and receives the response: 'Oui, [...] *mais par celle à qui vous devez le jour!*' ['Yes, [...] *but by the mother to whom you owe your life*'] (*LMR* III, 270–71).[100] On this occasion, the roses are accompanied by a letter proving all that we suspect regarding Rosalba's emotions. She begs Léocadie to meet her, reasoning 'O procure cet instant de bonheur à l'infortunée qui, depuis quinze ans, n'a connu de l'amour maternel que les inquiétudes et les douleurs qu'il peut causer!' ['Oh, grant this moment of happiness to the unfortunate woman who, for the past fifteen years, has known nothing of maternal love but the anxiety and grief it can cause' (*LMR* III, 264). Léocadie is requested to go to a certain tree, in the hollow of which, Rosalba will be concealed.

When Léocadie arrives at the tree, the reader witnesses the denouement of the mother-daughter correspondence:

> Ne sachant point si ma mère était arrivée déjà, je suivis ses ordres, je passai du côté du banc, et je m'arrêtai là, en m'appuyant sur l'arbre; j'avais un tel battement de cœur, qu'il m'était impossible de proférer une parole [...]. J'écoutais avec autant d'attention que de saisissement, lorsque j'entendis distinctement soupirer!... Je tombai à genoux, j'étendis les bras pour embrasser cet arbre cher et sacré! Un ruisseau de larmes inondait mon visage. 'O ma mère', m'écriai-je, 'mon âme entière est attachée sur cette écorce!...' A ces mots, ma mère ne répondit que par des sanglots et des gémissements. Ce que je sentis alors est inexprimable; [...] mes bras se détachèrent de l'arbre chéri que je pressais contre mon sein, mes yeux se fermèrent, et je m'évanouis. (*LMR* III, 275–76)

> [Not knowing if my mother had already arrived, I followed her orders. I passed the side of the bank and stopped there, leaning against the tree. My heart was beating so wildly that I could not utter a word [...]. I was listening with as much attention as astonishment, when I distinctly heard a sigh!... I fell to my knees, and stretched out my arms to embrace this dear, sacred tree! Tears streamed down my face. 'Oh mother', I exclaimed, 'my entire soul is tied to this bark!...' At these words, my mother replied only with sobs and whimpers. What I felt then is inexpressible; [...] my arms fell from the beloved tree which I was pressing against my breast, my eyes closed, and I fainted.]

Natural elements now permit Léocadie to contact her birth mother in return. As secrecy must be maintained to protect Rosalba's identity, she remains hidden in the hollow of the tree. Léocadie therefore embraces the tree and addresses both it and her mother concurrently. The tree is a powerful symbol with regard to the concept of roots and identity. Léocadie has never known her genuine family tree, and yet on the first opportunity that arises for her to speak to her birth mother, she returns to the 'roots' of her family. The tree, the mother, the family and the roots of her existence all become fused as one. When she embraces the tree, she embraces her true biological identity. Such emotion proves too great, and she collapses. Upon regaining consciousness, she discovers that her mother is holding her. In this way, the incident at the 'family tree' also enables physical contact to be established between mother and child.

The rose and the tree are significant aspects of the natural world employed by Genlis to establish a connection both emotionally and verbally between mother and daughter. As we saw in the opening to this chapter, McIntosh's 'third ingredient of the language [of gardens] relates to the plants in the garden and the meanings they are given'. Elements of nature in Genlis's novel not only have their own language, they actually have a language superlative to that of the characters. Nature enables the communication of emotions and feelings which may otherwise have remained unspoken due to their incommunicability via ordinary language. The discourse established through natural objects causes Rosalba to hope that the situation between mother and daughter can be resolved. Indeed, the two characters do obtain a close bond after this meeting.

Yet, ultimately, re-establishing contact with Léocadie will not resolve the fact that the child already has, and loves wholeheartedly, another mother. In paradoxical irony, the tree which permits discourse between Léocadie and her birth mother, is in fact a tree which has been linked with Pauline throughout the novel. The tree was christened 'L'arbre de Pauline' ['Pauline's tree'] (*LMR* I, 183) when the latter was a child herself, and subsequently became Léocadie's tree when Pauline adopted the baby girl: 'Léocadie s'est emparée de mon vieux chêne' ['Léocadie has taken possession of my old oak'] (*LMR* II, 227), says Pauline. 'Elle soutient qu'il est à elle, et depuis cette usurpation il s'appelle *l'arbre de Léocadie*' ['She insists that it is hers, and since this appropriation it has been called *Léocadie's tree*'] (*LMR* II, 227).[101] The reconciliatory image of mother and daughter embracing at the point of symbolic natural roots is therefore fraught with maternal complications, a factor which echoes Léocadie's association of the first rose with Pauline and not Rosalba. In placing herself inside *l'arbre de Pauline*, Rosalba has in fact been attempting to displace a mother figure which already existed and a mother-daughter relationship which was already positive. Rosalba finally realizes that in order for Léocadie to be happy, she must be left to continue in the manner in which she grew up: with Pauline as her mother. The only possibility left to Rosalba is to attempt to atone through faith, and to confine herself in a convent, endeavouring to achieve spiritual salvation rather than earthly happiness.

Conclusion

Krüdener and Genlis capture the Rousseauesque Zeitgeist regarding motherhood that was prevalent in the late eighteenth and early nineteenth centuries. Their novels *Valérie* and *Les Mères rivales* combine images of the human mother with those of Mother Nature, and praise women who conform to the ideal of the loving, nurturing mother advocated by Rousseau. However, these women writers do not merely echo Rousseau's ideas, rather, they expand on them. They write landscapes of maternal loss through which they expose the problems that mothers continued to face in their contemporary world and which now frequently carried greater emotional consequences because of this new ideal. Krüdner and Genlis employ several techniques in order, persuasively, to build on Rousseau's ideas and to address the problems these ideas caused.

Firstly, they construct their landscapes of maternal loss in settings which were then in vogue and which, in fact, can be linked to Rousseau and his thought. The choice of spatial settings which carry already familiar associations allows Krüdener and Genlis to maximize the impact of their arguments. This is because they turn these spatial associations into the foundations for building a weighted meaning, specific to the plight of the mother in question.

Garden deathscapes that contain, for example, a private tomb or memorial at their heart, were very much in keeping with the early Romantic fashions of the day. By incorporating such a space into *Valérie,* Krüdener is able to engage with the nation's sense of increasingly personalized grieving, a concept vital to her depiction of maternal suffering. The fact that such a garden appears on an island also implicitly references Rousseau's own final resting place. In this way, within the very same natural space, Krüdener references the demands that are made on women to conform to the ideals of motherhood, and combines these with an evocation of the painful realities for which women were not prepared by those ideals. As a result, the cruel irony of Valérie's situation, that she embodies Rousseau's maternal ideal but has no child to mother, is more persuasively presented to the reader.

In *Les Mères rivales*, Genlis alludes to the long-established argument, well-recognized in eighteenth-century French thought and vital in the works of Rousseau, that nature constitutes a morally virtuous space. She simultaneously draws on the contemporary understanding that the art of designing gardens itself was 'une science morale' ['a moral science'].[102] In so doing, she is able to construct a landscape which both applauds and teaches virtue, using elements of the garden, such as the labyrinth, pathways and signposts, to assert that it is a woman's moral duty to conform to the image of the ideal mother. In other words, through the written landscape, she creates a mouthpiece by means of which to exert ethical pressure on mothers. However, also crucial to Genlis's written landscape is the equally common eighteenth-century association of nature with emotion. The ability to feel and express emotion at the heart of natural landscapes was a key element of Rousseau's writing.[103] This link between nature and emotion, like the link between nature and morality, permeated down to the level of garden design, which itself constituted 'une source [...] de délicatesse pour le sentiment' ['a source

[...] of delicacy for sentiment'].[104] Genlis taps into this contemporary understanding, employing features of the natural landscape (the cave, the stream, the poppies, the *roses mousseuses*, the hollow of the tree) in order to expose the intense, raw emotion of the woman who has been forced to give up her child. By using nature to highlight Rosalba's guilt, sense of loss, and continuing love for a lost child, Genlis reminds the reader that the ideal of motherhood did not prepare women for these issues, and simultaneously invokes the reader's sympathy for Rosalba's plight.

Secondly, Genlis and Krüdener build on and challenge Rousseau's ideas by re-working the metaphor from *Émile ou de l'Education,* presented in the epigraph to this chapter. They show that motherhood is much more complicated than this simple metaphor would have us believe. Krüdener and Genlis, like Rousseau, show the mother figure as a gardener; however, where Rousseau's metaphor has the mother-gardener cultivating her child as she would a plant, Krüdener and Genlis show the mother-gardener cultivating plants because she *cannot* nurture her infant. Valérie and Rosalba assume the role of landscape gardeners in order to come to terms with the loss of their child, to deal with their own emotion, and to communicate important messages to two specific audiences. They wish, not only to convey messages of love to the child itself but also to convey their pain to those in the wider world who do not understand the consequences of losing one's child. Everything plays a significant role, from the physical situation of the garden and its boundaries, through the objects placed within it, to the plant life itself. These elements, as McIntosh points out, form three pillars of garden language and endow gardens with intended meaning. However, as has been shown, not only are features of the natural world used as a means of achieving communication, but, in fact, communication can take place via nature where ordinary language does not suffice. Nature is therefore often the only means of conveying linguistically inexpressible concepts. Indeed, Genlis herself argued as much: 'pour faire parler l'amour maternel [...] il n'existe qu'un seul langage; c'est celui de la nature [...]; et nul lecteur ne peut le méconnaître' ['there exists only one language which might give voice to maternal love [...]: that of nature [...], and no reader can be unaware of this'] (*LMR* II:26).[105] Therefore, by not only writing a landscape, but also by writing their female protagonists' act of designing that landscape, Krüdener and Genlis use Rousseau's own maternal metaphor to bring to light the problems which confronted women in relation to the eminent philosopher's ideal of motherhood.

Thirdly, Krüdener and Genlis are able to address the issues resulting from Rousseau's imposed ideal of motherhood by constructing the gardens within their novels as middle spaces. As we have seen, a natural landscape which possesses both public and private spatial connotations constitutes a perfect example of a 'landscape of one's own': a space which acts as a platform from which women might address the preoccupations of their sex with respect to socio-political issues. In this case, those issues concern Rousseau's pigeonholing of women and his imposed maternal ideal. Valérie's garden is both private and public. The garden itself is on an island and is thus a space apart from the rest of the world, separated physically by the boundary of the sea and inside the gated enclosure. This reminds us that Valérie is isolated from the rest of the world because she no longer fits the expected model, and because of her pain, with which she can only come to terms in private. However, the garden is also continually on public display in Valérie's home in the form of the painting, thereby conveying that pain and her ironic situation to all around her. Rosalba's garden is also private and public. It incorporates both aesthetic and utilitarian features, which, respectively, allow Rosalba to deal with private emotion stemming from her own personal past and to convey advice to the visiting public. These gardens also allow Krüdener and Genlis to engage simultaneously with both the private and the public spheres. Through the communications achieved via the landscape, Krüdener and Genlis underline how socio-political decisions taken within the public sphere regarding gender roles have psychologically negative effects in the private sphere. Furthermore, Krüdener and Genlis expose the pain of the private sphere to a public audience: their readership.

The gardens are also middle spaces because, complementing the fusion of public and private, instruction and emotion, is a fusion of intertexts, historical eras and religious images. Symbolism from different historical periods, including antiquity, the Middle Ages, the early-modern period and the early nineteenth century, is invoked to endow the pillars of garden language with meaning. So too are different types of intertext: Valérie engages with Biblical imagery, particularly the Biblical symbolism of willow trees and the picture of an idyllic afterlife, in order to express inner emotion; Rosalba, on the other hand, conveys inner emotion with the help of an Ovidian intertext, and interacts with Biblical and English Protestant references in order to convey a didactic message instead. By choosing to convey the woman's voice through landscapes which refuse to be categorized, Krüdener and Genlis show that, when it comes to defining the roles played by women in society, political limitations, social conditioning and gender pigeonholing are artificial.

Through their triple technique of drawing on common associations with different types of garden space, writing the very the act of landscape design, and speaking from a platform which itself refuses to be categorized, Krüdener and Genlis take the established link between mothers and nature further. Nature, rather than simply being a metaphor for an ideal mother figure, is in fact shown to possess the power to communicate the problems women faced in the light of the new ideal of motherhood itself.

Notes to Chapter 2

1. Rousseau, *Émile*, II, pp. 399–400.
2. Margaret H. Darrow, 'French Noblewomen and the New Domesticity, 1750–1850', *Feminist Studies*, 5:1 (1979), 41–65 (p. 44).
3. See Vincent Houdry, 'Sermon 24: Du soin des enfants' (1696), in Élisabeth Badinter, *L'Amour en plus: Histoire de l'amour maternel (XVIIᵉ–XXᵉ siècle)* (Paris: Flammarion, 1980), p. 60; Jacques-Bénigne Bossuet, 'Fragment sur la brièveté de la vie et le néant de l'homme', in Jacques-Bénigne Bossuet, *Œuvres*, 43 vols (Versailles: J.A. Lebel, 1816), XII, p. 704.
4. Jennifer J. Popiel, *Rousseau's Daughters: Domesticity, Education, and Autonomy in Modern France* (Durham, New Hampshire: University of New Hampshire Press, 2008), p. 5.
5. Roger Mercier, *L'Enfant dans la Société du XVIIIe siècle (Avant Émile)* (Dakar: Université Faculté des Lettres et Sciences Humaines, 1961), p. 40.

6. Élisabeth Badinter, *L'Amour en plus: Histoire de l'amour maternel (XVIIe–XX^esiècle)* (Paris: Flammarion, 1980), p. 69.
7. Ibid., p. 19.
8. Popiel, p. 4; Darrow; Badinter, *L'Amour en plus*; Maria Mann, *La Mère dans la littérature française 1678–1831* (New York: Peter Lang, 1989).
9. Badinter, *L'Amour en plus*, p. 55.
10. Popiel, p. 5.
11. Rousseau, *Émile*, II, p. 406.
12. Darrow, p. 42.
13. Popiel, p. 2.
14. Badinter, *L'Amour en plus,* p. 85.
15. Mann, pp. 10–11.
16. Carol Duncan, 'Happy Mothers and Other New Ideas in French Art', *The Art Bulletin*, 55:4 (1973), 570–83 (p. 577).
17. McMillan, p. 13.
18. Isabelle Brouard-Arends, *Vies et images maternelles dans la littérature française du 18e siècle. Studies on Voltaire and the Eighteenth Century* (Oxford: The Voltaire Foundation, 1991), p. 329.
19. Jordanova, p. 210.
20. Jean-Jacques Rousseau, *Les Confessions* (Paris: Charpentier, 1862), Partie II, Livre XII (1765), p. 637.
21. Duncan, p. 583.
22. This can be seen in Genlis's *Adèle et Théodore* and Cottin's *Élisabeth, ou les exilés de Sibérie* as well as in Krüdener's *Valérie* and Genlis's *Les Mères rivales*.
23. Brouard-Arends; Bonnie Arden Robb, *Félicité de Genlis: Motherhood in the Margins* (Newark: University of Delaware Press, 2008); Lesley H. Walker, *A Mother's Love: Crafting Feminine Virtue in Enlightenment France* (Lewisburg: Bucknell University Press, 2008); Carol L. Sherman, *The Family Crucible in Eighteenth-Century Literature* (Burlington, VT; Aldershot, UK: Ashgate, 2005).
24. Jordanova; Kadish; Mann; Popiel; Sherman; Walker.
25. Christopher McIntosh, *Gardens of the Gods: Myth, Magic and Meaning* (London: I.B. Tauris & Co Ltd., 2005), p. 3.
26. Yves Blayo, 'La mortalité en France de 1740 à 1829', *Population*, 1 (1975), 123–42 (p. 133).
27. Geneviève Masuy-Stroobant and Michel Poulain, 'La variation spatiale et temporelle du déclin de la mortalité infantile dans nos régions', *Espace, populations, sociétés*, 1 (1983), 67–73.
28. Blayo, pp. 138–39.
29. Ibid.
30. Voltaire, *Lettres philosophiques* (Amsterdam: E. Lucas, 1734), Lettre XV, Comment XLVI, p. 372.
31. John McManners, *Death and the Enlightenment: Changing Attitudes to Death among Christians and Unbelievers in Eighteenth-Century France* (New York: Oxford University Press, 1981), p. 334.
32. Charlton, *New Images*, pp. 88–89.
33. McManners, p. 304.
34. Charlton, *New Images*, p. 96.
35. Ibid., p. 97.
36. Ibid., p. 97.
37. McManners, pp. 344–45.
38. Elizabeth MacArthur, 'The Tomb in the Garden in Late Eighteenth-Century France', *Dalhousie French Studies*, 29 (1994), 97–111 (p. 98).
39. McManners, p. 348.
40. Charlton, *New Images*, p. 97.
41. Ibid., p. 95.
42. McIntosh, p. 3.
43. Fred Hagenender, *The Meaning of Trees: Botany, History, Healing, Lore* (San Francisco: Chronicle Books, 2005), p. 181.

44. Ibid.
45. Psalms 137. 1–2, *The Bible, Authorized King James Version with Apocrypha*, ed. by Robert Carroll and Stephen Prickett (Oxford: Oxford University Press, 1997), p. 716.
46. McManners, p. 351.
47. Charlotte de La Tour, *Le Langage des fleurs* (Paris: Garnier Frères, 1858), p. 304.
48. Hagenender, p. 180.
49. See entry 'Rose', in Jean Chevalier and Alain Gheerbrant, *A Dictionary of Symbols* (Oxford; Cambridge, MA: Blackwell, 1994).
50. Ibid.
51. Stéphanie Félicité de Genlis, *La Botanique historique et littéraire: suivie d'une nouvelle intitulée Les fleurs, ou les artistes* (Paris: Maradan, 1810), I, p. 161.
52. Northrop Frye, *Anatomy of Criticism: Four Essays* (Princeton, NJ: Princeton University Press, 1957).
53. Le Borgne, p. 75.
54. Bakhtin, p. 84.
55. Ibid., p. 225.
56. Ibid., p. 225.
57. McIntosh, p. 3.
58. Carlota Vicens-Pujol, 'Du jardin à l'île, de l'île au jardin: un parcours (1760–1875)', in *Jardins Et Intimité Dans La Littérature Européenne (1750–1920): Actes Du Colloque Du Centre De Recherches Révolutionnaires Et Romantiques, Université Blaise-Pascal* (Clermont-Ferrand, 22–24 Mars 2006), ed. by S. Bernard-Griffiths, F. Le Borgne and Daniel Madelénat (Clermont-Ferrand: Presses universitaires Blaise-Pascal, 2008), pp. 117–28 (117).
59. Nigel Harkness, Lisa Downing, Sonya Stephens and Timothy Unwin, 'Introduction', in *Birth and Death in Nineteenth-Century French Culture*, ed. by Nigel Harkness, Lisa Downing, Sonya Stephens and Timothy Unwin (Amsterdam; New York: Rodopi, 2007), pp. 9–16 (pp. 9–10).
60. Mercier, *L'Enfant dans la Société du XVIIIe siècle*, p. 56.
61. Ibid.
62. Claude Delasselle, 'Les enfants abandonées de l'Hôtel-Dieu de Paris: l'année 1793', *Enfance abandonnée et société en Europe, XIVᵉ-XXᵉ siècle. Actes du colloque international de Rome (30 et 31 janvier 1987)* (Publications de l'École française de Rome), 140:1 (1991), 503–12 (p. 503).
63. Monique Maksud and Alfred Nizard, 'Enfants trouvés, reconnus, légitimés: Les Statistiques de la filiation en France, aux XIXe et XXe siècles', *Population*, 6 (1977), 1159–1220 (p. 1165).
64. McIntosh, p. 1.
65. Monique Mosser and Georges Teyssot, 'Introduction: The Architecture of the Garden and Architecture in the Garden', in *The History of Garden Design: The Western Tradition from the Renaissance to the Present Day*, ed. by Monique Mosser and Georges Teyssot (London: Thames and Hudson Ltd., 1991), pp. 11–23 (p. 11).
66. Original emphasis.
67. Vicens-Pujol, p. 121.
68. Ibid.
69. Paolo Santarcangeli, *Le Livre des labyrinthes* (Paris: Gallimard, 1974 [1967]), p. 94. (Original emphasis).
70. Stephen Bending, *A Cultural History of Gardens in the Age of Enlightenment* (London: Bloomsbury, 2013), p. 153.
71. Ibid.
72. Ibid.
73. Simon-Nicolas-Henri Linguet, *Voyage au labyrinthe du jardin du roi* (La Haye: Libraires Associés, 1755), p. 21.
74. Ibid., p. 23.
75. It is uncertain as to whether Genlis possessed a copy of Linguet's text. However there are connections between the two writers via the Girondist Jacques-Pierre Brissot de Warville, who collaborated with Linguet on the latter's *Annales politiques, civiles et littéraires*, published between 1777 and 1792; see Simon Burrows, 'The Innocence of Jacques-Pierre Brissot', *The*

Historical Journal, 46:4 (2003), 843–71 (p. 862). Genlis was the former employer of Brissot's wife (see: Robert Darnton, 'The Grub Street Style of Revolution: J.-P. Brissot, police spy', *Journal of Modern History*, 40:3 (1968) 301–27 (p. 303) and intervened upon Brissot's imprisonment in the Bastille to facilitate his release (J.-P Brissot de Warville, A. Brissot de Warville, and F . Montrol, *Mémoires de Brissot sur ses contemporains et la Révolution française*, 2 vols (Paris: Ladvocat, 1830), II, pp. xxvi–xxx.

76. Gillian Dow, 'The British Reception of Madame de Genlis's Writings for Children: Plays and Tales of Instruction and Delight', *British Journal for Eighteenth-Century Studies*, 29 (2006), 367–81 (p. 371).

77. Mme de Genlis, *Herbier moral, ou receuil de fables nouvelles et autres poésies fugitives* (Hamburg: Pierre Chateauneuf, 1799), pp. xiv–xvi. (Original emphasis.)

78. Bending, *Green Retreats*, p. 70.

79. Alexandre de Laborde, *Discours sur la vie de la campagne et la composition des jardins* (Paris: Delance, 1808), p. 4.

80. Bending, *Green Retreats*, p. 23.

81. Anon, *Letters to Honoria and Marianne, on Various Subjects*, 3 vols (London: J. Dodsley, 1784), I, p. 57. See: Bending, *Green Retreats*, p. 23.

82. Bending, *Green Retreats*, pp. 23–24. (Original emphasis.)

83. Bending, *A Cultural History of Gardens*, p. 143.

84. At first it may seem unusual that Genlis, a Catholic, should engage intertextually with a Protestant writer like Bunyan. However, at the end of her 1782 novel *Adèle et Théodore*, Genlis compiles a list of everything Adèle has read between the ages of six and twenty-two, in which is included another seventeenth-century English Protestant text: John Milton's *Paradise Lost*. See: Mme de Genlis, *Adèle et Théodore, ou Lettres sur l'éducation, contenant tous les principes relatifs aux trois différents plans d'éducation, des princes, des jeunes personnes, et des hommes*, 3 vols (Paris: Chez M. Lambert et F. J. Baudouin, 1782), III, p. 419. Genlis even has several English characters in *Adèle et Théodore* exclaiming that 'le Paradis perdu est le plus beau poème qui existe dans aucune langue vivante' ['*Paradise Lost* is the most beautiful poem that exists in any living language'], Ibid., III, p. 24. Genlis did encourage the reading of such material, therefore. This, coupled with Genlis's renown as an Anglophile who spent much time in Britain in the early 1790s, and the striking similarities between her descriptions of the allegorical garden in *Les Mères rivales* and parts of *The Pilgrim's Progress*, suggests both that Genlis was aware of Bunyan's text and that her engagement with it is deliberate.

85. Original ellipsis.

86. John Bunyan, *The Pilgrim's Progress* (London: Penguin, 1987), p. 27.

87. John Bunyan, *Le Pèlerinage d'un nommé Chrétien, écrit sous l'allégorie d'un songe*, trans. anon (Paris: Frères Estienne, 1772), p. 35. (My emphasis.)

88. Original emphasis.

89. Original ellipses.

90. Bunyan, *The Pilgrim's Progress*, p. 39.

91. Ibid., p. 104.

92. Original emphasis.

93. Ovid's *Metamorphoses* is also on Adèle's reading list at the end of *Adèle et Théodore*. See: Stéphanie-Félicité de Genlis, *Adelaide and Theodore, or Letters on Education*, ed. and trans. by Gillian Dow (London: Pickering and Chatto, 2007), p. 516, n. 12. In fact, in addition, *L'Instruction sur les Métamorphoses d'Ovide* by Ragois is one of the works Adèle copies out by hand. See Genlis, *Adèle et Théodore*, III, p. 413. Genlis was clearly very familiar with Ovid's text. Representations of the *Metamorphoses* in the design of real gardens in this period were in fact not uncommon. Even Versailles's Latona fountain 'represents an episode from Ovid's *Metamorphoses*'. See: Bending, *A Cultural History of Gardens*, p. 54.

94. Ovid, *Metamorphoses* XI, ed. by G. M. H. Murphy (Bristol: Bristol Classical Press, 1979), p. 36. (Translation my own.)

95. Ibid., p. 36. (Translation my own.)

96. Mosser and Teyssot, p. 11.

97. Original emphasis.

98. La Tour, p. 303.

99. Original emphasis.

100. Original emphasis.

101. Original emphasis.

102. Laborde, *Discours sur la vie de la campagne*, p. 4.

103. For details on nature and emotion as a key element of Rousseau's work (particularly of Julie, ou la nouvelle Héloïse), see: Mornet, pp. 195–217; Russell Goulbourne and David Higgins (eds.), *Jean-Jacques Rousseau and British Romanticism: Gender and Selfhood, Politics and Nation* (London: Bloomsbury, 2017), p. 55.

104. Le Ménahèze, p. 43.

105. C.f. Alphonse comte de Fortia de Piles and Stéphanie Félicité comtesse de Genlis, *Esprit de Madame de Genlis, ou, portraits, caractères, maximes et pensées, extraits de tous ses ouvrages publiés jusqu'à ce jour* (Paris: Porthmann, 1814), p. 289.

CHAPTER 3

❖

Landscapes of Rebellion: Natural Madhouses

Une remarque essentielle, c'est qu'il se trouve moins de fous furieux dans les hôpitaux et les pensions de Paris, que de folles furieuses. [...] Je conclus en conséquence que, par rapport à la construction des hôpitaux, il faut y préparer plus de logements pour les femmes, que pour les hommes.

[It should be noted that there are fewer raving madmen in the hospitals and institutions in Paris, than there are raving madwomen. [...] Consequently, I have concluded that, when it comes to constructing hospitals, we must ensure that we create more quarters for women than for men.]

TENON, *Mémoires sur les hôpitaux de Paris.*[1]

The Feminization of Madness

In addition to exposing the problems faced by women in post-revolutionary French society, nature also helps women to rebel against the patriarchal dominance which causes those problems. Nature's ability to assist feminine rebellion through madness will form the focus of the present chapter.

For the Romantics in France, as in Britain, '[t]he victimized madwoman became almost a cult figure'.[2] Many scholarly analyses draw on Victorian studies of insanity to discuss portrayed links between women and madness in the English nineteenth-century novel.[3] Yet, surprisingly little exists documenting the novelistic portrayal of madness as a feminine concept in early nineteenth-century French fiction. Through an analysis of Cottin's *Malvina* and *Mathilde,* and of Krüdener's *Valérie,* this chapter fills a small part of this void. Specifically, it examines how these authors construct natural landscapes within their novels in order, firstly, to strengthen the arguments made regarding the causes, results and treatment of the protagonists' madness, and in order, secondly, to bring those arguments beyond the boundaries of the novels themselves.

Among the novels penned by late eighteenth- and early nineteenth-century French female writers, madness features prominently in those which discuss women's oppression. One possible reason for this is simply that women were more likely to be pathologized and institutionalized than men. Madness and incarceration themselves, then, can be added to our list of the problems that women faced in this period, alongside arranged marriages, confinement to the domestic sphere and pressure to uphold the ideal of motherhood. Secondly, however, madness is not only a problem in its own right, it is also a direct consequence of the oppression, rejection or grief that women had faced in other areas of their lives. We can argue either that madness is an inevitable result of the depression caused by the problems which precede it, or — as the present chapter will show — we can argue that madness is used as a form of active feminine protest against the dominant, patriarchal society which provokes a woman's unhappiness. Both Cottin and Krüdener portray madness as a product of oppressive male-dominated society, and, as a result, the characters in their novels who suffer insanity are female or effeminate.

An alteration in the way madness was viewed during the late eighteenth and early nineteenth centuries made the subject especially relevant for women: 'in nineteenth-century England and France madness was constructed as a "female malady"'.[4] A discussion of the ways in which insanity became constructed as feminine in this period must take three things into account. Firstly, the number of women incarcerated on the grounds of mental illness was significantly higher than the number of men. This, it should be noted, remained the case no matter what political faction controlled the country between 1789 and 1815, and indeed remained the case throughout the rest of the nineteenth century as well. The gender imbalance in asylums was commented upon in 1788 when Jacques-René Tenon published data from the records of all the Paris hospitals, providing a table (see Table 3.1) detailing the numbers of mad men and women confined to each hospital. Tenon's own conclusions were that insanity is more common among women, and that consequently more space must be provided for women in mental institutions, as the epigraph to this chapter illustrates. Indeed, by the late nineteenth century, women in fact 'represented the majority of those incarcerated in asylums'.[5]

Our second consideration must take into account the simple reason for this imbalance in numbers according to gender: women were thought to be more susceptible to insanity than men. It had been believed since the time of the Greeks that hysteria was caused by the womb (ὑστέρα [hystera]) wandering through the body. However, even though the term was not new, hysteria was to assume a fundamental role in issues of women's health throughout the eighteenth and nineteenth centuries. In fact, the disease came to be 'the most commonly diagnosed "female malady"' of the age.[7] In large part, this was because '[a]t the end of the eighteenth century the link between the womb and madness became established as scientific "fact", which, as Foucault notes, resulted in "the entire female body" being "riddled" by "a perpetual possibility of hysteria"'.[8]

The supposed link between hysteric madness and the female body was discussed by many scientific minds of the day. In his medical texts, Jean-Baptiste Louyer-Villermay defined hysteria as follows: 'une affection de l'utérus, et, comme toutes les maladies de cet organe, elle ne peut être observée que chez les femmes' ['an affliction of the uterus, and, like all diseases of this organ, can only be observed in women'].[9] This link between feminine biology and mental instability was coupled with the opinion that women were more susceptible to madness because they were a more emotional sex than men. Ironically, women's susceptibility to insanity was also thought to be increased by the very restrictions that society placed upon them:

Table 3.1. 'État des fous furieux, des folles furieuses, des imbéciles, des épileptiques renfermés dans les Maisons de force et les Hôpitaux de Paris.' [Account of the raging madmen, raging madwomen, imbeciles and epileptics shut up in the Houses of Detention and the Hospitals of Paris].[6]

	Fous furieux	Folles furieuses	Hommes imbéciles	Femmes imbéciles	Hommes épileptiques	Femmes épileptiques
A l'Hôpital de la Salpêtrière		150		150		300
A Bicêtre	92		138		15	
A la Maison des Frères de la Charité à Charenton	1		77		4	
Aux Petites-Maisons	22	22				
Dans les Pensions du faub. S.-Jacques [In the private hospitals of the Faubourg St. Jacques]						
Pension du St Massé, à Montrouge		2	16	2		
Pension du St Bardot, rue neuve Sainte-Geneviève			5	4		
Pension de la veuve Rolland, route de Villejuif			4	8		
Pension de la Dlle Laignel, cul-de-sac des Vignes				36		
Pension du St des Guerrois, rue vieille Notre-Dame				17		
Pension du St Teinon, rue Copeau			5	1		
Dans les Pensions du faub. S.-Antoine [In the private hospitals of the Faubourg S.-Antoine]						
Pension de la dame de Saint-Colombe, rue de Picpus			28			
Pension de St Esquiros, rue du chemin-verd			12	5	2	
Pension de la veuve Bouqueton, au petit Charonne		3	10	10		
Pension du St Picquenot, au petit Bercy	2		15	16		
Pension de la dame veuve Marcel, au petit Bercy	1		5	1		

	Fous furieux	*Folles furieuses*	*Hommes imbéciles*	*Femmes imbéciles*	*Hommes épileptiques*	*Femmes épileptiques*
Pension du St Bertaux, au petit Bercy	3		2	1		
Couvent des Religieux Picpus			3			
Pension du St Cornillieaux, à Charonne			1	1		
Dans les Pensions du quartier Montmartre [In the private hospitals of Montmartre]						
Maison de S. Lazare, faub. S. Denis				17		
Pension de la Dlle Douay, rue de Bellefonds		5		15		
Pension du St Huguet, rue des Martyrs				6	3	
A l'Hôtel-Dieu	42	32				
TOTAL	*163*	*214*	*346*	*286*	*22*	*300*

'The French psychiatrist Philippe Pinel agreed that hysteria was the product of a restrictive and rigid bourgeois family life'.[10] Forbidden from participating in the public sphere, and confined to a life of very little, women appeared more susceptible to madness, having no outlet for their so-called nervous energy. The notion that restriction upon a person can result in their turning to madness is certainly reflected very clearly in the novels of women writers.

The third reason why insanity became a significant preoccupation for women in the late eighteenth century and throughout the nineteenth concerns the use of art and literature to transmit the image of madness as female into the public consciousness. According to Jane E. Kromm:

> [W]hen asylum statistics first confirmed the perception that female inmates were likely to outnumber their male counterparts, figures of madwomen, from Victorian lovestruck, melancholic maidens to the theatrically agitated inmates of the Salpêtrière, already dominated the cultural field in representations of madness.[11]

The public, in both Britain and France, not only became accustomed to seeing images of madwomen, they were in fact continually exposed to the very personification of madness as a female figure.[12] According to Elaine Showalter:

> [T]he dialectic of reason and unreason took on specifically sexual meaning, and [...] the symbolic gender of the insane person shifted from male to female. For the Augustans, the cultural imagery of the lunatic was male. In the middle of the eighteenth century, the most famous representations of madness were the two manacled male nudes sculpted by Caius Gabriel Cibber for the gates

FIG. 3.1. Tony Robert-Fleury, *Pinel délivrant les aliénés à la Salpêtrière en 1795* [*Pinel Freeing the Insane at the Salpêtrière in 1795*]. Image courtesy of the U.S. National Library of Medicine.

of Bethlem Hospital, then in Moorfields. [...] In the course of the century, however, the appealing madwoman gradually displaced the repulsive madman, both as the prototype of the confined lunatic and as a cultural icon. [...] By 1815, Cibber's male statues had been hidden away from public view behind curtains that were drawn aside only by special request. These disturbing images of wild, dark, naked men had been replaced by poetic, artistic, and theatrical images of a youthful, beautiful female insanity.[13]

Across the Channel, the French painter Théodore Géricault was asked by Dr Georget, a member of staff at La Salpêtrière, to depict the mentally ill. He painted ten portraits of lunatics between 1821 and 1822. One of the most famous of the surviving paintings is that of a madwoman: *La Monomane de l'envie* [*Portrait of a Woman Suffering from Obsessive Envy*].[14] Later in the nineteenth century, artistic portraits and theatrical portrayals of Ophelia, Shakespeare's 'document in madness',[15] took France by storm. Madeleine LeMaire famously painted the Shakespearian heroine, as did the Romantic painter Eugène Delacroix, and, on the Paris stage, Harriet Smithson's Ophelia became a sensation. By the end of the nineteenth century, the French cast a retrospective glance at the 1780s and 1790s — the era of celebrated psychologist Philippe Pinel — and argued that this was the definitive moment at which the stereotypical personification of madness as a feminine form arose. This is perhaps typified in Tony Robert-Fleury's famous 1876 painting (Fig. 3.1), as Showalter has observed.[16]

This painting portrays the stereotype which had been gaining precedence since Pinel's own time: rationality and control were male, whilst female madness was dishevelled, disorientated, wild, even erotic. The female figures in the painting exhibit no control over events, or over themselves; they sit huddled in a corner, lean seemingly senseless against a wall, kiss the hand of the man who has unbound them from their chains, or stand puppet-like supported by a male attendant as he removes their irons. Their clothes are untidy, loose, or simply falling away. The woman on the right is missing a shoe; the female in the centre is depicted with her dress falling from her shoulders. In contrast, the men are neatly and elaborately dressed in coats, jackets, lace neckcloths and rings, showing no part of their figure exposed. According to Showalter:

> In Robert-Fleury's painting, the irrationality Pinel frees from its fetters is thus visually translated into its most recognizable sign: the beautiful woman, whose disordered body and mind are exposed — and opposed — to the scrutiny of the man who has the authority to unchain her.[17]

The opposition of rational male and irrational female is therefore made explicit, as is the stereotypical picture of the madwoman. Such representations of female hysteria were not exclusive to the visual arts; they also appeared in literature. In an age accustomed to arguing that women were more vulnerable to madness than men, many literary heroines' deaths were often attributed to hysterical madness, to which they were susceptible on account of their extreme emotional behaviour:

> Le monde romanesque du début du XIXe siècle foisonne de décès qui ne se laissent pas réduire à des causes physiques. Comme il s'agit le plus souvent de jeunes femmes, on pourrait en conclure que les romans en question se réfèrent, le plus souvent implicitement, au modèle de l'hystérie.

> [In the fictional world of the early nineteenth century, there was an abundance of deaths which cannot simply be explained away by physical causes. These deaths were most frequently those of young women, and we might therefore conclude that the novels in question referred, most often implicitly, to hysteria].[18]

It is in such a climate that Cottin and Krüdener were writing, and it is thus unsurprising that when madness appears in their novels it is associated strongly with this feminine stereotype.

The personification of madness as a female figure has been thoroughly analysed by literary criticism and feminist theory, both of which

> call attention to the existence of a fundamental alliance between 'woman' and 'madness'. They have shown how women, within our dualistic systems of language and representation, are typically situated on the side of irrationality, silence, nature and the body, while men are situated on the side of reason, discourse, culture, and mind. They have analysed and illuminated a cultural tradition that represents 'woman' as madness, and that uses images of the female body, as in the Pinel painting, to stand for irrationality in general.[19]

The references to silence and nature made in this statement are also particularly intriguing, as both are key to understanding the discussion about feminine madness generated in the novels of Cottin and Krüdener.

The following two sections of this chapter investigate Cottin's exploration of madness as a form of female rebellion in *Malvina* and *Mathilde* respectively. Cottin draws her readers' attention to the subjugation and silencing of women at the hands of patriarchal society, echoing in fiction the reality of her contemporary era.[20] Hysteria becomes for women a method of communicating their opinions and feelings at their enforced situation in the only way they can. This chapter also investigates how this communication is facilitated by the natural world. Cottin employs two different types of natural landscape as symbolic replacements for the conventional madhouse: the tamed nature of a walled, domestic garden in *Malvina,* and the wild, hostile nature of the Middle Eastern desert in *Mathilde*. In so doing, she creates spaces that her fictional madwomen are able to re-appropriate in order to voice their oppression and aid their rebellion. Through engaging with different contemporary theories in each case, Cottin is able to illustrate whether and how such female rebellion against the patriarchy might successfully endure.

As the final section of this chapter will show, it is not only women who feel the oppression of patriarchal dominance and who wish to rebel. Janet Beizer declares that, in the eighteenth and nineteenth centuries, '[w]hen hysteria was attributed to men, it retained its identity as a female complaint'.[21] The type of man to suffer hysteria was unlikely to be a strong, controlling, patriarchal figure. Instead, male hysterics were considered to be inactive, emotional, weak. They were consequently also viewed as effeminate, since the aforementioned characteristics were stereotypically associated with lives of women:

> As a male affliction, it was usually ascribed to the effeminacy of the victim or of his life-style. Sydenham, for example, declares: '[...] such male subjects as lead a sedentary or studious life, and grow pale over their books and papers, are similarly afflicted'.[22]

The madman, therefore, in Romantic and pre-Romantic writing, displays the link between femininity and madness every bit as much as the female lunatic, as Showalter states:

> While the name of the symbolic female disorder may change from one historical period to the next, the gender asymmetry of the representational tradition remains constant. Thus madness, even when experienced by men, is metaphorically and symbolically represented as feminine: a female malady.[23]

This notion is particularly significant for Krüdener's *Valérie*. As this chapter shows, Krüdener underlines both the link between effeminacy and madness, and also the bond between woman and nature through the degenerative sanity of a male character. The Romantic hero, Gustave, rejects the masculine authority of society and indeed even his own masculine identity. In order to protest, he turns to the feminine worlds of hysteria and nature.

The Garden *intra muros*: The Madwoman and the Natural Asylum in Cottin's *Malvina*

Philip W. Martin argues that the

> myth of women's madness [...] tells a simple tale: the woman is left or found alone, a widow, a bereaved mother, a deserted wife or a jilted lover. Her mind is vulnerable to the disturbances caused by an obsession with past happiness or promises, perhaps an excessive desire for the lost object of her love. In some cases this disturbance leads to insanity and eventually even death. In others it leads to physical illness, fever or derangement.[24]

Similar arguments were made in the nineteenth century, when, based on his own observations of patients, the physician Paul Briquet stated: 'On ne devient hystérique qu'après avoir souffert' ['You only become hysterical after suffering'].[25] The eponymous heroine of Cottin's *Malvina* and the character Agnès in Cottin's *Mathilde* reflect the situation of many real mad and melancholic women of the day: both have been abandoned by their lover, feel powerless against the oppression of the society in which they live, suffer shock and loss, and believe themselves to be failures. It can be argued that an overall feeling of powerlessness leads these characters to depression and then to madness; in Malvina's case, it also leads to death.

For Malvina, depression and a feeling of failure are brought on by the combination of her husband's infidelity, society's oppressive treatment of her, and the traumatic experience of losing her daughter. The latter event proves to be the ultimate catalyst for Malvina's descent into insanity, unsurprisingly so, since there is a definable 'link between trauma and its common representation or manifestation as madness', as described by Sarah Anderson.[26] Jean Laplanche and J.-B. Pontalis identify trauma as '[un] événement de la vie du sujet qui se définit par son intensité, l'incapacité où se trouve le sujet d'y répondre adéquatement, le bouleversement et les effets pathogènes durables qu'il provoque dans l'organisation psychique' ['an event in the subject's life, defined by its intensity, the inability of the subject to respond to it adequately, and the devastation and lasting pathogenic effects that it provokes in the psychological makeup of the subject'].[27] We witness the intensity of the traumatic event which contributes to Malvina's madness in the violent removal of the person Malvina loves most in the world. Unable to respond adequately, Malvina resorts to desperate, panicked measures: screaming and throwing herself in front of the wheels of Birton's carriage. Her pleas are ineffectual; she is deprived of the right to contest the decision to remove Fanny. The devastation caused by the enforced separation destroys Malvina's reason for living, and the fact that there are lasting effects on the psychological health of the subject is proved when Malvina becomes insane. In her last moments of sanity, the description focuses upon her despair, her guilt, and the oncoming madness: 'Le coup est porté', dit-elle, 'et mon sort est rempli; je l'ai bien mérité'. Mistriss Clare, effrayée de sa résignation, s'approche, lui parle, l'embrasse: elle ne répond pas; ses joues sont pâles et glacées, son regard fixe et égaré' ['The blow has been delivered', she said, 'And my fate is sealed; I have certainly deserved it'. Mistress Clare, frightened by Malvina's resignation, approached her, spoke to her and embraced her. She did not reply, her cheeks were pale and icy, her gaze fixed and disorientated'] (*M* IV, 119).

Darwinian psychiatry argues that if a woman transgressed her role or disobeyed the will of patriarchal society, as Malvina does, then the madness to which she is doomed is in fact inevitable: 'Mental breakdown [...] would come when women defied their "nature"'.[28] However, both the Darwinian argument and Martin's theory of how women come to suffer from madness passively as the result of depression, are not the only models applicable. Nor indeed, are they perhaps the most relevant. The following analysis will argue that Malvina (and Agnès after her) resorts to madness as a form of feminine protest. Showalter states:

> For a feminist analysis, we have to turn the question around. Instead of asking if rebellion was mental pathology, we must ask whether mental pathology was supressed rebellion. [...] Was hysteria [...] a mode of protest for women deprived of other social or intellectual outlets or expressive options?[29]

Similarly, Hélène Cixous argues in *La Jeune Née* that hysteria is the 'nuclear example of women's power to protest'.[30] This certainly fits with Philippe Pinel's notion that nineteenth-century women were susceptible to madness when restricted and oppressed. In the case of Malvina, hysteria is the only action left when she has been subdued into silence. 'According to feminists-of-difference such as Moira Gatens, Luce Irigaray, and Hélène Cixous, hysteria is a last resort when other avenues of communication have failed',[31] and it certainly restores to Malvina a method of communicating her suffering: by providing her with a means of protesting against the situation into which she has been forced and of protesting against the male-dominant society responsible.

Before losing her reason, Malvina makes every attempt to persuade Mistress Birton not to take Fanny away. She begs frantically, screaming repeatedly, before finally throwing herself in front of Birton's carriage in desperation, in order to prevent her from leaving with the child:

> 'Non, je ne te quitterai pas', lui cria Malvina en se jetant sous les roues de la voiture; 'ils m'écraseront, les barbares! avant de t'enlever à ta mère'. 'Faites retirer madame', dit froidement mistriss Birton aux gens qui l'entouraient; 'vous voyez bien qu'elle perd l'esprit. [...] Faites retirer madame', répéta mistriss Birton avec une voix tremblante de colère [...]. Malvina s'apercevant qu'on se préparait à l'éloigner de force, se lève, tombe aux pieds de mistriss Birton, et s'écrie: 'Au nom du ciel! Au nom de l'humanité! au nom de votre propre repos! ne m'ôtez pas mon enfant! Je ne survivrai pas à sa perte. Voulez-vous avoir ma mort à vous reprocher? Voulez-vous que mon sang crie éternellement contre vous?' (*M* IV, 179–80)

> ['No, I will not leave you', Malvina cried to her, throwing herself under the wheels of the carriage. 'They will crush me, the barbarians, before removing you from your mother!' 'Remove your mistress. You can clearly see that she is losing her mind', said Mistress Birton coldly to the people surrounding her. [...] 'Remove your mistress', repeated Mistress Birton in a voice trembling with anger [...]. Malvina, upon perceiving that they were about to force her to move, stood up, fell at the feet of Mistress Birton, and cried out 'In Heaven's name! In

the name of humanity! For your own peace of mind! Do not snatch my child away from me! I will not survive her loss. Do you wish to be the cause of my death? Do you want my spilt blood to haunt you forever?']

The desperation in Malvina's voice, emphasized by the exclamations, imperatives and rhetorical questions is outweighed by the cold, simple repetition of Birton's words. Malvina's voice falls on deaf ears: 'Birton, sur le visage de laquelle se peignait ce que la colère et l'effroi ont de plus hideux, se hâta de s'éloigner' ['Birton, on whose face anger and dread had painted the most hideous image, hastened to leave'] (M IV, 181). Malvina's efforts at ordinary communication have, therefore, failed. Since there is no longer any concrete or legal means by which she might protest against her situation — rejected wife, failed mother and social outcast — she protests against reality instead, and turns to insanity. Madness provides the only method left open to her through which she can make the world see and understand her pain. Contrasting acutely with the loud and violent communication in the scene in which Fanny is torn from her, linguistic communication henceforth fails Malvina, who is often characterized during her madness as silent: 'Affreux silence! oh! qu'est donc devenue ma Malvina? [...] tout est changé, elle n'a plus rien à me dire' ['Terrible silence! Oh! What has become of my Malvina? [...] Everything has changed, and she no longer has anything to say to me'] (M IV, 185). The only way in which Malvina can now communicate is through her hysterical behaviour and the 'landscape of one's own' that she inhabits during her madness.

Malvina retreats to the garden surrounding her house: the same garden which had once provided a space of bliss for her new-found marital happiness. The first description presented of this natural space immediately after the heroine descends into insanity is very dark. Edmond returns home to find that the nature in the garden in which Malvina wanders has significantly altered:

> Depuis son départ, les arbres ont perdu leur parure, les fleurs ont disparu, les oiseaux ne chantent plus; un froid piquant a succédé à l'air doux et embaumé qu'on y respirait. Dans son chemin, il aperçoit quelques cyprès religieux, quelques sombres sapins dont les tiges pyramidales conservent un reste de verdure; du haut de leurs sommets le cri du hibou s'est fait entendre; ce son a retenti dans le vaste silence de la nuit, l'écho l'a répété. (M IV, 156–57)

> [Since his departure, the trees have lost their foliage, the flowers have disappeared, the birds no longer sing. A piercing cold has replaced the sweet, perfumed air they once breathed there. On the path in front of him, he perceives some funereal cypress trees and sombre pines, whose pyramid-like appearance preserve a vestige of greenery. From their highest treetops, the cries of the owl could be heard, and the sound rang out in the night's vast silence, with the echo repeating it.]

Because she is unable to bring the outside world into her mind, Malvina chooses to inhabit an outside world that represents her state of mind and allows her suffering to become manifest. In this way, when anyone seeks her, they too will be able to experience the coldness and darkness of her despair, for the garden becomes a mouthpiece for the voice of her insanity. This is made apparent when Malvina's voice emanates from the natural world itself: 'une voix douce et faible [...] semble sortir du bosquet' ['a soft, feeble voice [...] seems to issue from the grove'] (*M* IV, 158). The contrast in the garden between the vast silence of the natural world and the echoing dull cries of the nocturnal owl are further symbolic representations of the silence enforced upon Malvina and the repeated cries she makes to be heard in the dark space of her insanity.

Malvina's garden also contains a stereotypical image of insanity. Every occasion when this garden is presented to the reader after Malvina has lost her mind occurs in moonlight. The moon is an aspect of nature long associated with insanity, to which the etymology of the word 'lunacy' bears witness. At the full moon, insanity supposedly presents itself at its full strength. Whilst this connection between the moon and madness is not exclusive to the eighteenth or nineteenth centuries, it should be noted that during the studies of insanity made throughout this period, experiments were conducted into whether or not the moon actually did influence madness. In 1791, Dr Joseph Daquin concluded, after several investigations: 'd'après les observations rédigées sur mon journal, il est très certain et très prouvé, que la folie est une maladie, sur laquelle la lune exerce une influence constante et réelle' ['from the observations drawn up in my journal, there is strong evidence to show that madness is an illness on which the moon exerts a constant and real influence'].[32] The moon's connection to insanity had therefore become both an increasing subject of scientific study, and, at least in the minds of the psychiatric physicians of post-revolutionary society, proven fact. The moon is also associated with women and their menstrual cycle, and, as has earlier been noted, women's biological makeup was thought to be one of the principal causes of hysteria. The moon is a doubly appropriate natural image to employ here, therefore, embodying, as it does, both madness and femininity.

The moon, hitting the dishevelled Malvina from directly above, causes Edmond to perceive how much his wife has altered: 'la lune frappe aplomb sur son visage, et [...] Edmond fixe sa femme chérie et aperçoit tous ses traits altérés par la main du malheur' ['the moon strikes Malvina's face from directly above, and [...] Edmond fixes his gaze on his beloved wife and perceives all her features transformed by her unhappiness'] (*M* IV, 162). The moon is also employed here to draw our attention to the coldness and violence of the society which has forced Malvina into insanity. This is achieved through the play on words created by 'frappe aplomb'. The violence is clearly indicated by the use of the verb 'frapper' ['to strike']. 'Aplomb' ['vertical'] underlines the directness of the blows; however, it also creates a play on words which leads to an impression of intense coldness. Combining la lune ['the moon'] with the sound of the word 'aplomb' reverses the French expression 'un soleil de plomb': an intense sun whose heat weighs down on those beneath it like lead. 'Une lune qui frappe aplomb', can therefore be interpreted as a moon whose coldness (this passage takes place on a wintry night in Scotland) and ability to encourage insane behaviour both beat down so hard directly upon Malvina that they oppress her. Through his contemplation of the garden in which Malvina is now housed, Edmond is able to understand, therefore, the cold, cruel, trauma-inducing forces which have brought her there. Silenced, Malvina cannot express her state of mind to him through words, and so features of the natural landscape achieve this communication for her.

In addition to conveying the woman's ability to protest her situation through hysteria, the construction of a natural asylum in *Malvina* also helps the reader understand how Cottin engages with theories in her own contemporary society regarding the new purpose and design of insane asylums and the practices employed therein. In the late eighteenth century, the perception of madness underwent radical reviews, resulting in a re-evaluation of the institutions in which the mad were housed. In the seventeenth and eighteenth centuries, tolerance of certain groups amongst the lower echelons of society, including the poor, the criminal and the insane, had waned dramatically. The Enlightenment period, with its focus on reason and rationality, encouraged the ostracization of those who did not conform to the norms of the social order.[33] The spaces inhabited by social outcasts were constructed to hide them physically from view, as much as to exclude them socially, and as such, the 'houses of confinement were located in the periphery [...]. Madness, indigence, and crime were reduced to a single category and expelled from the visual horizon'.[34] The public saw insanity as 'a danger to be contained and neutralized'.[35] Methods and tools of punishment employed in insane institutions are detailed in article twelve of the edict of 1656, which founded the *Hôpital général*. They included gallows, irons, prisons, dungeons within the hospital, and many other forms of detention and chastisement. Foucault refers to these tools in his seminal work on the history of madness, as he declares that 'l'Hôpital général est un étrange pouvoir que le roi établit entre la police et la justice, aux limites de la loi: le tiers ordre de la répression' ['the *Hôpital général* is a strange power, established by the king, somewhere between the police and the justice system, situated at the outer limits of the law. As such, it is the third order of repression'].[36]

The advent of the Revolution witnessed a change in public consciousness regarding the mad. The political freedom called for by the Revolution would bring to a close the seventeenth- and early eighteenth-century age of confinement. Jill Harsin asserts:

> France and Britain were the early leaders in the field [of psychiatry], and in both countries events occurred in the late eighteenth century that focused attention on the issues of madness. [...] In France [...] the crisis that focused attention on insanity — and opened a career to the outsider Pinel — was more thoroughgoing and profound: the French Revolution, which seemed at first to promise liberation for all those, including beggars, vagabonds, and the insane, who had been caught up in what Michel Foucault has referred to as the 'great confinement.' A few believed, if only briefly, that creating a new world free from oppression would end all causes of insanity.[37]

Freedom from oppression would certainly lead to the physical liberation of the insane, but it was thought that such freedom might also liberate them mentally. Doctors and legislators alike shared similar beliefs, calling for the liberation of the state, the people, and, in particular, the imprisoned. Foucault talks of the 'espace social dont rêvait la Révolution' ['social space of which the Revolution dreamed'], saying:

Il y a donc convergence spontanée, et profondément enracinée, entre les exigences de *l'idéologie politique* et celles de la *technologie médicale*. D'un seul mouvement, médecins et hommes d'État réclament en un vocabulaire différent, mais pour des raisons essentiellement identiques, la suppression de tout ce qui peut faire obstacle à la constitution de ce nouvel espace.

[There is, therefore, a spontaneous and profoundly rooted convergence between the demands of *political ideology* and those of *medical technology*. With the same impulsion, doctors and statesmen call for — using different language, but for essentially identical reasons — the suppression of everything which might stand in the way of the constitution of this new space'].[38]

Many insane patients, however, presented a danger to themselves and society, and it was deemed irresponsible to allow them to live at large with the general population. Consequently, there was no easily definable alternative to confinement, and for some time it was unsure how madness should be classified or treated:

Elle [la folie] a surtout embarrassé le législateur, qui ne pouvant manquer de sanctionner la fin de l'internement, ne savait plus en quel point de l'espace social la situer — prison, hôpital ou assistance familiale. Les mesures prises immédiatement avant ou après le début de la Révolution reflètent cette indécision.

[Above all, it [madness] was an embarrassment for the legislators. Unable not to sanction the end of internment, they no longer knew what type of social space was appropriate to situate madness within: prison, hospital, or amid family assistance. The measures taken immediately before or after the beginning of the Revolution reflect this indecision].[39]

Discussions over how to handle the insane culminated in science taking precedence in the treatment of madness where law and punishment had previously dominated. Madness now became a topic for medical study, whereas '[l]ongtemps, la pensée médicale et la pratique de l'internement étaient restées étrangères l'une à l'autre. [...] À la fin du XIIIe siècle, ces deux figures se rapprochent, dans le dessin d'une première convergence' ['for a long time, medical thought and the practice of internment had remained strangers to one another. [...] At the end of the eighteenth century, these two figures were brought closer together, laying the groundwork for their first true convergence'].[40] Thus, the close of the Ancien Régime saw the beginnings of a desire to care for and cure the mentally ill, a state of affairs which had certainly not existed previously:

Two of the fundamental bases of the profession in the nineteenth century — the notion that the insane might be 'curable,' and the idea of the hospital, or asylum, as a *machine à guérir* [*curing machine*] — had been put forward in the last years of the ancien regime, whose administrators had devoted two wards of the Hôtel Dieu to the curable insane.[41]

Finding the balance between the new ideas and the previous state of affairs was not simple. Madness constantly struggled to find a place in society, somewhere between criminality and malady, between contempt and sympathy, between imprisonment and hospitalization. Even as the Revolution dawned, prisons for the mad were still being designed. Jacques-Pierre Brissot de Warville and Louis-Michel Musquinet de la Pagne created geometric, rigid, and cruel designs to confine those they considered to be 'perturbateurs du repos public' ['disturbing the public peace'].[42] Yet simultaneously, others were arguing that madness was to be pitied and that cruelty was not the approach it merited. The Revolution had taught people that the public needed to be liberated, yet it was too dangerous to return the insane to the streets and so a caring atmosphere in which they might be detained was created. Foucault declares:

> Il faut donc trouver une voie moyenne entre le devoir d'assistance que prescrit une pitié abstraite, et les craintes légitimes que suscite une épouvante réellement éprouvée; ce sera tout naturellement une assistance *intra muros*, un secours apporté au terme de cette distance que prescrit l'horreur, une pitié qui se déploiera dans l'espace ménagé depuis plus d'un siècle par l'internement et laissé vide par lui.

> [It is necessary therefore to find a compromise between the duty of care prescribed by abstract pity, and the legitimate fears provoked by genuine terror. This will naturally be an *intra muros* assistance: help provided at the distance that horror imposes, and pity that will be displayed within the space that confinement has provided for more than a century and that it has now left empty].[43]

The term '*intra muros* assistance' proves a useful lens through which to read the creation of symbolic natural asylums in Cottin's *Malvina*.

A key moment in the birth of French psychiatric history occurred in the Revolutionary decade, when physicians such as Pinel visited asylums. Pinel's philosophies have become celebrated through his legendary 'freeing of the insane' in 1793, when he is said to have personally liberated the mad prisoners of Bicêtre and La Salpêtrière from their chains, thus abrogating confinement and suffering, and even curing patients in the process. Artistic licence has embellished Pinel's story, and a myth has arisen projecting him as a saviour figure. Harsin describes 'Pinel's *semimythical* decision to strike off the chains of the inmates of Bicêtre'.[44] Showalter's choice of phrase also indicates that historical fact may be distorted: 'Pinel, *so the story goes*, first removed the chains of several male inmates; some weeks later, he got around to the women'.[45] This statement also highlights the gender inequality which existed even within the new thinking. What Pinel did and did not achieve, however, is not the subject of this chapter. What I aim to establish here, is that the undeniable change in the perception of madness, the new theories regarding an asylum's function, and the new methods used to treat madness, all of which arose at the time Pinel was practising, surface clearly in Cottin's work when she writes about insanity and constructs her fictional landscape-asylums.

One might justifiably ask whether Cottin was aware of these changes. Tili Boon Cuillé, in her monograph on musical tableaux in eighteenth-century texts, talks of Cottin and Krüdener's 'awareness of the increasingly widespread use of music in mysticism and medical science to contest the hold that sickness, death, madness, and the forces of the occult exercised over the soul of the listener'.[46] Indeed, in *Malvina*, musical interludes, songs and flutes assist in the treatment of the heroine by providing palliative care. Cuillé's reference to Cottin and Krüdener's knowledge of the use of music in medicine draws our attention to the writers' awareness of the contemporary views on treatments for mental alienation. If these two writers were sensible of the use of music *within* medical science to contest the forces of madness, then it follows that they were aware of the work of medical science with regard to madness in the first place, and that they would therefore likely be aware of the changes in perceptions of madness and its treatment which had taken place within their own lifetimes.

With regard to the new perception of madness which emerged at the end of the eighteenth century, Jean Khalfa states: 'Madness, which has been alienated by society, is now defined as psychological alienation, an alienation of the self from itself and the space of confinement a space where the self can gather itself again'.[47] Malvina has certainly become alienated from her own self in Cottin's text. She admits as much to Edmond, who, upon asking her 'Malvina, est-ce toi que je vois? est-ce toi que j'entends?' ['Malvina, is it you whom I see? Is it you whom I hear?'], receives the reply 'Non, [...] je ne suis plus Malvina' ['No, [...] I am no longer Malvina'] (*M* IV, 158). Yet do we also see the space of confinement become a space where self and sanity are restored? The simple answer to this question is an affirmative one. However, to understand how Malvina's madness is brought under control, and thence eliminated, we must return to Foucault's definition of the new conceptions in the late 1700s and early 1800s of what a mental asylum must constitute. The new institution would be an asylum in both senses of the word: a space of confinement where the mad could safely be detained at a distance from the rest of society for the latter's protection, and a space of shelter in which the mad might be cared for. This conclusion was reached in 1785 by two of the most notable medical men of the day, Jean Colombier and François Doublet, who influenced the minds of psychologists and physicians working under the Republic and Empire, and who played a large role in the modernizing of insane institutions.[48]

The tamed nature of Malvina's garden replaces the conventional madhouse in both its functions: a space of confinement and a space of treatment. The first function is clearly visible in the description provided of it when Edmond returns home:

> [I]l arrive, il aperçoit le mur du jardin, il s'arrête devant la petite porte dérobée dont il n'a pas perdu la clef, et, pendant que sa voiture fait le tour pour entrer dans les cours de la maison, il entre dans l'enclos. (*M* IV, 156–57)

> [[H]e arrived, and saw the wall of the garden. He stopped in front of the small, concealed door whose key he still possessed, and, while his carriage proceeded to go around in order to enter the courtyard of the house, he went into the enclosure].

The initial aspect to meet Edmond's gaze is the wall surrounding the garden and not the garden itself, which is hidden from view. In this wall is a door to the prisoner's 'cell', a door which is hidden and therefore difficult to find, and which must be opened with a key. Furthermore, the garden, once entered, is described as an 'enclos' ['enclosure']. Its inhabitant, Malvina, is therefore to be prevented from leaving. This, coupled with the sombre nature of the trees and the reference to their

trunks and great height — creating the image of prison bars — adds the final touch
to the impression of the garden as an imprisoning mental institution.

When Edmond first encounters Malvina's insanity in this horticultural prison,
he discovers to his dismay that she has lost so much of her mind that she no longer
recognizes him:

> 'O Malvina! reconnais-moi par pitié! je suis Edmond, ton Edmond, ton époux,
> qui revient pour ne plus te quitter!' Malvina s'assit sur une pierre, et le regardant
> avec un souris [sic] amer: 'Pourquoi criez-vous ainsi, je suis Edmond? je suis
> Edmond?' (*M* IV, 159)

> ['Oh Malvina! Recognize me for pity's sake! I am Edmond, your Edmond, your
> husband, who has returned and will never leave you again!' Malvina sat on a
> rock and looked at him with a bitter smile, saying: 'Why do you shout thus, I
> am Edmond, I am Edmond?']

Edmond hopes that reversing the situations which provoked the madness will cure
Malvina. He reiterates that he is by her side and brings Fanny back, reasoning that
'peut-être la vue de Fanny, en calmant sa conscience, réveillera sa raison' ['perhaps
the sight of Fanny will reawaken her reason by calming her conscience'] (*M* IV,
168). However, neither of these attempts is successful. Whilst Malvina does at least
recognize Fanny, the child is sensible of her mother's altered mental status, and asks
'pourquoi ne me caresses-tu pas comme autrefois?' ['why do you not pet me as you
used to do?'] (*M* IV, 214). Malvina does not realize that Edmond has returned at all.
At this point, she therefore rejects the male figure demanding her return to reason.
She recognizes neither her husband's re-appearance, nor his authority.

The doctor summoned to treat Malvina then decides to stage Edmond's return
afresh, stating that the false return must take place in the garden. He puts an end
to allowing Malvina to wander aimlessly in her garden asylum, with the natural
world reflecting her mind-set, whilst he and Edmond merely visit her there.
Instead, he transforms the garden into a space of healing to echo the new type of
asylum advocated in the early nineteenth century. As Foucault states, the cure, like
the confinement, must take place *intra muros*: in this case in the enclosure within
the garden walls. Edmond waits in the garden, performing music on a flute (*M* IV,
220–22) and thus partaking (as Cuillé has argued) in the curing process himself,
while the doctor escorts Malvina into the space of healing:

> '[V]ous l'allez revoir: des méchants avaient emmené votre enfant et votre
> époux, tous deux vous sont rendus; voici Fanny près de vous, et Edmond est
> dans le jardin [...]; il vous attend' [...]. [E]lle approchait [...] à l'entrée du bosquet
> [...]. A ce moment la lune, au haut d'un ciel pur, éclairait tous les objets de ses
> rayons vifs et argentés: [...] Malvina fait un pas vers le bosquet; il [Edmond] en
> sort, elle le voit, le reconnaît, et s'écrie, en se précipitant dans ses bras: 'Oh!
> c'est lui! c'est bien lui! mes yeux ne me trompent point, et mon Edmond est
> revenu'. (*M* IV, 217–23)

> [[Y]ou will see him again. The villains had taken away your child and your
> husband, but now both have been returned to you. Here is Fanny by your side,
> and Edmond is in the garden [...] waiting for you' [...]. [S]he approached [...] the
> entrance of the grove [...]. At that moment, the moon, high up in a clear sky, was

illuminating all the surroundings with its bright silvery rays. [...] Malvina takes
a step towards the grove. He [Edmond] comes out from within, she sees him,
recognizes him, and cries out, flinging herself into his arms: 'Oh! It is him! It
is definitely him! My eyes do not deceive me; my Edmond has returned']

Where other attempts to heal Malvina failed, now, within the walls of the garden-
asylum, under the control of the physician, the patient is treated and her sanity
restored. The reference to the moon is again significant here. Whilst the moon
is indeed a symbol of insanity, paradoxically, it also has the power to enlighten,
as is seen in the above quotation. The moon casts its light on both Edmond and
the garden and, in so doing, it symbolically enlightens Malvina as to the truth.
Malvina's cure is made all the more vivid by the change in tense. The historic past
and imperfect tenses make way for the use of the present tense as Malvina enters
the healing space of the garden and recognizes her husband. The movement from
past to present reflects the movement of Malvina's mind from distant obscurity to
present reality. Her protest against reality through madness is over. In the sentence
which describes Malvina's arrival at the grove, the enumeration of verbs, combined
with the paucity of words between the commas as the sentence progresses both
serve to highlight the speed with which the action takes place, and the speed of
Malvina's thoughts now that her mind has been restored to her.

Casting a light upon the truth was considered acutely important in healing the
mad, as Foucault explains: 'L'internement doit donc être espace de vérité tout autant
qu'espace de contrainte, et ne doit être celui-ci que pour être celui-là' ['Internment
must be a space of truth as much as it is a space of constraint, and must only be the
latter in order to be the former'].[49] Creating the space of confinement was necessary
in order that the truth about madness, and about the individual suffering insanity,
could be revealed therein. This is precisely the function of Cottin's walled garden in
Malvina. In Britain the same philosophy for curing the insane existed as in France.
Opened in 1796, the Retreat, founded by the English expert on mental illness
William Tuke, was established in order both to confine and heal the mad. It had
five steps in the procedure to curing the insane, of which the fifth stated:

C'est parce qu'elle ramène la folie à une vérité qui est à la fois vérité de la folie
et vérité de l'homme, à une nature qui est nature de la maladie et nature sereine
du monde, que la *Retraite* reçoit son pouvoir de guérir.

[The *Retreat* possesses the power to heal because it brings madness back to truth,
a truth which is both the truth of the madness and the truth of man, and to a
nature which is both the nature of the illness and the serene nature of the world].[50]

If the new type of asylum was thought to bring the insane back to the truth of the
natural world, it is fitting, then, that in *Malvina* it is the natural world itself which
recalls this truth to the mind of the madwoman. Not only is the space of healing a
garden filled with natural features, but an aspect of nature — the moon — is the
tool employed to reveal the truth so crucial to the healing process. As the doctor
escorts Malvina into the garden, it therefore becomes an example of the new type
of early nineteenth-century asylum in which the power of the male scientist, figure
of rationality and authority, can restore sanity and end madness.

On the one hand, we might argue here that Cottin shows how the new type of asylum, in which care and concern for the mad meet the need to contain them, can result in the healing of insane, institutionalized women. However, on the other hand, it becomes evident that, as the doctor and Edmond take over the garden and turn it into a curative asylum, Malvina's own control over the space is relinquished. Furthermore, and as a consequence, as the male characters assume control over the natural asylum — Edmond using it to perform curative music, the doctor using it to enlighten the madwoman as to the truth — so, too, do they assume control over the woman within it. Malvina's attempts at protest are removed and she loses her ability to use the garden to convey her voice. Like the madwomen in Robert-Fleury's painting of Pinel at the Salpetrière, the disheveled Malvina is 'freed' from her mental prison, but only at the cost of allowing herself to be dominated by masculine power and control. Almost as proof, the instant that Malvina regains her sanity and recognizes Edmond, she begins to lose her voice again, and falls at the latter's feet, symbolically highlighting the husband's dominant position: 'Alors, sa voix s'affaiblissant tout à coup, elle coula entre les bras d'Edmond, et tomba sans mouvement à ses pieds' ['And so, her voice suddenly growing weaker, she sank into Edmond's arms and fell, motionless, at his feet'] (*M* IV, 224). Such a situation would later be echoed in the Robert-Fleury painting, which depicts a liberated woman kneeling at Pinel's feet and kissing his hand. Both the silencing of Malvina's voice and the description of her weakness are echoed further when she wakes from her faint: 'Elle ne put en dire davantage, et la chaleur qu'elle venait de mettre à sa touchante prière, lui occasionna une faiblesse qui dura quelques heures' ['She could say no more, and the energy which she had put into her moving prayer brought on a weakness which lasted for several hours'] (*M* IV, 235). Now, physically powerless, and without even the means of insanity to rebel against her situation and the suffering she has endured, she resorts to the only path left by which she might escape oppression: death.

The Desert Asylum: A Space of Enduring Female Rebellion in Cottin's *Mathilde*

It is fitting that Malvina's relinquishing of control take place in a tamed, walled garden; for, just as the garden has been contained and controlled by mankind, so too has the madwoman within it. Should the madwoman wish both her rebellion and her voice to endure, however, a different space must mark out her natural asylum, as Cottin illustrates in her later novel *Mathilde*.

Published in 1805, *Mathilde* is a historical novel set during the Crusades. The story involves two strong female opponents: Mathilde, Princess of England, and Agnès, Princess of Jerusalem. Although Agnès is a Christian princess, she falls in love with the Islamic warrior Malek-Adhel. Christian society forbids her desires, and attempts to force her into submission. However, in her love for Malek Adhel, Agnès is prepared to abandon the three staple loyalties expected of her: her family, her country and her God: '[S]i tu savais quelle félicité je goûtais à oublier près de lui ma patrie, ma famille, mes crimes et mon Dieu même!' ['If you knew what delight

I would taste to forget, when next to him, my fatherland, my family, my crimes and even my God!'] (*Mat* I, 274). She is thus cast out of Christian society, hated and condemned for joining Malek-Adhel's harem as one of his wives. Unfortunately for Agnès, when Mathilde arrives in the Holy Land, Malek-Adhel's passion turns from the wives in his harem to Mathilde alone, with whom he falls deeply in love. Agnès struggles to deal with the rejection. She attempts to declare her feelings for her husband on several occasions. Each time, she is spurned and reminded that, as his wife, she must obey his orders. Agnès thus suffers two attempts to subjugate her: that of Christian society and that of her husband. Agnès chooses to rebel against such enforced subjugation, and once other attempts at rebellion have been made, madness becomes the strongest means of protest available to her.

Agnès's first attempts at rebellion are directed towards Christian, Western society. She states her desire to take up arms against all she previously held dear:

> J'ai désiré *l'anéantissement* de l'empire du Christ, parce qu'il peut s'élever contre celui de mon amant; j'ai désiré voir cet amant régner seul sur tous les rois et les mondes *enchaînés*; j'allais le suivre à l'armée [...] *lever l'épée* contre mon propre sang, et le Dieu de mes pères. (*Mat* I, 286)

> [I desired the *annihilation* of Christ's empire, because it can rise up against that of my lover; I wished to see my lover reign alone over all kings and all worlds *in chains*; I was going to follow him into battle [...] *raising my sword* against my own blood, against the God of my fathers.][51]

Each staple of her society of origin — family, country and religion — has a male figure at the pinnacle of the hierarchy: father, king and God. Agnès wishes to attack each of these ultimate representatives of male authority. She does indeed take up her sword in protest, and, in so doing, rejects the domestic space which, as a woman, she is expected to occupy, in favour of the battlefield: a space associated with masculinity. Her first rebellion against her oppression as a woman is not through madness, therefore, but through attempting to escape her femininity altogether. She dresses as a male warrior and attacks the Christians in the desert in the hope of returning Malek-Adhel to her by killing Mathilde. Agnès is so brutal in her combat, so convincing in her attire, that the Christian soldiers take her for a man without question, and are shocked when they discover the truth:

> [J]amais la victoire n'a fait attendre Montmorency: son ennemi est renversé, il lève le bras, il va lui ôter la vie. 'Frappe, Montmorency', s'écrie d'une voix sourde le guerrier vaincu; 'enfonce ton poignard dans le sein d'une femme.' A ce nom, le héros français s'arrête, il doute de ce qu'il entend, car la force qu'on vient de lui opposer est celle d'un soldat. (*Mat* III, 26)

> [Montmorency has never had to wait for victory. His enemy thrown back, he raises his arm and is about to kill him. 'Strike, Montmorency!' cries the weak voice of the vanquished warrior. 'Sink your dagger into the breast of a woman.' At this word, the French hero stops, doubting what he hears, for the strength with which the enemy has just opposed him is that of a soldier].

Agnès rejects the feminine role of subordinate, in which she has been unhappy, and chooses to undertake an action reserved for men. Judith Butler states: 'gender proves to be performative — that is, constituting the identity it is purported to be. In this sense, gender is always a doing'.[52] Agnès's choice of deed certainly defines her new gender role. Her protest is also literal, however, as the masculine deed she undertakes in order to perform that gender, is hand to hand combat. According to Butler, '[t]hat the gendered body is performative suggests that it has no ontological status apart from the various acts which constitute its reality'.[53] Agnès seeks to be recognized in her manly role as a warrior where she and her self-identity have merely been cast aside in her role as a woman. Performing as a male warrior gains her the desired respect, but this performance neither lasts, nor ultimately succeeds in resolving her problems. Despite her convincing performance, she is defeated in combat and identifies herself as a woman in order to live. Her failure to uphold a combative male agency in the desert eventually results in her employment of the only other rebellious option available to her: she turns to feminine hysteria in order to protest through madness.

Before doing so, Agnès attempts one final time to plead with Malek Adhel, hoping that she might once again be recognized by him as a wife. It is significant that Agnès's final attempt to escape her oppressive and depressing situation is through words, since, as we have seen, Gatens, Irigaray, and Cixous argue that 'hysteria is a last resort when other avenues of communication have failed'.[54] In this respect, Agnès's situation echoes that of Malvina. Malek Ahdel refuses to listen to Agnès's pleas: '[E]lle a suivi Malek Adhel à Césarée, mais Malek Adhel refusa de la voir [...] ses forces ne résistèrent point à tant de fatigues, de chagrins et d'affronts. Sa tête s'aliéna' ['She followed Malek-Adhel to Cesarea, but Malek-Adhel refused to see her [...], her strength could in no way resist so much exhaustion or so many sorrows and insults, and she lost her mind'] (Mat IV, 78). Her hand stayed by the Christians, her voice silenced by her husband, Agnès engages in a second protest. She becomes the stereotypical madwoman, rolling deranged on the floor, her hair wild and dishevelled, beating her breasts and crying curses to those not present.

As in Malvina, Cottin constructs an asylum for her madwoman at the heart of the natural world. Whilst sharing certain properties with the natural asylum of her earlier novel, the overriding image of the natural asylum in Mathilde is very different. As a result of this combination of similarities and differences, Cottin shows not only how the madwoman re-appropriates nature as a platform from which to voice her oppression, but also how she retains this space in order to permit her rebellion to continue. The natural asylum must both reflect female oppression, as did Malvina's natural asylum, but must also resist domination by powerful male figures, which Malvina's space did not. In order to construct such a space, Cottin returns us to the stage of Agnès's first attempted rebellion — in which she herself was permitted to assume a male role — the Palestinian desert. By engaging not with contemporary theories of asylum space on this occasion but with contemporary theories of the Middle Eastern desert landscape, Cottin manages to create for Agnès a 'landscape of one's own' which permits continued rebellion against her own personal treatment, and which is also able to make subtle comments on the treatment of women in patriarchal society in general. Understanding the ways in which the Middle Eastern landscape was viewed in late eighteenth- and early nineteenth-century France will ultimately help us to understand some of the more subtle arguments Cottin is able to make because of this choice.

According to Barre, the fascination with desert space in late eighteenth- and early nineteenth-century France stemmed from two types of travel writer: those engaged in 'enquêtes' ['investigations'] and those engaged in quêtes ['quests']. In other words, descriptions were provided both by regional explorers such as Volney, Ali Bey and Denon, and by those who ventured to desert space for reasons of personal interest or religious pilgrimage, such as Chateaubriand. When analysing the literary depiction of Oriental deserts in particular, we must bear in mind several connotations associated with this landscape by both types of traveller.

The first connotations derive from the Orientalist discourse of explorers and colonists. This period witnessed Napoleon's invasion of the Middle East and North Africa, bringing scientists and scholars with the specific desire to describe and record the region for the Europeans.[55] They stereotyped the Orient, its characteristics, its landscape and its people, and, in so doing, both created a dichotomous notion of 'Self' (European) and 'Other' (non-European), and painted a sweeping picture of the 'Other' in which 'les notions ethniques sont confuses' ['ethnic concepts are muddled'],[56] with no allowance for regional difference. This Orientalism, as it has been famously labelled by Edward Said, is easily identifiable in the travel writing of Volney and other French writers.[57] Indeed, Said specifically 'dates the rise of modern Orientalism to the French invasion of Egypt in 1798' by Napoleon,[58] and much of the latter's information came from Volney's work.[59] Volney and his contemporaries presented the Orient as dangerous and uncivilized in contrast to a progressive and developed West; the local people were often depicted as oppressed;[60] Volney, in particular, presented a very hostile description of the Islamic religion;[61] and the desert landscape was frequently portrayed as 'un milieu hostile et inhospitalier' ['a hostile and inhospitable environment'].[62] Volney writes:

> Pour se peindre ces déserts, que l'on se figure sous un ciel presque toujours ardent et sans nuages, des plaines immenses et à perte de vue, sans maisons, sans arbres, sans ruisseaux, sans montagnes: quelquefois les yeux s'égarent sur un horizon ras et uni comme la mer.

> [In order to picture these deserts, you must imagine, beneath an almost continually burning, cloudless sky, immense and endless plains without houses, trees, streams or mountains: sometimes the eye becomes lost in a uniform, flat horizon, like the sea].[63]

One of the descriptions of the desert and its Bedouin peoples in Volney's work to reveal perhaps the most blatant Orientalist discourse appears in the first volume of his travels through Egypt and Syria:

> Dans notre Europe, et surtout dans notre France, où nous ne voyons point de peuples errants, nous avons peine à concevoir ce qui peut déterminer des hommes à un genre de vie qui nous rebute. Nous concevons même difficilement ce que c'est qu'un désert, et comment un terrain a des habitants s'il est stérile.

> [In our Europe, and above all in our France, where there are no nomadic peoples, we find it difficult to conceive what might induce men to the type of

life that repels us. We even find it difficult to conceive precisely what a *desert* is, and how a sterile terrain might come to have inhabitants].[64]

His language — the reference to '*notre* Europe' [*our* Europe] and '*notre* France' ['*our* France'], the continual repetition of 'nous' ['us'], and the striking use of the verb 'rebuter' ['repel'] — could hardly make the creation of a Self-Other binary more obvious.

The knowledge of the Orient produced by explorers and scientists shaped the understanding of the region by the Europeans, who then used these presented images as justification for intervention in and dominion of the Orient. The hegemonic power the Europeans possessed over the area to describe and stereotype it was thus deepened further, and, in turn, as political power increased, so too did the ability to dominate the knowledge produced about the region.

Cottin's *Mathilde* is impregnated with the type of Orientalist discourse employed by explorers and scholars of the time. The novel was first published in 1805 by Giguet et Michaud of Paris. Joseph Michaud, himself a leading intellectual figure and non-fiction author, as well as an admirer and friend of Cottin, later published a lengthy and detailed *Histoire des Croisades* between 1811 and 1822,[65] as well as the *Correspondance d'Orient: 1830–1831* in which he discussed Napoleon's involvement in the Middle East and engaged with some of Volney's work.[66] Michaud approved Cottin's decision to set her novel during the Crusades, encouraged her writing,[67] and even prefaced *Mathilde* with an introduction entitled 'Tableau historique des trois premières croisades' ['Historical Sketch of the Three First Crusades']. We may never be sure whether Cottin read Volney's work directly;[68] however, the stereotypes of the Middle East which had disseminated owing to his work appear throughout *Mathilde* (and indeed also throughout Cottin's earlier prose poem *La Prise de Jéricho, ou la pécheresse convertie*). Indeed, Cottin even writes to her cousin: '*Mathilde* réussira: il y a de l'intérêt dans l'ouvrage, et il est dans le goût du jour' ['*Mathilde* will succeed: there is interest in the work, and it corresponds to contemporary taste'].[69] Like Volney, Cottin presents both the desert and people of the Orient as uncivilized and savage: 'Savez-vous qu'une fois arrivée au Caire, il vous faudrait traverser un désert brûlant, aride, immense, semé de soldats indisciplinés et d'Arabes homicides?' ['Do you know that, once you arrive in Cairo, you will have to cross an immense, burning, arid desert, filled with undisciplined soldiers and homicidal Arabs?'] (*Mat* II, 131). Elsewhere in the novel, followers of Islam are described as cowardly and fanatical:

> Troublée par la frayeur et le fanatisme, la troupe entière fait bientôt entendre que tant de malheurs ne leur sont envoyés que pour les punir des soins extraordinaires qu'on les force de prodiguer à une chrétienne; ils vont même jusqu'à dire que si elle demeure plus longtemps parmi eux, Mahomet les engloutira tous dans le sable. (*Mat* II, 227–28)

> [Disturbed by both terror and fanaticism, the entire troop soon lets it be known that they are being sent so many misfortunes purely as punishment for the extraordinary care that they are forced to bestow on a Christian woman. They even go so far as to say that, if she remains with them for much longer, Muhammad will engulf them all in sand.]

Echoes of Volney's criticism of Islam are clear. Further similarities with Volney's opinions occur in Cottin's discussion of the treatment of Islamic women. The Archbishop of Tyr asserts: 'Ce titre d'épouse [...] est très-loin d'être aussi saint chez les Musulmans que chez les chrétiens' ['The title of wife [...] is far from being as sacred in the Muslim world as it is in the Christian one'] (*Mat* I, 264). *Mathilde* portrays the Islamic woman living in an oppressive, patriarchal society which treats her unfairly and denies her freedom. Indeed, in this respect, *Mathilde* contains echoes of nineteenth-century opinions on Islamic women which have permeated down to the present day.[70] As we will see, however, it is through her portrayal of women's treatment in the East that Cottin is able to make subtle and powerful comment on the treatment of women in the West.

The second connotations tied to the desert at the time of Cottin's writing are Romantic ones. For many at this time, seeking out desert space was another means of escaping society, of exhibiting the desire to return to nature so prevalent in the eighteenth century:

> Dès la fin du XVIIIe siècle, le souci du sujet de restaurer ses liens avec la vraie nature, loin de la société industrielle, favorise la quête d'espaces vierges, immaculés, encore intacts ou présumés tels, dont le désert, qui réclame une description *ad hoc*. Dès que le voyage en Afrique du Nord ne répond plus qu'à des exigences d'exploration, mais qu'il devient tour [...], un chiffre progressivement croissant d'Européens élit le désert en tant que destination favorite.

> [From the end of the eighteenth century, concern about restoring one's connection with real nature, far from industrial society, promotes the quest for untouched, immaculate spaces which are still intact or which are at least presumed to be so. The desert can be described perfectly in just this way. As soon as travel to North Africa was no longer a matter of fulfilling the demands of exploration, but became a matter of tourism, a progressively increasing number of Europeans chose the desert as their favourite destination.][71]

Essentially, we witness here a desire to seek a wild, aesthetically sublime space of retreat, rather than a utopian garden. Desert space appealed to the emerging Romantic consciousness, and thus descriptions of it became Romanticized, associated with exoticism, with a personal connection to the natural world, with an emphasis on the self.[72] The very notion of a *quête* or pilgrimage implies a journey made to satisfy personal needs and to embark upon self-discovery and reflection. Said argues:

> Unlike Volney and Napoleon, the nineteenth-century French pilgrims did not seek a scientific so much as an exotic yet especially attractive reality. This is obviously true of the literary pilgrims, beginning with Chateaubriand, who found in the Orient a locale sympathetic to their private myths, obsessions, and requirements.[73]

Possessing these connotations, the desert becomes the perfect space to which Cottin's heroines might withdraw for the purposes of gathering the thoughts which will give birth to their rebellion. Agnès's introspection in the desert turns her thoughts towards both rebellion through madness and escape through death:

> [L]a douleur de sa honte s'accroissait par le souvenir de sa célébrité, et cette
> nécessité irrévocable qui la liait à sa pensée, et la forçait à vivre avec elle-même,
> la jetait dans des accès de désespoir, auprès desquels la folie et la mort eussent
> été de grands biens. Si quelquefois l'image de Malek-Adhel venait la détourner
> de sa propre image, ce n'était que pour lui présenter un nouveau malheur. (*Mat*
> I, 283)

> [[T]he pain of her shame increased with the memory of its fame, and that
> irrevocable necessity which bound her to her own thoughts and forced her to
> live with herself threw her into fits of despair, compared with which madness
> and death would have been great comforts. If the image of Malek-Adhel
> occasionally distracted her from her own self-reflection, it only served to
> present her with new sorrow.]

Mathilde is also able to contemplate her own private meditations while in the
desert:

> Jamais tant d'idées nouvelles ne se présentèrent à son esprit; car maintenant,
> loin de les rejeter, elle les accueille et les examine. [...] C'est dans cette longue
> suite de méditations et de rêveries qu'elle passe tout le jour et une partie de la
> nuit. (*Mat* II, 86)

> [Never have so many new ideas come to her mind; for now, far from rejecting
> them, she welcomes and examines them. [...] And so, she spends the whole day
> and part of the night in reverie and a long series of meditations.]

In fact, Mathilde even undertakes a pilgrimage through the desert in order to
examine both her emotions and her very soul itself. The desert — a space of
pilgrimage in biblical scripture and medieval literature — also became a space
of pilgrimage for the Romantics, including Chateaubriand in his *Itinéraire* from
1811 and Byron in his semi-autobiographical *Childe Harold's Pilgrimage* (1812–1818).
Mathilde's pilgrimage is peppered with Romantic imagery similar to that which
surfaces in the works of later writers: including tempestuous nature, ruins reclaimed
by the natural landscape, and the appearance of God within nature.[74] These vestiges
of early Romanticism are employed to help reveal to Mathilde the power that
nature might have in assisting her own rebellion against oppression. Furthermore,
in the works of the canonical Romantic writers, there is also a notable link to the
Orientalist discourse propagated by explorers. 'Leask points to the connection
between the expansion of [...] colonial rule [...] and the principal exponents of
Romanticism'.[75] Travellers such as Chateaubriand, and later also Lamartine and
Hugo, depict the Orient as savage, boundless and barren, as mysterious, timeless
and unprogressive. Canonical Romantic writers also frequently portray the Islamic
treatment of women in an unfavourable light.[76] Cottin's *Mathilde* is no different in
this respect. The early Romantic aesthetics within *Mathilde*'s desert are often linked
to the connotations derived from Orientalist discourse. This is fitting, for Cottin
uses both Orientalist discourse and Romantic imagery to contribute to the same
arguments: to highlight the patriarchal dominance over women in both the East and
the West, and to promote the power of women to rebel against their oppression.

Cottin was aware of the early roots of the Romantic movement in France.
Rousseau's works profoundly influenced her own, and sentimental and aesthetic

responses to nature permeate her earlier novels.[77] Cottin was captivated, too, by the writing of Chateaubriand, particularly his desert scenes in *Atala*.[78] She also spoke English[79] and was familiar with other sublime and wild Romantic landscapes in the works of eighteenth-century British writers, such as those in James Macpherson's Ossian cycle. However, *Mathilde* was published before the major canonical Romantic writing set in the East: six years before Chateaubriand's discussion of the Oriental desert in *Itinéraire de Paris à Jérusalem et de Jérusalem à Paris* [*Itinerary: Record of a Journey from Paris to Jerusalem and Back*], seven years prior to Byron's *Childe Harold's Pilgrimage: a Romaunt*, eight years prior to Byron's *Eastern Tales,* thirteen years prior to Percy Shelley's 'Ozymandias', twenty-four years prior to Hugo's *Les Orientales* [*Oriental Poems*], thirty years prior to Lamartine's *Voyage en Orient* [translated into English as *Visit to the Holy Land, or Recollections of the East*], forty-six years prior to Gérard de Nerval's *Voyage en Orient* [*Voyage to the Orient*] and fifty-one years prior to Lamartine's poem 'Le Désert' ['The Desert']. Therefore, the Romantic imagery which permeates the descriptions of the desert in *Mathilde* prefigures most of that which has become better known to us.

The third connotations associated with the desert at the time of *Mathilde*'s publication were religious. The subjective experience of individual travellers to the Middle East (particularly Chateaubriand) was often religious, influenced by biblical images of the desert and by the desire to undertake a journey through the desert as part of a pilgrimage to the Holy Land. Therefore, biblical images penetrate Oriental desert space when it is described in subjective fiction of the late eighteenth and early nineteenth centuries, building on those which were already prevalent in European medieval literature:

> [L]'effort de fournir un tableau exhaustif et objectif du désert fait la place à des connotations partielles de l'environnement, liées tour à tour, à l'expérience qu'en fait le voyageur, à ses attentes, ou aux images biblico-littéraires qui en filtrent la perception.

> [[T]he effort of providing a comprehensive and objective picture of the desert makes way for partial connotations of its environment, linked in turn to the way that travellers experience it, their expectations, or the biblical and literary images which influence their perception of the space].[80]

Such biblical and literary images include those which present the desert as a space of crusade, a space of hellish difficulty, and a wilderness in which to repent.

Cottin's knowledge of the Crusades was undoubtedly reinforced by her conversations with Michaud. However, *Mathilde* not only presents the desert as a historical space of battle; its plotline also echoes those of medieval romances, for, '[t]he Crusades were particularly fertile for European cross-cultural love stories between Christians and Muslims'.[81] Cottin's knowledge of biblical Palestine is clear from her religious fervour. In a letter to M. Azaïs in 1806, Cottin writes: 'La religion et l'amitié, voilà désormais toute ma vie: chaque nouveau jour ajoute une force de plus à mes sentiments de piété' ['Religion and friendship will henceforth constitute my life: every new day adds further strength to my pious sentiments'].[82] She was a keen reader of the Bible, and of the *Vie des Saints*, both of which made her aware of the depictions of the desert as a space of repentance.[83] In medieval literature, too, according to Wogan-Browne — and particularly that which tells of the lives of saints — '[c]ell and desert function as versions of each other in [...] metaphorics of penance'.[84] There are strong echoes with Mary of Egypt in Cottin's portrayal of Agnès.[85] Mary spends over forty years repenting in the desert for her sinful life as a fallen woman. Cottin's Agnès is forced to live out her days in a space which is both cell (in the form of a cave) and desert, after being cast out by Christian society for prioritizing her carnal desires and joining the harem of Malek-Adhel. Cottin's correspondence in fact reveals her use of the *Vie des Saints* in her research for *Mathilde*. She requests that her brother-in-law André send her 'quelques volumes de la *Vie des Saints*' [several volumes of the *Lives of the Saints*], stating: '[J]'ai un besoin très pressant de savoir positivement la vie qu'ils menaient dans les déserts de la Thébaïde, et surtout dans les cavernes du Liban' ['I have a most pressing need to know for certain the lives that they led in the Theban [Egyptian] deserts, and particularly in the caves of Lebanon'].[86] Upon reading *Mathilde*, it becomes clear why.

In order to construct a 'landscape of one's own' in *Mathilde* from within which the primary female characters, Agnès and Mathilde, might both voice their oppression and protest against it, Cottin engages with the imagery from all three connotations attached to Palestinian desert space — Orientalist, Romantic and religious — frequently mixing them. Let us begin by noting how she constructs the desert as a space through which women's oppression might be voiced.

Echoing Volney's presentation of Islam and its treatment of women, Cottin shows how Agnès has neither rights nor voice as an Islamic woman, but rather must defer to her husband's will. Malek-Adhel, wishing to remove Agnès from his seraglio and force her into marriage with another man, states:

> En vous donnant à moi [...], en adoptant le culte de Mahomet, vous êtes devenue esclave, et les lois du sérail m'interdisent de vous rendre la liberté. Choisissez donc, ou de l'époux que je vous propose, ou d'une éternelle captivité. (*Mat* I, 248)
>
> [In giving yourself to me [...], in adopting the faith of Muhammad, you have become a slave, and the laws of the seraglio forbid me from restoring your liberty. Choose, then, either the husband whom I propose for you, or eternal captivity].

Refusing the enforced marriage, Agnès therefore finds herself the eternal captive instead. She is confined to a desert asylum, in an *enclos,* surrounded by a hedge of wild trees, in order to prevent escape:

> A peu de distance de la cabane il mit pied à terre avec la princesse, et il la conduisit dans un enclos entouré d'une haie de citronniers sauvages; au milieu était une chétive demeure, où tout respirait la tristesse et la misère. [...] Ils s'avancèrent vers un sombre enfoncement que quelques roches formaient à l'extrémité de l'enclos, et qu'ombrageaient quelques sapins épars. (*Mat* IV, 69–70)
>
> [A short distance from the cabin, he alighted with the princess, and directed her into an enclosed area of land surrounded by a row of wild lemon trees. In the centre was a poor dwelling, where everything breathed sorrow and misery. [...]

They advanced towards a gloomy recess formed by several rocks at the furthest side of the enclosure, shadowed by a few pine trees growing here and there.]

The space is stereotypically barren; the trees are few, but grow in two rows — one surrounding the entrance to the cave and the other surrounding the enclosure itself — thereby serving more as a reminder of prison bars, than of verdant life. Nature highlights here the oppression which has brought Agnès to the point of insanity: her lack of freedom as a woman. The similarities with the natural asylum in *Malvina* with its symbolic walled enclosure and tree-trunk-prison-bars are evident. Also like Malvina's garden, the desert landscape itself is able to transmit the pain the madwoman feels in response to her lack of freedom. The landscape is imbued with misery and gloom; the desert's barren rocks, dust, and oppressive heat encourage a feeling of hopelessness, as deserts in the works of travel writers so often did. Unable to make the world understand her pain, Agnès has the natural landscape around her inspire it in others, speaking for her.

Yet, Cottin's argument extends further than the portrayal of a mere symbolic landscape. For, it is through her portrayal of the East, its subjugation of women and its oppressive landscape, that she is able to provide subtle critique of Western society and its own treatment of women. As already established, Cottin was writing in an extremely patriarchal Western society which denied women the rights of citizenship, often forced women into unhappy marriages against their will, and in which wives were legally powerless to prevent physical abuse.[87] Even Cottin's best friend, Julie Verdier, had been mistreated and abused by her husband, and Cottin had provided Julie with assistance. Cottin had also written about neglectful husbands and unhappy wives in her earlier novels *Claire d'Albe*, *Malvina* and *Amélie Mansfield*. Her private life, correspondences and previous fiction writing all, therefore, serve to remind the reader of Cottin's awareness that the 'titre d'épouse' was often very far from 'saint' in European society, contrary to the statement made in *Mathilde* by the Archbishop of Tyr. Therefore, when we hear the latter comment further 'nous ne sommes point ici en Europe, où les femmes [sont] libres dans leur choix, [...] mais en Orient, où les femmes sont assujetties à un maître qui en dispose à son gré' ['we are not in Europe here, where women, [...] are free in their choice [...]. We are in the Orient, where women are subjected to a master, who disposes of them at will'] (*Mat* I, 240–41),[88] his words seem altogether too ironic.

As if to emphasize the irony of this statement, Cottin's portrayal of the treatment of women in Islamic society is matched by her portrayal of the treatment of women in the West. Richard, Mathilde's brother and king, demands that his sister marry a French crusader whom she does not love: '[E]lle connaît trop ses devoirs et mes droits pour avoir osé s'engager; seul je dispose d'elle, et j'en ai disposé: [...] Lusignan sera son époux, et je jure qu'elle n'en aura point d'autre.' ['[S]he knows her duty and my rights too well to dare to become engaged to another; I alone may dispose of her, and I have done so: [...] Lusignan will be her husband, and I swear that she will have no other'] (*Mat* II, 85). Richard's wife is accustomed to deferring to his will, and does not envision Mathilde avoiding a similar fate: ' "[I]l vous contraindra à lui obéir." "Il me contraindra", reprit fièrement la princesse, "et quel est son droit, quelle sera sa force?" "Ses ordres suffiront"' ["[H]e will force you to obey him." "He will force me", repeated the Princess boldly, "And what right, what power will he have?" "His orders will suffice."'] (*Mat* III, 148). Malek-Adhel's patriarchal power over the women in his harem is echoed here in King Richard's over Mathilde, emphasized by the repeated use of the words 'disposer de' ['dispose of'], 'force' ['power'], and 'contraindre' ['to force'].

Cottin's critique of European society through her direct descriptions of an Eastern one becomes clearer when we analyse the contemporary stereotypes of the Orient she employs in her description of Mathilde's own experiences in the Palestinian desert. Like Agnès, Mathilde finds herself pushed towards the desert by a society which forbids her freedom of choice. Mathilde believes that loving the Muslim Malek-Adhel is a sin because she has been so informed by those around her, and therefore attempts to seek redemption by undertaking a pilgrimage to visit a hermit in the desert. Also like Agnès, she finds the desert a dangerous, hostile space, which mirrors the oppression and threats that brought her there. She encounters the 'horreurs [...] du désert ['horrors [...] of the desert'] (*Mat* II, 166), and 'le passage le plus dangereux' ['the most dangerous part'] of her journey is considered to be 'dans le vaste désert de sable' ['through the vast sandy desert'] (*Mat* II, 222). Cottin describes the desert climate with an emphasis on violent language, in order to highlight the hostility of the space:

> Ils marchent tout le jour au sein de ces landes sablonneuses que les feux d'un soleil ardent frappent aplomb, et dont la réverbération réfléchit un éclat qui blesse les yeux, et une chaleur si terrible, que les hommes les plus robustes ont peine à la supporter. La nuit ne leur apporte presqu'aucun soulagement; car alors les vents cessant de souffler, le calme les laisse exposés aux exhalaisons suffocantes des sables embrasés qui leur servent de lit. (*Mat* II, 163)

> [They walk all day amid the sandy landscape that the fiery rays of the burning sun strike directly from above, fiery rays whose reverberation reflect a glare which hurts their eyes, and in a heat so terrible that even the strongest of men can scarcely endure it. The night brings them almost no relief; for, as the winds cease to blow, the still air exposes them to the suffocating emissions from the bed of burning sand on which they lie.]

The phrase 'frappe aplomb' creates an image of violence in the text here which echoes that in the natural madhouse in *Malvina*. In Cottin's earlier novel the moon beats down upon the face of the heroine, reflecting the oppression of the society which has forced her into rebellion via madness. Now, the violently oppressive sun beats down upon Mathilde, reflecting her own lack of freedom and the attempts to force her to do society's bidding. In addition, the focus on the multiple directions from which the discomfort in the desert originates creates an image of the travellers hemmed in on all sides, as though they are prisoners of the hostile climate. The sun causes them pain from above because of its heat; from all sides because its brightness reflects around them, hurting their eyes; and from below, when, even at night, its retained heat causes the sand to burn underneath them as they sleep. There is no escape from the suffering in terms of either space or time. As if to reinforce the perception of the landscape as an oppressive gaol, vertical columns of sand appear, creating the image of prison bars closing in: 'à peine les premiers rayons du jour commencent-ils à éclairer la terre, qu'on aperçoit d'énormes colonnes de sable qui tantôt courent avec une prodigieuse rapidité, tantôt s'avancent avec une majestueuse lenteur' ['scarcely do the first rays of dawn begin to shine on the earth before it is possible to perceive enormous pillars of sand which at times move with prodigious speed, and at times advance majestically slowly'.] (*Mat* II, 227). The images of oppression and imprisonment which later appear in Agnès's natural asylum are therefore prefigured by Mathilde's own experiences in the desert. The fact that Mathilde's treatment at the hands of Richard matches that of Agnès at the hands of Malek-Adhel is highlighted by the similarity of the landscapes which proclaim that treatment. By voicing a Western woman's oppression via an Eastern landscape, whose stereotypes dictated such oppression be expected, Cottin achieves what Meyda Yegenoglu describes as the 'representation of the West to *itself* by way of a detour through the other'.[89] It is Cottin's engagement with Oriental discourse which allows the Palestinian desert to become the mouthpiece for the unspoken criticism of European oppression of women.

Cottin's Orientalism is not, then, simply a matter of echoing inaccurate stereotypes propounded by others. It is an attempt to claim power. Said's discussions show us that

> [t]he Orient has been 'Orientalised' or described as 'Oriental' not merely because it has displayed the characteristics Westerners associate with 'the Oriental', *but because it could be*. The point is that this imbalance of power is discernible in *writing*. [...] What is important about Orientalism, then, is its quasi-material density and *persistence*, and its capacity thereby to monopolise the field of representation of the Oriental.[90]

Cottin claims power for herself from her position as a Western writer, connected with European intellectual society, and uses it to Orientalize the Middle East in her work, promoting the stereotypes associated with the region. Capitalizing on that power, she uses those stereotypes to strengthen her announcement of female oppression. It has been argued that women, and indeed feminism itself, have been complicit in the process of Orientalism.[91] Joanna Liddle and Shirin Rai state that 'aspects of imperialist discourse on the colonised woman were taken up in Western women's writing at the time of "first wave" feminism, and reproduced in the "second wave"'.[92] Even if the term had existed during the period in which she was writing, Cottin, an ardent admirer of Rousseau, would not have described herself as a feminist. Nonetheless, she is certainly a Western woman writer discussing the oppression of her sex, and partaking in Orientalist discourse in order to do so in a more compelling manner. Highlighting East-West similarities regarding the treatment of women through the subtlety of writing the landscape not only strengthens her argument, but also makes it more palatable to her French readership. Other scholars have come to similar conclusions in their analysis of later nineteenth-century European women's writing. Zonana, for example, writes:

> [B]y calling Rochester a "sultan" and herself a "slave," Jane [Eyre] provides herself and the reader with a culturally acceptable simile by which to understand

and combat the patriarchal 'despotism' central to Rochester's character. Part of a large system of what I term feminist orientalist discourse that permeates *Jane Eyre*, Charlotte Brontë's sultan/slave simile displaces the source of patriarchal oppression onto an 'Oriental,' 'Mahometan' society, enabling British readers to contemplate local problems without questioning their own self-definition as Westerners and Christians.[93]

Such a displacement is particularly apt for Cottin's novel, for herein lies another way in which it, in her own words, 'est dans le goût du jour' ['corresponds to contemporary taste']. Regarding attitudes towards the Orient, '[t]he underlying anxiety in much of the discourse [...] was that Europe was not as free, nor as different from the Orient, as Europeans might wish. This was especially voiced in French criticisms of monarchical power and the growing centralization of the state'.[94] In *Mathilde,* it is voiced in French criticism of the patriarchal power of post-revolutionary society.

However, Cottin not only highlights the similarities between Agnès's and Mathilde's oppression by way of the desert landscape. She also writes it in such a way that both women are able to employ it as a podium from which they might voice an ongoing protest against the patriarchal dominance of Western society.

Like Malvina in Cottin's earlier novel, Agnès protests through madness, re-appropriating her desert-asylum in order to do so. Indeed, the landscape itself and its atmosphere even directly transmit the madwoman's suffering and protesting cries: the archbishop 'fut interrompu [...] par cette infortunée, qui, d'une voix aiguë et déchirante, faisait retentir les airs' ['was interrupted [...] by this unfortunate woman, whose shrill, harrowing voice made the very air resound'] (*Mat* IV, 71). Each time Agnès's mad voice is mentioned, it is coupled with reference to the landscape. It is when she is 'étendue sur le sable' ['sprawled on the sand'] that she 'ne cessait de répéter "Malek-Adhel!"' ['did not cease to repeat "Malek-Adhel!"'](*Mat* IV, 71). Similarly, when Mathilde recognizes the voice, Agnès is 'pâle, échevelée, couchée sur la poussière, et qui se meurtrissait le sein en poussant de lugubres mugissements' ['a pale, dishevelled woman, lying in the dust, beating her breasts and howling dolefully] (*Mat* IV, 70). The resemblance of her desert floor to a padded cell reminds us that Agnès's voice can now only be heard through her mad protest, and that it is the desert which gives her the ability to voice that mad protest.

Unlike Malvina, however, once Agnès has made her decision to protest, she refuses to resubmit to the control of male, powerful figures, including the doctor who repeatedly attempts to treat her and the Archbishop who wishes to force her to repent. We are told that 'le médecin [...] n'en espère presque rien; cependant il vient tous les jours' ['the doctor [...] holds out little hope; nonetheless he comes every day'] (*Mat* IV, 76), and that Agnès reiterates vehemently: 'je ne puis pas, non je ne puis pas me repentir' ['I cannot, no I cannot repent'] (*Mat* I, 343). The refusal to relinquish the power granted to her by her rebellion becomes even more apparent in this same encounter with the Archbishop:

'[C]ette miséricorde, qui est partout, est encore là [...]; elle n'attend qu'un mot de repentir sincère pour vous reprendre au nombre de ses enfants. [...] O Agnès! ne déchirez pas mon cœur par votre silence'. La fille d'Amaury continuait à se taire. L'archevêque tomba à genoux. 'O mon Dieu! s'écria-t-il, 'daignez lui inspirer de la pitié pour elle-même: votre pardon est tout prêt; mais ce n'est pas assez encore, forcez son cœur à vous le demander'. Agnès continua à se taire. Guillaume se releva, [...] il dit: 'Ainsi le fruit de votre crime demeurera éternellement dans ce monde et dans l'autre, et [...] vous gémirez sans fin dans ces lieux terribles où le pardon n'entra jamais'. (*Mat* I, 344–45)

['This ubiquitous mercy is still there [...], it only waits for one single word of repentance from you in order to count you amongst its children. [...] O Agnès! Do not break my heart with your silence'. Amaury's daughter said not a word in reply. The Archbishop fell to his knees. 'O my God!' he cried. 'Deign to inspire her with self-pity: your forgiveness is ready; but it is not yet enough. Force her heart to ask it of you'. Agnès remained silent. Guillaume stood up [...]. He said: 'So the fruit of your crime will remain eternally in this world and the next, and [...] you will howl endlessly in those terrible places where forgiveness has never entered'.]

In a reversal of the situation in *Malvina,* here the male figure kneels at the feet of the rebellious woman, indicating clearly Agnès's continued control. Furthermore, although silenced by her oppression as a woman, Agnès even succeeds in turning that enforced silence to her advantage: it announces her resolution to uphold her rebellion, and thus increases her power.

Given her determination to resist attempts to force her to resubmit to patriarchal control, it is fitting that Agnès's natural desert-asylum reflect this unshakeable decision. In this respect, Agnès's natural asylum differs starkly from Malvina's. Firstly, in order for the madwoman within it to refuse treatment from the male representative of the scientific world, the natural asylum must not become the curative, controlled space *intra muros* advocated by Pinel. The landscape which stages Agnès's rebellion through madness is therefore not to be found within the safe space of a walled garden, but rather within the wilderness of the desert. Cottin capitalizes on Orientalist stereotypes of desert space as savage and uncivilizable in order to construct a 'landscape of one's own' suitable for a prolonged rebellion through madness. The enclosure is created by trees growing wild in dusty sand, not by trees planted by man himself in a verdant garden; Agnès is surrounded by scattered desert rocks amid a barren wilderness, not by the uniformly placed stones of a manmade wall in the grounds of a manor house. The landscape's wildness mirrors the wild, mental depravity of the prisoner confined within it: her savage nature is clear when we see her beating her breasts and moaning, and is highlighted by her dishevelled appearance. Thus, the space which resists mankind's domination becomes the perfect habitation for the madwoman who also refuses domination: when the doctor approaches her in this space, he fails in his attempts to eliminate her mad protest.

Secondly, Cottin plays on the religious associations with desert space in her construction of Agnès's 'landscape of one's own'. It is expected that the desert will provoke repentance in Agnès's soul, as it did for Mary of Egypt. The Archbishop's words clearly link the act of repentance with desert space: 'si *du sein de sa demeure elle laissait échapper un mot de repentir,* tout ne serait pas perdu encore' ['if, *from the heart of her dwelling, she uttered one word of repentance,* all would not yet be lost'] (*Mat IV*, 73).[95] However, Agnès vehemently refuses, instead reasserting her right to rebel against Christian society. Therefore, in order for her to re-appropriate her desert-asylum, it must become a landscape in which Hell is repeatedly invoked, declaring her determination to follow the consequences of her refusal to repent. The first hint that the depraved Agnès inhabits a hellish space appears when the Archbishop and Mathilde must descend to a lower level in order to reach her: '[J]e désirerais qu'avant de rentrer à Ptolémaïs, votre altesse voulût descendre avec moi dans une de ces cabanes placées au pied de la colline' ['Before returning to Ptolemais, I would like Your Highness to descend to one of the shacks at the foot of the hill with me'] (*Mat IV*, 68). As they approach, the Archbishop indicates clearly that Hell and its punishments are to be found in this landscape asylum: 'je veux que vous mesuriez vous-même la profondeur de l'abîme où les passions peuvent entraîner, et quel châtiment Dieu réserve aux coupables qui y tombent' ['I want you to measure for yourself the depths of the abyss into which passion can lead, and the punishment that God reserves for the guilty parties who fall into it'] (*Mat IV*, 69). The space is in fact so infernal that even demonic spirits seem to be found within: 'quand la nuit vient, c'est un train, un vacarme.... on dirait que tous les démons sont après elle' ['when night comes, it is at such a pace and with such a din that you would have thought every demon were after her'] (*Mat IV*, 76).[96] The dark and ominous hollow, rocky recess which Agnès inhabits is reminiscent of the cave at the gateway to Hell through which Virgil's Aeneas and the Sibyl enter the Underworld. It forms the beginning of her own descent into the bowels of the Earth: her madness takes place in an antechamber to the Hell which she is determined to enter when dead if this is what is required for continued rebellion.

Linking Agnès's determination to rebel against both church and science, the images of punishment and demonic torture created by her personal Hell also result in her prison greatly recalling the madhouses of the Ancien Régime rather than the care and treatment of Pinel's institutions. Thus, Cottin further imbues Agnès's natural asylum with necessary properties for a prolonged rebellion through madness, ensuring that the madwoman's voice — which imparts the novel's crucial dual message that women have long been oppressed and that they have the right to resist that oppression — continues.

It is notable that the longer Agnès's rebellion endures the more it is directed with increasing intensity towards male representatives of the West and their attempts to re-subjugate her. As a result, when Agnès reappropriates the natural landscape for the podium of her protest, she retains the desert's Eastern stereotypes whilst deliberately reversing the expected Christian image of the desert as a space of repentance. This reiterates Cottin's use of Orientalism as the means of critiquing the West, for now she has not only employed Orientalist discourse to reflect Mathilde's oppression at the hands of Western patriarchy, she has also employed it to ensure Agnès's continued rebellion against the West.

Mathilde also comes close to protesting through madness: 'sa raison parait aliénée' ['her reason seemed to have deserted her'] (*Mat II*, 143) and, as she becomes more agitated, 'son désordre toujours croissant' ['her ever increasing mental disturbance']

(*Mat* II, 144) threatens to overtake her. However, she ultimately decides to embark upon a pilgrimage in order to save herself, and, as she does so, the desert landscape becomes for her an asylum in a different sense. She rejects the lunatic asylum in favour of a sanctuary. She employs the same retreat to nature as many others in the early Romantic period in order to escape society, and, as she re-appropriates the desert landscape for her own purposes, the early Romantic imagery with which the landscape is infused assists in her protest.

At the destination of Mathilde's pilgrimage lie ruins, a familiar trope of Romanticism.[97] As in many Romantic literary works, such as Staël's *Corinne*, Byron's *Childe Harold*, Shelley's 'Ozymandias', and the oriental poems of Hugo and Lamartine, the ruins provoke reflection on a past easily destroyed by the passage of time:

> Chacun [...] s'avance alors au milieu des décombres [...]. Ils regardent autour d'eux, et contemplent, sans pouvoir se lasser, ces colonnes éparses, brisées, ces pilastres entassés, ces vestiges d'une magnificence passée, et ces innombrables débris qui étonnent l'imagination par leur grandeur, comme ils attristent l'âme par leur ruine. 'Hélas! mon père', s'écrie l'un des guerriers, 'cette nef auguste qui subsiste encore en partie, ce double rang de piliers, et cette arcade si élevée, que l'œil se fatigue à en mesurer la hauteur, tout cela aussi se détruira-t-il?' Il dit, et du sein du silence qui règne dans ces vastes ruines, une pierre ébranlée se détache, tombe, et lui répond. (*Mat* II, 183–84)

> [Each one [...] advances amid the ruins; [...] They look around them, and contemplate, without wearying of doing so, the sparse, broken columns, the piles of pilasters, the remains of a past magnificence, and the innumerable fragments whose grandeur both stuns the imagination and saddens the soul by their ruined state. 'Alas Father!' cries one of the warriors, 'This august nave which still exists in part, this double row of pillars, and this elevated vault which is so high that it tires the eye to measure it, will all this also be destroyed?' He speaks, and from the heart of the silence which reigns amid these vast ruins, a loose stone detaches itself and falls in answer to him.]

The monastery ruins are, in fact, in the process of being reclaimed by nature: '[d]eux pêchers sauvages croissent parmi les décombres' ['two wild peach trees grew among the ruins'] (*Mat* II, 168). Emphasizing this fact, the hermit reminds the travellers that whilst human life and achievement are ephemeral, nature is eternal:

> [E]ncore un peu de temps, et ce corps misérable retournera en poudre comme ces colonnes qui rampent sur la terre après avoir touché jusqu'aux cieux; encore un peu de temps, elles et moi nous nous dissoudrons en entier, et il ne restera de nous qu'un peu de poussière qui ira se mêler et se perdre avec les sables du désert. (*Mat* II, 185)

> [Before long this wretched body will return to dust like the columns that lie on the ground, where once they touched the sky; before long, they and I will dissolve entirely, and nothing will remain of us but a little dust which will mingle with and be lost among the sands of the desert.]

The ruined manmade construction, coupled with the vision of the male figure turning to dust, symbolizes the transience of patriarchal rule. Ultimately, even this will fall prey to the landscape, consumed by the sands of the desert. Thus, the early Romantic imagery here stresses the advantage of turning to nature (aptly associated with the feminine), rather than civilization (aptly associated with the masculine), for the empowerment and immortality of the female voice protesting against such rule. We now notice further reasons for the desert landscape's suitability as a space of female protest, beyond that of its wildness reflecting the woman's own rebellious desire. Firstly, the Romantic-Orientalist view of the desert as a timeless space helps us to see how, by utilizing such a space for the podium of her protest, a woman's rebellion will also endure. Secondly, just as Agnès reversed Malvina's submissive situation by forcing the male authoritative figure to kneel at her feet, now, in yet another reversal of *Malvina* (which saw male authoritative figures assert their power over the landscape, taming both it and the woman within it to their will), in Cottin's *Mathilde* the desert landscape not only resists man's efforts to tame it, it actually possesses the power to reclaim control over mankind and his constructs.

While in the desert, Mathilde thus finds the strength and ability to defy her brother's will to join her to Lusignan, and to call God to witness her promise to marry Malek-Adhel: '[T]u es digne d'être mon époux; je jure de n'en avoir jamais d'autre que toi, je le jure à ce Dieu qui, en ce moment, remplit de son immensité et de sa toute-puissance et ce désert et ton cœur' ['[Y]ou are worthy of being my husband; I swear never to have any other but you, I swear it to God, who, in this moment, fills both this desert and your heart with his immensity and great power'] (*Mat* II, 244). Although Mathilde avoids madness in her protest, the moon — stereotypically connected with both madness and femininity — is still present in her rebellion. Indeed, as she calls God into her desert space of retreat, its power is reinforced:

> [L]a lune verse son feu tranquille sur toute l'étendue du désert; aucun bruit, aucun son n'en interrompt le silence; il semble qu'au sein de ce calme et de cette solitude, Dieu doit mieux entendre les prières de l'âme qui l'implore, et l'âme qui l'implore y mieux entendre sa voix. (*Mat* II, 243–44)

> [[T]he moon pours its tranquil light over the whole desert; no noise, no sound at all interrupts the silence; it seems as though, at the heart of that calmness and solitude, God must better hear the prayers of the soul which implores him, and the soul which implores him must better hear his voice.]

The light of the moon was employed by the physician in *Malvina* to reveal to the madwoman the truth of her madness, assisting in her treatment. In *Mathilde,* the moon reveals another truth: God's truth. The Romantic notion of finding God within nature furnishes Mathilde's desert rebellion with one final key resource: it allows her protest to be approved. Thus, it is in the desert that the Archbishop eventually joins Mathilde's and Malek-Adhel's hands in marriage (*Mat* IV, 247), and in the desert that Mathilde chooses to live out her days after her husband's death, remaining in a monastery by the side of his grave, rather than returning to England with her brother. It is also worth noting that, like Agnes's re-appropriated desert asylum, that of Mathilde has also turned silence from a mark of repression to a mark of power.

A space which was both Eastern and Western in terms of its criticism of oppression now again possesses elements of both. In order to write the landscape in such a way that it might be used by both of her female protagonists as a podium for their protest, Cottin has married to her engagement with Oriental discourse an engagement with both the religious and Romantic associations possessed by desert space in the period in which she was writing. The desert asylum in *Mathilde* is therefore a middle space in two respects: in terms of imagery and in terms of criticism. Neither wholly Eastern nor wholly Western, but rather a space which can be defined in more than one way, the desert landscape is perfect for women to re-appropriate in order to highlight the fact that they, too, must not be restricted or pigeonholed. In fusing multiple images of desert space, calling on its contemporary associations with retreat and religion, East and West, oppression and rebellion, powerful and untameable nature, Cottin succeeds in writing a landscape which voices women's oppression, holds out against any attempt to dominate it, and which even extends female protest beyond the boundaries of the constructed 'landscape of one's own' itself and out in to the wider world.

Rejecting the Masculine World for the Feminine World: Nature and the Male Hysteric in Krüdener's *Valérie*

Gustave Linar, the twenty-two year old male protagonist of Krüdener's novel, suffers from unrequited love for the title character Valérie. He is therefore subject to the same problematic situation faced by women which we have previously seen highlighted by Martin: rejection by a loved one. Gustave, unlike Cottin's Malvina and Agnès, however, is not cast out by society as a punishment for a forbidden love. Rather, it is he who rejects patriarchal society, rebelling against the authoritative masculinity that society so greatly exhorts. Just as the female characters of Cottin's novels protest against their oppressive situation through madness, so too does Gustave. As he rejects masculinity, he assumes elements of effeminacy, resorts to the 'feminine malady' of hysteria in order to convey his desire to protest, and turns to the traditionally feminine natural world in order to find an asylum, an ally and a voice.

Whilst Showalter's discussion of male hysteria as a method of rejecting masculinity focuses on post-traumatic shock experienced during and after the First World War, her arguments are nonetheless applicable to the Romantic hero of the period in the aftermath of the French Revolution. Showalter asserts that '[w]ar neurosis was "an escape from an intolerable situation"', a means of deliverance from the horrors of war.[98] Gustave has not suffered the trauma of war; however, he experiences symptoms in reaction to his own intolerable situation similar to those described by Showalter, allowing us to argue that male hysteria is linked to a rejection of a masculine order long before the aftermath of the Great War. Such male hysteria was, according to Showalter:

> a disguised male protest [...] against the concept of 'manliness' itself. While
> epidemic female hysteria [...] had been a form of protest against a patriarchal

society that enforced confinement to a narrowly defined femininity, epidemic male hysteria [...] was a protest against the politicians, generals, and psychiatrists. The heightened code of masculinity that dominated in wartime was intolerable to surprisingly large numbers of men.[99]

Gustave rejects manliness and rebels against masculine authority throughout the novel for several reasons. Before looking at the natural asylum he seeks out in his madness, we must first understand the processes which cause Gustave to descend into insanity.

The first factor to be considered is Gustave's sexual frustration. Gustave is driven mad by his love for Valérie, whom he cannot possess because she does not return his love, and because she is already married. To compound matters, Valérie is in fact married to a man whom Gustave holds in high esteem: a count who was a close friend of Gustave's late father, and who has promised to care for Gustave as if the boy were his own son. The count represents patriarchal dominance in the novel. Gustave begins by extoling the virtues of this father figure in a letter to his friend Ernest, stating his debt to the count and describing him in elaborate terms as the best and most educated of men:

> Il se plaît dans l'idée que nous ne nous séparerons pas, qu'il pourra me guider lui-même dans cette nouvelle carrière où il a voulu que j'entrasse, et qu'il pourra, en achevant lui-même mon éducation, remplir le saint devoir dont il se chargea en m'adoptant. Quel ami, Ernest, que ce second père! Quel homme excellent! [...] Le comte sait tout, connaît tout. (*V*, pp. 26–27)

> [He is pleased by the idea that we will not be separated, that he will be able to guide me himself in the new career he wishes me to enter, and that, in completing my education himself, he will be able to fulfil the sacred duty that he undertook on adopting me. What a friend, Ernest, this second father is! What an excellent man! [...] The count knows and understands everything.]

However, Gustave's respect and admiration for the count are gradually dispelled as the novel progresses, and as Gustave finds his situation with respect to his guardian increasingly intolerable. The existing marriage between Valérie and the count places a restraint upon Gustave's love, and so tensions begin to arise. Gustave's desire to rebel against his replacement father is driven by jealousy and sexual frustration, the latter of which is a recognized characteristic of male hysteria:

> Robert Brudnell Carter had attributed hysteria to sexual repression and frustration, and noted that male hysterics were often celibate, 'a circumstance which may have assimilated the effects of emotiveness upon them to those which are constantly witnessed in the female'.[100]

Indeed, in his own seminal analysis, Freud argues that 'the traumas that produced hysteria were exclusively sexual in nature'.[101] Gustave begins to show signs of hysterical protest against the count, born from childish capricious fantasies: the desire to obtain what he cannot have, and to gain vengeance upon the man who forces what he considers to be an impossible and unacceptable situation on him. Gustave witnesses the count scold Valérie for excessive fear when a wave rocks the gondola in which they are travelling. Whilst the count's intelligence was praised so strongly when it came to dealing with Gustave's own education, now his head for business stands in the way of his concern for his wife, and therefore earns Gustave's disgust:

> Le comte, préoccupé des affaires publiques, ne s'occupa qu'un instant de Valérie. [...] [E]lle était sur son sein, il respirait son souffle, son cœur battait contre le sien, et il restait froid, froid comme une pierre! Cette idée me donna une fureur que je ne puis rendre. (*V*, p. 129)

> [The count, preoccupied with public business, attended to Valérie for only a brief moment. [...] [S]he was pressed against his chest, he was breathing in the air she exhaled, his heart beat against hers and yet he remained cold, as cold as stone! This idea filled me with inexpressible rage.]

Gustave's previous extolling of the count's manly, authoritative qualities now mutate in fact into anger, hatred and utter rejection of the same representative of patriarchal society that he had once admired:

> [J]e m'accrochai aux branches d'un buisson, et je vis avec délice couler mon sang de mes mains meurtries, que j'enfonçai dans les épines: une espèce de rage indéfinissable me poussait; il s'y mêlait une sorte de volupté; [...] ma jalousie était avide de nouveaux tourments: je sentais aussi que je rompais les dernier liens de la vertu en commençant à haïr le comte. (*V*, p. 130)

> [I clung to the branches of a bush, and, with delight, I saw blood run from my wounded hands, which I thrust into the thorns: an indefinable rage urged me on, mixed with a sort of exquisite pleasure; [...] my jealousy was hungry for new torments, and I felt, too, that I was breaking my remaining links to virtue by beginning to hate the count.]

Here, Gustave makes use of nature to enable his rebellion against masculine authority. His hysteria becomes apparent through his desire for violent self-harm, and it is the natural world which permits this. He pushes his hands deeply into the thorns of the bush at the side of the canal, drawing his own blood in a Christ-like image which conveys his belief in his martyrdom to love. He tortures himself physically just as the count — representative of patriarchal authority and permitted lover in Valérie's bedchamber — tortures him mentally. In this way, Gustave's situation is reminiscent of that of Malvina and Agnès, both of whom employ aspects of the natural world to communicate their protest against powerful male figures.

Gustave not only displays a lack of sexual power, he also displays a lack of any political, economic or social power. Whereas his sexual powerlessness causes him to turn against masculine authority, his lack of political, economic or social power in fact strips him of his own masculine identity. The antithesis of the count who possesses the masculine power of the husband, the patriarch, and the business man, Gustave is a wandering figure, without effectual purpose in the public sphere, continually described, even in his own voice, as weak: 'Je suis le plus faible des hommes' ['I am the weakest of men'] (*V*, p. 62, see also p. 96). As Thomas Sydenham declares, the male hysteric 'lead[s] a sedentary or studious life'.[102] This is precisely the case for the solitary Gustave, who, since adolescence, has spent his time meandering in the wilds of the Romantic North, in the Swedish countryside, engaging in personal introspection and 'longues rêveries' ['long reveries'] (*V*, p.188), reading Romantic poetry rather than turning his head to business or politics: ' "Avec qui es-tu donc, mon fils, dans tes courses solitaires?" Il a tiré Ossian; et [...] dit: "Avec les héros [et] la nature" ' ["Who are you with on your solitary walks, my son?" He took out a copy of Ossian, and [...] said: "With the heroes [and] with nature"] (Ibid.). He has displayed a tendency towards the feminine world of nature from an early age therefore, and in so doing, he has also demonstrated his desire to distance himself from the male-dominated sphere of public service. As a result, in later life he finds himself powerless and dependent on a more masculine figure for financial support and shelter. Showalter notes the ways in which powerlessness might cause a man to lose his sanity:

> What happened to make these men so unstable, so emotional, in a word, so feminine? Women understood the lesson of [hysteria] better than their male contemporaries: that powerlessness could lead to pathology, that a lasting wound could result when a person lost the sense of being in control, of being 'an autonomous actor in a manipulable world'.[103]

Gustave's situation, arising from a refusal to undertake the masculine role expected of him, is compounded when he realizes that not being able to control his emotion aligns him with a feminine stereotype, thus robbing him further of his own male identity. It becomes apparent that Gustave himself associates a lack of courage to stem emotions with a non-male identity when he retreats to la Chartreuse de B., renting a room in a small house overlooking the convent. In this room he discovers the story of the life of one of the saints. Despite the sufferings this saint underwent, his great courage enabled him to resist the carnal need for sexual passion. This is something Gustave has never been able to do, and so the comparison between the two men is striking. Gustave refers to the saint as follows:

> Je viens de lire la vie d'un saint que j'ai trouvée dans une des armoires de ma chambre. *Ce saint avait été homme, il était resté homme:* il avait souffert; il avait jeté loin de lui les désirs de ce monde, après les avoir combattus avec courage. (*V*, p. 151)

> [I have just read the life of a saint, which I found in one of the closets in my bedchamber. *This saint had been a man, and he had remained a man:* he had suffered; he had cast his worldly desires far from him, after courageously fighting them].[104]

Gustave's view that the saint was, and always remained, a man, owing to his ability to display courage, reveals much about how Gustave views himself: he sees personal weakness in the face of intense emotion and feels emasculated. Gustave's own opinions on courage as a masculine virtue correspond in fact with those of theorists of male hysteria:

> When all signs of physical fear were judged as weakness and where alternatives to combat — pacifism, conscientious objection, desertion, even suicide — were viewed as unmanly, men were silenced and immobilized and forced, like women, to express their conflicts through the body. Placed in intolerable

circumstances of stress, and expected to react with unnatural 'courage,' thousands of soldiers reacted instead with the symptoms of hysteria.[105]

This is what befalls Gustave. He is expected to repress both his emotional desires and his fears that those desires will never become a reality, and he finds that he cannot do so.

A man's knowledge of his own powerlessness next to the masculine authority which he is expected to display, is worsened when he finds himself silenced, just like women who suffer a similar lack of power and voice in male-dominant society. Like Malvina and Agnès, Krüdener's Gustave is forced into silence by his situation. After being asked by the count to explain the reason for his apparent suffering, he writes to Ernest: 'Je pris ses mains avec impétuosité; je les pressai sur mon sein; et ma voix, enchaînée comme ma langue, ne put produire un seul son' ['I took his hands impetuously; I pressed them to my breast; and my voice, as tied as my tongue, could produce not a single sound'] (V, p. 132). The choice of the passive 'enchaînée' ['tied'] here is significant, implying that the silence is forced upon him and that he is powerless to counteract it. As a response to the silence that he cannot overcome, Gustave expresses his internal suffering and conflict the only way he can: by reacting to stress through hysteria, like the madwoman. As Showalter declares, where words are no longer possible, discourse transmits itself through the mind and body:

> To be reduced to a feminine state of powerlessness, frustration, and dependency led to a deprivation of speech as well. [...] Thus shell shock may actually have served the same kind of functional purpose in military life — defusing mutiny — that female hysteria served in civilian society.[106]

Gustave's retreat into insanity defuses the explosive situation which may have occurred had he acted upon his desires and made love to Valérie, or had he confessed his love either to the count or to Valérie herself. Forced into silence, stripped of his masculine identity, and angrily desiring to reject the masculine dominance of society in any case, Gustave finds, like the victims of post-war neurosis, that the only answer is to perform the feminine act of hysteria. As Butler argues that performance and action dictates gender, we therefore see Gustave assume a feminine identity where he is robbed of a masculine one.

As a consequence, during his madness Gustave finds himself seeking out the supposedly feminine world as a replacement for the masculine world that he has rejected. As he retreats further away from his adoptive family, both physically (as he travels to la Charteuse de B. and then to Pietramala) and mentally (by losing his reason), he seeks out Mother Nature, turning to the wild natural landscape of the countryside for asylum and aid. Again, just as for the female hysterics Malvina and Agnès, nature provides the perfect asylum for the emasculated hysteric Gustave:

> J'arrivai ici au milieu des Apennins, hier dans la journée. Le site de Piétra-Mala est presque sauvage. Ce bourg est caché dans des gorges de montagnes; mais j'aime ce lieu qui paraît oublié du monde entier. [...] [J]e respirais avec plus de liberté; l'air est si pur dans ces montagnes! J'ai été voir une petite maison qui appartient à mon hôte, et qui me plaît beaucoup. Un torrent, destructeur

comme la passion qui me dévore, a renversé près de la maison de hauts pins et de vieux érables. (*V*, p. 157)

[I arrived here, in the middle of the Apennines, yesterday during the day. The area of Pietramala is almost wild. The small town is concealed in mountain gorges, but I love this place which seems as though it has been forgotten by the entire world. [...] I have been able to breathe more freely; the air is so pure in these mountains! I have been to see a cottage which belongs to my host, and which I find delightful. A mountain torrent, as destructive as the passion which devours me, has uprooted tall pines and old maple trees near the house.]

The wild natural madhouse has several powerful functions for Gustave. Firstly, as we see in the above quotation, it acts as a symbolic representation of the wildness of his mind. The destructive power his emotions have upon his mind is equalled only by the destructive power of the torrential waters which uproot the trees from the earth. His own desire to rebel against the patriarchal dominance of the count through violent self-harm finds its equivalent in nature's violent rebellion and self-harm as its storms uproot its trees. The kindred spirit that Gustave finds in the wilds of nature is comforting to him. He has more in common with Mother Nature, the traditionally feminine world, than he did with the supposedly masculine world of courage, action and business. He continues to seek out nature throughout his madness, up to the very moment of his death, repeatedly asking to be taken closer to the window, or rising from his bed to rush into the garden. He exclaims: 'Que la nature est belle! quel calme elle répand dans tout mon être! [...] Comme elle m'a consolé, cette nature si sublime!' ['How beautiful nature is! With what tranquillity it fills me! [...] How this sublime nature has consoled me!'] (*V*, p. 180).

Secondly, the natural madhouse sought by Gustave protects him by the fact that it is 'caché' ['hidden'] and 'oublié' ['forgotten'], concealing him from the world. It performs the same functions as the natural madhouses in *Malvina* and *Mathilde* in this respect. In addition to these factors, nature has a third power to offer Gustave, one which he has lost: the ability to speak. Gustave finds his own voice silenced by the horror of his unvirtuous thoughts, and so seeks out instead the voice of nature as a replacement. The power of nature's voice is seen in the nouns and verbs attributed to it: 'Que j'ai vécu ici, Ernest! combien j'y ai pensé! J'ai vu hier un orage: le tonnerre, avec sa terrible voix, parcourut toutes ces montagnes, répéta, gronda, éclata avec fureur' ['How I have lived here, Ernest! How much I have thought here! Yesterday, I saw a storm: the terrible voice of the thunder travelled right across the mountains, reverberating, rumbling, exploding with fury'] (*V*, p. 153). Endowing the thunder with a voice and the ability to repeat itself serves to anthropomorphize it. Furthermore, describing the voice as terrible and furious underlines the fact that nature has a more acutely powerful human voice than Gustave has ever possessed. As was true in Cottin's novels, therefore, Krüdener shows that hysterics are able to find a replacement for their silenced voice within nature. For all these reasons, it is only at the heart of nature that Gustave truly feels at home in his madness. As F. C. Green states, 'Nature offers some solace, and [Gustave] seems to find a sympathetic echo in the silence of the mountains and in the ceaseless rush of their torrents'.[107]

It should be noted here, however, that despite the calm induced in him by the landscape, the natural asylum in which Gustave finds himself is a wild one. This was also the case with Agnès, and, like Agnès, Gustave also prolongs his rebellion with the aid of nature.

Gustave's retreat into nature in the hour of his madness is significant for another reason, however. Gustave has become insane, not only because of the dual lack of power and speech owing to his rejection of masculinity, and not only as another means of rejecting masculinity in itself, but also because the object he loves is an illusion. The illusion he seeks was conceived in, and is intricately connected with nature. Fragments from the journal of Gustave's mother describe a particular instance in his childhood when he confesses his invention of an ideal woman: 'J'ai été avec un être idéal, charmant; je ne l'ai jamais vu, et le vois pourtant; mon cœur bat, mes joues brûlent; je l'appelle; elle est timide et jeune comme moi, mais elle est bien meilleure' ['I was with an ideal, charming being, whom I have never seen, but whom I do see nonetheless. My heart is pounding and my cheeks burning. I call her. She is shy and young, like me, but she is infinitely better'] (V, p. 188). This explanation appears at the end of the novel, and explains much of the difficulty Gustave has faced. It was on to Valérie that Gustave projected this imagined ideal created in his adolescence. As Stephanie M. Hilger states, 'Gustave attempts to subdue his gradually increasing passion by constructing her as an ideal, an ethereal rather than physical being'.[108] Specifically important is the fact that Gustave constructed the ideal image of woman whilst walking alone amid nature, for nature plays an integral part in his conception of the feminine ideal. The link between the ideal woman and nature is reiterated throughout the novel. One of the factors which makes Valérie fit so aptly with Gustave's ideal construct is her connection with nature: 'Ernest, je sentais que si je l'aimais ainsi, c'était parce qu'elle était restée près de la nature' ['Ernest, I felt that the reason I loved her so much was because she remained close to nature'] (V, p. 82). Finally, towards the end of the novel, Gustave writes to Valérie, at last declaring his love for her:

> Tu étais la vie de mon âme: longtemps elle avait langui après toi; et en te voyant, je ne vis que ta ressemblance; je ne vis que cette image que j'avais portée dans mon cœur, vue dans mes rêves, aperçue dans toutes les scènes de la nature, dans toutes les créations de ma jeune et brûlante imagination. (V, p. 166)

> [You were the very life of my soul: it pined for you for a long time; and in seeing you, I only saw your resemblance, I only saw this same image that I had carried in my heart, seen in my dreams, perceived in all natural scenes, in all the creations of my young, fiery imagination.]

Having perceived Valérie in nature, in his state of madness brought on by his inability to possess the real woman, he therefore retreats to nature to seek out instead her resemblance there.

There is one final argument to be made regarding Gustave's notion of the ideal woman. In a manner reminiscent of Freud's notion of Oedipal desire, 'defined as a constellation of desire for the mother as a sexual object and hate of the father as a rival',[109] the ideal woman that Gustave constructs must, he notes, be the image of his mother. In his youth, Gustave informs his mother: 'Il faudra que la femme qui sera ma compagne vous ressemble, pour qu'elle aie [sic] toute mon âme' ['The woman who is to be my companion must resemble you in order for her to possess all my soul'] (*V*, p. 188). The Oedipus Complex from which Gustave suffers appears further highlighted when Gustave states: 'Errant comme Œdipe je ne cherche comme lui qu'un tombeau' ['Wandering like Oedipus, I look only for a tomb, as did he'] (*V*, p. 158). Whilst Krüdener's reference is evidently not a direct reference to the Oedipus Complex itself, coined by Freud roughly a hundred years after the publication of *Valérie*, the recollection of the wandering Theban figure is nonetheless striking for the modern reader, recalling, as it does, the appropriateness of the application of Freud's complex to Gustave's situation. If Gustave's ideal woman is the representation of his own mother, and Valérie becomes the embodied human form of that ideal, consequently, she must remind him of his mother, either in physical resemblance, or in her possession of similar qualities. This being the case, the reason for Gustave's rejection of the count becomes abundantly clear: he hates and rejects the father figure as his rival, as he has explicitly stated himself. He is jealous of the patriarchal figure's possession of the maternal representation. It is Gustave's Oedipus complex, then, (in parallel with his Freudian sexual frustration) that causes him to reject masculinity. Both his emasculation and the chimerical illusion forbidden to him result in his descent into insanity, which in turn allows him further possibility to reject the masculine world, by embracing the feminine one. Therefore, in his insanity, when he looks to inhabit a natural asylum, he is not only seeking out the resemblance of Valérie in the natural world, and not only seeking out aspects of nature which mirror his intense passion and his madness, he also seeks out the mother he cannot have. He no longer has his real mother, who died long ago. He cannot have the mother-image that is Valérie because she belongs to another man and does not return his love. Consequently, he seeks out the only other representation of a mother possible: Mother Nature. He declares: 'Ici la nature semble me plaindre et s'attendrir sur moi. Elle me recevra dans son sein, et fidèle amie, elle gardera mes tristes secrets' ['Here, nature seems to pity me and to be moved by me. She will hold me to her breast, and, faithful friend that she is, she will keep my sad secrets'] (*V*, p. 158). He finds consolation in the bosom of nature as he would wish to find solace in the bosom of a mother. If hysteria is a rejection of the masculine patriarchal world, Gustave goes mad in order to regain the matriarchal world he so desires, and uses nature to prolong this rebellion in order to continue his relationship with it.

Butler argues that 'the identity categories often presumed to be foundational to feminist politics [...] simultaneously work to limit and constrain in advance the very cultural possibilities that feminism is supposed to open up'.[110] In extending the feminine protest against patriarchal power through madness to a male character, *Valérie* shows that women are not alone in suffering because of the strict gender roles and boundaries imposed in post-revolutionary society. Moreover, in blurring the boundaries between male and female in the conveying of this argument, *Valérie* further conveys how inappropriate it is to restrict someone to a particular space according to their gender.

Conclusion

Astbury writes that '[t]he prevalence of madness as a plot device in the Directory period suggests in fact that it is another indication of the psychological response of authors to the Revolution'.[111] In women's writing of the first decade of the nineteenth century, however, it can be seen more as a response to post-revolutionary society's oppression of women and its general demands to conform to imposed gender roles. Cottin and Krüdener both portray powerless, oppressed female or emasculated male characters who use madness as a means of rebelling against patriarchal society and rejecting masculine authority. There are several conclusions to be drawn from the analysis of how such protests through madness are presented.

Firstly, the novels' engagement with the question of gender stereotypes and gender authority must be considered. Both writers engage with the feminization of insanity investigated and developed in their contemporary society. This includes the supposed link between moon, menstruation and madness, the disheveled madwoman with wild hair and her clothes in tatters, and the belief that an inability to control emotion (a supposedly womanly flaw) led to hysteria. Playing to these stereotypes grants the protagonists' mad rebellion a pre-established feminine quality, thereby making madness an apt means of presenting both female rebellion against the patriarchy and male rejection of masculine expectations or authority.

Side-by-side analysis of Cottin and Krüdener's work also raises intriguing discussion of the crossing of gender boundaries. Cottin's Agnès crosses into a masculine domain and agency, performing the role of a male warrior in order to protest against the oppression of her womanly role and to attack those who attempt to force it on her. This is momentarily successful, but when she is forced to identify once more as a woman, she finds that madness provides her with a better opportunity to protest. Krüdener's Gustave fails to live up to the masculine role expected of him and which he expects of himself, and so he resorts both to the feminine world of madness in order to protest, and to the feminine world of Mother Nature as a replacement for the patriarchal world that he shuns. These spaces restore some of the power previously stripped from him. Ultimately, madness becomes portrayed as a female malady on the part of Agnès and Gustave because it arises once a masculine agency has been, respectively, lost or rejected, and because madness provides what that masculine agency was not able to provide.

Further interesting comparisons can be drawn between *Mathilde* and *Valérie* regarding the gender identities of their mad characters because of the novels' brief, yet significant, engagement with the lives of saints. Agnès and Gustave are portrayed as distinct opposites to, respectively, Mary of Egypt and the unnamed saint in the book discovered in Pietramala. When Gustave reads the story of the saint, he appears less of a man in his own eyes. The comparison thus further underlines his emasculated status, and pushes his consequent desire to retreat into the stereotypically feminine worlds of madness and nature. Agnès, in her madness, adopts a persona which deliberately contravenes expectations of a repentant, female, desert sinner. The implicit comparison to Mary of Egypt thus highlights Agnès's determined rejection of a masculine authority that she had previously tried to assume.

Secondly, we must consider the vital importance of natural landscapes to the novels' arguments. Ultimately, it is through their engagement with nature that Cottin and Krüdener achieve their presentation of madness as a form of protest. Nature provides a symbolic landscape-asylum in place of a conventional madhouse: a space to which the oppressed woman or emasculated male can safely retreat, one which mirrors the mad characters' state of mind, one whose features enable rebellion, one which restores the voice that patriarchal society has removed, and, ultimately, one which can therefore be reclaimed by the mad protagonist for the purposes of protesting against the socio-political status quo regarding gender oppression. This chapter has further shown that, whilst both tamed and wild natural landscapes permit rebellion against male authority through madness, the rebellion is precluded from enduring in the tamed landscape, because of the very fact that it has, itself, submitted to the control of man. On the other hand, a wild landscape which resists domination proves to be a more successful long-term podium for protest through madness.

Yet, as the direct comparison of Cottin's two novels clarifies, the argument regarding prolonged rebellion extends deeper than a simple tamed-wild dichotomy. Engaging with late eighteenth- and early nineteenth-century theories regarding the two spaces she elects to portray as fictional madhouses adds crucial subtle layers to Cottin's arguments. Malvina's walled garden-asylum is constructed to mirror the *intra muros* space of assistance advocated by physicians such as Pinel, and so brings into focus the contemporary debates over how madness was to be treated. Cottin makes clear that woman is still subject to male domination even within a space which purports to offer care to her whilst she suffers. Because Cottin's natural asylum — so clearly a representative of the era's new types of mental institution — is, itself, an area controlled by authoritative male figures, any successful treatment of madness within it comes at a price: the madwoman's own relinquishing of control to masculine authority. In *Mathilde*, Cottin writes the desert as a middle space, not clearly definable as wholly one thing or another, which is consequently well suited for staging the prolonged, successful rebellion of women who oppose their own pigeonholing and lack of freedom to shape their own identity and destiny. Furthermore, because of her engagement with theories of the Orient in particular, Cottin grants significant power to the desert asylum to convey the woman's plight. For the purposes of her own argument, she portrays a Middle Eastern landscape which is barren, arid, uninhabitable, hostile, dangerous, and full of savage Arab Bedouins, untrustworthy, corrupt infidels, and followers of a religion which is presented as uncivilized, fanatic, and oppressive of women. Bourdieu states that the power of words is 'nothing other than the *delegated power* of the spokesperson and his speech'.[112] This is indeed the case with Orientalist discourse; the power of the stereotypes produced stems from the power delegated to the Western speaker who disseminates them. *Mathilde* shows Cottin using this transfer of power to the woman's advantage. As a Western writer she has the power to disseminate Orientalist discourse; that discourse, then, in turn, strengthens her announcement of female oppression and empowers her subtle critique of her own society. In other words, partaking in imperialism and drawing on the power to disseminate Orientalist discourse, gives the Western speaker the power to critique the West via presentation of the East. Thus, through the very means of constructing both her natural asylums — drawing on contemporary theories to give them their relevant characteristics — Cottin in fact extends the arguments about women's desire and right to protest against their oppression beyond the boundaries of the asylums themselves. The natural asylum has therefore played a vital role in the conveying of the novels' arguments.

Notes to Chapter 3

1. Jacques-René Tenon, *Mémoires sur les hôpitaux de Paris* (Paris: L'Imprimerie de PH.-D. Pierres, 1788), pp. 219–20.

2. Elaine Showalter, *The Female Malady: Women, Madness and English Culture, 1830–1980* (London: Virago, 1987), p. 10.

3. Helen Small, *Love's Madness: Medicine, the Novel, and Female Insanity, 1800–1865* (Oxford: Clarendon Press, 1996); Sandra M. Gilbert & Susan Gubar, *The Madwoman in the Attic: The Woman Writer and the Nineteenth-Century Literary Imagination* (New Haven & London: Yale University Press, 1979); R. A. Houston, 'Madness and Gender in the Long Eighteenth Century', *Social History*, 27:3 (2002), 309–26.

4. Jane E. Kromm, 'The Feminization of Madness in Visual Representation', *Feminist Studies*, 20:3 (1994), 507–35 (p. 507).

5. Jill Harsin, 'Gender, Class, and Madness in Nineteenth Century France', *French Historical Studies*, 17:4 (1992), 1048–70 (p. 1051).

6. Reproduced from Tenon, p. 218.

7. Jane M. Ussher, *The Madness of Women* (London and New York: Routledge, 2011), p. 8.

8. Ibid., p. 18.

9. Jean-Baptiste Louyer-Villermay, *Traité des maladies nerveuses, ou vapeurs et particulièrement de l'hystérie et de l'hypocondrie* (Paris: Méquignon, 1816), p. 11.

10. Ussher, p. 23.

11. Kromm, p. 507.

12. See: Showalter, *The Female Malady*, pp.8–10, and Margaret Miller, 'Géricault's Paintings of the Insane', *Journal of the Warburg and Courtauld Institutes*, 4:3–4 (1941–1942), 151–63 (p. 151).

13. Showalter, *The Female Malady*, pp. 8–10.

14. Miller, p. 151.

15. A description provided by Laertes in *Hamlet*. See *The Library of Shakespeare II (Tragedies)* (London: Midpoint Press, 2005), II p. 133.

16. Showalter, *The Female Malady*, pp. 1–2.

17. Ibid., p. 3.

18. Anne Amend-Söchting, 'La Mélancolie dans *Corinne*', in *Madame de Staël, Corinne ou l'Italie, 'l'âme se mêle à tout'*, ed. by José-Luis Diaz (Paris: Sedes, 1999), pp. 101–10 (p. 107).

19. Showalter, *The Female Malady*, pp. 3–4. (Original emphasis). C.f.: Shoshana Felman, 'Women and Madness: The Critical Phallacy', *Diacritics*, 5 (1975), 2–12.

20. It should be noted here that women are not necessarily silent by virtue of their being feminine; on the contrary, women have often been stereotyped throughout the ages as garrulous: even in the *Encyclopédie*, 'several contributors remark upon woman's proclivity to talk'. Terry Smiley Dock, *Woman in the* Encyclopédie: *A Compendium* (Potomac, MD: Studia Humanitatis, 1983), p. 86. However, when society represses their voice and refuses to hear their complaints, then, Cottin's female protagonists often turn to madness as a conscious rebellion.

21. Beizer, p. 6.

22. Ibid., p. 6.

23. Showalter, *The Female Malady*, p. 4.

24. Philip W. Martin, *Mad Women in Romantic Writing* (Sussex: The Harvester Press; New York: St. Martin's Press, 1987), p. 1.

25. P. Briquet, *Traité Clinique et thérapeutique de l'hystérie* (Paris: J.-B. Baillière et fils, 1859), p. 190.

26. Sarah Anderson, *Readings of Trauma, Madness and the Body* (New York: Palgrave Macmillan, 2012), p. 3.

27. Jean Laplanche and J.-B. Pontalis, *Vocabulaire de la psychanalyse* (Paris: Presses Universitaires de France, 1971), p. 499.

28. Showalter, *The Female Malady*, p. 123.

29. Ibid., p. 147.

30. Hélène Cixous and Catherine Clément, La Jeune Née, trans. by Betsy Wing (London: I. B. Tauris, 1996), p. 154. See also: Elaine Showalter, 'Hysteria, Feminism, and Gender', in *Hysteria Before Freud*, ed. by Sander L. Gilman (California: University of California Press, 1993), p. 332.

31. Megan Jennaway, *Sisters and Lovers: Women and Desire in Bali* (Lanham, MD: Rowman & Littlefield, 2002), p. 28.

32. Joseph Daquin, *La Philosophie de la folie, ou Essai philosophique sur le traitement des personnes attaquées de folie* (Paris: Librarie Née de la Rochelle, 1792), p. 85.

33. José Monleón, *A Specter is Haunting Europe: A Sociohistorical Approach to the Fantastic* (Princeton: Princeton University Press, 1990), p. 29.

34. Ibid. p. 25.

35. Yannick Ripa, *Women and Madness: The Incarceration of Women in Nineteenth-Century France* (Cambridge: Polity Press, 1990), p. 12.

36. Michel Foucault, *Histoire de la folie à l'âge classique* (Paris: Gallimard, 1972), p. 61.

37. Harsin, pp. 1049–1050.

38. Michel Foucault, *Naissance de la clinique* (Paris: PUF, 1963), p. 37. (Original emphasis.)

39. Foucault, *Histoire de la folie*, p. 440.

40. Ibid., p. 447.

41. Harsin, p. 1053. (Original emphasis.)

42. Foucault, *Histoire de la folie*, p. 449.

43. Ibid., pp. 452–53.

44. Harsin, p. 1050. (My emphasis.)

45. Showalter, *The Female Malady*, p. 2. (My emphasis.)

46. Tili Boon Cuillé, *Narrative Interludes: Musical Tableaux in Eighteenth-Century French Texts* (Toronto: University of Toronto Press, 2005), p. 147.

47. Jean Khalfa, 'Introduction', in Michel Foucault, *History of Madness*, trans. by Jonathan Murphy and Jean Khalfa (Oxford and New York: Routledge, 2009), pp. xv–xvi (p. xviii).

48. Jean Colombier and François Doublet, *Instruction sur la manière de gouverner les Insensés, et de travailler à leur guérison dans les Asyles qui leur sont destinés* (Paris: L'Imprimerie Royale, 1785).

49. Foucault, *Histoire de la folie*, p. 456.

50. Ibid., p. 496. (Original emphasis.)

51. My emphases.

52. Judith Butler, *Gender Trouble* (New York: Routledge, 2007), p. 34.

53. Ibid., p. 185.

54. Jennaway, p. 28.

55. Edward W. Said, *Orientalism* (London: Penguin, 2003) p. 81.

56. Henry Laurens, 'L'Orientalisme des Lumières', in *Penser l'Orient: Traditions et actualité des orientalismes français et allemands*, ed. by Youssef Courbage and Manfred Kropp (Beirut: Presses de l'Ifpo, 2004), pp. 103–28 (p. 112).

57. Barre; Said, pp. 166–97; Rachida El Diwani, *Le Discours Orientaliste de Volney* (Morrisville, NC: Lulu Press Inc., 2008).

58. Conor McCarthy, *The Cambridge Introduction to Edward Said* (Cambridge: Cambridge University Press, 2010), p. 77.

59. Bonaparte even 'cites Volney directly in his own *Campagnes d'Egypte et de Syrie*, dictated during his exile on St Helena'. McCarthy, p. 77.

60. '[U]ne intervention militaire européenne permettra le déclenchement d'un puissant movement

de liberation des peoples de l'Orient'. ['[E]uropean military intervention will open up the way for the beginning of a powerful movement which will liberate the peoples of the Orient]. Laurens, p. 111.

61. Volney, II, pp. 420–21.

62. Barre, p. 41.

63. Volney, I, p. 350. Elsewhere, Volney writes: 'une grande partie du Liban est composée de rochers incultivables, et [...] le terrain même aux lieux cultivés est rude et peu fertile' ['A large part of Lebanon is made up of rock which cannot be cultivated, and [...] even the terrain in the cultivated places is harsh and not very fertile']. (Ibid., II, p. 19), and: 'Palmyre [...] se trouve située si singulièrement, étant en quelque sorte une Isle séparée de la terre habitable, par une mer de sables stériles' ['Palmyra [...] is situated very peculiarly, being like an island separated from habitable land by a sea of sterile sand']. (Ibid., II, p. 265) and describes the 'désert aride et sec' ['arid and dry desert']. (Ibid., II, p. 267). Volney does distinguish some exceptions, noting that certain areas of the desert in Egypt and Syria, particularly those close to the sea, can be cultivated.

64. Ibid., I, p. 348 (Original emphasis).

65. See: Sykes; p.66, and David J. Denby, *Sentimental Narrative and the Social Order in France, 1760–1820* (Cambridge: Cambridge University Press, 1994), p. 60.

66. Joseph F. Michaud and Baptistin Poujoulat, *Correspondance d'Orient 1830–1831*, 8 vols (Brussels: Gegoir, Wouters and Co., 1841), VIII, pp. 59; 91–97; 143.

67. See: Cottin and Michaud's correspondence between 1802 and 1806, in Sykes, pp. 369–87.

68. It is likely that she had. She certainly loved to read travel literature, and had not only read Chardin's *Voyages en Perse*, but had even used it when teaching her cousin's children. Ibid., p. 38.

69. Mme Cottin to Mme Verdier. Ibid., p. 394. Although this letter is not dated, Sykes estimates it to be from around August 1805.

70. '[T]he West's concern for the subservient position of women in the Islamic world does not reflect a genuine compassion for Muslim women, but is just another arrow in the armor of criticism towards Islam'. Erich Kolig, *Conservative Islam: A Cultural Anthropology* (Lanham, MD: Lexington Books, 2012), p. 121. See also: Omero Marongiu-Perria, *En finir avec les idées fausses sur l'islam et les musulmans* (Ivry-sur-Seine: Éditions de l'Atelier, 2017).

71. Barre, p. 334.

72. Said, p. 173.

73. Ibid., p. 170.

74. 'Unlike the deistic God, the Romantic God is typically more dynamic and more immediately present, both in nature and in the self'. Andrew Swensen, 'Theology and Religious Thought', in *Encyclopedia of the Romantic Era, 1760–1850*, ed. by Christopher John Murray, 2 vols (New York: Fitzroy Dearborn, 2004), II, pp. 1128–1130 (p. 1129).

75. Hsu-Ming Teo, *Desert Passions: Orientalism and Romance Novels* (Austin: University of Texas Press, 2012), p. 50. Teo refers here to Nigel Leask, *British Romantic Writers and the East: Anxieties of Empire* (Cambridge: Cambridge University Press, 2000).

76. See: Teo, pp. 50–58; Emily Haddad, *Orientalist Poetics: The Islamic Middle East in Nineteenth-Century English and French Poetry* (London; New York: Routledge, 2017); Sarga Moussa, 'Imaginary Hybridities: Geographic, Religious and Poetic Crossovers in Victor Hugo's "Les Orientales"', in *Hybridity: Forms and Figures in Literature and the Visual Arts*, ed. by Vanessa Guignery, Catherine Pesso-Miquel and François Specq (Newcastle: Cambridge Scholars Publishing, 2011), pp. 280–90; Monica Katiboglu, 'Constructing the Orient: Pierre Loti's Re-interpretations in Aziyadé', in *French Orientalism: Culture, Politics, and the Imagined Other*, ed. by Desmond Hosford and Chong J. Wojtkowski (Newcastle: Cambridge Scholars Publishing, 2010), pp. 135–36.

77. See: Michael J. Call, *Infertility and the Novels of Sophie Cottin* (Newark: University of Delaware Press; London: Associated University Presses, 2002), p. 18.

78. Cottin writes of Atala 'Il y a là-dedans tout ce que j'aime: le désert, la mélancolie, la religion et l'amour'. ['Within it is everything that I love: desert, melancholy, religion and love']. Mme

Cottin to M. Devaines. See: Sykes, p. 338. The similarities with the motifs and topics of her own *Mathilde* are clear.

79. She even teaches English to Julie Verdier's children. See: Arnelle, pp. 209–10.

80. Barre, p. 248 and following.

81. Teo, p. 31.

82. Sykes, p. 368.

83. Ibid., p. 38.

84. Jocelyn Wogan-Browne, 'Chaste Bodies: Frames and Experiences', in *Framing Medieval Bodies*, ed. by Sarah Kay and Miri Rubin (Manchester: Manchester University Press, 1994), pp. 24–42 (p. 39).

85. The story of Mary of Egypt was also know to French audiences because, in twelfth-century France, the life of Mary the Egyptian had been written as a courtly romance. See: Peter F. Dembowski (ed.), *La Vie de Sainte Marie l'Égyptienne: versions en ancien et en moyen français* (Geneva: Droz, 1977); Sylvia Huot, *Madness in Medieval French Literature: Identities Found and Lost* (Oxford: Oxford University Press, 2003).

86. Mme Cottin to M. André Cottin. Sykes, p. 324. This letter is taken from a bundle dated between 1798 and 1800.

87. Abuse even extended as far as uxoricide, according to le Père Duchesne, who writes circa 1790: 'Comment, foutre, encore une femme assassinée par son mari! Cette mode-là prend bougrement' ['What! Damn! Another wife murdered by her husband! This fashion is bloody catching']. Le Père Duchesne, *L'Indignation du Père Duchesne contre l'indissolubricité du mariage, et sa motion pour le Divorce* (Paris: Tremblay, c.1790), p. 1.

88. The full discussion of the Eastern view of women in *Mathilde*, here, resembles aspects of Volney's own discussion of the treatment of women in the Middle East. Cf. Volney, II, p. 443.

89. Meyda Yegenoglu, *Colonial Fantasies: Towards a Feminist Reading of Orientalism* (Cambridge: Cambridge University Press, 1998), p. 1. (Original emphasis).

90. McCarthy, p. 70. (Original emphasis).

91. Yegenoglu, p. 86.

92. Joanna Liddle and Shirin Rai, 'Feminism, Imperialism and Orientalism: the challenge of the "Indian Woman"', in *Women's History Review*, 7:4 (1998), pp. 495–520 (p. 495).

93. Joyce Zonana, 'The Sultan and the Slave: Feminist Orientalism and the Structure of *Jane Eyre*', in *Signs*, 18:3 (1993), pp. 592–617 (p. 593). In fact, the similarities between *Mathilde* and *Jane Eyre* are numerous. They both invite postcolonial readings; they both present patriarchal society's oppression of women; they both tell of the love of two women for the same man; they both present a madwoman from a distant land, locked in a private asylum, who is positioned in opposition to a moral, yet passionate virgin.

94. Teo, p. 57.

95. My emphasis.

96. Original ellipses.

97. The growing feelings of Romantic melancholy which gripped the nation 'coincided with the beginnings of organized archaeological investigation, so that ruins became sentimentally fashionable and technically interesting simultaneously'. McManners, p. 343. The paintings of Hubert Robert, *surnommé* 'Robert des Ruines', became widely popular, inviting the nation to contemplate the transience of human existence. A certain pleasure was to be found in experiencing melancholy emotions whilst gazing upon reminders that 'our own pomp will go down to the same doom'. Ibid., p. 341.

98. Showalter, *The Female Malady*, p. 170.

99. Ibid., p. 172.

100. Ibid., p. 172.

101. Gerald N. Izenberg, 'Seduced and abandoned: The rise and fall of Freud's seduction theory', in *The Cambridge Companion to Freud*, ed. by Jerome Neu (Cambridge: Cambridge University Press, 1991), pp. 25–43 (p. 30).

102. Beizer, p. 6.

103. Showalter, *The Female Malady*, p. 190.

104. My emphasis.
105. Showalter, *The Female Malady*, p. 171.
106. Ibid., p. 175.
107. F. C. Green, *French Novelists From the Revolution to Proust* (London & Toronto: J. M. Dent & Sons Ltd., 1931), p. 39.
108. Stephanie M. Hilger, *Women Write Back: Strategies of Response and the Dynamics of European Literary Culture, 1790–1805* (Amsterdam; New York: Rodopi, 2009), pp. 135–36.
109. Bennett Simon and Rachel B. Blass, 'The Development and Vicissitudes of Freud's Ideas on the Oedipus Complex', in *The Cambridge Companion to Freud*, ed. by Jerome Neu (Cambridge: Cambridge University Press, 1991), pp. 161–74 (p. 163).
110. Butler, pp. 200–01.
111. Astbury, p. 125.
112. Pierre Bourdieu, *Language and Symbolic Power*, trans. by Gino Raymond and Matthew Adamson, ed. by John B. Thompson (Cambridge, MA: Harvard University Press, 1991), p. 24. (Original emphasis.)

CHAPTER 4

❖

Landscapes of Autonomy and Escape: Female Power in Death

[J]'ai des accès de tristesse noire [...]. Je ne puis exprimer l'espèce de malaise qui me poursuit, mon bon ami, je voudrais bien finir d'exister; non, il n'est point d'instant dans la journée où je ne reçusse la mort avec volupté.

[I have bouts of intense sadness [...]. I cannot express the kind of oppression that pursues me, my good friend. I would very much like my existence to end; no, there is no moment of the day when death would not provide a welcome release.]

MME COTTIN to M. Gramagnac.[1]

Rien cependant n'inspire autant d'horreur que la possibilité d'exister uniquement, parce qu'on ne sait pas mourir.

[Nothing, however, inspires so much horror as the possibility of living simply because one does not know how to die.]

MME DE STAËL, De l'influence des passions.[2]

Natural Deathscapes, Untenable Situations, and the Power of Suicide

Literary deaths form a crucial point of analysis in this study of French women's writing of the late eighteenth and early nineteenth centuries for two, interlinked, reasons. Firstly (as was noted in Chapter 2), the period witnessed an increasing fascination with mortality and grief, and, in literature and paintings alike, both women and nature were images frequently associated with this new fascination. Secondly, death, like madness, occurs for the female protagonists of novels of this period in response to the problems faced throughout their lives, and is most often sought and found at the heart of nature. Ultimately, as this chapter will argue, women writers make use of the first point to highlight the second. In other words, they draw on the contemporary fashion for viewing and contemplating a woman's death in natural landscapes and build on this, politicizing those landscapes by turning them into 'landscapes of one's own' in which a woman's oppression might be announced, her autonomy and voice restored, and her escape ensured and eased. With the aid of the natural world, death, like madness, becomes a means of rebellion.

Corresponding with the late eighteenth- and early nineteenth-century fashion for seeking out areas of nature in which death might be contemplated (discussed in

Chapter 2), literature also began to include imagery of natural deathscapes. Where tombs appeared in fiction, they often did so amid natural scenery. This is seen most famously perhaps in Bernardin de Saint-Pierre's *Paul et Virginie* and Chateaubriand's *Atala*, both of which portray a male protagonist burying his lover at the heart of the natural world. As the eighteenth century progressed, nature's role in the deaths of literary heroines became increasingly apparent. Either there were significant links between the natural world and the lifeless corpse of the heroine, or nature itself had a hand in the woman's death. Manon Lescaut succumbs to the harshness of the climate and landscape; Rousseau's Julie dies after jumping into water to save the life of her child; Virginie perishes in the sea, following a shipwreck. When we reach the publication of *Atala* in 1802, the heroine's body is encircled by nature as she lies on the grass, surrounded by mountains, with flowers in her hair. Natural deathscapes also appear in the works of women writers, as we have seen: Krüdener's Valérie places her child's tomb in an island garden and then landscapes this garden to her wishes, and Souza's Adèle buries her husband in her *jardin à l'anglaise*. However, it is women writers' use of nature in their novels to expose and discuss the death of the heroine herself, as well as the situation surrounding it, which forms the main focus of this chapter.

The events which, according to Pasco, typically befall the Romantic hero, are also appropriate for the Romantic heroine,[3] and particularly for the heroines of women's novels between 1789 and 1815:

> [They] eventually decide to settle for the love of a woman (or man) who for one reason or another is inappropriate and unavailable. [...] When reality fails to measure up to their hopes, they fall prey to melancholy. When reason betrays them, they turn to imagination and dreams. Frequently they come to yearn for death.[4]

The initial stages of this process certainly occur for the heroines of the novels analysed in Chapter 1, who find themselves facing unrequited love, disappointment with the reality of arranged and forbidden marriages, and consequent melancholy. The Romantic heroines discussed in Chapter 2 faced further depression when confronted with some of the harshest realities of motherhood and further examples of lost love (albeit of a different kind) at the death or removal of their child. In its analysis of madness as a means of protest, Chapter 3 then outlined how Pasco's subsequent stage — the onset of insanity — also befalls the female heroines of women writers. However, for those characters who (like Amélie Mansfield, Claire d'Albe and Delphine) do not become insane, for those who (like Corinne) only suffer a momentary delusion, or for those who (like Malvina) are cured of their insanity, another, final escape from their problematic, depressive situation must be found. This final escape is sought in death, and thus Pasco's final stage is also fulfilled.[5]

Given the melancholy these women experience throughout their lives, a yearning for death is not unexpected. Indeed, even their creators were known to experience it, as can be seen in the quotations which open this chapter, taken from Cottin's correspondence and Staël's treatise *De l'influence des passions* [*On the influence of the Passions*]. These authors' heroines, Corinne, Claire d'Albe and Malvina, allow themselves to waste away on account of forbidden love, an expectation to conform unquestioningly to restrictive roles, an inability to fit into society, a feeling of personal failure, and melancholic depression. Others choose to end their own lives in a more dramatic fashion: Amélie Mansfield throws herself headlong into the Danube, while Delphine deliberately takes poison. Death as a means of escape was, then, common in women's literature of this period. Whilst the deaths of Corinne, Claire d'Albe and Malvina are not the result of an act of suicide in the same manner as those of Amélie Mansfield and Delphine, their deaths are nonetheless willed, and, as the results of personal choice, they are understood to be brought about by the protagonist's own hand.[6] They can thus be considered a 'quasi-suicide': the term Patrick Vincent employs to describe Corinne's death.[7]

In Staël's discussions on suicide, although she is careful not to praise and encourage it, she explains nonetheless that she views it as understandable and, on occasion, advantageous, as this chapter's second epigraph indicates. Margaret Higonnet's analysis of Staël's works notes that the latter show suicide to be 'a form of mastery'.[8] Particularly influential in drawing this conclusion is Staël's reflection in *De l'influence des passions* that:

> [I]l serait si difficile de ne pas s'intéresser à l'homme plus grand que la nature, alors qu'il rejette ce qu'il tient d'elle, alors qu'il se sert de la vie pour détruire la vie, alors qu'il sait dompter par la puissance de l'âme le plus fort mouvement de l'homme, l'instinct de sa conservation.

> [[I]t would be difficult not to find interesting the man who is greater than nature, when he rejects what he has received from it, when he uses life to destroy life, when he can master by the power of the soul the strongest human action: the instinct of self-preservation].[9]

According to Higonnet, suicide was, in Staël's opinion, a particularly empowering action for women of this period, for the very reason that it constitutes death by the exercising of free will. Firstly, willing to die opens up a possible escape from the oppression and pigeonholing that women suffered, because 'the act — or the idea of suicide — serves as a condition for freedom. [...] The very *thought* of suicide is enabling'.[10] Secondly, actively pursuing death also allows it to become a form of rebellion against domination and imposed limitations, for it restores both voice and autonomy (and consequently power) to a repressed person in much the same way as does madness:

> Staël consistently theorizes and analyzes the social reaction to women's other (unmentionable) 'lack': namely, women's disbarment from speech and other forms of public action. The point is critical. For under the circumstances Staël describes, suicide may ultimately become for a woman the only available means of speaking or acting.[11]

(The fact that suicide also directly contravened the teachings of, and was therefore condemned by, the church made it a still more a rebellious act against the patriarchal order). Staël shows that '[w]here women's words and actions are persistently misread and repressed by men, suicide becomes the final authorizing signature that guarantees transmission of a message'.[12] Ultimately, then, Staël argues that suicide can be seen as a form not only of mastery but also of self-preservation. This occurs in the cases of her own heroines Corinne and Delphine, and also for Cottin's Claire d'Albe and Amélie Mansfield. Arguments that death provides both a voice and a means of establishing autonomy are reinforced by Foucault's and Elisabeth Bronfen's analysis of the understanding of death in this period. According to Foucault, the eighteenth century saw death provide a means of restoring language, creating a moment 'where an otherwise incommunicable secret could be made visible'; indeed, 'Michel Foucault argues that an epistemic shift occurred at the end of the eighteenth century, and sees as one of its traits the rediscovery [...] that knowledge is possible on the basis of death'.[13] In addition to this, according to Bronfen, death in the late eighteenth century is

> constitutive of singularity and offers an escape from a dull, average life. Death emerges as that moment in a person's life where individuality and absolute rarity could finally be attained, in a singular and unique severment from common or collective affiliation.[14]

Death therefore 'ascribes a certain autonomous power to the dying person' in this period, since 'the form of death, which can be shaped by the dying person, comes to determine her or his individuality'.[15] These arguments certainly fit comfortably alongside Higonnet's analysis of Staël's discussions when it comes to examining female suicides.

Staël was not alone in refusing to condemn suicide. Despite (or perhaps because of) its contravention of religious doctrine, suicide had not been unacceptable in the minds of the eighteenth-century *philosophes* with whose writing she often engaged:

> To Enlightenment thinkers like Montesquieu, Rousseau, and Voltaire, Richard and Bridget Smith's decision to end their lives was perfectly reasonable [...]. In an age that [...] put a premium on the rights of the individual, suicide seemed an essential human liberty.[16]

Furthermore, the Romantics in Britain and Germany had been obsessed with the idea of suicide for at least thirty years prior to Staël's own discussions on the subject: 'If dying young was glamorous, suicide was the ultimate thrill. The act showed an enviable, even heroic refusal to accept the banality of the world'.[17] Where the Enlightenment notion of suicide as an essential human liberty meets the Romantic notion of suicide as a heroic refusal to accept the world, we find the rebellious self-willed deaths of post-revolutionary women writers' heroines, desiring to obtain their own freedom and right to self-determination and to reject the ideals imposed upon them.

It seems that the gender oppression which provoked literary suicides reflected that responsible for real suicides. In the late eighteenth century, Siméon-Prosper Hardy, Parisian printer and bookseller, kept a journal in which he recorded details about 'the alleged epidemic of suicide' which seemed to have gripped the nation.[18] The cases mentioned by Hardy (41 attempted and 218 realized suicides in Paris), reveal several interesting points about female suicides. Firstly, 'as many as 16 percent of the women (7 of 45) killed themselves because they were rejected, abandoned, or otherwise thwarted in matters of the heart'; secondly, '22 percent (10 of 45) of the women were abused or deserted by their husbands'; thirdly, '[a]t least two of the female suicides were unmarried and pregnant when they took their own lives'.[19] In fact, '[t]he percentage of women who committed suicide because of problems with persons of the opposite sex, spouses, parents, relatives, children, or friends (23 of 45 or 51 percent) was more than twice the percentage of men', and consequently, Hardy, 'who usually refrained from moralizing, complained more than once about the "deceitfulness and inconstancy" of men and the victimization of [...] women in his time'.[20]

The deaths which occur in the fiction published throughout the eighteenth and nineteenth centuries are most often those of the heroines, not the heroes.[21] Ruth P. Thomas notes that Montesquieu's Roxanne, Prévost's Manon, Voltaire's Mlle de St. Yves, Laclos' Mme de Tourvel, Rousseau's Julie and Bernardin's Virginie all perish in novels published during the eighteenth century.[22] Similarly, Nancy Rogers cites Staël's Corinne, Constant's Ellénore, Sand's Valentine, Stendhal's Madame de Rênal, Sainte-Beuve's Madame de Couaën and several of Balzac's female protagonists as frequent examples of dying heroines in the nineteenth century.[23] Bertrand-Jennings in fact describes Genlis's *Mademoiselle de Clermont* (1802) as unusual for terminating the life of the hero rather than that of the heroine.[24] As the century progressed, an increasing number of female heroines were being described in death, so that by the end of the eighteenth century and the turn of the nineteenth, images of deathbed scenes and of the lifeless bodies of female figures were frequently portrayed. Whilst the corpses of Manon, Roxanne and Julie are not presented at all, in later decades Bernardin's Virginie and Chateaubriand's Atala are described in death in some detail. With the obvious exceptions of those in Gothic tales, such as Jean-Joseph Regnault-Warin's *La Caverne de Strozzi* [*The Cave of Strozzi*], women were presented as both beautiful and tranquil in death, not as cold and decaying. The view of the dead female body was also very common in visual art, indeed, '[t]he pictorial representation of dead women became so prevalent in eighteenth- and nineteenth-century European culture that by the middle of the latter century this topos was already dangerously hovering on the periphery of cliché'.[25] Images of women in death often also included natural scenes. Two engravings which appeared in 1831 of Atala's burial, for example, portray the dead heroine about to be entombed by her lover, and in each case surrounded by a detailed depiction of the natural countryside of North America.[26] Many of the engravings and paintings of Virginie's corpse also featured the landscape and seashore of the Île de France.[27]

One significant reason why the deaths of fictional women outnumber those of men is due to the fact that female protagonists of this era, like their extra-fictional counterparts, were frequently faced with irreconcilable choices. One example of such a choice is presented by Thomas, who argues that women were trapped in an untenable situation, subject to an impossible feminine ideal comprising both 'angel and sexual object'; she elaborates: 'At the same time, she must be virgin and whore. [...] Chastity is required, promiscuity rewarded'.[28] Expecting a woman to fit into extreme binary opposites does not allow for the normality of anything in between. Unsurprisingly, therefore, 'beset by conflicting voices, the woman finds her position untenable'.[29] Either the woman falls from grace, desiring to please masculine society as a sexual object, and wishes to die upon realising her fall, or she is so virtuous that she is compelled to die because she is too good for the world. The heroines discussed by Thomas are the constructs of male authors and all perish in novels published in pre-revolutionary France. Thomas argues that 'in murdering their heroines, they were, wittingly or not, re-enacting the social drama taking place on a larger stage in the eighteenth century'.[30] However, Thomas's notion of an untenable position leading to death proves equally true for the heroines of the novels of post-revolutionary society. Not only is Cottin's Claire d'Albe forced very clearly into the 'angel-whore' situation, as this chapter will outline, but there is also a second, very similar, example of a woman's irreconcilable choice which arises in the later sentimental novels of Cottin, Genlis, Krüdener, Souza and Staël. This is the choice between personal happiness or duty to family and society.[31] Should a woman break free from the constraints of society to pursue her own happiness (whether in terms of love or career) and be punished by society for doing so, or should she conform to the dutiful domestic tasks and marriage expected of her and remain forever unfulfilled? Again, women are described as fulfilling one of two very distinct possibilities, allowing for no middle ground which might incorporate their personal happiness as autonomous individuals, their respect for family, and society's respect for the women in turn. Corinne, Delphine, Claire d'Albe and Amélie Mansfield are all faced with this internal debate, and therefore they, too, find themselves in untenable situations, 'beset by conflicting voices'.[32] The duty-happiness debate occurs commonly in sentimental and early Romantic fiction, because, as Cohen argues '[i]n representing individual happiness in tension with collective welfare, sentimental novels give poetic expression to a central preoccupation of Enlightenment liberalism'.[33] This statement both reinforces Thomas's argument that the drama taking place in society at large is re-enacted within novels, and extends it into the nineteenth century. Caught between the requirements of social duty and the desire for personal contentment, finding that they desire to undertake elements of both but that a choice must be made, Corinne, Delphine, Claire d'Albe and Amélie Mansfield all find, ultimately, that death is the only way out.

It could be argued that such dilemmas are not unique to eighteenth- and nineteenth-century women, and that a woman's position has been irreconcilable for centuries. Beauvoir argues:

> Voilà donc pourquoi la femme a un double et décevant visage: elle est tout ce que l'homme appelle et tout ce qu'il n'atteint pas [...]. Il projette en elle ce qu'il désire et ce qu'il craint [...]. [E]lle est Tout sur le mode de l'inessentiel: elle est tout l'*Autre*. Et, en tant qu'autre, elle est aussi autre qu'elle-même, autre que ce qui est attendu d'elle.

> [This is the reason why woman has a double and duplicitous face: she is everything that man desires and everything that he does not obtain [...]. He projects on to her both what he desires and what he fears. [...] She is Everything

on the inessential plane: she is all the *Other*. And, as the other, she is also other
than herself, other than what is expected of her].[34]

It is this 'otherness' which makes a happy ending impossible, because of the woman's
inability to fulfil two extremes at the same time. However, this dilemma comes to
the fore in the eighteenth century (and consequently in its novels), an era which
famously attempts to force women into the pigeonhole of domestic virtue and duty,
and yet which is replete with sexual *libertinage*. The literary deaths are necessarily
feminine, because it was the woman upon whom the pressure of an ideal was
forced: 'The victim is necessarily a woman, for eighteenth-century society defines
social relationships in terms of the erotic yet, at the same time, distrusts passion
and demands that marriage be based on a more stable and rational foundation'.[35]
Female protagonists of eighteenth- and early nineteenth-century French novels
die, essentially, as a product of the socio-historical era in which their novels are
produced, and the demands that this era makes on women.

This chapter examines the consequences provoked by these demands. Firstly, it
analyses the fatal consequences of the male creation of a feminine ideal in Cottin's
Claire d'Albe. It is argued that, throughout the novel, Cottin writes a landscape
which continually voices the conflicting positions forced upon Claire: angel and
whore. Since nature has been used to highlight her oppression, it is to nature that
Claire turns for assistance as she is dying. Secondly, the chapter addresses the deaths
of the eponymous heroines in Staël's *Corinne* and Cottin's *Amélie Mansfield*, also
making several comparisons with Staël's *Delphine*. Whilst Claire d'Albe attempts,
and ultimately fails, to uphold the domestic feminine ideal and the angelic virtue
expected of her, Corinne and Amélie refuse from the outset to conform to society's
demands. Their untenable situations appear, therefore, once they need the approval
of that society for their love. In other words, they refuse their expected duty and
are, in turn, refused their desired happiness. It will be shown that the 'landscapes
of one's own' which permit Corinne's and Amélie's escape and which restore their
voice and autonomy are centred around bodies of water which act as spaces of
mediation, or middle spaces.

The Death of an Ideal: The Case of *Claire d'Albe*

In 1797, Cottin writes to her cousin Julie Verdier: 'A quelques exceptions près, tous
les hommes n'ont-ils pas dit, d'un accord unanime, ce qu'était la vertu pour les
femmes?' ['With a few exceptions, have not all men stated, in unanimous agreement,
what virtue was for a woman?'].[36] The following year, she writes to Julie in even
more animated statements, directly highlighting the harm that the attitudes of
men, when derived from convention, could cause her sex: 'Parce qu'il est dit dans
les livres que les femmes tourmentent les hommes, cette ridicule espèce se venge
de ces douces créatures en les tourmentant réellement' ['Because it is written in
books that women torment men, this ridiculous species avenge themselves on those
gentle creatures by really tormenting them'].[37] Clearly aware of the domination
and pigeonholing suffered by her sex, months later, Cottin publishes *Claire d'Albe*,

in an era still dominated by the influential thinking of the eighteenth-century men of letters (Rousseau in particular,[38] but also Restif de la Bretonne, Antoine Léonard Thomas, and Bernardin de Saint-Pierre)[39] and of science (including Roussel, Cabanis and La Mettrie), who discussed the qualities and roles of the perfect woman. In this, her first novel, Cottin has her male characters carry out the same process, and, by doing so, she draws the reader's attention to the consequences which arise on account of a projected and enforced womanly ideal.

Nineteen-year-old Frédéric, born and raised in the mountains, arrives in the Loire Valley to take up a position in the factory run by his relative and benefactor, M. d'Albe. There are obvious parallels with Krudener's later novel, *Valérie*. Like Gustave, Frédéric is a young Romantic, with little head for business; both young men create an image in their mind of an 'ideal woman'; both proceed to project this image on to their replacement father's young wife, with whom they soon fall in love; M. d'Albe, like Krüdener's count, believes in traditional gender roles; and the two 'ideal' women, Claire and Valérie, even both name their sons Adolphe. The previous chapter established how the attempt to create a feminine ideal drove Krüdener's Gustave mad, and the consequences of Frédéric's and M. d'Albe's attempts to impose a feminine ideal on to a real woman are no less tragic. Claire is forced into an untenable situation, and both M. d'Albe and Frédéric lose the object of their affection when she seeks the escape and autonomy that death provides. 'No-one remains unscathed', writes Thomas, 'when the inhuman ideal is imposed upon the real world'.[40]

D'Albe's opinions remind the reader starkly of the common eighteenth-century argument that a woman must not concern herself with public affairs, and that nature itself has ordained this:

> [U]ne femme, en se consacrant à l'éducation de ses enfants et aux soins domestiques, en donnant à tout ce qui l'entoure l'exemple des bonnes mœurs et du travail, remplit la tâche que la patrie lui impose [...]. C'est aux hommes qu'appartiennent les grandes et vastes conceptions, c'est à eux à créer le gouvernement et les lois; c'est aux femmes à leur en faciliter l'exécution, en se bornant strictement aux soins qui sont de leur ressort. Leur tâche est facile; car, quel que soit l'ordre des choses [...], elles sont sûres de concourir à sa durée, en ne sortant jamais du cercle que la nature a tracé autour d'elles; car, pour qu'un tout marche bien, il faut que chaque partie reste à sa place. (*C d'A*, p. 28)

> [In devoting herself to the education of her children and to domestic concerns, in providing an example of good behaviour and actions to all around her, a woman fulfils the task that the nation has imposed on her [...]. It is to men that great and vast projects belong. It is up to men to create government and laws. It is up to women to facilitate their execution, by confining themselves strictly to the cares which fall under their remit. Their task is easy; for, whatever the order of things, women are sure to contribute to its duration by never leaving the sphere that nature has drawn up around them. This is because every part must remain in its place in order for the whole to work well.]

D'Albe underlines his wife's perfect compliance with this model: 'contemplez bien cette femme, [...] elle s'est retirée à la campagne, seule avec un mari qui pourrait être son aïeul, occupée de ses enfants, ne songeant qu'à les rendre heureux par sa douceur et tendresse' ['behold this woman, [...] she retired to the countryside, alone with a husband old enough to be her grandfather, busy with her children and thinking only of how to make them happy with her gentleness and tenderness'] (*C d'A*, p. 31).

Immediately following this declaration, the reader learns that the young Frédéric has long since created in his own mind the image of an ideal woman. He comments:

> Dans les premiers beaux jours de ma jeunesse [...] je me créai l'image d'une femme telle qu'il la fallait à mon cœur. Cette chimère enchanteresse m'accompagnait partout; je n'en trouvais le modèle nulle part; mais je viens de la reconnaître dans celle que votre mari a peinte. (*C d'A*, pp. 31–32)

> [In the spring of my youth [...] I created the image of a woman such as I needed her to be in my heart. This enchanting dream accompanied me everywhere; nowhere did I find its incarnation. However, I have just recognized it in the image your husband has painted.]

Frédéric's ideal woman thus also conforms strongly to the eighteenth-century desired stereotype.[41] Furthermore, and unsurprisingly, given the importance that the traditional woman-nature connection had in reinforcing the eighteenth-century image of the ideal woman, when Frédéric conjures a feminine ideal in his mind, he not only creates a model of virtue, happy to be fulfilling her familial duty, he also establishes a link between her and nature:

> [J]e lui donnais des traits; je la douais de toutes les vertus; je réunissais sur un seul être toutes les qualités, tous les agréments dont la société et les livres m'avaient offert l'idée. Enfin, épuisant sur lui tout ce que la nature a d'aimable et tout ce que mon cœur pouvait aimer, j'imaginai Claire! (*C d'A*, p. 69)

> [I gave her features; I endowed her with all virtues; I assembled together in one single being all the qualities and charms which society and books had presented to me. Finally, endowing her with all the graces that nature has to offer and everything that my heart could love, I imagined Claire!]

In fact, Claire and her perfection are so intertwined with nature that, during his walks in the French countryside, Frédéric perceives her everywhere within it:

> [L]a terre ne m'offrait que l'empreinte de vos pas; le ciel, que l'air que vous respiriez; un voile d'amour répandu sur toute la nature m'enveloppait délicieusement, et me montrait votre image dans tous les objets que je fixais. (*C d'A*, p. 73)

> [[T]he Earth offered me only the imprint of your steps, and the sky only the air you breathed. A veil of love spread over all of nature enveloped me delightfully, and showed me your image in everything upon which I gazed.]

In projecting his ideal on to Claire, Frédéric causes her to assume, in his mind, the role of a virtuous angel. Throughout the novel, he refers to her as 'un ange' ['an angel'] (*C d'A*, pp. 30; 58; 97), 'l'image vivante de la divinité' ['the living image of the divinity'] (*C d'A*, p. 97), and 'une déité bienfaisante' ['a benevolent deity'] (*C d'A*,

p. 74). In addition to embodying the divine, Claire is also 'la plus parfaite de toutes les créatures' ['the most perfect of all creatures'] (*C d'A*, p. 97). The apt application of the label 'angel' is even apparent in 'la pureté que contient symboliquement le nom de la première héroïne de Mme Cottin: Claire d'Albe (Claire, de "clarus", blanc brillant, et Albe, de "albus": blanc mat)' ['the purity symbolically contained in the name of Mme Cottin's first heroine: (Claire, from "clarus", bright white, and Albe, from "albus": matt white'].[42] In fact, Claire's name further ties her to the notion of feminine virtue in its intertextual reference to Rousseau's *Julie ou la Nouvelle Héloïse*, for Claire d'Albe is but two letters away from Claire d'Orbe, the name of Julie's cousin in the eminent philosopher's bestseller. It is from Claire d'Orbe, who remains dutiful and faithful to her husband despite being no more in love with him than her namesake is with M. d'Albe, that the notoriously virtuous Julie draws inspiration for her own qualities:

> Un coup d'œil jeté par hasard sur monsieur et madame d'Orbe [...] m'émut plus puissamment encore que n'avaient fait tous les autres objets. Aimable et vertueux couple [...] [l]e devoir et l'honnêteté vous lient: tendres amis, époux fidèles.

> [An incidental glance towards Monsieur and Madame d'Orbe [...] moved me even more powerfully than any of the other objects. Kind and virtuous couple [...] [d]uty and honesty bind you: tender friends, faithful spouses].[43]

Cottin makes a thinly-veiled second comparison to Rousseau's model of feminine virtue when her heroine proves herself willing to risk her life to save that of her child. Claire is walking with her family and Frédéric in the meadows around the Loire, in a scene of seeming perfection: 'Le temps était superbe; les prairies, fraîches, émaillées, remplies de nombreux troupeaux, offraient le paysage le plus charmant' ['The weather was superb; the fresh meadows adorned with flowers were filled with flocks and presented the most charming of landscapes'] (*C d'A*, p. 55). Suddenly a bull charges towards her son, and Claire throws herself in front of the boy (*C d'A*, p. 56) in a manner reminiscent of Julie's sacrifice, when the latter throws herself into a dyke to save her son from drowning.[44] In *La Nouvelle Héloïse,* Julie 'is presented not only as the ideal woman, but also as the ideal human being',[45] and clearly, in both d'Albe's and Frédéric's minds, Claire fits this model well.

Yet, the ideal is doomed because of its very creation. On account of her deemed angelic perfection and virtue, Claire becomes an object of sexual desire, and thus typifies Thomas's angel-whore paradox. Frédéric himself indicates clearly how Claire embodies both angel and object of sexual desire:

> Claire! Seule tu réunis ce mélange inconcevable de décence et de volupté qui éloigne et attire sans cesse, et qui éternise l'amour. Seule tu réunis ce qui commande le respect et ce qui allume les désirs. (*C d'A*, pp. 96–97).

> [Claire! You alone combine this inconceivable mixture of reserve and sensual delight which endlessly draws away and attracts, and which eternalizes love. You alone bring together that which commands respect and that which inflames desire.]

Claire reciprocates Frédéric's love, and, as his repeated advances cause her feelings to intensify, she begins to fall from grace in society. Her friend Elise writes of Frédéric 'c'est lui qui a porté le trouble dans cette âme céleste, et qui a terni une réputation sans tache' ['it is he who has troubled this heavenly soul, and who has tarnished her spotless reputation'] (*C d'A*, p. 144). Elise's statement makes clear that Claire's desirability, like her angelic perfection, derives from Frédéric's mind and is attributed to her according to his whim. In other words, as Beauvoir would later argue in a more general sense: 'Il [l'homme] projette en elle [la femme] ce qu'il désire et ce qu'il craint' ['He [man] projects on to her [woman] what he desires and what he fears'].[46] Frédéric both projects the image of perfect angelic virtue on to Claire and desires her to fall from that virtuous position in order that he might lie with her. He both desires her to be the perfect ideal and fears that she will retain this position, leaving his love unrequited. Simultaneously, he both desires to possess her in her perfection and fears that, if he does so, she will lose it. As a joint application of Beauvoir and Thomas's arguments would indicate, therefore, it is the male creation of the ideal and his desire to possess that ideal which causes Claire to be caught in an untenable situation. Indeed, according to the writer of the introduction to the 1831 edition of *Claire d'Albe*, Frédéric's culpability lies even deeper: 'Un jeune homme, quelque passionné qu'il soit, est toujours inexcusable de choisir le moment où une femme est à moitié morte pour satisfaire son amour. [...] [I]l y a réellement là une brutalité qui fait mal' ['There is no excuse for a young man, no matter how impassioned he may be, to choose the moment when a woman is half dead to satisfy his love. [...] [T]his is a truly painful form of brutality'].[47] The writer refers here to the climax of the novel: Claire has fallen seriously ill as a result of the combined pain she feels at Frédéric's supposed infidelities and her own guilt at loving a man who is not her husband.[48] Frédéric returns to the house, and, despite Claire's weakened state and her reservations, persuades her to make love to him. Cottin herself seems to underline Frédéric's guilt at this moment in her description of Claire as 'oppressée' ['oppressed'] (*C d'A*, p. 147).

Just as Cottin employed nature to highlight Claire's embodiment of the feminine ideal, she also employs it to highlight Claire's embodiment of the unvirtuous woman. Nature begins to lose its charm and idyllic qualities as the heroine feels her own reputation begin to crumble and her guilt to consume her:

> Où est donc la verdure des arbres? Les oiseaux ne chantent plus. L'eau murmure-t-elle encore? Où est la fraîcheur? Où est l'air? Un feu brûlant court dans mes veines et me consume [...]. J'irai lentement errer dans la campagne; là, choisissant des lieux écartés, j'y cueillerai quelques fleurs sauvages et desséchées comme moi, quelques soucis, emblèmes de ma tristesse: je n'y mêlerai aucun feuillage, la verdure est morte dans la nature, comme l'espérance dans mon cœur. (*C d'A*, p. 130)

> [Where, then, is the green foliage of the trees? The birds no longer sing. Does the water still murmur? Where is there any coolness? Where is there any air? A burning fire runs through my veins, consuming me [...]. I will wander slowly in the countryside; there, selecting isolated spots, I will pick some wild flowers which are withered like I am, some marigolds, emblems of my sadness. I will

not combine any leaves with them; greenery is dead in nature, just as hope is dead in my heart.]

Nature is also the site of Claire's ultimate fall from grace: the moment of 'brutalité qui fait mal' ['painful brutality'], when Frédéric's and Claire's sexual passion seals her fate as an adulteress. After 'Claire [...] s'était fait conduire au bas de son jardin, sous l'ombre des peupliers qui couvrent l'urne de son père' ['Claire [...] had arranged to be taken to the bottom of the garden, under the shade of the poplar trees which covered her father's urn'] (*C d'A*, p. 145), she is discovered there by Frédéric, and the couple make love on the site of her father's grave. Cottin employs nature, therefore, to draw attention to both positions forced upon Claire — the angel of virtue and the guilty object of sexual desire — which eventually lead to an untenable situation. As she would continue to do in her later novels, in *Claire d'Albe* Cottin writes a landscape which forms a site from which she might make known the suffering of her sex.

The only escape is death. As Cohen argues, 'Claire dies to mark the impossibility of reconciling the collective good with individual freedom'.[49] She cannot be happy conducting her expected wifely duties and ignoring her passion, but nor can she live freely knowing she has been persuaded to abandon the virtuous position of which she was so proud. However, death provides more than just a simple escape. Thomas asserts, in a manner similar to Higonnet, Bronfen and Foucault, that '[o]nly by choosing death [...] can the woman gain her autonomy'.[50] In life Claire has to endure the desires of others imposed on her, but death permits her to reclaim her voice and exercise her individual right to be heard. Her death becomes rebellion against established male authority, 'an attack on the ideology of fatherhood and phallus',[51] because she uses it to regain autonomy, even to punish. M. d'Albe finds her choice to die even harder to endure than her adultery: 'le seul tort que je ne vous pardonne pas est de souhaiter une mort qui me laisserait seul au monde' ['the only wrong that I cannot forgive you is that of wishing for a death which will leave me alone in the world'] (*C d'A*, p. 152). Frédéric is horrified to find himself condemned by his lover when he hears Claire say: 'il te hait ce cœur plus encore qu'il ne t'a aimé; ton approche le fait frémir, et ta vue est son plus grand supplice; éloigne-toi, va, ne me souille plus de tes indignes regards' ['this heart hates you now more than it has loved you; it trembles at your approach, and the sight of you causes its greatest torture. Go away, go, do not sully me any longer with your unworthy gaze'] (*C d'A*, p. 149). Claire finally makes Frédéric aware of the damage his imposed gaze has caused her. Where, then, Claire had previously submitted to the expectations voiced by men, now, their voices are second to her own: 'la voix de Frédéric ne va plus à son cœur' ['Frédéric's voice no longer reaches her heart'] (*C d'A*, p. 149). After making love to Frédéric in the garden, Claire chooses the path to death, and from this moment on it is she who dictates the subsequent course of events. Frédéric, D'Albe and Elise must simply listen and follow.

All three are desperate to hear her voice; Frédéric 'se tait, il ne respire pas, il étouffe les horribles battements de son cœur pour mieux écouter, il attend la voix de Claire' ['is silent, he holds his breath, he stifles the dreadful fluttering of his heart in order to hear her better, he awaits Claire's voice'] (*C d'A*, p. 150), and Elise says to d'Albe: 'Craignez qu'elle ne s'éteigne avant de nous avoir parlé' ['Fear lest she die before she has spoken to us'] (*C d'A*, p. 153). This desperation not only finally accords Claire's voice the right to be heard, but also places it in a position of great power. She uses this power to influence the future of her relatives. She gives Elise instructions for the care and education of her daughter, thus entrusting her with the future generation: ' "O toi, mon Elise!" continua-t-elle avec un accent plus élevé, "toi qui vas devenir la mère de mes enfants [...] veille sur ma Laure, que son intérêt l'importe sur ton amitié" ' [' "Oh, Elise!" She continued in an elevated tone, "You who will become the mother of my children [...] watch over my Laure, and may your friendship take on her best interests" '] (*C d'A*, pp. 155). For Frédéric, she provides peace by granting the forgiveness for which he longs: 'Enfin, ces mots [...] viennent frapper ses oreilles et calmer ses sens: *Va malheureux, je te pardonne*' ['Finally, these words [...] reach his ears and calm his senses: *Go wretched man, I forgive you*'] (*C d'A*, p. 150; original emphasis). She also issues final instructions to d'Albe, ensuring that he sees the 'effrayante fatalité qui [la] poursuit' ['terrifying destiny which pursues [her]'] (*C d'A*, p. 154) and that he, too, will not condemn Frédéric (*C d'A*, p. 157).

Claire's newfound autonomy and power is to be found amid the nature already employed to draw attention to her oppressive situation. Frédéric finds himself imprisoned by the natural landscape around them until Claire has had the last word: '[I]l ne peut sortir du bois épais qui les couvre sans l'avoir entendue encore une fois' ['He is unable to leave the thick wood covering them without hearing her voice one more time'] (*C d'A*, p. 150). Her voice may be feeble and dying, but it is carried through nature: 'Enfin, ces mots faibles, tremblants, et qui percent à peine le repos universel de la nature, viennent frapper ses oreilles et calmer ses sens' ['Finally, his senses are calmed upon hearing these faint, trembling words, which barely pierce the universal calm of nature'] (*C d'A*, p. 150). This same natural space also reveals the truth of the situation to d'Albe. Not only is it at the heart of nature that he discovers his wife on the point of death, but nature also literally enlightens him as to the tragic consequences of Claire's situation: 'la lune éclairait faiblement les objets [...] à la lueur des rayons argentés qui percent à travers les tremblant peupliers, il aperçoit un objet [...] c'est Claire étendue sur le marbre et aussi froide que lui' ['the moon casts a feeble light on the surrounding objects [...] by the light of its silvery rays which shine through the gaps in the trembling poplars, he makes out an object [...]; it is Claire, just as cold as the marble on which she is lying'] (*C d'A*, p. 151). Therefore, whereas Claire was previously both idealized because of her supposed connection to nature and overwhelmed by her male lover in a site of nature, as she dies, she reclaims the landscape for her own, using it to stage the recovery of her voice and power.

Waterscapes and Death in Staël's *Corinne* and Cottin's *Amélie Mansfield*

'Mme de Staël's novels are concerned with the sufferings of woman in a cold, frivolous, egotistical society',[52] declares Winegarten. *Corinne* provides a prime example of such suffering. When attempting to live in British society, Corinne is unhappy on account of its condemnation of her chosen profession. However, attempting to pursue her own happiness by continuing to write and perform, and by refusing to conform to society's imposed domestic duty results only in further unhappiness. She is ostracized from the society whose expectations she has rejected and consequently forbidden from marrying the man she loves. Caught in an untenable and melancholic situation, unable to live without her talent or her lover, she chooses to waste away, aggrieved by her lot, and uses her death to voice that grievance. To some extent, *Corinne*'s untenable situation underlines the author's own. Whilst society did not forbid Staël her choice of lover on account of her decision to pursue her talents, she did find herself exiled on account of her writing: 'Unhappy when not writing (because it was her *raison d'être*), unhappy through writing (because it brought expulsion and censorship), she was caught in a double bind of freedom and necessity'.[53]

Similarly, 'Amélie's story is one of an angry woman who attempts to isolate herself from patriarchal society, only to be drawn back into it with disastrous results', says Call.[54] Like Corinne, Amélie finds that the path to death is precipitated by an untenable situation forced upon her by an oppressive, aristocratic society. The untenable situation is even underlined for Amélie by her brother Albert, who declares: '[N]e pense jamais qu'ayant été moins sage, tu eusses été plus heureuse: par une faiblesse, une femme accroît ses maux et n'en évite aucun' ['Do not ever think that you would have been happier had you been less virtuous. Through weakness a woman increases her misfortunes and is never spared any] (*AM* III, 128). Amélie was betrothed from birth to her cousin Ernest de Woldemar, for reasons of family fortune. However, as Ernest is violent and capricious, Amélie refuses the marriage and elopes with M. Mansfield, a poet far beneath her social status. As a result, she is cast out from the family, receiving the strongest condemnation from Ernest's mother. Some years later, Ernest, masquerading under the name Henry Semler, seduces the now widowed Amélie. Ignorant of his true identity, she falls deeply in love, and allows Ernest to draw her further and further away from her son. When the truth is revealed, Amélie suffers Mme de Woldemar's terrible retribution, and must also deal with her own guilt at failing in her motherly duty. Amélie is thus caught in an untenable situation on account of the demands of patriarchal society: torn between her desire to free herself from aristocratic tyranny and the need for the approval of that society for her love. The only escape for Amélie, as for Corinne, is death, and so she commits suicide.

In attempting to break free from society's constraints, both Corinne and Amélie bring calamity upon themselves. They seek death because no other route is left open to them, and they ultimately welcome death as it both brings them escape from the oppression and depression they suffer, and also restores to them a means of communicating that suffering. For Amélie and Corinne, as for Julie, Virginie and Manon before them, nature plays a significant role in their deaths. Similarly, as is the case with Rousseau's and Bernardin's heroines, Corinne and Amélie find that the prevailing natural deathscapes they encounter are those centred around bodies of water. *Corinne* and *Amélie Mansfield* each portray three waterscapes which serve to dramatize the heroine's path to death by representing one of three stages on that path. Firstly, water is used to announce the imminent death. The waterscapes both make the heroine aware of the inevitability of her death, and also provide her with the means of communicating to others that death will be the only available option to her. Secondly, waterscapes permit a contemplation of suicide and a consequent near-death experience. As a result, these second waterscapes also permit a view into the afterlife and cause the heroine to realize that death will provide peace, and is therefore something to be looked upon favourably. Finally, a third waterscape is employed to permit the heroine's actual death and her consequent transition to the 'other side'. In all three stages, the waterscapes also underline society's responsibility for bringing the heroine to the point of death. The waterscapes thus restore to women a means by which they might communicate their oppression and its cause.

A connection between woman and water, like that between woman and nature, has long been established in literature, philosophy, and mythology in societies throughout the world, 'les propriétés des fluides étant, historiquement, abandonnées au féminin' ['the properties of fluids being, historically, surrendered to the feminine'].[55] Bachelard remarks that water possesses 'un caractère profondément féminin' ['a profoundly feminine nature]', and also that '[l]es formes féminines naîtront de la substance même de l'eau' ['[f]rom the very substance of water, feminine forms are born'].[56] The strong connection arises partially because of the association of water with the amniotic fluid of pregnancy, and the reminder that '[l]'eau nous porte. L'eau nous berce. L'eau nous endort. L'eau nous rend notre mère' ['[w]ater carries us. Water cradles us. Water sends us to sleep. Water gives us back our mother'].[57] French philosophy has also established a woman–water connection based on the homophony of 'mer' ['sea'] and 'mère' ['mother']. Both Julia Kristeva and Cixous have written on this subject.[58] The grammatical gender of the words 'eau' ['water'] and 'mer' ['sea'] and of the names of most French rivers has also provoked a similar philosophical-linguistic connection.[59] In addition, the woman–water relationship often has the notion of spiritual purification at its heart,[60] or that of governance, custodianship and provision, since water-carriers have traditionally been women. Finally, the connection is made at the level of power: both women and water have been thought to provide an unmasterable force.[61] It is appropriate, therefore, to see waterscapes used in women's literature both to voice women's concerns and to restore autonomy and power to the female protagonist.

There is also a common link drawn in literature, philosophy, mythology, and ancient tradition between water and death. Bachelard argues that '[l]'imagination du malheur et de la mort trouve dans la matière de l'eau une image matérielle particulièrement puissante et naturelle' ['[t]he imagination of misfortune and death finds an especially powerful and natural material image in the substance of water'].[62] 'L'eau' ['Water'], he states, 'communique avec toutes les puissances de la nuit et de la mort' ['communicates with all the powers of night and death'].[63] This ability to communicate powerfully renders a waterscape a highly suitable medium for restoring a woman's lost voice at the moment of her death. Also relevant for the present argument is Bachelard's description of the 'tragique appel des eaux' ['tragic summons of the waters']; he states that '[q]ui joue avec l'eau perfide se noie, veut se noyer' ['[h]e who plays with treacherous water drowns and wants to drown'].[64] There are, therefore, 'des images où l'eau dans la mort nous apparaît comme un *élément désiré*' ['certain images where water in death appears as a *desired element*'], and the summons of this element is so powerful that 'il peut nous servir à déterminer des types de suicides bien distincts' ['it can assist when it comes to determining certain distinct types of suicide'].[65] It thus becomes highly appropriate for waterscapes to form the natural areas in which female literary protagonists might contemplate the benefits of suicide.

In his discussion of fluvial myths, Simon Schama associates waterscapes not only with death but also with rebirth,[66] a dual image which owes its origins to the ancients, who associated the river Nile with fertility and plenty, but also with the cult of Osiris, the god of the underworld and the dead. Therefore, 'with Seneca, Pliny, Plutarch, Strabo, and Diodorus, an entire genre of Nile literature — a rich slurry of myth, topography, and history — inaugurated the Western cult of the fertile, fatal river'.[67] Furthermore, the notion of reaching the afterlife by crossing a body of water surfaces in many European traditions, both northern and southern — including Greco-Roman,[68] Norse,[69] and Celtic[70] — and also in Eastern belief systems.[71] Indeed, 'Bruce Lincoln has gathered convincing evidence for an underlying Indo-European concept of a guide to the Afterworld, known as the "ferryman of the dead"'.[72] The rivers, cascades and waterways which appear in *Corinne* and *Amélie Mansfield* are, therefore, clear indications not only that the heroines are approaching death, but also that there will be a future, more hopeful life awaiting them on the other side. Thus, whilst society is guilty of killing the heroine, nature provides the peaceful afterlife.

Bachelard, in his discussion of *Hamlet*, writes: 'L'image synthétique de l'eau, de la femme et de la mort ne peut pas se disperser' ['The synthetic image of water, woman, and death cannot be broken up'].[73] This same unbreakable three-way connection captured the imagination of eighteenth- and early nineteenth-century France, as did the Shakespearian play which prompted it. The period witnessed a fascination not only with Ophelia's madness, as was seen in the previous chapter, but also with her death: suicide by drowning in a brook. According to Helene E. Roberts, '[m]any of the Romantic paintings of death were inspired by literature. William Shakespeare's Ophelia is one such character depicted in both French and English iconography'.[74] Two of the most famous French sentimental heroines of the day, Rousseau's Julie and Bernardin's Virginie, also die as a result of falling into bodies of water. In addition, Staël's Corinne contemplates drowning herself in a river, Delphine contemplates death at the edge of a waterfall, Cottin's Amélie Mansfield throws herself into a river, and Claire d'Albe resolves to die on an island surrounded by a large stream (when she is found, it is at first believed that she has already perished here). In fact, in eighteenth-century France, water was not only frequently associated with the (often voluntary) deaths of literary women, but also with those of real women. Water became a common way to enable female suicides at this time: for example, 'The Seine offered unhappy Parisians a simple way to kill themselves [...]. A disproportionate number of women attempted suicide in this way'.[75] Comparing the means of suicide employed by each sex, Hardy's eighteenth-century journal noted that men tended to shoot themselves, whilst '[a] third of the women [...] chose the arguably less violent and frequently more convenient death by drowning'.[76]

The first descriptions of waterscapes in *Corinne* and *Amélie Mansfield* to be analysed here are those which announce the heroines' forthcoming death, and voice the fact that society's oppression is responsible for that death. In Corinne, it is the Venetian waterways which are endowed with the power of communication and which portend Corinne's fate. Preparing her reader for these announcements, Staël clearly establishes nature's ability to communicate messages to the beholder early in her novel, even before the couple reach Venice:

> 'Ne trouvez-vous pas', dit Corinne en contemplant avec Oswald la campagne dont ils étaient environnés, 'que la nature en Italie fait plus rêver que partout ailleurs? On dirait qu'elle est ici plus en relation avec l'homme, et que le créateur s'en sert comme d'un langage entre la créature et lui'. (*C*, p. 141)

> ['Do you not find', said Corinne, as she and Oswald gazed at the countryside around them, 'that nature in Italy makes you dream more than anywhere else? Here nature seems more closely related to mankind, and the Creator seems to use it as a language between his creatures and himself'.]

In the later Venice episode, therefore, Staël is able to draw on the foundations she has built, and carry the landscape's power of communication further, using it to make specific and targeted proclamations, both to Corinne and, once the latter has accepted them, to others on Corinne's behalf.

From the moment of arrival into the floating city, Corinne is aware of the fatal announcement that the landscape imparts. We are told: 'Un sentiment de tristesse s'empare de l'imagination en entrant dans Venise' ['a feeling of sadness captures the imagination on entering Venice'] (*C*, p. 420), and Corinne asks Oswald: 'D'où vient la mélancolie profonde dont je me sens saisie en entrant dans cette ville? N'est-ce pas une preuve qu'il m'y arrivera quelque grand malheur?' ['Where does the profound melancholy that I've felt since arriving in this city come from? Is it not proof that some great tragedy will befall me?'] (*C*, p. 421). She comprehends the revelation of her fate and ensures that Oswald hears it too: 'croyez-moi, les fleurs de la vie sont pour toujours jetées derrière moi' ['believe me, the flowers of life have, once and for all, been cast behind me'] (*C*, p. 422). She is able to do so visually as well as verbally, for the presentiment that the Venetian landscape inspires in her seems to bring the shadow of death across her at that very moment, in a manner which is both visible and tangible for Oswald: 'Oswald sentit ses mains froides dans les siennes, et une pâleur mortelle couvrait son visage' ['Oswald felt her cold hands in his, and her face assumed a deathly pallor'] (*C*, p. 422). As long as she remains in Venice, the comprehension of impending death strengthens, and it is the landscape which both inspires this and transposes it on to her body for others to read the same message: 'le spectacle de la nature, qui porte à la rêverie, redoublait encore sa peine. [...] Les tourments de son âme ne se trahissaient plus que par sa mortelle pâleur' ['the natural scenery, which provokes reverie, intensified her suffering. [...] Her soul's torments were now only revealed through her deathly pallor'] (*C*, p. 474).

Intimations of death surround Corinne in the Venetian landscape nowhere more than on its waterways: 'Ces gondoles noires qui glissent sur les canaux ressemblent à des cercueils [...], à la dernière [...] demeure de l'homme. [...] On dirait que ce sont des ombres qui glissent sur l'eau' ['These black gondolas which glide on the canals resemble coffins [...], man's final resting place. [...] They are like shadows gliding on the water'] (*C*, p. 421). Once the gondolas have filled Corinne's mind with images of ghostly shadows, death and coffins, the heroine then continues to see such images all about her in Venice, and knows that they portend her own demise:

> Une fois, en entrant à l'église de Saint-Marc [...], elle se retournait, elle aperçut un cercueil qu'on apportait dans l'église. A cet aspect elle chancela, ses yeux se troublèrent, et, depuis cet instant, elle fut convaincue par l'imagination que son sentiment pour Oswald serait la cause de sa mort. (*C*, p. 472)

> [Once, as she entered Saint Mark's church [...], she turned round and saw a coffin being brought inside. At this sight, she staggered, her vision became cloudy, and, from that moment, her imagination convinced her that her feelings for Oswald would be the cause of her death.]

In making this connection between the gondolas (aspects unique to the Venetian waterscape) and death, Staël draws on previous comparisons. As Marie-Madeleine Martinet explains, 'à Venise, Mme de Staël adapte l'épigramme de Goethe sur la gondole comme cercueil' ['In the Venice episode, Mme de Staël adapts the epigram in which Goethe likens the gondola to a coffin'].[77] Staël's choice to make the Venetian landscape the natural herald of Corinne's fate is therefore apt because of the pre-established perception of this region in eighteenth-century France which stemmed from the influence of the German Romantic writer. Goethe's *Venetian Epigrams*, and in particular 'la V et la VIII, sur les gondoles, thématisent l'association souvent reprise de ce bateau et d'un cercueil' ['the fifth and eighth epigrams, on the gondolas, establish the common comparison of this boat to a coffin'].[78] In fact, the 'échos goethéens de *Corinne*' ['the echoes of Goethe in *Corinne*'] [79] themselves serve as a bridge, influencing the works of other Romantic writers and later novelists. Where Staël draws on the work of Goethe, Byron draws on Staël. Byron writes: 'Didst ever see a Gondola? [...] / It glides along the water looking blackly. / Just like a coffin clapt in a canoe',[80] and 'Byron's version of the gondola owes most to Madame de Staël's *Corinne*'.[81] The self-same image also later arises in the work of Staël's compatriot Chateaubriand, who writes in his 1849–50 *Mémoires d'outre tombe* that 'les gondoles ressemble à des bières' ['the gondolas resemble coffins'],[82] and in Thomas Mann's 1912 novella *Der Tod in Venedig* [*Death in Venice*] which, in turn, draws inspiration from Byron's *Beppo*.[83]

As well as announcing Corinne's inevitable death, Staël's waterways and gondolas simultaneously highlight for the reader the role that society plays in causing that death. They achieve this, firstly, by providing the ominous setting for the events, put in place by external society, which commence the decline to the dénouement itself:

> Dans *Corinne* [...] l'épisode vénitien, avec son écho de Goethe, se place dans
> la deuxième moitié du roman, partie du déclin, après les épisodes de Rome et
> de Naples et en prélude au second voyage et à la mort. Le thème qui était une
> épigramme chez Goethe a pris dans *Corinne* son sens de mort soutenu par sa
> place et son rôle structurel, maintenant celui d'amener la conclusion funèbre.
> Venise devient alors une fin de voyage tandis qu'elle était un début.

> [In *Corinne* [...] the Venetian episode, with its echoes of Goethe, takes place
> during the second half of the novel, the decline: after the episodes in Rome and
> Naples, and before the second voyage and Corinne's death. The theme which,
> for Goethe, was merely epigrammatic, takes on a truly deathly dimension in
> *Corinne* on account of its place and structural role within the novel: that of
> leading towards the fatal conclusion. Venice therefore becomes the end of a
> journey whereas it was originally a beginning].[84]

It is here that Oswald leaves Corinne, ending their relationship (and, consequently,
also their happiness) forever. Forbidden from continuing his Romantic wanderings,
he must instead join his regiment and undertake the stereotypically masculine role
of a soldier. This is soon to be followed by an obligation to assume his role as a
husband, wedding Lucile, the woman that society has marked out for him. On
the canals, Corinne reveals the pain that Oswald's announcement brings her: 'Dès
qu'ils furent ensemble dans la gondole, Corinne, dans son égarement, dit à lord
Nelvil "Hé bien, ce que vous venez de m'apprendre est mille fois plus cruel que
la mort"' ['As soon as they were together in the gondola, Corinne, in a state of
turmoil, said to Lord Nelvil "Indeed, the information you have just imparted to
me is a thousand times more cruel than death"'] (*C*, p. 437). As the painful events
triggered by this parting begin to unfold, Corinne does in fact successfully will
her own death. Philippe Monnier describes the eighteenth century's vision of the
gondola as a 'frail, unsteadfast symbol of love's coffin'.[85] This image suits *Corinne*
very well, for not only do the Venetian gondolas (as we have seen) inspire visions
of Corinne's literal coffin, they also firmly provide the scene for 'love's coffin', and,
ultimately, it is 'love's coffin' which eventually begets Corinne's real coffin.

Secondly, Staël's waterways and gondolas also highlight society's role in causing
Corinne's death by, themselves, becoming agents of society's will. It is a gondola
which irrevocably removes Oswald from Corinne's side, carrying him away from
her towards his political and social duty, forever precluding the realisation of a
union between them:

> [L]orsque Oswald lui eut dit que la gondole viendrait le prendre à trois heures
> du matin, et qu'elle vit à sa pendule que ce moment n'était pas très éloigné, elle
> frémit de tous ses membres; et sûrement l'approche de l'échafaud ne lui aurait
> pas causé plus d'effroi. (*C*, p. 440)

> [When Oswald told her that the gondola was coming for him at three o'clock in
> the morning, and when she noticed on her clock that this moment was not far
> off, her whole body trembled. Surely even the approach of the scaffold would
> have provoked less terror in her].

The comparison of the gondola to the scaffold is striking, and not only because it
marks the second time the gondola is likened to a macabre object. Whilst the coffin

is a passive receptacle for those already dead, the scaffold plays an active role in causing death, and, furthermore, does so on the orders of society. Yet, the gondola appears even more threatening than the scaffold itself. Rather than providing a swift death, it glides silently, slowly nearer, forcing Corinne to look on as it executes society's orders to remove Oswald from her, thus triggering unendurable pain. She does indeed watch his departure in the gondola, until he disappears out of sight.

In *Amélie Mansfield*, water also announces the heroine's fatal future. This announcement is made to her lover Ernest, in a moment of hallucination whilst he is ill with fever.

> [I]l me semblait que toute cette eau s'était formée des larmes d'Amélie... Un frisson m'a saisi... cette eau était glacée, glacée comme la mort. Je vois bien qu'Amélie n'existe plus, me disais-je, et je sentais remonter vers mon cœur quelque chose qui le serrait en le perçant. (*AM* IV, 6–7)

> [It seemed to me as though all this water were formed of Amélie's tears... I shivered uncontrollably... This water was icy, icy as death. I told myself I could see clearly that Amélie was no longer alive, and I felt something rising up to my heart, tightening around it and piercing it].[86]

Thanks to the vision, Ernest knows, even in his delirious state, that once he reveals his true identity to Amélie and she is faced with the retribution of society, the situation will destroy her. Whilst clearly an illusion, the pool of icy tears foreshadows Amélie's fate highly accurately, for she will meet her death in the icy waters of the Danube. Bachelard argues that water has a significant connection for the death of women because '[l]'eau est le symbole profond, organique de la femme qui ne sait que *pleurer* ses peines et dont les yeux sont si facilement "noyés de larmes"' '[[w]ater is the profound, organic symbol of the woman who can only *cry* over her sorrow and whose eyes are so easily "drowned in tears"'].[87] This is particularly pertinent for our analysis of *Amélie Mansfield*. Amélie cannot fully put into words the pain caused by patriarchal society's oppression, the ways in which it has affected her past, or the injustice which will bring about her downfall. Instead, it is water, which, in a vision, transforms into her tears, that voices injustice on her behalf, and which symbolizes her pain and announces her consequent death by drowning.

The second step on both Corinne's and Amélie's path to death involves the allaying of their fear of death, and takes place during a near-death experience enabled by another waterscape. This near-death experience permits the heroines to contemplate the 'other side', a commonly-used term which highlights the fact that 'relationships between the living and the dead have been spatialized in modern western society', in which we frequently articulate 'an "imagined geography" of the living and the dead'.[88] Both *Corinne* and *Amélie Mansfield* spatialize the worlds of the living and dead; both present these two realms as separated by a clearly definable border, and both use bodies of water to construct those borders. In Staël's novel, the two worlds are imagined to occupy the opposing banks of the same river. In Cottin's novel, the border is to be found at a tumultuous waterfall. Both Corinne and Amélie feel drawn towards death whilst hovering on these waterscape-boundaries.

Hidden in the shadows, Corinne observes Oswald and Lucile at a ball on Oswald's estate. She then wanders across his land until she comes to a river. Gazing upon it, she contemplates suicide, and, as she does so, she is permitted a vision of the world of the dead. It is not unusual that Staël should present such an image; according to Bronfen, '[i]t is a literary convention of the nineteenth century that in their last moments the dying have a vision of the after-life'.[89] Although Corinne does not throw herself into the water, the serious consideration of ending her life suffices nonetheless for her to gain, in this moment, a window onto the afterlife and the imagined world of the dead. Amid the natural scenery of Oswald's estate, the worlds of the living and dead are juxtaposed and the boundary between the two begins to dissolve.

> Le château était placé sur une hauteur, au pied de laquelle coulait une rivière. Il y avait beaucoup d'arbres sur l'un des bords, mais l'autre n'offrait que des rochers arides et couverts de bruyère. Corinne en marchant se trouva près de la rivière; elle entendit là tout à la fois la musique de la fête et le murmure des eaux. La lueur des lampions du bal se réfléchissait d'en haut jusqu'au milieu des ondes, tandis que le pâle reflet de la lune éclairait seul les campagnes désertes de l'autre rive. On eût dit que dans ces lieux, comme dans la tragédie de Hamlet, les ombres erraient autour du palais où se donnaient les festins. L'infortunée Corinne, seule, abandonnée, n'avait qu'un pas à faire pour se plonger dans l'éternel oubli. 'Ah!' s'écria-t-elle, 'Si demain, lorsqu'il se promènera sur ces bords [...] ses pas triomphants heurtaient contre les restes de celle qu'une fois pourtant il a aimée, n'aurait-il pas une émotion qui me vénérait, une douleur qui ressemblerait à ce que je souffre'? (C, p. 499)

> [The manor was situated on higher ground, with a river running below. On one bank of the river there were many trees, but on the other were only arid rocks covered with heather. As Corinne walked on, she found herself by the river, where she could hear both the music from the ball and the murmuring of the water. The light from the lanterns at the ball reflected from above across to the middle of the water, whilst only the pale reflection of the moon illuminated the deserted landscape on the opposite bank. Just like in the tragedy of Hamlet, it was as though ghosts wandered around the palace in which festivities were taking place. Miserable, abandoned and alone, Corinne had only to take one more step to throw herself headlong into eternal oblivion. 'Oh!' She cried. 'If tomorrow, when walking along these banks [...] his triumphant steps were to stumble upon the remains of the woman he once loved, would he not revere me, would he not suffer a similar pain to my own?']

In addition to the clear link drawn by Staël between water, death and the female figure, and to the reference to Hamlet in this respect (echoed, as we have seen, over a century later by Bachelard) two significant points must be noted here regarding Corinne's vision and the role of nature in creating it. Firstly, contrast between an oppressive society which brings Corinne to the point of destruction and a natural world which provides hope that life will continue beyond that destruction is achieved through the comparison of two lights and two sounds. At the river's edge, Corinne hears the noise of the gathering at the ball behind her and the sound of murmuring water in front of her. Society pushes her forwards towards destruction, whilst nature draws her onwards towards the afterlife. Similarly, the lamplight illuminating the ball is reflected in the water, and the natural light of the moon lights up the *autre rive*. The lights, therefore, indicate the same progression: society brings Corinne to the water's edge, and so it is the light of society which illuminates the river, focusing Corinne's attention on the possibility of suicide, whilst the lunar light illuminates the afterlife. The moon is an appropriate light to guide the way to the world of the dead, being only a dead light source itself, a mere reflection of the light of the sun.

Secondly, we must consider the importance of the river itself. According to Mary Murray, a 'near death experience seems to take place in liminal 'other worldly' space. It is a space [...] that appears to lie somewhat betwixt and between the land of the living and the land of the dead'.[90] The importance of the boundary between antithetical spaces is also highlighted by Mieke Bal, who states that 'a special role is played by the boundary between two opposed locations. [...] The shop as a transitory place between outside and inside, the sea between society and solitude [...] function as mediators'.[91] The boundary space in Staël's *Corinne* between the two opposing spaces of the living and the dead is not the sea, but rather another natural space of water. A river is a particularly relevant choice of inter-world mediator. As the above discussion of fluvial myths has indicated, the river is a motif long associated with the liminal space between the worlds of the living and dead. Staël was certainly aware of the ancient Greek and Roman belief that these two worlds were separated by the River Styx, and that the ferryman, Charon, must be paid to carry the dead across. She draws our attention to the Styx's function as a gateway to the underworld earlier in *Corinne* (C, p. 60), when discussing the work of Dante. Staël was also aware of another celebrated myth associated with the Styx: that of the waters rendering Achilles invulnerable when he was dipped into them, the only remaining vulnerable part being the heel by which he was held and which consequently was not washed by the river. In *Reflexions sur le suicide*, Staël writes of being able 'dans le Styx, s'y rendre invulnérable' ['in the Styx, to render oneself invulnerable'].[92] The river on Oswald's estate conveys a twofold symbolic meaning in *Corinne*, therefore, because of its mythological echoes. In providing a window on to the figurative other side, the river indicates to Corinne that there is another life awaiting her, thus allaying her fears. This figurative window can be visually traversed because nature provides a light to illuminate what lies beyond. Together, the river and moon bring comfort in the death that society has ordered. The river's strong resemblance to the Styx also reminds Corinne that in death, in crossing this symbolic boundary, she will become invulnerable, beyond the reach of the pain society causes. In other words, crossing the river will not only provide an escape from an untenable situation to a happier one, it will also restore power to the heroine, who has hitherto been oppressed and silenced.

Contrary to the tranquil river of *Corinne,* in Cottin's *Amélie Mansfield*, the waterscape which permits a near-death experience is harsh and savage, and constitutes an example of nature's unmasterable force. Nonetheless, it still permits the heroine to contemplate the peace she would experience upon death, and to contrast this with the turmoil she experiences in life. Accompanied by Ernest,

Amélie visits a grotto in the Swiss mountains. She hurries towards a waterfall by the grotto specifically in order to hide her disquiet at Ernest's declarations of love and simultaneous reminders of obstacles to their union. She is thus brought to the space of her near-death experience in much the same manner as Corinne: by the obstacles created by an oppressive society. On arriving at the waterfall, Amélie comes perilously close to plunging to a violent death. The description of the power and hostility of the natural landscape leave us in no doubt that Amélie would have died had she fallen:

> Je marchais très vite; je suis arrivée la première, et pour mieux voir l'effet du torrent qui bouillonne entre deux roches vives taillées à pic, je me suis appuyée le corps en avant sur le tronc d'un vieux pin posé sur deux pieux pour servir de balustrade. Il était pourri sans doute: M. Semler, l'ayant vu s'ébranler, s'est élancé vers moi, m'a saisie par le milieu du corps, et m'a arrachée à une mort certaine, car l'arbre est tombé au même instant avec fracas dans le gouffre. (*AM* II, 167–68)

> [I walked very quickly and so arrived first. In order to see the effect of the torrent which churned between two sharp, vertically cut rocks, I leaned forward on the trunk of an old pine tree placed across two posts to form a railing. The pine was undoubtedly rotten, and M. Semler, seeing it give way, rushed towards me, seized me around the waist and snatched me from certain death, because, at that very moment, the tree fell with a great crash into the gorge.]

The border between life and death is represented in this instance by the pine tree over the waterfall, yet nature permits that border to become permeable: the power of the waters have weakened the tree, and it crumbles away, leaving the way to death clear. The unmasterable force of nature at the waterfall becomes, for a moment, a potential space of rebellion for Amélie. Ernest, however, acts to prevent Amélie leaving the earthly realm. It soon transpires that Amélie would have been more grateful to the natural landscape for claiming her life, and thus permitting her desired rebellion, than she is to Ernest for saving it. Immediately after this incident, she declares: '[U]ne prompte mort m'eût épargné bien des douleurs, et le sort que je prévois me la fera regretter souvent' ['A swift death would have spared me much suffering, and the fate that I see ahead of me will often make me regret that I did not die'] (*AM* II, 169). Furthermore, the near-death experience made possible by nature allows Amélie to comprehend fully what would happen if she were to perish: she would suffer no longer. She compares this lack of suffering with the painful future she sees unfolding before her because of her untenable situation. Whereas the human hand that saves Amélie's life brings her nothing but disquiet, the tumultuous waterscape ironically provides a glimpse of peace, and thus permits Amélie to contemplate with equanimity the possibility of death. From this point on, she positively welcomes it: '[J]e n'ai pas peur des tombeaux; tout ce qui est insensible et mort me fait envie; je voudrais être cette pierre insensible, ce monument glacé, cette ruine qui s'écroule' ['I am not afraid of tombs. I envy everything which is dead or incapable of feeling. I wish to be this unfeeling stone, this icy monument, this crumbling ruin'] (*AM* IV, 130–31). A lack of fear of death after a near-death experience is a common reaction:

> Once back in the world of the living, many, if not most, of these other worldly travellers report profound psychological or spiritual changes affecting their sense of themselves and their personal inner space. Those experiencing [near death experiences] often say that they have lost their fear of death.[93]

Amélie has lost her fear because she now understands what nature has attempted to show her: that death will provide the rebellion she seeks, a path to solve her pain and problems, and the only escape from the untenable situation that society has forced upon her. Suffering her own *mal du siècle,* after this incident Amélie not only exhibits suicidal thoughts in the manner of a Romantic hero, she eventually does take her own life — in another waterscape.

The near-death experiences which occur at waterscapes in both *Corinne* and *Amélie Mansfield* are highly reminiscent of a passage from Staël's *Delphine,* which also involves a watery landscape, and in which the heroine also admits her desire for her life to end: 'je vous le dis, l'action de vivre m'agite trop' ['I tell you, the act of living upsets me too greatly'] (*D* II, 229). She concludes that 'il ne faut pas lutter plus longtemps contre le malheur' ['I must no longer struggle against unhappiness'] (Ibid.). Yet, she does not commit suicide at this point; rather, she resolves to enter a convent. Although this initially seems (as it does for Souza's Eugénie, the desperate nun of *Adèle de Sénange*) to be but another way of ending her life, the situation is not so simple:

> Les anciens croyaient que les âmes qui n'avaient pas reçu sur la terre les honneurs de la sépulture, erraient longtemps sur les bords du fleuve de la mort; il me semble qu'une situation presque semblable m'est réservée. Je serai sur les confins de cette vie et de l'autre. (*D* II, 230)

> [The ancients believed that souls which had not received burial rites on earth would long wander on the banks of the river of death; it seems to me that an almost identical situation awaits me. I will remain on the border between this life and the next.]

In *Corinne,* Staël would later push this image further, writing her own Stygian waterscape which might permit her heroine to contemplate death itself with equanimity. In *Delphine,* the image of the border river permits the heroine to perceive that entering the convent would only place her in limbo. Staël thus highlights yet another untenable situation faced so often by women of her era: the pressure to enter a convent when unable to marry. Delphine's foresight here proves only too accurate, and her retreat to the life of a nun does indeed only trap her further. She is neither a part of the world, nor truly apart from it: prevented by her vows from marrying Léonce once his first wife has died, but unable to drive her love for him out of her mind. Truly belonging with neither the living nor the dead, she walks the line between the two worlds. This is because, as Delphine herself states, she has not received burial rites: inevitably so, as she is not yet dead. Staël therefore implies that true escape can only be found in death itself, and Delphine's eventual escape, like that of Amélie, will be suicide.

The necessity of death is made clear as Delphine gazes over the edge of the tumultuous cataract by which she contemplates these issues:

[M]es promenades rêveuses me conduisirent jusqu'à la chute du Rhin près de Schaffhouse; je restai quelques temps à la contempler, je regardais ces flots qui tombent depuis tant de milliers d'années [...]. De tous les spectacles qui peuvent frapper l'imagination, il n'en est point qui réveille dans l'âme autant de pensées. Il semble qu'on entend le bruit des générations qui se précipitent dans l'abîme éternel du temps. [...] 'Oh!' M'écriai-je, 'd'où vient donc que j'attache à mon avenir tant d'intérêt et d'importance? Voilà l'histoire de la vie! Notre destinée, la voilà! Des vagues engloutissant des vagues, et des milliers d'êtres sensibles, souffrant, désirant, périssant, comme ces bulles d'eau qui jaillissent dans les airs et qui retombent. [...] Qui donc entendra mes cris? est-ce la nature?' (*D* II, 229)

[Strolling and musing, I found myself at the waterfall on the Rhine, near Schaffhouse. I stayed there a little while, contemplating it; I gazed at the torrent which had been cascading for thousands of years [...] Of all the sights which strike the imagination, there is none which arouses so many thoughts in the soul. It seems as though you can hear the sound of generations falling headlong into the eternal abyss of time. [...] 'Oh!' I cried, 'whence comes my need to attach so much interest and importance to my future? Here is the story of life! Here is our destiny! Waves submerging waves, and thousands of sensitive beings, suffering, longing, dying, like these bubbles of water which gush forth into the air and then fall back down. [...] Who then will hear my cries? Is it nature?']

As its power is revealed, nature both voices the inevitability of death and reveals its own sensitivity to the sufferings of the masses; thus, again, nature both breaks down the boundaries between the worlds of the living and the dead (which taking religious vows cannot), and eases the passage from one world to the next. Staël's focus on the sublimity of the natural landscape and on the transience of human life in the face of nature's everlasting power reveals clear Romantic overtones which she harnesses to show that Delphine's suffering can only be communicated via nature and that only nature can help this trapped woman to escape her fate.

The final step on both Corinne's and Amélie's mortal path is also marked by a landscape in which water is a dominant feature. In Corinne's case, a reminder of a previously experienced seascape works to break down the boundary between the worlds of the living and dead at the very moment of her passing, allowing her to cross from this world to the next. On her deathbed, Corinne takes Oswald's hand and draws his attention to the clouds and the moon:

Elle leva ses regards vers le ciel, et vit la lune qui se couvrait du même nuage qu'elle avait fait remarquer à lord Nelvil quand ils s'arrêtèrent sur le bord de la mer en allant à Naples. Alors elle le lui montra de sa main mourante, et son dernier soupir fit retomber cette main. (*C*, p. 586)

[She lifted her gaze to the heavens, and saw there the moon covered by the same cloud to which she had drawn Lord Nelvil's attention when they stopped by the seashore on the way to Naples. On her death bed, she raised her hand to point it out to him again, and, as she drew her final breath, her hand fell back down.]

As has been noted in previous chapters, deathscapes permit time and space to become confused. This was the case in Adèle's garden, where the inclusion of

Sénange's tomb allowed past, present and future to be juxtaposed; it was also the case in Valérie's memorial garden, where the seasons became intertwined and time could be cheated. Now, the nature connected to Corinne's dying moments also permit the transcendence of space and time. Thus, the heroine is transported to the edge of the sea in the Neapolitan countryside by the reappearance of the very same cloud which she once saw there. On that occasion, the two lovers wandered through the countryside by the sea, enjoying each other's company and declaring their love. The description of the seascape that Staël provides holds several interesting points of analysis.

Firstly, it provides another clear example of the sublime in nature:

> On voyait, on entendait [...] la mer dont les vagues se brisaient avec fureur. Ce n'était point l'orage qui l'agitait, mais les rochers, obstacle habituel qui s'opposait à ses flots, et dont sa grandeur était irritée. [...] Ce mouvement sans but, cette force sans objet qui se renouvelle pendant l'éternité, sans que nous puissions connaître ni sa cause ni sa fin, nous attire sur le rivage où ce grand spectacle s'offre à nos regards; et l'on éprouve comme un besoin mêlé de terreur de s'approcher des vagues et d'étourdir sa pensée par leur tumulte. (C, pp. 286–87)

> [You could see and hear [...] the sea, whose waves were breaking violently. It was not the storm which stirred them, but rather the rocks, an obstacle which habitually confronted the waters, and enraged the magnificence of the sea. [...] That aimless movement, that directionless force, endlessly replenished, without our knowing its cause or end, attracts us to the shore where this great spectacle meets our eyes, and we experience an urge mingled with terror to approach the waves and make our minds spin with their chaos.]

The simultaneous fear and awe inspired in the onlooker by the power of the sea echoes Burke's definition of the sublime:

> Whatever is fitted in any sort to excite the ideas of pain and danger; that is to say, whatever is in any sort terrible, or is conversant about terrible objects, or operates in a manner analogous to terror, is a source of the *sublime;* that is, it is productive of the strongest emotion which the mind is capable of feeling. [...] [A]t certain distances, and with certain modifications, it may be, and it is delightful.[94]

The representation of the sublime in Staël's description is significant. For Burke there is 'nothing sublime which is not some modification of power'.[95] The woman's attraction to a space in which nature reveals its great power reflects her own desire to regain a power which has been stripped from her. Sublime nature becomes a space of rebellion here, firstly, because it is unmasterable, and secondly because its forceful chaos makes it a space to which one might turn in order to dull the pain of external, societal factors. In this respect, it echoes Delphine's and Amélie's waterfalls clearly. It is significant that we are returned to this point as Corinne dies, for Corinne assumes great power at her death, as is explored in Chapter 5. Bronfen states that, in the nineteenth-century, the moment of death not only commonly brought visions of the afterlife, but also, '[a]t the same time a central part of the deathbed ritual includes [...] the redistribution of social roles'.[96] Corinne achieves exactly this;

drawing power from the sublime nature of which she is reminded as she dies, she not only manipulates the futures of Oswald and Lucile, but also bequeaths her own role as a talented female artist to their daughter Juliette, and, in so doing, influences the education of future women. As will be argued in Chapter 5, Corinne's actions upon her death pave the way for Staël to make even wider arguments with regard to women's education and its vital importance in the foundation of a nation's true liberty. Therefore, by extension, Corinne's redistribution of social roles as she dies also reminds us that Staël herself is exposing the need in her own era to redistribute social roles and, specifically, to think less about defining these roles according to gender.

Secondly, the temporal and spatial transcendence to the seashore at Terracina also, as with the other dominant waterscapes in the novel, reminds the reader of the role that patriarchal society plays in bringing Corinne to the point where death is her only option. As the day closes, Corinne turns her gaze to the Heavens, and sees there an omen informing her that her love will be condemned:

> La lune que je contemplais s'est couverte d'un nuage, et l'aspect de ce nuage était funeste. J'ai toujours trouvé que le ciel avait une impression, tantôt paternelle, tantôt irritée, et je vous le dis, Oswald, ce soir il condamnait notre amour. (C, p. 289)

> [As I gazed at the moon, a cloud covered it, and the sight of this cloud was ominous. I have always thought of the heavens as being at times paternal, at other times irate, and I tell you, Oswald, that evening they condemned our love.]

The clouds and moon permit the barrier between the worlds of the living and dead to become porous, thus giving rise to visions of deceased family members which would otherwise be impossible. The paternal and angry aspect to the heavens reflects the displeasure at the couple's union on the part of both protagonists' fathers from beyond the grave, and therefore casts a shadow over the light of the lovers' happiness, just as the cloud casts a shadow over the moon. Corinne, in contemplating the visions of the dead that nature has permitted, reads and comprehends both that her love is forbidden by patriarchal society and that the dead will call her to them as a result of her unrequited love. This vision only applies to the female protagonist, however. Oswald is shut out from the expressive communication with nature, and therefore from the call to death. When Oswald declares that he does not believe in the vision, Corinne replies, 'Eh bien, tant mieux, si vous n'êtes pas compris dans ce présage [...] il se peut que ce ciel orageux n'ait menacé que moi' ['Well, so much the better, if you are not included in this omen [...] it may be that this stormy sky has only threatened me'] (C, p. 290). The reappearance of this identical vision at the moment of Corinne's passing confirms that the barrier between the geographies of the living and dead is indeed broken down by the natural world in order that Corinne may be called to join the dead.

Once again, however, nature provides tranquillity in the death that society has ordered. For the final reminder provided by the seascape at Terracina is one of the peace which may be found in death. Towards the evening, once the waves have become more calm, we are informed:

Le sable [...] contenait un grand nombre de petites pierres ferrugineuses qui brillaient de toutes parts; c'était la terre de feu conservant encore dans son sein les traces du soleil, dont les derniers rayons venaient de l'échauffer. Il y a tout à la fois dans cette nature une vie et un repos qui satisfont en entier les vœux divers de l'existence. (*C*, pp. 287–88)

[In the sand [...] there were a large number of ferruginous stones shining everywhere. It was as though the fiery earth still retained within it traces of the sun, whose rays had only just heated it. This nature contains both life and rest all at the same time, which wholly satisfy the diverse desires of existence.]

Death, as well as life and powerful vitality, are to be found here. Posited in opposition to 'life', 'rest' has clear simultaneous connotations of both eternal rest and restorative relaxation, and therefore the natural landscape to which Corinne is metaphysically transported on her deathbed reminds her that death will ease her pain and will provide a warmth which she has not received from her family or from the cold society which has condemned her talent and her love.

Like Corinne, Amélie Mansfield obtains death amid nature. The final waterscape which appears in Cottin's *Amélie Mansfield* to dramatize the heroine's path to death is centred on the river Danube, employed by Amélie as the agent of her suicide. The Viennese river in Cottin's novel, like the Scottish river in Staël's *Corinne*, becomes a Stygian liminal space between the realms of the living and dead.

[Ernest] arrive sur le bord du Danube; il appelle Amélie: nulle voix ne répond: c'est le silence de la mort [...]; il croit apercevoir un corps lutter contre l'onde; il se jette, plonge avec lui sous les eaux, le saisit: c'était elle. (*AM* IV, 149–50)

[Ernest] arrives at the edge of the Danube. He calls Amélie, but hears no voice in reply. Instead he hears only the silence of death [...]. He thinks he sees a body struggling against the waves, throws himself into the river, dives under the water, and seizes the body. It was her.]

Ernest knows immediately that this is a space of death, because death's silence surrounds the river. Like Agnès in Cottin's *Mathilde*, who, although silenced by her oppression as a woman, succeeded in turning that enforced silence to her advantage, Amélie also finds that the silence of death which surrounds the waterscape in which she commits suicide conveys her resolution to uphold her rebellion, and thus increases her power. This silence contrasts sharply with Ernest's voice: 'Il crie comme un insensé; sa tête est perdue; il implore du secours; plusieurs personnes l'entendent de loin' ['He shouts like a madman; he has lost his mind; he begs for help; several people hear him from a distance'] (*AM* IV, 149). Whilst Ernest's voice is so loud it can be heard from afar, it contains neither control nor power: instead, it exhibits a lack of clear thought and reliance upon the assistance of others. With their aid, Ernest pulls Amélie from the water. However, her determination to die is so great that it overcomes Ernest's efforts to save her. Her fall into the river provokes serious illness to which she soon succumbs. The water of the Danube permits the boundary between the worlds of the living and dead to become porous, and thus allows Amélie to traverse to the other side. In facilitating Amélie's execution of her final resolve, the waterscape provides the heroine with power and autonomy. For, in this scene, Cottin 'shows us a woman who defies both God and society in deciding to kill herself; she acts as she herself and she alone judges best'.[97]

There are further echoes here of *Delphine*. Both Delphine and Amélie eventually commit suicide in the first editions of the novels because of their impossible situations.[98] The former, unlike the latter, does not drown herself. She takes poison just as her lover is about to be executed. However, for Delphine, just as for Amélie, death becomes a means of reasserting her own authority. Knowing Léonce is condemned to death, Delphine attempts to obtain a pardon for him. Whilst her speeches and pleadings fall on deaf ears, her suicide stays the hands of the firing squad:

> Les soldats eux-mêmes [...] semblaient ne plus songer à remplir leur cruel emploi; quelques-uns même s'écriaient: 'Non, nous ne tuerons pas ce malheureux homme, c'est bien assez que sa pauvre maîtresse ait péri de douleur; non, qu'il s'en aille, nous ne tirerons pas sur lui'. (*D* II, 334).

> [The soldiers themselves [...] seemed to think no more of carrying out their cruel task; some even cried: 'No, we will not kill this miserable man, it is enough that his poor mistress has died of grief; no, let him go, we will not fire upon him'.]

Had Léonce not demanded that the soldiers take his life, provoking and insulting them in order to realize his own desire to die, Delphine would have succeeded in using the moment of her own death, and the power that this death brings about, to overturn the law itself and to save Léonce's life.

Similarly, in both *Amélie Mansfield* and *Delphine*, the hero and heroine are reunited happily post-mortem. Amélie's death brings her the peace promised earlier by the natural world. Through grief, Ernest himself perishes moments after Amélie, and thus the lovers are permitted happiness together in the eternal realm. Albeit a slightly macabre scene, the presentation of Amélie's corpse in her coffin, entwined with that her lover, proves to the reader that the heroine has achieved comfort in her eventual death, and that she has finally escaped the oppression of society: 'Une sorte de sérénité paraissait répandue sur leurs traits, comme s'ils eussent encore senti le bonheur d'être ensemble' ['A kind of serenity appeared across their features, as though they still felt the happiness of being together'] (*AM* IV, 283). The death which the natural elements and landscape announced as the only possible escape has, as promised, proved blissful and peaceful in its arrival. Léonce and Delphine are peacefully reunited in a waterscape after their deaths: 'M. de Serbellane rendit à ses amis les derniers devoirs. Il les réunit dans un tombeau qu'il fit élever sur les bords d'une rivière, au milieu des peupliers' ['M. de Serbellane paid his last respects to his friends. He reunited them in a tomb which he had erected on the banks of a river, amid poplar trees'] (*D* II, 334). Fulfilling the lovers' final wishes and burying them by the river renders them happy in death, which Serbellane is able to perceive (*D* II, 336). Furthermore, the river once again plays an important role as a liminal space:

> [Un]n soir que j'étais assis près de la tombe où reposent Léonce et Delphine [...], je n'en puis douter, du haut du ciel mes amis [...] écartaient de moi les fantômes de l'imagination qui nous font horreur du terme de la vie; il me semblait qu'au

clair de la lune, je voyais leurs ombres légères passer à travers les feuilles sans les agiter. (*D* II, 336)

[One evening, as I was sitting by Léonce and Delphine's tomb [...], I cannot doubt that, from the heavens above, my friends [...] removed from my mind the imaginary spectres that make us terrified of life's end. It seemed to me as though I could see their ghostly figures by the moonlight, passing through the leaves without disturbing them.]

This river, like that which would appear on Oswald's estate in *Corinne*, permits a window on to the afterlife, thereby allowing Serbellane the opportunity to connect with his dead friends, to catch a sight of their ghosts, and to understand their thoughts. Whilst entering a convent did not provide the required escape, instead placing Delphine in limbo, death and burial do permit the liminal space to be crossed and happiness finally to be voiced. Furthermore, Serbellane's statement here is, in itself, an implicit challenge to the traditional view that those who commit suicide are eternally doomed, and thus the success of the heroine's challenge to patriarchal demands is reinforced in the final moments of the novel.

Conclusion

As Thomas states, '[w]hile the Enlightenment recognized the woman's natural [...] needs and attacked the unreasonable demands made on her through marriages of convenience and the like, it stopped short of granting her what men had — complete autonomy'.[99] As the eighteenth century drew to a close, Staël and Cottin were only too aware of the ideals which society continued to impose on women, and the impossible position in which women often found themselves due to the repression of their voice and a lack of self-determination or of power to resist society's demands. Staël, for example,

was acutely conscious of the sometimes paralyzing conflict between woman's assigned place in society, with all the sacrifices it may entail, and her right to something more. Self-sacrifice, effectively or actually suicide, features as prominently as it does in her fiction (*Mirza, Zulma, Pauline,* and *Sappho* as well as *Delphine* and *Corinne*) because she knew the extreme and deadly pressures that male orthodoxy and authority imposed upon women.[100]

The same can be said of Cottin, who had complained to Julie Verdier about the unfortunate lot of women and the fact that what constituted a woman's virtue was dictated by men. Her heroines — Claire, Malvina and Amélie — all meet similar fates to those of Staël's eponymous protagonists because Cottin knew of the same pressures. Both authors reflected at some stage in their lives on the power and release that death might provide, and both grant these deaths to their female protagonists.

Claire d'Albe, Amélie Mansfield, Corinne and *Delphine* illustrate that when society places obstacles in the way of a woman's self-determination, her career choice, her power to select a marital partner, or her motherhood, death becomes a means of escape. Yet, the demise of each of the eponymous heroines is not as pathetically tragic as it may at first seem. Maria Fairweather argues that

> Corinne's tragic end demonstrates yet again that the society of the time would not tolerate such women. For one with a lifelong belief in progress, it may seem paradoxical that her [Staël's] heroines do not triumph over the odds.[101]

It is, however, not so paradoxical when we take into account, as Staël herself did, the power which a self-willed death might grant. The deaths chosen by Claire, Amélie, Corinne and Delphine establish their individuality, accentuate their determination, and restore their voice. Viewed through this lens, death does not only provide a way out; it also restores the autonomy denied to the eighteenth- and early nineteenth-century woman in the wake of some of the Enlightenment's failings. At the moment of death, women are able to make known the suffering that has been inflicted upon them and to make significant changes for the future of others. Indeed, even the moments preceding Staël's own death reveal the strength of her autonomy and voice:

> Depuis quelques jours, elle ne quittait plus son sofa; les taches livides dont son visage, ses bras, ses mains était couverts n'annonçaient que trop la décomposition du sang. Je sentais la pénible impression d'un adieu éternel et sa conversation ne roulait que sur des projets d'avenir. Elle était occupée de chercher une maison où sa fille, la duchesse de Broglie, grosse et prête d'accoucher, serait mieux logée. [...] [L]e contraste de cet aspect si plein de mort et de ces paroles si pleines de vie était déchirant.

> [She had not left the sofa for several days. The livid blotches with which her face, arms and hands were covered signalled only too clearly the decomposition of her blood. I had the painful impression of an eternal goodbye, yet her conversation turned only on her future plans. She was concerned with finding a house where her daughter, the Duchess of Broglie, who was pregnant and whose baby was imminently due, might be better accommodated. [...] [T]he contrast between her appearance so full of death and her words so full of life was harrowing].[102]

Throughout her life, Staël 'triumphed over her enemies' attempts to suppress her voice through censorship and her person through banishment',[103] and it is clear that, at the moment of her death, she was equally as determined to assert it.

In *Claire d'Albe,* nature is the site of Claire the angel and Claire the adulteress: it thus exposes the imposed ideals which bring the heroine to her untenable situation. For the very reason that nature is used to highlight the domination of her voice by the male figures in her life, it then also becomes the site she seeks as she dies, when attempting to re-establish her own voice. Throughout the novel, Cottin turns to nature to strengthen her arguments that the imposition of a feminine ideal is unrealistic, problematic, and ultimately tragic not only for the woman who is expected to uphold it, but also for the man who wishes to project his desires on to her. The lover who forced Claire into the untenable position soon follows her to the grave, and the husband who was so keen to see the stereotypical eighteenth-century domestic ideal upheld loses his adored wife.

In the preface to the novel, Cottin claimed that writing *Claire d'Albe* allows her to take refuge in an ideal world, away from the fears of the real world, and particularly of the Terror, in which she had seen relatives and friends executed or disappear: 'Le dégoût, le danger ou l'effroi du monde ayant fait naître en moi le besoin de me retirer dans un monde idéal, déjà j'embrassais un vaste plan qui devait m'y retenir longtemps' ['Since disgust, danger or fear of the world had aroused in me the need to retreat into an ideal world; I was already forming a vast plan that would keep me from the real world for a long time'] (*C d'A*, p. 3). Yet, despite these claims, in reality, Cottin's novel does tap into problems that were prevalent within the wider world: whilst the Terror does not invite its way into her idyll, the socio-political preoccupations of women certainly do. As Stewart argues, it is 'surely worth noting that she abandons a real world that inspires "fear" to create a fictional universe where the morbid resolution of events is hardly less daunting'.[104] With this in mind, the natural landscape Cottin describes within *Claire d'Albe* — the beautiful, perfect scenery with which Claire is connected by Frédéric, and which consequently heightens her own perfection — assumes one final significance. As Jean Gaulmier argues:

> [L]e paysage qu'elle évoque [...] au début de *Claire d'Albe*, [...] ne doit pas être compté comme promesse d'une idylle, mais [...] comme une source de contraste où le visage pacifique de la nature fera ressortir plus fortement le sort tragique de Claire.

> [[T]he landscape she evokes [...] at the beginning of *Claire d'Albe* [...] must not be viewed as a promised idyll, but rather [...] as a source of contrast where the peaceful appearance of nature emphasizes Claire's tragic fate more strongly].[105]

Building on this, we can argue that the early natural idylls of *Claire d'Albe* not only draw our attention to the ideal imposed on Claire, they also serve to emphasize the contrast to this ideal at the end, when, far from conforming to expectations, Claire establishes her own autonomy and power.

In *Amélie Mansfield*, *Corinne* and *Delphine*, Staël and Cottin portray the untenable situations caused when women are forced to choose between perceived duty and desired happiness. They also portray the heroines' methods of dealing with such situations. In order to achieve these ends, the authors construct — by engaging both with age-old traditions of associating death, water and women, and with contemporary associations of gondolas and coffins established by the German Romantic writer Goethe — three 'waterscapes of one's own' which their heroines might appropriate for their own ends. The first is endowed with the power of communication, announcing that society's oppression will cause the only way forward for the heroine to be death; the second provides a window on to the realm of the dead, allaying any fears; the third breaks down the barrier between the spaces of the living and dead in order to allow the heroine the death she desires. In so doing, it restores autonomy and power to her, and brings the peace that society has denied her. The written waterscapes incorporate rivers, torrential waterfalls, parks, woods, meadows and seashores. They include both tranquil areas of nature and those areas which contain the Romantic, 'harsh and haunting beauties of Nature', whose sublimity inspire melancholic and fearful *frisson*,[106] proving that both types are equally capable of voicing a woman's concerns and affirming her voice. Indeed, this is highly appropriate, as woman herself can be categorized as neither wholly domestic nor wholly wild; rather, she possesses many characteristics and desires.

Not only does each heroine have recourse to multiple types of scenery, but she often also finds the greatest power is to be found in a 'space in between'. As previously noted, middle spaces assume a crucial importance when women reclaim their voice. When Staël and Cottin choose the middle spaces for the construction of their 'waterscapes of one's own', they again draw on long-established traditions: the notion of liminal areas between the worlds of the living and dead, and, particularly, the historical and mythological connection of such spaces with water. Again they build on images and associations already prevalent and use these to the heroine's advantage. The ability of such liminal spaces to provide a window on to the other world permits the heroine to see the advantages that death will bring her, and their tradition of ferrying souls from one world to the next permits the heroine to cross eventually to the world beyond, thus bringing about the very moment of autonomy that she seeks and that accompanies death.

The fact that a middle space assumes a key role in presenting both the woman's escape from her untenable situation and the reclaiming of her autonomy highlights the need to consider more than opposing extremes as far as women's lives are concerned. The female protagonists of these three novels resist the attempts to pigeonhole them into one extreme or another (be that angel or whore, dutiful wife or seeker of personal liberty). Thus a space which belongs neither to one world nor another, but which lies somewhere in between, is the most appropriate space that might permit these resisted attempts to succeed. Furthermore, forcing women to choose between public duty and private happiness reinforces the dichotomy of the public and private spheres. As outlined in the introduction to this book, this dichotomy does not account for women's true essential being, which bridges both spheres. Therefore, writing a middle space which permits a woman to escape the necessity to choose between two extremes allows the woman to voice her objection to being forced to choose (and to being condemned for choosing the 'wrong' role). The creation of this middle space in a waterscape lends a particular power to the woman's rebellion. The Styx, we should remember, in addition to forming the border between the realms of the living and dead, is also the river capable of bestowing invulnerability, as Staël knew.[107] If both women and water are considered unmasterable forces, then, when the two join together, the autonomy and self-identity established within them carry symbolic weight.

This chapter has approached its analysis of the deaths of literary heroines through a combined application of Thomas' notion of the 'untenable situation' and examination of late eighteenth- and early nineteenth-century French views both on deathscapes and on suicide (including the views of Enlightenment thinkers, of Romantic writers, and of Staël herself). As a result, it demonstrates that, in writing land- or waterscapes which ease the path to death or which form the very site of death, women writers create a space which restores to their heroines both autonomy and voice. In turn, the literary scenery of their novels becomes the site from which the novelists themselves might regain autonomy in an eighteenth- and nineteenth-century world which denied their sex autonomy and voice. For example, just as the heroines retreat from the world through death and find power in their voice as they do so, Cottin also seeks an escape from the real world and finds that this very escape provides her with the means to voice her own concerns to that world. Similarly, Corinne's redistribution of social roles as she dies also reminds us that Staël herself exposes the need in her own era to redistribute social roles and, specifically, to avoid defining these roles according to gender. The final chapter of this book will examine the redistribution of social roles in the wake of the deaths of heroines more closely, examining the writing which is left behind, and the future which is bequeathed to women writers.

Notes to Chapter 4

1. Mme Cottin to M. Gramagnac, April 1795. Arnelle, pp. 93–94.
2. Mme de Staël, *De l'influence des passions sur le bonheur des individus et des nations* (Lausanne: J. Mourer, 1796), p. 307.
3. Lanser has argued that female Romantic heroes appear in the works of Staël, [Mary] Shelley and Sand. However, in the period 1789–1815, Staël was not alone in portraying female protagonists who underwent similar experiences to the male Romantic hero, as this book has outlined. Susan Sniader Lanser, *Fictions of Authority: Women Writers and Narrative Voice* (Ithaca: Cornell University Press, 1992), pp. 161–62.
4. Pasco, pp. 7–8.
5. Other heroines, who do not die, find a method of removing themselves from the world, which ultimately amounts to a death of sorts: Rosalba and Mathilde enter convents, shutting themselves away, and preparing, through prayer and repentance, for death.
6. In this respect, the present analysis aligns itself with the stance adopted by Ruth P. Thomas, who argues similarly that, since the deaths of Manon, Julie, Mlle de St. Yves, Mme de Tourvel, and Virginie are willed by the heroines themselves, they can be classed as suicides. Ruth P. Thomas, 'The Death of an Ideal: Female Suicides in the Eighteenth-Century French Novel', in *French Women and the Age of Enlightenment*, ed. by Samia I. Spencer (Bloomington: Indiana University Press, 1984), p. 321.
7. Vincent, p. 491.
8. Margaret Higonnet, 'Suicide as Self-Construction', in *Germaine de Staël: Crossing the Borders*, ed. by Madelyn Gutwirth, Avriel Goldberger, and Karyna Szmurlo (New Brunswick, NJ: Rutgers, 1991), pp. 69–81 (p. 71).
9. Staël, *De l'influence des passions*, p. 245.
10. Higonnet, p. 74. (Original emphasis).
11. Ibid., p. 70.
12. Ibid., p. 75.
13. Elisabeth Bronfen, *Over Her Dead Body: Death, femininity and the aesthetic* (Manchester: Manchester University Press, 1992), pp. 76–77.
14. Ibid., p. 77.
15. Ibid., p. 77.
16. George Howe Colt, *November of the Soul: The Enigma of Suicide* (New York: Scribner, 2006), p. 167.
17. Ibid., p. 175.
18. Jeffrey Merrick, 'Patterns and Prosecution of Suicide in Eighteenth-Century Paris', *Historical Reflections*, 16:1 (1989), 1–53 (p. 5). See also: Siméon-Prosper Hardy, et al. *Siméon-Prosper Hardy: Mes Loisirs, ou journal d'événements tels qu'ils parviennent à ma connaissance (1753–1789)* (Québec: Presses de l'Université Laval, 2008).
19. Merrick, 'Patterns and Prosecution of Suicide', pp. 14–15.

20. Ibid., pp. 15–16.
21. See: Godelieve Mercken-Spaas, 'Death and the Romantic Heroine: Chateaubriand and de Staël', in *Pre-text, Text, Context: Essays on Nineteenth-Century French Literature,* ed. by Robert L. Mitchell (Columbus, OH: Ohio State University Press, 1980), pp. 79–86 (p. 79). C.f. Michel Vovelle, *La Mort et l'Occident de 1300 à nos jours* (Paris: Gallimard, 1983), p. 445.
22. Thomas, pp. 321–31.
23. Thomas and Rogers argue that these heroines give up on life after what they have endured, and that their deaths are thus 'self-willed'. Rogers, p. 246; Thomas, p. 321.
24. Bertrand-Jennings, p. 49.
25. Bronfen, p. 3.
26. François-René de Chateaubriand, *Atala* (Paris: Lordereau, 1831).
27. Including Augustin Legrand's late eighteenth-century *La Mort de Virginie,* and James Bertrand's 1869 identically titled painting.
28. Thomas, pp. 322–23.
29. Ibid., p. 323.
30. Ibid., p. 330.
31. Cohen, *The Sentimental Education of the Novel.*
32. Thomas, p. 323.
33. Margaret Cohen, 'Introduction', in Sophie Cottin, *Claire d'Albe,* ed. by Margaret Cohen (New York: The Modern Language Association of America, 2002), pp. vii–xxii.
34. Beauvoir, I, p. 320. (Original emphasis).
35. Thomas, p. 329.
36. Mme Cottin à Mme Verdier, June 1797. Sykes, p. 315.
37. Mme Cottin à Mme Verdier, March 1798. Ibid., p. 320.
38. See: Trouille, p. 40; Jean-Louis Lecerle, 'La femme selon Jean-Jacques', in *Jean-Jacques Rousseau: Quatre études* (Neuchâtel: Editions de la Baconnière, 1978), p. 42.
39. See: Trouille, p.43.
40. Thomas, p. 328.
41. One might argue that Frédéric's dislike of Claire's status as a mother (he states disgustedly that her baby daughter smells of sour milk (C d'A, p. 18)) renders his image of the ideal woman somewhat contrary to that propounded by Rousseau. However, Frédéric does not disapprove of the female figure as a mother per se; rather, he is jealous of the fact that Claire already has a husband and family. Claire's children are simple reminders that she is not available to him.
42. Catherine Cusset, 'Sophie Cottin ou l'écriture du déni', *Romantisme,* 77 (1992), 25–31 (p. 26).
43. Rousseau, Julie, p. 261.
44. Ibid., p. 535.
45. Trouille, pp. 40–41.
46. Beauvoir, I, p. 320.
47. H.D. 'Introduction' to Mme Cottin, *Claire D'Albe* (Paris: Hiard, 1831), p. 8.
48. In order to separate Claire and Frédéric, Elise and M. D'Albe conjure a lie, informing Claire that Frédéric has been unfaithful to her.
49. Margaret Cohen, 'Women and fiction in the nineteenth century', in T. Unwin (ed.), *The Cambridge Companion to the French Novel: From 1800 to the Present* (Cambridge: Cambridge University Press, 1997), pp. 54–72 (p. 60).
50. Thomas, p. 324.
51. Stewart, p. 186.
52. Winegarten, *Mme de Staël,* p. 85.
53. Goodden, p. 306.
54. Call, p. 87.
55. Luce Irigaray, *Ce sexe qui n'en est pas un* (Paris: Éditions de minuit, 1977), p. 113.
56. Gaston Bachelard, *L'Eau et les rêves* (Paris: Librairie José Corti, 1942), pp. 144–45.
57. Ibid., p. 150.
58. Julia Kristeva, *The Impudence of Uttering: The Mother Tongue,* trans. by Anne Marsella, <http://www.kristeva.fr/impudence.html> [Accessed 13 March 2018]. Deborah Jenson, "Hélène

Cixous, Translator of History and Legend: '*Ce transport vertigineux*'", in *Joyful Babel: Translating Hélène Cixous*, ed. by Myriam Díaz-Diocaretz and Marta Segarra (Amsterdam: Rodopi, 2004) pp. 197–204 (p. 197).

59. Wendy O'Shea-Meddour, 'Gaston Bachelard's *L'Eau et les rêves*: conquering the feminine element', *French Cultural Studies*, 14:1 (2003), 81–99 (p. 83).

60. Susan Napier, *The Fantastic in Modern Japanese Literature: The Subversion of Modernity* (London; New York: Routledge, 1996), p. 35.

61. Lynda Haas, 'Of Waters and Women: The Philosophy of Luce Irigaray', *Hypatia*, 8:4 (1993), 150–59 (156); C.f. O'Shea-Meddour.

62. Bachelard, *L'Eau et les rêves*, p. 105.

63. Ibid., p. 106.

64. Ibid., pp. 96–97.

65. Ibid., p. 95. (Original emphasis.)

66. Simon Schama, *Landscape and Memory* (London: Harper Collins, 1995), pp. 257–60.

67. Ibid., p. 255.

68. Lorena Stookey, *Thematic Guide to World Mythology* (Westport, CT; London: Greenwood Press, 2004), p. 3.

69. Ibid.

70. Shan M. M. Winn, *Heaven, Heroes and Happiness: The Indo-European Roots of Western Ideology* (Lanham, MD: University Press of America, 1995), p. 174.

71. Michael C. Brannigan, *The Pulse of Wisdom: The Philosophies of India, China, and Japan* (Belmont, CA: Wadsworth, 1995), p. 344.

72. Winn, p. 174.

73. Bachelard, *L'Eau et les rêves*, p. 102.

74. Helene E. Roberts, *Encyclopedia of Comparative Iconography: Themes Depicted in Works of Art* (Chicago; London: Fitzroy Dearborn, 1998), p. 229.

75. Jeffrey Merrick, 'Rescued from the River: Attempted Suicide in Late Eighteenth-Century Paris', *Social History*, 49:98 (2016), 27–47 (p. 30).

76. Merrick, 'Patterns and Prosecution of Suicide', p. 10.

77. Marie-Madeleine Martinet, *Le Voyage d'Italie dans les littératures européennes* (Paris: Presses Universitaires de France, 1996), p. 130

78. Ibid., p. 129.

79. Ibid., p. 125.

80. George Gordon Byron, *Beppo: A Venetian Story* (London: John Murray, 1818), p. 10.

81. Tony Tanner, *Venice Desired* (Cambridge, MA: Harvard University Press, 1992), p. 48.

82. François René de Chateaubriand, *Mémoires d'outre-tombe*, 6 vols (Paris: Dulfour, Mulat and Boulanger, 1860), VI, p. 187.

83. Mark Sandy, 'Reimagining Venice and Visions of Decay in Wordsworth, The Shelleys and Thomas Mann', in *Venice and the Cultural Imagination: 'This Strange Dream Upon the Water'*, ed. by Michael O'Neill, Mark Sandy and Sarah Wootton (Oxford: Routledge, 2016), pp. 27–42 (pp. 38–40).

84. Martinet, pp. 130–31.

85. Philippe Monnier, *Venice in the Eighteenth Century* (London: Chatto & Windus, 1910), p. 65 (Original italics.)

86. Original ellipses.

87. Bachelard, *L'Eau et les rêves*, p. 98. [Original emphasis.]

88. Mary Murray, 'Laying Lazarus to Rest: The Place and the Space of the Dead in Explanations of Near Death Experiences', in *Deathscapes: Spaces for Death, Dying, Mourning and Remembrance*, ed. by Avril Maddrell and James D. Sidaway (Surrey, UK; Burlington VT: Ashgate, 2010), pp. 37–54 (p. 37).

89. Bronfen, p. 77.

90. Mary Murray, p. 39.

91. Mieke Bal, *Narratology: Introduction to the Theory of Narrative* (Toronto; Buffalo; London: University of Toronto Press, 1997), pp. 216–17.

92. Mme de Staël, *Réflexions sur le suicide* (London: Schulze and Dean, 1813), p. 20.
93. Mary Murray, p. 40.
94. Edmund Burke, *A Philosophical Inquiry into the Origin of Our Ideas of the Sublime and Beautiful; with an Introductory Discourse Concerning Taste* (New York: Harper and Brothers, 1844), pp. 51–52.
95. Ibid., p. 81.
96. Bronfen, p. 77.
97. Call, pp. 97–98.
98. In the second editions of both novels, neither heroine dies directly by her own hand, but both still will their deaths. Amélie's death is still enabled by the Danube, to which she proceeds intending to kill herself: she collapses on the river bank and succumbs to illness. In the second edition of Staël's novel, Delphine dies of melancholy.
99. Thomas, p. 330.
100. Goodden, p. 300.
101. Maria Fairweather, *Mme de Staël* (London: Constable and Robinson, 2006), p. 327.
102. Comtesse de Boigne, *Mémoires*, 5 vols (Paris: Émile-Paul Frères, 1921), II, pp. 293–94.
103. Goodden, p. 294.
104. Stewart, pp. 185–86.
105. Jean Gaulmier, 'Sophie et ses malheurs ou le Romantisme du pathétique', in *Romantisme*, 3 (1971), 3–16 (p. 9).
106. McManners, p. 334–35.
107. Staël, *Réflexions sur le suicide*, p. 20.

CHAPTER 5

❖

Writing the Landscape:
The Ossianic North and the Debate over
Women's Writing and Education

[C]e n'est point sous le rapport littéraire que je prétends juger les *femmes-auteurs*, mais sous le rapport plus intéressant de la morale. Convient-il bien à une femme dont le devoir le plus sacré est d'être épouse fidèle et mère tendre [...] de sortir de cette douce obscurité dont son état lui impose la loi, pour livrer son existence tout entière à un public qui après s'être établi juge de ses écrits, a le droit de devenir juge de ses actions?

[[I]t is not from the literary perspective that I claim to judge *women writers*, but from the more interesting moral perspective. Is it fitting for a women whose most sacred duty is to be a loyal wife and tender mother [...] to step out of this sweet obscurity, to which she is bound because of her position in society, in order to give her whole existence over to a public audience which, after establishing itself as the judge of her writings, has the right to judge her actions as well?]

ANON., 'Variétés', *Journal des Débats*.[1]

Women Writers and Gendered Spheres

Aside from madness or suicide, a third way in which women might express their rebellion against the patriarchal dominance which pigeonholed them was through writing. Cottin, Genlis, Krüdener, Souza and Staël all defied the social order by stepping out of the domestic sphere and entering the public one through writing and publishing. So, too, do the women writers who feature in their novels (Staël's Corinne, Cottin's Mistress Clare and Genlis's Natalie). This chapter exposes the connections established by Staël and Cottin between their written landscapes and their fictional women writers and argues that, through these connections, Staël and Cottin bequeath power to the women writers of the future.

The Republic and Empire saw an increased gendering of the public and private spheres, and a consequent division of societal roles. The obsession with the medical distinctions between the sexes which began to take hold of French eighteenth-century scientists, had a profound influence on defining women's place. According to Robert A. Nye:

> Between 1770 and 1830, biologists and doctors were engaged in a kind of bio-ethnography, compiling lists of male and female attributes, identifying [...] sexually differentiated pathologies, warning of occupational or professional hazards [...], or speculating about male and female contributions to procreation. [...] The obsession with maleness and femaleness that drove these writers boils down again and again to fertility.[2]

Medical research comprised investigations to determine bone strength, analyse bodily fluids, and compare reproductive systems. The physicians responsible for these investigations, including Pierre Roussel, Pierre J. G. Cabanis and Julien-Joseph Virey, concluded that woman was categorically what man was not and man was what woman was not. These two opposites could not overlap, nor should their everyday roles interchange, any more than could their physical distinctions.

Roussel believed that women's bone density, muscle tone and pale skin made them more suited to home-making than to exterior pursuits, and that their internal organs and bone structure rendered them ideally suited to bearing children. Women's comparatively weaker frame and mentality were, he argued, not suited to the world of physical or intellectual work. Cabanis drew almost identical conclusions. Such scientific research played a key role in the subordination of women. Yet this subordination was not simply marital. Rather, 'concerns about sexual difference [...] are inextricably interwoven with a host of other anxieties that arose out of changes in the social and familial division of labor, in class relations, and in the workplace'.[3] As Susan K. Foley states, 'biology now became destiny for women'.[4] They were granted no political or juridical rights, and were expected to undertake no role outside domestic life. Women writers were aware of the changes which resulted in the subordination of their sex. Staël admits: 'depuis la révolution [sic], les hommes ont pensé qu'il était politiquement et moralement utile de réduire les femmes à la plus absurde médiocrité' ['since the Revolution, men have thought it to be politically and morally useful to reduce women to the most absurd mediocrity'].[5]

Following the conclusions drawn by such medical research, one major public sphere activity from which women were expected to refrain was writing and publishing. The education a woman received was even questioned, in order to discourage her from writing. As Hesse explains:

> Based on these new theories, a full-blown assault was launched [...] specifically on *women writers* after the French Revolution. And this new mode of argumentation [...] went right to the heart of cultural life itself, questioning the capacity of women for moral self-regulation and their suitability for the production of knowledge through reading and writing. Proponents of the new biology advocated a very limited education for women, tailored narrowly to their maternal role.[6]

Women's desire to continue to write and publish, despite expectations that they should not, led to much controversy. The strength of opinion behind the citation from the *Journal des Débats* at the opening of this chapter, indeed the very appearance at all of the debate over women's writing in such a publication in 1800, substantiates this.

One political figure who firmly believed in reserving the world of publishing for men was Joseph de Maistre. He writes to his daughter in 1808 that women must not concern themselves with the public world of writing and publishing because they are incapable of creating great works.[7] In Maistre's mind, the only thing women could, and therefore should, excel at was the domestic role of mother and wife. Restif de la Bretonne also stressed how men and women are marked out for different roles in life, and described how their educations should be correspondingly dissimilar. Women's education should, he argued, be limited, particularly regarding writing: 'A douze accomplis, les filles riches apprendront la danse, la musique et les autres choses d'agrément, ensuite, à lire, et même les langues, mais non à écrire' ['At twelve years old, rich girls learn dancing, music, and other agreable pastimes, and then reading, and even languages, but they are not taught to write'].[8] Sylvain Maréchal takes this argument further with his 1801 treatise *Projet d'une loi portant défense d'apprendre à lire aux femmes* [*Proposal of a law to forbid women from learning how to read*].[9] Although such a law never came into being, its proposal nonetheless testifies to the seriousness of such beliefs.

The situation regarding women's education in fact worsened in the decades between Restif's and Maréchal's arguments. Whilst even as early as 1791, under the Constitutional Monarchy, the post-revolutionary era was concretising women's subordination by denying them citizenship, at least in this year there had been provision for women's education. However,

> [b]y 1799 the flow of projects for the organisation of women's education, that had been almost a torrent to *le comité de l'instruction publique* in 1791, had completely dried up. Convention deputies [...] vocally opposed to women having any role outside the home, let alone equal chances in education, had succeeded in having women's societies closed and women excluded from all public debates.[10]

Indeed, under the Terror, '[r]adical women like Olympe de Gouges, Pauline Léon and Claire Lacombe had gone to the guillotine or disappeared into hiding, so that voices in support of women's education were very few in number'.[11] It is hardly surprising, therefore, to find that women writers such as Staël, Genlis and Cottin often (at least outwardly) presented their chosen career paths as unsuitable for their sex.

Cottin argues that a woman's first duty is to her husband and family, despite the fact that she was a successful female author. In a letter to her sister-in-law Mme Jauge, Cottin confesses:

> Ne croyez pas pourtant, ma sœur, que je sois partisane des femmes auteurs, tant s'en faut... Il me semble que la nature ne donna un cœur si tendre aux femmes, qu'afin de leur faire attacher tout leur bonheur dans les seuls devoirs d'épouse et de mère [...]; que s'il est permis à quelques-unes d'exercer leur plume, ce ne peut être que par exception, et lorsque leur situation les dégage de ces devoirs.

> [Do not think, sister, that I am in favour of women writers. Far from it... It seems to me that nature only granted women such a tender heart in order to make them pin all their happiness on the sole duties of wifehood and motherhood [...], and that if it is permissible for some women to exercise their

pen, it can only be by exception and when their situation releases them from these duties].[12]

Yet, in the same letter, she states why she feels it necessary to voice this opinion: 'pour m'excuser à vos yeux, je sentais que j'avais besoin de toutes les circonstances qui peuvent me justifier d'avoir [sic] entré dans cette carrière' ['in order to excuse myself in your eyes, I felt that I needed all the circumstances that could justify my having entered this profession'].[13] Cottin fears harsh judgement from family and friends for entering a profession reserved for men. Did she passionately believe women should not write, or did she simply feel compelled to justify her career choice? When it later transpired that Mme de Staël had seen herself in a passage of *Malvina*, which also articulated that women should only write when they had no domestic duties, Cottin was horrified at having offended her fellow writer. She wrote afterwards: 'Mme de Staël ne pouvait deviner que, si j'eusse cédé au très vif désir d'écrire une note sur elle, je n'aurais fait qu'un éloge' ['Mme de Staël could not have guessed that, had I had given in to my strong desire to write anything about her, I would only have praised her'].[14] If Cottin not only refused to condemn one of the most active and outspoken women writers of her generation, but also in fact desired to praise her, then it is unlikely that she passionately believed in discouraging women from writing.

Whilst many were disdainful of women writers, some praised female creativity. Marie-Joseph de Chénier, for example, remarked that 'ce sont des femmes qui figurent avec le plus de distinction parmi les romanciers modernes' ['it is women who figure with the most distinction amongst modern novelists'].[15] Certainly, despite the many arguments maligning women writers, the number of women's publications increased post-Revolution, according to Hesse.[16] This does not mean that the number was great, particularly when compared to the number of male writers: 'While the ranks of published female authors doubled during the Revolutionary period, they rose from only two to four per cent of the total'.[17] Nor does it mean that publication was always smooth; as Béatrice Slama states, for women writers, 'se faire éditer n'est pas facile' ['getting a work published was not easy'].[18]

In such a society, female authors were skilled at depicting the debate around women's writing. Genlis's *La Femme auteur* [*The Woman Writer*] (1806) depicts a female writer, Natalie, being shunned by society and her family. Staël's *Corinne* tackles the issue of talented women possessing influence in the public sphere. The eponymous heroine is an actress, writer, poet and singer, who does not conform to the society into which she wishes to marry, because of her chosen career. The heroine of Cottin's *Malvina* also fails to satisfy the society in which she lives because of her desire for education, to read poetry and mythological tales, to take an interest in the workings of the local forge, hospital and school, and to befriend a female author. The issue of women's writing comes under scrutiny in volume two when Malvina meets this female author, Mistress Clare, for the first time, and they discuss whether women should write.

Women and Writing as Reflected in Contemporary Views of Britain and Scotland in *Malvina* and *Corinne*

Cottin and Staël confront women's preoccupations regarding writing and education through engaging with the northern British natural landscape chosen as the setting for their novels. The reason for the attribution of such importance to this landscape as a site of socio-political critique is twofold. Firstly, Britain is a relevant spatial setting for the discussion of women's writing due both to allegorical suitability and to intertextuality. Secondly, contemporary fascination for the region assured its appearance in popular literature and ensured that its connotations would be easily recognized. The dichotomous representation of Britain as both ordered and wild mirrors both the restrictions placed on women and the rebelliousness of the women writers who did not yield to them. Furthermore, Scotland's Ossianic literature, frequently referenced in Staël and Cottin's work, included a female bard.

In the early eighteenth century, Voltaire and Montesquieu had admired Britain's stable political organization,[19] which was thought to be greatly responsible for the seriousness in routine displayed in British society as a whole. According to McManners, '[o]ne inspiration of the Anglomania which became prevalent in French society [...] was an admiration of the gravity of the English, assumed to be connected with their solid constitutional arrangements in government.'[20] According to Pierre Carboni, Anglomania continued into late eighteenth- and early nineteenth-century France, with British fashions becoming popular on the continent.[21] Seeing Paris as a declining city, Jean-Baptiste-Antoine Suard 'compares contemporary Paris to Rome in the late Empire, and sees only England [Britain] and printing as possible instruments of a regeneration that could not have taken place in Rome'.[22] Furthermore, concerning industry and commerce, the British Industrial Revolution was envied; indeed one of the most famous industrial inventions of the period was the brainchild of a Scotsman: James Watt's steam engine. This admiration did not die with the eighteenth century, the early nineteenth still 'saw a steady procession of French visitors to England and Scotland [...] most of these visitors were [...] savants mainly interested in the state of British society, its industry, science and commerce'.[23] The factors most noted by French visitors to Britain for many years, then, were its stable political organisation and industry, its social order and its structured routine.

The 'règles' ['rules'], ordre ['order'], and habitudes ['habits'] which have become unwritten rules in society and industry form recurring leitmotifs in *Corinne* and *Malvina*. Staël, for example, notes Oswald's observations of Britain upon returning from Italy:

> Dès qu'il eut mis le pied sur la terre d'Angleterre, il fut frappé de l'ordre et de l'aisance, de la richesse et de l'industrie qui s'offraient à ses regards; les penchants, les habitudes, les goûts nés avec lui se réveillèrent avec plus de force que jamais. (*C*, pp. 447–48)

> [As soon as he set foot in England, he was struck by the order and prosperity, by the affluence and industry which met his eyes. The inclinations, habits and tastes which were born with him now came back stronger than ever.]

We see a similar vision of order when Corinne lives with her stepmother in Britain. The house of M. Maclinson, the fiancé intended for Corinne by her stepmother, possesses a very regulated system: '[I]l y avait tant d'ordre dans sa maison, tout s'y faisait si régulièrement, à la même heure et de la même manière, qu'il était impossible à personne d'y rien changer' ['[T]he house was so ordered, everything was done so regularly, at the same time and in the same manner, that it was impossible for anyone to change anything'] (*C*, p. 374). Aspects of everyday life are forbidden to change, in particular regarding women, who must constantly conform to what is expected, 'prêtes à recommencer le lendemain une vie qui ne différait de celle de la veille que par la date de l'almanach. [...] Les femmes vieillissaient en faisant toujours la même chose, en restant toujours à la même place' ['ready to start again the next day a life that differed from that of the previous day only by the date on the calendar. [...] The women grew older always doing the same thing, always staying in the same place'] (*C*, pp. 368–69).

Unable to cope with the pressure exerted on her by society because of such regulations, Corinne asks: '[E]st-il vrai que le devoir prescrive à tous les caractères des règles semblables?' ['[I]s it true that duty prescribes the same rules to all personalities?'] (*C*, p. 366). Corinne's nature makes her find it impossible to follow such rules, and she will therefore never be considered suitable marriage material for Oswald in their families' eyes. Corinne is a misfit because she is a female writer and artistic genius, a woman who partakes in activities declared unsuitable for her sex. Staël's presentation of Britain's order, rules and routine in *Corinne* becomes an allegory for her own homeland, in which women were relegated to the status of second-class citizens, deemed unfit to involve themselves in the public sphere of writing.

Cottin's *Malvina* depicts Britain's order to a similar end: to represent the gender ideologies of her homeland, and the consequent effect on women who did not abide by them. Malvina visits the industries and charitable organisations established by her benefactress, Mistress Birton, and is pleasantly struck by their order and well-kept nature: 'Le lendemain, Malvina, accompagnée de sa cousine et de M. Prior, fut visiter l'infirmerie, l'école et la forge [...]. Elle fut assez contente de l'ordre et de la propreté qui régnaient dans les divers établissements' ['The next day, Malvina, accompanied by her cousin and M. Prior, visited the infirmary, the school and the forge [...]. She was quite content with the order and cleanliness throughout the different establishments'] (*M* I, 39). However, after seeing the manner in which Birton's workers are treated and observing the lacuna between their poverty and Birton's comfortable wealth, the order and rules of Birton's establishments appear less congenial. After questioning Birton's methods of running her establishments, Malvina is told: '[J]usqu'à présent tous les étrangers que j'ai conduits ici ne se sont pas cru le droit de suivre leur penchant, ni de déroger aux règles que j'y ai établies sans avoir commencé par obtenir mon aveu' ['[U]p until now any stranger I have brought here has not felt entitled either to follow their whim or to depart from the rules that I have established without first obtaining my permission'] (*M* I, 82). Birton frowns upon Malvina for condescending to make friendly conversation with the workers, for in so doing, she has broken the rules of the social order. Although

Malvina is not a woman writer, nonetheless, like Corinne, she deviates repeatedly from established social rules throughout the novel, promoting women's education, even befriending a woman writer. Thus, Malvina is also a misfit.

Any novel delineating the situation of female misfits requires a backdrop composed of a society to which the rebellious women cannot adapt. The stereotypical view of ordered Britain proves a more useful setting to Staël and Cottin than France because Britain has something France does not: the wild Scottish natural scenery and the poetry allied with it, which form a striking contrast to ordered civilization. For, the fascination with Britain is not entirely accounted for by the country's order and stability. Andrew Hook and Pierre Carboni attribute much of the Anglomania in eighteenth- and nineteenth-century France to a contemporary taste for Scottish landscape and an admiration of Ossian.[24]

Previous to the mid eighteenth century in France, there had been a distinct 'sense of repulsion, displeasing irregularity or, at best, disinterested boredom' felt in reaction to mountain scenery.[25] Yet, the works of Louis Ramond de Carbonnières and Albrecht von Haller played a significant role in causing attitudes to change. So, too, did the fashion for undertaking the Grand Tour, which familiarized travellers with mountainous landscapes.[26] The works of J. A. Deluc, Horace Bénédict de Saussure, M.-T. Bourrit, as well as of Ramond, lent particularly enticing and beautiful descriptions to the Alpine scenery they viewed, inspiring the population, since '[l]eurs ouvrages [...] révélèrent, avec leurs audaces d'alpinistes et leurs observations de savants, l'incomparable poésie des déserts glacés' ['their works [...] revealed, with their mountaineer's daring and their scholarly observations, the incomparable poetry of frozen deserts'].[27] And it was not only the Alps and Pyrenees whose landscapes were now revered. The Scottish Highlands and the influence of the sublimity of the natural landscape in the Ossian poems quickly began to play a major role in changing French attitudes to wild and stormy mountain scenery.[28]

In 1760 the Scottish poet James Macpherson published an English translation of what he claimed to be original epic verse by the third-century poet Ossian. Despite controversy over the supposedly apocryphal nature of these poems, the text, *Fragments of ancient poetry, collected in the Highlands of Scotland, and translated from the Gaelic or Erse language*, was instantly successful. Other works in the same cycle followed: *Fingal* (1761) and *Temora* (1763), and many shorter poems. They were translated into French almost immediately:

> Le début de l'ossianisme français est à peu près contemporain de la naissance même de l'Ossian anglais. A peine Macpherson a-t-il publié ses *Fragments* que le *London Chronicle* en donne quelques extraits; le journal tombe sous les yeux de Turgot qui, intéressé par une poésie si nouvelle, envoie deux morceaux traduits, et accompagnés de ses propres réflexions, au *Journal Étranger* (1760).

> [The beginning of French Ossianism is more or less contemporaneous with the emergence of Ossian in English. No sooner had Macpherson published his *Fragments* than the *London Chronicle* published several extracts from them. This paper came to the attention of Turgot who, interested in such new poetry, sent two translated passages accompanied by his own reflections to the *Journal Étranger* (1760)].[29]

Several partial translations emerged over the next two decades, with the entire Ossianic cycle appearing in 1777, translated by Le Tourneur. The poems were popular both amongst the general public and the famous names of the day. Diderot, for example, 's'extasie, à son ordinaire, devant les *chansons écossaises* qui lui paraissent l'essence même de la poésie' ['went into raptures, as usual, at the *Scottish songs*, which seemed to him to be the very essence of poetry'].[30] Napoleon was such a fervent reader of Ossian that he carried a copy whenever he went into battle.[31] Contemporary women writers also regarded the poetry of Ossian highly: Staël, for example, 'was as much an Ossian enthusiast as her archenemy Napoleon'.[32]

    The French public's affinity for Ossian can largely be attributed to the poems' exquisite depictions of nature, coupled with the fact that both the type of landscape and the manner of its description were novel. Scotland became revealed to the French as a land of wildness and melancholy: 'Macpherson opened a world of stormy mountain scenery, full of the grandeur and terror demanded by the new taste for the Sublime'.[33] The setting of the Ossian canon was in keeping with the fashion promoted by Rousseau in the same decade: the desire to return to nature, of which Ossian 'offre de parfaits modèles' ['offers perfect models'].[34] Yet these models are not the utopian Arcadias of a valley, meadow or garden. The Ossianic poems provide a very different return to nature: a return to wilderness, to barren, stormy landscapes, dominated by rugged mountains, bracken, mist and snow, resounding with the howling wind. Thus, the dissemination of the Ossianic poems engendered a vogue for a new type of nature which had not previously featured in French eighteenth-century novels: wild nature.

> La découverte d'Ossian aura également une influence sur le regard porté sur la nature. Si Haller, Rousseau et Saussure avaient mis les paysages alpins à la mode et transformé le jugement du public sur la montagne, Ossian acclimatera en France les mers tempétueuses, le vent, les rochers, les landes de bruyère et le brouillard.

> [The discovery of Ossian would also influence views on nature. If Haller, Rousseau and Saussure had made alpine landscapes fashionable and transformed the public's opinion of mountains, Ossian would accustom France to the stormy seas, wind, rocks, heather-covered moor, and fog].[35]

Van Tieghem describes in more detail the particular type of wild countryside in the Ossianic poems that appealed to the French nascent Romantic consciousness:

> Son paysage vague et vide, mais émouvant dans sa solitude et sa mélancolie; le spectacle monotone d'une mer orageuse et sombre, d'un ciel gris que parcourent perpétuellement des nuages, de montagnes désertes que recouvre le brouillard ou qu'un pâle soleil du Nord éclaire tristement; ces bruyères, ces rochers, ces torrents, ces chênes solitaires, ces chevreuils errant sur la mousse; ces tombeaux abandonnés, ces ruines de châteaux et de villes jadis prospères: tout cela était absolument nouveau pour la sensibilité européenne, et pour celle de la France en particulier.

> [Its landscape, indistinct and empty, yet moving in its solitude and its melancholy; the monotonous view of a gloomy and stormy sea, or a grey sky perpetually crossed with clouds, of desolate mountains covered with fog or

sadly lit up by a pale northern sun; the heather, the rocks, the torrents, the lonely oaks, the deer roaming over the moss; the abandoned tombs, the ruins of castles and once prosperous towns: all of this was absolutely new to European sensibility, and to that of France in particular].[36]

One feature which wild nature evokes, and which is important to bear in mind for *Corinne* and *Malvina,* is a preponderance towards melancholy. Indeed, for some travellers to Scotland, Ossian transformed their visit, bringing alive the melancholy countryside. Without Ossian, Scottish nature was just not the same:

> *Le Mercure* publie une traduction d'un *Voyage en Écosse:* l'auteur, qui est une dame, écrit d'Oban, en juin 1810, qu'elle veut croire à l'existence d'Ossian, comme à celle de Guillaume Tell, sans quoi 'les montagnes de la Suisse et celles de l'Écosse perdront' pour elle 'la moitié de leurs charmes'.

> [*Le Mercure* published a translation of *Voyage en Écosse:* the author, a woman, wrote in June 1810 about Oban and stated that she wished to believe in the existence of Ossian and that of William Tell, without which 'the mountains in Switzerland and those in Scotland would lose' for her 'half of their charm'].[37]

As Scotland increased in popularity with travellers and readers, it also grew in popularity with women writers, who portray the northern countryside because of its relevance to their writing. *Corinne* and *Malvina* are two perfect examples of novels which draw on well-recognized features of this wild nature and include direct references to the Ossianic stories. This allows their authors to heighten the arguments they contribute to the debate over women's writing. The Ossian cycle was already part of intellectual discussion on women's writing in England because of its employment in the meetings of the Bluestockings and its imitation in the works of writers like Catherine Talbot.[38] The Bluestockings, an English society founded by a feminine intellectual elite, had a particular affinity for Ossian:

> [They] began holding eccentric dinner parties, during which guests 'had the feast of shells and drank out of a nautilus shell to the immortal memory of Ossian.' In honour of Ossian, the recently rediscovered Highland bard, [Elizabeth] Montagu recreated — down to the unconventional stemware — the ceremonial meals of the Highland warriors described by Ossian's self-proclaimed translator [...]. Montagu's feasts are just one example of the Bluestockings' passion for Ossian, a passion that crops up repeatedly in their voluminous correspondence.[39]

Ossian enjoyed reverence amongst female intellectuals because of the poems' lack of bias regarding gender roles:

> In many ways, the Ossian poems provided a template for Bluestocking salons, where both sexes debated issues of literary, social, and political interest. [...] With the exception of their military exploits, popular heroines from the Ossian poems such as Malvina and Darthula acted remarkably like these first-generation Bluestockings.[40]

Not only did the Ossianic poems show women participating alongside men in feasting, drinking, politics, military campaigns, and intellectual discussions, but they also displayed open-minded tolerance towards female writers and poets:

> The poems also provided women writers on the Celtic periphery with a role
> model of a woman patriot poet who celebrates the history of her nation: the
> female bard, Malvina. [...] She is the addressee of many of Ossian's poems and,
> more importantly, a bard in her own right and Ossian's poetic heiress until her
> own premature demise.[41]

A set of epic poems which included tales of a female bard could hardly fail to appeal
to women publishing in an age which attempted to forbid them from, or condemn
them for doing so.

Almost every critic to comment upon the love of Ossian in late eighteenth- and
early nineteenth-century France alludes to Staël's *De la Littérature,*[42] and its notion
that there exist 'deux littératures tout à fait distinctes, celle qui vient du Midi et
celle qui descend du Nord; celle dont Homère est la première source, celle dont
Ossian est l'origine' ['two literatures, completely distinct from one another, the one
stemming from the South and the other from the North. Homer is the source of the
former, and Ossian the origin of the latter'].[43] Some, albeit few, of these critiques
also mention Staël's *Corinne* and Cottin's *Malvina*. However, no analysis exists of
both these novels in terms of their trio of common themes: depiction of Scottish
nature, reference to Ossian and discussion of women's writing. For centuries French
male writers had commented upon and imitated the male dominated works of
Homer and other ancient writers, yet,

> [u]sing the Ossian poems as evidence, conjectural historians portrayed the
> Highlands in the time of Ossian as an idyllic space where relative gender
> equality led to a refined sociability that eliminated the rough treatment of
> women found in Homer's ancient Greece.[44]

It is understandable, therefore, that Ossian should represent for French eighteenth-
and nineteenth-century women writers what, for centuries, Homer had represented
for men: a flattering vision of their sex and ambitions, and a revered hero to
emulate.

The Ossianic landscape and the Woman Writer in *Malvina*

Like Cottin, Mistress Clare (the woman writer in *Malvina*) argues that women
should only write when they have neither husband nor children to care for:

> [L]e motif de ma conduite [...] tient à un secret si important, que le monde
> entier, que mon père même l'ignore. [...] [P]renez bien garde que je ne permets
> d'écrire qu'à celles qui se trouvent dans ma situation [...]. Les épouses, les mères
> de famille composent la plus grande partie de notre sexe; l'importance de leurs
> devoirs ne leur laisse pas le temps de s'occuper des ouvrages de l'imagination.
> (*M* II, 84–90)

> [[T]he motive of my conduct [...] is linked to a secret so important that nobody
> in the world, not even my father, knows it. [...] [U]nderstand fully that I only
> permit women to write when they find themselves in my situation [...]. Wives
> and mothers make up the largest number among our sex; the importance of their
> duties does not leave them the time to deal with works of the imagination].

Yet, confusion emerges in *Malvina* because only four years after the publication of the first edition, a second edition was printed, in which the chapter incorporating the discussion about women's writing was removed. Had Cottin changed her mind about the reasons given? Had the removal of the heated topic been requested? The answer may perhaps never be entirely clear, but it is certain that Cottin's publisher did not demand the chapter's removal. On the contrary, Maradan states in a letter to Cottin: 'Madame, votre ouvrage a eu assez de succès pour me décider d'en faire une 2de édition sans changements et corrections' ['Madame, your book has been successful enough for me to decide to publish a second edition without amendments or corrections'].[45] It seems, then, that removing the chapter was Cottin's own decision. This implies that either she no longer felt it necessary to excuse her writing career, or that she no longer believed the reasons she had proffered. Either way, the only reason remaining in the second edition of *Malvina* regarding Mistress Clare's decision to write is the 'secret si important' ['secret so important'].

Mistress Clare initially refuses to confess this secret; however, she admits towards the end of the novel that she writes in order to raise money to support her sister Louise (*M* III, 57–58). Having been abandoned by Edmond Seymour after bearing his illegitimate child, Louise is left penniless and dying. Mistress Clare's writing provides Louise and her child with a roof over their heads. Interestingly, this roof is a natural one — 'creusée dans la roche et masquée de verdure' ['dug into the rock and covered with greenery'][46] — in the midst of the Scottish wilderness. Bianciardi describes the scene thus: 'la nature, protectrice, prend en charge la jeune femme, rejetée hors de la société' ['Nature protects and takes care of the young woman who has been rejected by society'],[47] and so we see Mistress Clare coupled with nature as they both protect Louise. This linking of the woman writer, nature and shelter recurs throughout the novel.

The notion of a woman justifying her writing through charitable necessity was not unique to Cottin's writing. The protagonist in Genlis's *La Femme Auteur*, sells her work in order to provide funds and security for those who need it:

> L'ouvrage, dès le soir même porté chez l'imprimeur, fut imprimé avec une extrême célérité [...]; l'édition entière fut enlevée en moins de douze jours: plusieurs personnes bienfaisantes, sachant à quel usage on en destinait le produit, ne se contentèrent pas de donner le prix fixé; un Russe, entre autres, envoya deux cents louis pour un seul exemplaire. Tout cet argent fut porté chez l'avocat des prisonniers, qui s'était chargé du soin de vendre l'ouvrage. Les quatre mille francs étaient complétés; Natalie, heureuse et triomphante, fut délivrer les prisonniers.

> [The book, taken to the printers that very evening, was printed with the greatest speed [...]; the entire edition was snapped up in less than twelve days: several kind people, knowing for what use the book was intended, were prepared to pay above the fixed price. A Russian, amongst others, sent two hundred louis for a single copy. All this money was taken to the prisoners' lawyer, who had been charged with taking care of the sale of the book. The four thousand francs were raised; Natalie, happy and triumphant, went to free the prisoners].[48]

Cottin also wrote to support others, in particular her cousin and closest friend

Julie Verdier. After Julie and her husband had separated due to the latter's violence, Julie lived with Cottin and 'dépendait vraisemblablement des secours que Sophie était heureuse de lui accorder' ['in all likelihood depended on the help with which Sophie was happy to provide her'].[49] Therefore, the theme of a woman writing in order to provide charity recurs both in the lives of authors and those of their protagonists. Perhaps such a selfless reason for entering the public sphere was deemed somewhat more admissible to others, or perhaps it simply appeared more acceptable, or flattering, to women writers themselves.

Sykes has argued that the presence of the Scottish landscape in Cottin's *Malvina* is a mere backdrop, of no importance to the story: 'l'Ecosse [...] n'est guère pour [*Malvina*] qu'un pays de montagnes escarpées et sauvages, où l'hiver est d'une rigueur extrême. Les descriptions de paysages sont fort rares et toutes conventionnelles' ['Scotland [...] for [*Malvina*] is only a country of steep and wild mountains where winter is extremely harsh. The descriptions of the landscape are very rare and all conventional'].[50] Paul Pelckmans believes Ossian no more relevant to the plotline than Scotland. He declares that, in *Malvina* (and in Staël's *Corinne*), '[l]a note ossianique [...] reste à peine moins incidente que ces allusions à la Révolution ou aux intrigues jacobites' ['[t]he Ossianic note [...] remains scarcely less incidental than the allusions to the Revolution or to the Jacobite intrigues'] in Mme de Charrière's *Les Ruines de Yedburg*.[51] Pelckmans describes the allusions to the Revolution and Jacobite intrigues in the latter novel as rare and hardly relevant at all. However, Ossian surfaces at particularly intriguing points within *Malvina*, rendering him far from insignificant. My discussion aligns itself with Van Tieghem's statement that 'le paysage des landes écossaises jou[e] un grand rôle dans le roman' ['the landscape of the Scottish moors plays a large role in the novel'].[52]

The wildness of the Scottish countryside contrasts starkly with the British order and routine in *Malvina*. The 'paysage vague et vide' ['vague and empty landscape'], the 'mer orageuse et sombre' ['gloomy and stormy sea'], the 'ciel gris' ['grey sky'], the 'montagnes désertes' ['desolate mountains'], the clouds, fog, rocks, heather, torrents and lonely oaks described by Van Tieghem resurface throughout Cottin's novel from the opening pages. Numerous features of the landscape, and the adjectives which characterize them, present Scotland as barren, remote, wild and cold to the extreme. To avoid confusion, the lengthier ensuing descriptions will be numbered, as they will be referred to in later analyses.

Quotation 1:

> [L]es eaux bleuâtres et transparentes du lac s'étendaient au loin, et les vapeurs qui s'élevaient de son sein ne permettaient pas d'apercevoir ses bornes. Sur un de ses côtés, les montagnes, couvertes d'une forêt de noirs sapins, dont les têtes robustes défieraient la fureur des tempêtes, entrecoupées de profonds ravins, du sein desquels de vastes et impétueux torrents se versaient à grand bruit, faisaient un contraste frappant avec le silence qui habitait les montagnes de l'autre rive; celles-ci, encombrées d'énormes blocs de granit, entassés les uns sur les autres, et sans aucun vestige de végétation, offraient à l'œil attristé l'image du chaos et de la destruction. (*M* I, 26)

> [The bluish and transparent waters of the lake extended into the distance, and

the vapour which rose from its heart made it impossible to discern its shores. On one side of the lake, the mountains — covered with a forest of black fir trees, whose sturdy treetops would defy the fury of the storms — interspersed with deep ravines, from the heart of which vast and impetuous torrents poured forth loudly, contrasted strongly with the silence which filled the mountains on the other side of the lake. These mountains, covered with enormous blocks of granite piled one on top of another, and lacking any trace of vegetation, presented to the saddened eye the image of chaos and destruction].

Images of wildness and fury abound in Cottin's juxtaposition of imposing mountains and rocky ravines, of storms and torrents. The forests do not have a cultivated or fresh greenery about them, they are black, and entirely enshroud the mountains. The granite stones and boulders are devoid of any vegetation, impressing upon the reader that attempts to civilize and cultivate this land would be futile. Similar pictures recur throughout *Malvina*. Where plant life does exist, it is just as untamed as the rocks.

Quotation 2:

> De hautes montagnes s'élevaient de tous côtés, et la voiture s'enfonçait dans une gorge sombre et solitaire. [...] [E]lle s'avança vers une roche assez élevée d'où pendaient, en festons et en guirlandes, des touffes de ronces et de plantes sauvages. (*M* III, 21–23)

> ['High mountains rose up on all sides, and the carriage sank into a gloomy, lonely gorge. [...] It headed towards a reasonably high rock from which hung, in festoons and garlands, clumps of brambles and wild plants].

Cottin describes only that which grows wild and free.

Nature's untamed liberty is not only apparent from its features, but also from descriptions of its characteristics. Cottin's use of pathetic fallacy in her portrayal of the fury of the storms and the impetuous torrents is striking. She imbues the Scottish landscape with the human characteristics and emotions necessary to paint it in a wild, impetuous light.

Quotation 3:

> Effrayée de la violence du vent qui faisait craquer ses croisées elle se levait, regardait le temps, et voyait la neige tomber à gros flocons. Elle se figurait qu'il y en avait au moins deux pieds d'épaisseur sur la terre, et que sir Edmond allait y être englouti: les torrents qui mugissaient au loin, lui semblaient des cris plaintifs, et le sinistre croassement des hiboux, des appellations douloureuses. (*M* I, 239)

> [Frightened by the violence of the wind crashing against her casement windows, she got up, looked at the weather, and saw the snow falling in large flakes. She imagined that the snow lay at least two feet thick on the ground, and that Sir Edmond would be submerged in it: the torrents which howled in the distance seemed like plaintive cries, and the sinister hooting of the owls like painful calls].

The savage, dominating, snow covered mountains, wild bracken and brambles, howling winds, storms and barren countryside give anything but an impression of order and stability. Indeed, contrary to the seventeenth- and early eighteenth-century notion of taming nature by imposing order on it, here the tempest threatens to destroy mankind and its order, with the howling gale battering the castle, and the snow potentially engulfing Edmond. The unfettered wildness of the landscape is the perfect metaphor for the female misfit who, similarly, struggles against society's rules, and it is therefore ideal for the social outcasts Malvina and her friend Mistress Clare to inhabit. The condemnation of Mistress Clare and her profession is obvious from the comments of Malvina's hostess:

> J'avais appris depuis peu qu'elle se mêle de faire des livres, et cette nouvelle lui a beaucoup nui dans mon opinion, car il me semble qu'une femme qui se jette dans cette carrière, ne sera jamais qu'une pédante ou un bel-esprit. (*M* II, 77)

> [I had only recently learned that she is involved in writing books, and this information has made me think far less of her, for it seems to me that a woman who launches herself into that career will never be anything other than a pretentious intellectual.][53]

Malvina also transgresses social boundaries and hierarchies, befriending the wild mountain men who work at the forge, and donating to their families when she is explicitly told to ignore them; she promotes women's reading and education; and she develops a close friendship with the female writer who is shunned by others.

There is a further reason why the landscape provides a fitting metaphor for the heroines struggling against the enforced rules of society. Eighteenth-century *philosophes* admired the political, religious and economic liberty of the English (male) population.[54] Béat Louis de Muralt noted in 1725 that 'l'Angleterre est un pays de liberté [...]: chacun y est ce qu'il a envie d'être' ['England is a country of freedom [...]: everyone there is what he wants to be'].[55] As a result of this freedom of expression and action, 'le peuple partage le gouvernement sans confusion' ['the people share the government without confusion'],[56] as Voltaire remarked. Britain was ordered and stable partly because of this political liberty and freedom of thought, meaning there was no need for political revolution. This liberty, so admired by the French, was believed to be rooted in the country's landscape and climate:

> French travellers [...] often viewed the English melancholy as inextricable from the very civic culture they so admired. Linking the 'melancholic disposition' of the English to the foggy climate, Le Blanc reasoned, 'this same tendency to melancholy prevents their ever being content with their fate, and equally renders them enemies to tranquillity and friends to liberty'. [...] Montesquieu argued in *L'Esprit des lois* (1748) that cold climate led the English [...] toward constitutional government.[57]

It is ironic that political liberty contributed to creating the social order that ultimately repressed women by dictating the roles they must fulfil and the rules they must obey. However, it is fitting that as a consequence of their own oppression, women should turn back to the wild landscape and climate that promote liberty in order to seek the freedom they desired.

Through use of pathetic fallacy, the landscape also reflects the female misfit's emotional reactions to her situation. In the description of the landscape in

Quotation 3, four sounds are repeated in immediate succession, all stemming from the weather, the flora and the fauna, and all suggesting pain and melancholy. The torrents 'mugissaient' ['howled'], this latter verb suggesting a noise made when suffering pain or grief. To confirm this suspicion, we are informed that such howlings resemble 'cris plaintifs' ['plaintive cries']. The 'sinistre croassement des hiboux' ['sinister hooting of the owls'] adds to the scene's eerie, wild aura, and yet simultaneously imbues it again with a sense of the inconsolable in its resemblance to 'appellations douloureuses' ['painful calls'].

The phrase 'offraient à l'œil attristé' ['presented to the saddened eye'] in Quotation 1 must be noted too. This phrase also appears as the novel opens: 'les arbres dépouillés de leurs feuilles, et le vaste tapis de neige qui couvrait la terre, offraient à l'œil attristé un austère et monotone tableau' ['the trees, stripped of their leaves, and the vast blanket of snow which covered the ground, presented to the saddened eye a sombre and dreary image'] (*M* I, 9). It both underlines the image of melancholy and simultaneously suggests that the natural scenery is particularly moving for those already susceptible to despondent emotions. The landscape, then, is an appropriate metaphor for the female misfit on account of its ability to display melancholia. The female misfit is doomed always to be melancholy if she must suffer others' condemnation. She is doomed also to be lonely, if society rejects her, and this, too, is echoed in Quotation 2, which describes the solitary nature of the gorges. Throughout the novel, Malvina displays the typically Romantic characteristics of feeling isolated and suffering melancholy. To begin with this is due to her friend Clara's death; subsequently it is when she befriends Mistress Clare and suffers condemnation from Mistress Birton and the latter's friends; finally she suffers melancholy loneliness when she is cast out from society altogether because of her marriage and when her daughter is removed from her.

Metaphor is only one technique employed to draw attention to the wild, melancholy, Romantic nature of Scotland, to the condition of the female misfit, and to the bond between the two. Attributing a human voice to the landscape means that it can speak not only *for* Malvina, but also *to* her. In other words, a discourse is established between the heroine and her *milieu*; natural space replies to Malvina, empathizes with her, comforts her, and provides her with a figurative asylum.

The landscape reassures Malvina that she is not alone, it experiences the same pressures she does. Furthermore, when Malvina is at her most melancholy and in need of comfort, Ossianic mythology becomes a recurring topos. According to Schama, the discourse between the landscape and the individuals who experience it can extend far deeper than the simple influence of one upon the other, or the projection of the sentiments of one onto the appearance of the other:

> [I]t should be acknowledged that once a certain idea of landscape, a myth, a vision, establishes itself in an actual place, it has a peculiar way of muddling categories, of making metaphors more real than their referents; of becoming, in fact, part of the scenery.[58]

Established in the Scottish countryside, the Ossianic myths provide rich descriptions of northern Britain's wild natural scenery. As Schama indicates, the presence of vestiges of mythology can build on and extend an author's use of spatial metaphor, with the result of creating a possibility of spatio-temporal transcendence through intertextuality. This enables Cottin to establish new links between Ossian, the wild landscape and the woman writer.

Ossian is first referenced in the opening chapter, as Malvina grieves for Clara. She feels alone in the world, and turns to the Ossianic countryside and the bard himself for solace:

> Malvina voyait avec une sorte d'intérêt cette antique Calédonie, patrie des Bardes, et qui brille encore de l'éclat du nom d'Ossian. Nourrie de cette lecture, il lui semblait voir la forme de son amie à travers les vapeurs qui l'entouraient: le vent sifflait-il dans la bruyère, c'était son ombre qui s'avançait; écoutait-elle le bruit lointain d'un torrent, elle croyait distinguer les gémissements de sa bien-aimée; son imagination malade était remplie des mêmes fantômes qui habitaient jadis le pays qu'elle traversait; son nom même, ce nom porté jadis par la fille d'Ossian, lui semblait un nouveau droit aux prodiges qu'elle espérait. [...] [D]ans ce moment sa douleur seule l'égarait. (M I, 12–13)

> [Malvina saw, with a kind of interest, this ancient Caledonia, homeland of the Bards, which still shines with the brilliance of Ossian's name. Stimulated by this reading, she thought she perceived the shape of her friend through the mist which surrounded her: when the wind whistled in the heather, it was her shadow approaching. She listened to the distant din of a torrent and thought she distinguished the groans of her beloved friend. Her fevered imagination was filled with the same spectres which previously inhabited the country she passed through. Even her name, the name borne long ago by the daughter of Ossian, seemed to give her new rights to the wonders for which she hoped. [...] [I]n this moment, only her pain led her astray].[59]

Malvina shares the name of Ossian's daughter-in-law, and draws comfort from this, feeling as though the landscape of Ossian understands her and her melancholia better because of it. Moreover, Cottin's choice to name her female protagonist Malvina permits the spatio-temporal gap between the narrative world of Cottin's novel and the mythical world of Ossian to be bridged, bringing them closer together. Cottin's ability to 'muddle the categories' in Schama's words, is further confirmed through comparison of the descriptions in *Malvina* with a passage from the Ossianic cycle itself, for there are striking resemblances. Cottin's Malvina is lamenting the death of her friend, when she imagines Clara's ghostly figure advancing through the mists, as the wind blows through the heather. One of Macpherson's poems, coincidentally entitled 'Malvina's Dream', depicts Malvina lamenting her husband's death. This Malvina, too, imagines her loved one's spectral form advancing through the wind and mist. The following quotation is taken from Le Tourneur's translation of Ossian, the French edition most readily available to, and most likely to have been read by Cottin:

> O vents, pourquoi avez-vous quitté les flots du lac? Vos ailes ont agité la cime de ces arbres, et le bruit a fait évanouir la vision. Mais Malvina a vu son amant; sa robe aérienne flottait sur les vents.

> [Oh winds, why did you leave the waters of the lake? Your wings shook the

tops of these trees, and the sound made the vision vanish. But Malvina saw her lover; his ethereal robe floating on the winds].[60]

The Ossianic Malvina shares emotions identical to those of her French literary name-sake, and thus the Ossianic myths are able to make Cottin's Malvina feel less alone.

Ossian appears a second time in Cottin's novel when Malvina is particularly troubled. Malvina feels guilty for distracting Edmond from his supposed fiancée, and worried about accusations of debauchery laid at his door. These concerns are compounded by feelings which she, herself, has for Edmond. Malvina thus proposes a walk in the Ossianic landscape to distract and comfort herself:

> Malvina rougit: la dernière phrase de M. Prior l'avait mise mal à son aise; [...] elle se leva [...] et retournant à la fenêtre: 'Monsieur Prior', dit-elle, 'je crois que, malgré l'excessive rigueur du froid, le soleil est si brillant, qu'il ferait beau au bord du lac; je n'y ai point été encore, et j'ai envie d'y hasarder une petite promenade'. (*M* I, 222)

> [Malvina blushed. M. Prior's last sentence had made her uncomfortable; [...] she got up [...] and, as she went back to the window, she said, 'Monsieur Prior, I think that, despite the bitter cold, the sun is so bright that it would be pleasant on the banks of the lake. I have not yet been, and I would like to venture there for a short walk'.]

On this walk, the landscape that she and the castle's other inhabitants traverse is so very Ossian-like that M. Prior is prompted to quote from one of Macpherson's poems, 'Carthon':

> Les arbres et les rochers, hérissés de glaçons et frappés par les rayons du soleil, brillaient des plus vives couleurs de l'arc-en-ciel; la neige qui couvrait le haut des montagnes, scintillait de feux éclatants, de sorte que les yeux étaient réellement éblouis de l'aspect de la campagne. En admirant les superbes effets de l'astre qui nous éclaire, s'écria monsieur Prior, en les admirant surtout dans ces montagnes, 'Qui ne respectera pas, avec moi, cette sublime invocation dont Ossian les fit retentir jadis?
> "O toi! qui roules au-dessus de nos têtes, rond comme le bouclier de nos pères, d'où partent tes rayons? O soleil! d'où vient ta lumière éternelle? [...] Tu te réjouis sans cesse dans ta carrière éclatante: lorsque le monde est obscurci par les orages, lorsque le tonnerre roule et que l'éclaire vole, tu sors de la nue dans toute ta beauté, et tu ris de la tempête"'. (*M* I, 224–26)

> [The trees and the rocks, glistening with ice and struck by the sun's rays, shone with the brightest colors of the rainbow. The snow which covered the mountain tops sparkled with fiery brilliance in such a way that the appearance of the countryside was truly dazzling to the eye. Admiring the superb effects of that star which illuminates us, and, particularly admiring its effects in the mountains, M. Prior exclaimed: 'Who will not observe, with me, that sublime invocation with which Ossian once made them resound?
> "Oh you who pass over our heads, as round as the shield of our fathers, from where do your rays originate? Oh sun! From where does your eternal light come? [...] You rejoice endlessly on your brilliant course: when the world is darkened by storms, when thunder rolls and lightning flies, you come out of the clouds in all your beauty, and you laugh at the storm"'.]

Thanks to the references to light and sunshine, the natural landscape becomes imbued with the happiness and security that we associate with light. Just as Malvina perceived through the window that the sun which brightened the day would cheer her mood, so too does Ossian write of the sun gracing the darkest hours. The sun of the Scottish landscape and that of the Ossian poem itself brightens Malvina. Again, the transcendence through space and time to the landscape of myth, permitted by intertextual references provides the female misfit with solace. Furthermore, the landscape is so Ossianic, the spatio-temporal gap so clearly bridged through intertextuality, that a strange figure resembling the Scottish bard himself appears within it. The similarity is so striking that it is practically a vision:

> A cet instant la conversation fut interrompue par l'aspect d'un homme qui parut sur une des hauteurs de la montagne. Il paraissait âgé, et sa marche incertaine pouvait faire présumer qu'il était aveugle. 'Ce maintien vénérable', s'écria M. Prior, 'cette barbe argentée, cette marche incertaine, et jusqu'à ce bâton qui l'aide au défaut de ses yeux, tout, dans ce vieillard, me rappelle l'image d'Ossian: tel il errait jadis dans ces mêmes lieux'. (*M* I, 229–30)

> [At that moment, the conversation was interrupted by the sight of a man who appeared on one of the mountain tops. He seemed old, and his unsteady walk could make one assume that he was blind. M. Prior exclaimed: 'That venerable bearing, that silvery beard, that unsteady step, and even that stick which assists him in the absence of his sight, everything about this old man reminds me of the image of Ossian, such as he was when he used to wander through these same places'.]

Ossian himself seems to appear to his daughter-in-law's namesake. As Edmond rushes to the aid of the blind figure that so resembles the Scottish bard, guiding his footsteps and ensuring he does not fall to his death, all Malvina's faith in and love for Edmond is restored. Thus, the Ossian figure temporarily causes all to right itself.

The reader familiar with Macpherson's poems will note a further link between Cottin's Ossianic landscape and the provision of comfort and shelter. *Malvina*'s natural scenery echoes very precisely one particular poem in the Ossian cycle, 'The Six Bards'. This poem, translated into French as 'Scène d'une nuit d'octobre dans le nord de l'Écosse' ['Scene from an October night in the North of Scotland'], recounts the story of five bards who arrive at the chief's home, seeking shelter on a bitter and unforgiving night. There are uncanny similarities between Macpherson's and Cottin's descriptions of the landscape:

> J'entends le bruit sourd et confus des vents dans la forêt lointaine; le torrent solitaire murmure tristement, au fond du vallon; la chouette glapissante crie au haut de l'arbre qui est auprès de la tombe des morts. [...] [D]eux torrents qui descendent de la montagne, se choquent et se mêlent en mugissant. [...] Le vent continue de mugir dans les creux des montagnes, et de siffler dans le gazon des rochers. [...] Écoutez comme la grêle tombe; des flocons de neige descendent en silence des nues: la cime des monts blanchit.

> [I hear the faint and muffled sound of the winds in the distant forest; the lonely mountain stream murmurs sadly at the bottom of the valley; the screeching

owl cries from the top of the tree near the grave of the dead. [...] [T]wo streams that flow down the mountain collide and roar as they merge. [...] The wind continues to howl in the mountain hollows and to whistle in the grass of the rocks. [...] Listen as the hail falls; snowflakes falling silently from the clouds: the summits of the mountains whiten over].[61]

The repeated references to the wind, the torrents, the howling, the mountains and the snow, all recall the characteristics of the wild landscape in Cottin's descriptions in Quotations 1–3. Even the endowing of the scenery with human voices and emotions is echoed: Macpherson's torrents murmur sadly, and the torrents howl and moan as if with pain or anger. Furthermore, the very theme of Macpherson's poem is the search for shelter. Each voice in the poem seeks shelter: the refrain 'recevez-moi, sauvez-moi de cette nuit!' ['let me in, protect me from this night!'] resurfaces three times. Cottin's novel echoes the Ossianic poem in which shelter is most notably sought, and her use of Ossianic space and myth in her own work provides her heroine with consolation and shelter when she most needs it.

According to Marko Juvan, 'intertextuality [...] remains one of the most powerful means of spatial transgression'.[62] Cottin evokes the extratextual time-space of Ossian and superimposes it onto Malvina's story, thus transgressing spatio-temporal boundaries and establishing a closer relationship between the landscape in her novel, the mythical aspects inherent within that landscape, and the female misfit. Juvan also asserts that '[t]he interplay of spaces and discourses constitutes identities and social relations'.[63] Toying with the boundaries of novelistic space, Cottin establishes discourse between the female misfit and Ossianic Scotland, which consequently helps both the reader and the misfit herself to discover the latter's characteristics and emotions. Through identification with the landscape, Malvina discovers her true self, in contradiction to, rather than in harmony with societal norms.

Yet, how is this focus on Ossian and comfort linked with the woman writer? As we have seen, one of the few circumstances in which Cottin advocated women writing was in order to provide charitable assistance or shelter for others. It is no surprise then, that in *Malvina*, an Ossianic landscape is not the only thing to provide Malvina with comfort and shelter. Mistress Clare reappears throughout the novel as a figure perpetually associated with this type of assistance. Her name often appears in conjunction with the word *asile*: 'je n'ai, dans ce moment, aucun autre asile que la maison de mistriss Clare' ['at this moment, I have no other asylum but that provided by the house of Mistress Clare'] (*M* II, 205). A bond is thus created between the woman writer and Ossian, owing to the similar roles that the two assume. Malvina approaches Mistress Clare several times when in need of help. When she is thrown out of Birton's estate and made homeless for declaring her wish to marry Edmond, she turns to Mistress Clare: 'je n'avais pas le choix des asiles, et dans la position où je me trouvais, celui que vous m'aviez si obligeamment offert était le seul qui me restât' ['I did not have a choice of shelters, and, in the position in which I found myself, the shelter with which you so obligingly provided me was the only one remaining to me'] (*M* II, 244–45). When Malvina receives a letter from Fanny's father stating his intention to remove Fanny from Malvina's care, Mistress Clare breaks her fall: 'son courage s'abattit, et fléchissant sous le poids de la douleur, elle

FIG. 5.1. Line engraving of Ossian and Malvina by Silvestre David Mirys, in *Ossian, Barde du IIIème siècle, Poésies galliques en vers français*, trans. by P. M. L. Baour Lormian (Paris: Giguet et Michaud, 1809).

tomba sans connaissance entre les bras de Mistriss Clare' ['her courage left her, and, collapsing under the weight of sorrow, she fell unconscious into the arms of Mistress Clare'] (*M* II, 259).

Perhaps the most significant time at which Malvina turns to Mistress Clare occurs as she is dying. Thus far, Malvina's protests against the suffering she has endured have failed, as we have seen in Chapter 3. Her rebellion through madness was quashed, and so she takes the only route left open to her: death. However, she uses what little strength remains to her to ensure the voice of women endures in a male-dominated world. She entrusts Fanny to the woman writer, asking her to raise and care for the child: 'Mistriss Clare, que son éducation vous soit confiée; ce devait être l'emploi de ma vie, il m'était bien doux; je n'ai rien de plus précieux à vous laisser pour tout le bien que vous m'avez fait' [Let her education be entrusted to you, Mistress Clare. It should have been my life's work, it was so very sweet to me. I have nothing more precious to leave you in return for all the good you have done for me] (*M* IV, 232). The significance of this request lies in the fact that Malvina entrusts both her future world (her adopted child and beloved next generation) and also her future voice (the instruction of Fanny) to the woman writer. In the Ossian myths, the bard himself similarly entrusts his own future voice and purpose — singing of the history of his homeland — to Malvina, the female bard. According to Leith Davis, Malvina is Ossian's poetic 'heiress': 'Ossian calls to Malvina: "Bring me the harp, O maid, that I may touch it when the light of my soul shall arise — Be thou near, to learn the song; and future times shall hear of Ossian".[64] An image depicting this very scene appears immediately following the title page of P. M. L. Baour Lormian's French translation of several of the poems in the cycle (see Fig. 5.1). Both the Malvina of the Ossian tales (the female bard) and the 'female bard' of Cottin's novel, Mistress Clare, hold the future in their hands. Cottin has ensured that her readers are aware of Malvina's name linking her to Ossian's daughter-in-law, and thus she creates a crucial succession: Ossian bequeaths his future to his daughter-in-law, Malvina. Now, Malvina (this time Cottin's Malvina) commits her future to a woman writer: her friend Mistress Clare. In giving her protagonist the name of Ossian's daughter-in-law, Cottin ensures that oral and written mythic past and tradition, comfort and safety, women's education, and the future are all passed on to women writers. In this way, Cottin takes Ossian's legacy — which he himself left with a female bard — and places it in the hands of her fellow female writers, thereby making a very strong statement about the importance and power of women's writing.

Further reference is made to Ossian when Birton informs her company of her disparaging opinions on women reading. When Malvina requests to borrow a book, she asserts: 'mon usage n'est pas de prêter mes livres aux femmes, qui ordinairement n'en ont aucun soin' ['it is not my practice to lend my books to women, who usually do not look after them'] (*M* I, 55). While she enjoys the privileges of her own place atop the social hierarchy (afforded to her by age, wealth and class), Birton believes that such privileges are not to be enjoyed by every woman. Rather, she represents a society which condemns women's education and writing and looks down on women readers. Consequently, she herself does not wish to encourage the

education of her sex by lending her books to women. Following this remark, M.
Prior, the curate, enquires about Malvina's own reading habits, and, in particular,
whether she is familiar with Ossian. The answer is yes. Following hard on the heels
of the condemnation of women's education is the confirmation that Cottin's misfit
heroine is well educated and enjoys reading Ossian, the poet associated with female
Bluestocking intellectuals and whose poems feature female bards. The contrast to
Birton's remark is a stark one.

It is unsurprising that Mistress Clare supports her sister and Malvina: she is an
intelligent and generous woman. However, it might appear odd that asylum should
be found in a wild landscape, and that this landscape should consequently reflect
the shelter-providing woman writer herself, especially when we have seen it rattle
the castle windows and threaten to bury Edmond in snow. Yet, as the introduction
to this book established, the term 'landscape' 'combine[s] a focus on the material
topography of a portion of land (that which can be seen) with the notion of vision
(the way it is seen)'.[65] Consequently, consideration of point of view sheds light
on the argument, and it is here that we begin to see the creation of an implied
reader. The landscape is certainly wild and threatening, but only to those who
avoid contemplating it. For those who are willing to gaze upon it and to explore
Macpherson's text, the landscape is sublimely beautiful, and does indeed provide
shelter. Whereas Malvina enjoys gazing out of her bedroom window at the scenery,
Birton refuses to do so, stating: 'Croyez-moi, il vaut mieux regarder le beau ciel de
France et d'Italie en peinture, que celui d'Ecosse en réalité' ['Believe me, it is better
to contemplate paintings of the beautiful skies of France and Italy than it is to look
upon the Scottish sky in reality'] (M I, 27). It is therefore Malvina who perceives the
comfort to be gained from the landscape, and who is able to hear the melancholy
in its voice, and discern its empathy. Birton, on the other hand, voluntarily blinds
herself to the landscape, and so the torrents and storms threateningly rattle the
casements of her castle.

Society further proves its voluntary blindness in the novel by exhibiting a
denial to read the poetry of Ossian. Malvina seems truly capable of appreciating
the Ossianic poems, because she makes the effort to comprehend the 'original'
language. Upon being offered lessons in Erse, 'Malvina accepta cette proposition
avec grand plaisir' ['Malvina accepted the proposal with great pleasure'] (M I, 70).
Birton at first reluctantly also agrees to attend the lessons, but never does. Birton's
friend, Kitty Melmor, is even more disparaging of Ossian, actively deriding him.
On observing M. Prior with a copy of his own translation, she rudely demands:
'Ah! fi! [...] comment avez-vous eu le courage d'écrire toutes ces tristes psalmodies?'
['Oh dear! [...] How could you bear to write all these sad dronings?'] (M I, 66–67).
She even boorishly interrupts his reply:

> 'Ne craignez-vous pas?...' 'Que l'esprit des collines, monté sur un coursier de
> vapeurs, ne me transperce de sa lance de brouillard?' interrompit miss Melmor
> en ricanant. 'Non, en vérité; et quand le soir viendra, que le vent sifflera dans
> la forêt, que les météores s'élèveront du sein du lac, et que les dogues hurleront
> dans la basse-cour, ce ne sera pas de la colère d'Ossian dont je serai effrayée'.
> (M I, 67–68)

['Are you not afraid?'... 'What? That the spirit of the hills mounted on a misty steed should run me through with his foggy lance?' interrupted Miss Melmor jeeringly. 'In all honesty, no. And when the evening draws in, the wind whistles through the forest, the meteors rise up from the bottom of the lake, and the guard dogs howl in the courtyard, it will not be Ossian's anger that I fear'.]

Cottin implies that only those who fully understand Ossian and who hear him speaking to them through the landscape, can also understand the natural countryside itself, and find solace in it. Appreciating the *written* landscape is therefore just as important as appreciating the physical one. For both Birton and Melmor the landscape will always be wild and threatening. They represent the social order against which the landscape and the female misfit, struggle to rebel. Thus they are incapable of viewing such rebellion as anything other than misbehaviour which must be repressed, whether this be by replacing the views out of the window with paintings of calmer, more socially acceptable views of France and Italy, by refusing to read Ossian, or by insisting that the female misfit conform to societal norms.

Intertextual references create an implied reader in *Malvina,* making apparent the importance of understanding these references. Kitty Melmor and Mistress Birton are ignorant of the Ossian poems, a situation against which Cottin clearly warns her reader. In so doing, she implies that the reader familiar with Ossian will comprehend allusions within her text that do not appear at first sight. Cottin confirms this with statements made by Mistress Birton and Kitty Melmor themselves:

> 'Miss Kitty', lui dit mistriss Birton avec un peu de hauteur, 'pour se mêler de juger un pareil ouvrage, il faut être en état d'en sentir les beautés, et en avoir lu plus de quelques pages, avant de se hasarder d'en parler'. (*M* I, 68)

> ['Miss Kitty', Mistress Birton said to her rather haughtily, 'to exercise the right to judge such a work, you must be capable of appreciating its beauties. You should also have read more than just a few pages of it before you venture to speak of it'.]

There is irony in Mistress Birton's retort. Although she is correct, she too has not read Ossian: ' "En ce cas", dit Miss Melmor tout bas, en se penchant vers l'oreille de Malvina, "elle ferait bien de n'en rien dire" ' [' "In that case", Miss Melmor said, leaning over to whisper in Malvina's ear, "she would do better to say nothing" '] (*M* I, 68). If you do not know Ossian, Cottin appears to say, you do not know my novel, and nor do you understand the arguments I contribute to the debate over the woman writer.

The Foundation of 'True Liberty' and the Importance of Women's Writing and Education in *Corinne*

According to Foley:

> *Corinne* was controversial at the time [...] because it dealt with the question of female talent and ambition. The heroine Corinne was a woman who challenged social norms and chose life as an author over marriage. [...] [The] plot raised questions about women's lives which daughters of the bourgeoisie were advised not to ask.[66]

As a female genius, Corinne is destined to endure the condemnation of others. Her alternate emotional states of suffering and happiness are reflected and inflected by the natural landscapes which surround her.

Corinne's mother was Italian and her father British, but her true love is for her mother's homeland. When in Italy, she feels that, although she is different, she is loved and respected. The warmth of her reception is mirrored in that of the climate, as Oswald notes:

> Un soleil éclatant, un soleil d'Italie frappa ses premiers regards, et son âme fut pénétrée d'un sentiment d'amour et de reconnaissance pour le ciel qui semblait se manifester par ces beaux rayons. [...] [O]n devait couronner le matin même, au Capitole, la femme la plus célèbre de l'Italie, Corinne, poète, écrivain, improvisatrice, et l'une des plus belles personnes de Rome. (C, p. 49)

> [Blazing sunshine, Italian sunshine, was the first thing to meet his eyes, and his soul was filled with love and gratitude for the sky which seemed to express itself through these beautiful rays. [...] [T]hat very morning, the most celebrated woman in Italy — Corinne, a poet, writer, improviser, and one of the most beautiful people in Rome — was to be crowned at the Capitol.]

Although her life does not conform to a woman's expected role, Corinne is happy in Italy. Italian nature encourages the woman writer's genius: her talents flourish in the warmth of the sun. Her situation is very different, however, in her adolescence, spent in England with her father's new wife, Lady Edgermond, and her half-sister Lucile. Here a woman's talent is not celebrated. Lady Edgermond proclaims:

> Il y a des actrices, des musiciens, des artistes enfin pour amuser le monde; mais pour des femmes de notre rang, la seule destinée convenable, c'est de se consacrer à son époux et de bien élever ses enfants. [...] [C]e pays lui est odieux; [Corinne] ne peut se plier à nos mœurs, à notre vie sévère. (C, pp. 458–61)

> [There are actresses, musicians and artists to entertain the world; but for women of our rank, the only appropriate destiny is that of devoting ourselves to our husbands and bringing up our children well. [...] [S]he detests this country; [Corinne] cannot bend herself to our customs or to our strict life.]

She thus confirms Corinne's status as a misfit for choosing authorship over domestic duties. The descriptions of British order in *Corinne* are similar to those in *Malvina*. Corinne notices the routine and rules of the society to which she is expected to adhere, and remarks: 'l'existence des femmes dans le coin isolé de la terre que j'habitais, était bien insipide' ['the existence of women in the isolated corner of the earth which I inhabited was very dull'] (C, p. 370). The situation for talented women in Britain, therefore, is very different from that in Italy:

> Il y a dans les plus petites villes d'Italie un théâtre, de la musique, des improvisateurs, beaucoup d'enthousiasme pour la poésie et les arts, un beau soleil; enfin, on y sent qu'on vit; mais je l'oubliais tout-à-fait dans la province que j'habitais, et j'aurais pu, ce me semble, envoyer à ma place une poupée légèrement perfectionnée par la mécanique; elle aurait très bien rempli mon emploi dans la société. (C, p. 369)

> [In the smallest Italian towns you will find a theatre, music, improvisers, great

enthusiasm for poetry and the arts, beautiful sunshine. Indeed, you feel alive there. However, I forgot this completely in the area where I lived, and it seems to me that I could have sent a delicately perfected mechanical doll to fill my role in society. Such a doll would have done very well in my place.]

Corinne explains how a woman who possessed any genius or desire for education soon had it eliminated from her in Britain:

> Il y en avait quelques-unes qui, par la nature et la réflexion, avaient développé leur esprit, et j'avais découvert quelques accents, quelques regards, quelques mots dits à voix basse, qui sortaient de la ligne commune; mais la petite opinion du petit pays, toute-puissante dans son petit cercle, étouffait entièrement ces germes: on aurait eu l'air d'une mauvaise tête, d'une femme de vertu douteuse, si l'on s'était livré à parler, à se montrer de quelque manière. (C, p. 370)

> [There were some women who, because of their nature and through reflection, had developed their minds, and I had discovered certain traces, certain looks, words uttered in low voices, which broke away from the norm. However, the small-mindedness of the small region, all-powerful in its own little circle, stifled these seeds entirely. Had one indulged in speaking or in making oneself conspicious in any way, one would have appeared difficult, a woman of dubious virtue.]

Not only is the order of British society not conducive to women's writing, it actively discourages it, stifling talented women with its cold reception. In this way, Staël, like Cottin, uses British society within her novel to represent her own nation. The order and regulations stereotypically attached to British society provide the perfect setting against which Staël can situate the story of a talented heroine wishing to break away from such misogynistic oppression.

It is not only the British people and society that are cold, but also the natural landscape and climate. The features of the wild landscape in themselves are similar to Cottin's. The pines enshroud the mountains in *Corinne* as in *Malvina*: 'les sapins couvraient les montagnes toute l'année, comme un noir vêtement' ['the pines covered the mountains all year long, like a black blanket'] (C, p. 378). Unlike the scenery in *Malvina*, however, the wild natural landscape in *Corinne* does not comfort the female misfit. The landscape is predominantly bleak, dismal and damp, features which are absorbed by the heroine: 'Le temps était humide et froid; je ne pouvais presque jamais sortir sans éprouver une sensation douloureuse' ['The weather was damp and cold; I could almost never go out without suffering'] (C, p. 367).

Corinne continually compares the frigid and depressing atmosphere of the British natural landscape with the warmth of that in Italy:

> Chaque jour j'errais dans la campagne, où j'avais coutume d'entendre le soir, en Italie, des airs harmonieux chantés avec des voix si justes, et les cris des corbeaux retentissaient seuls dans les nuages. Le soleil si beau, l'air si suave de mon pays était remplacé par les brouillards; les fruits mûrissaient à peine, je ne voyais point de vignes, les fleurs croissaient languissamment à long intervalle l'une de l'autre. (C, p. 378)

> [Every day I would wander in the countryside, where, in the evening in Italy, I was accustomed to hearing harmonious tunes, sung with such perfect

voices, and the squawks of crows resounding alone in the clouds. My country's beautiful sunshine and sweet air were replaced by fog. Fruit hardly ripened, I could not see any vines at all, flowers grew languidly and sparsely.]

The contrast between the two landscapes is highlighted in both vocabulary and sentence structure. The repetition of *si* in the description of the Italian climate to reinforce the warmth and beauty of the country and its landscape is outweighed in the second part of the sentence by the triple combination of 'à peine' ['hardly'], the negative 'ne point' ['not at all'] and the adverb 'languissamment' ['languidly']. It is unclear whether the Italian nature referred to here is tamed or untamed, however what is certain is that whilst flora and fauna flourish in Italy, fruits, vines and flowers hardly appear in Britain: Britain's is a landscape that, in Corinne's opinion, cannot be tamed. In fact, the British landscape in Staël's novel 'est d'abord et avant tout un paysage sombre' ['is first and foremost a gloomy landscape'].[67] This is very different from Cottin's novel, in which the sun shone brilliantly on Malvina's lakeside walk, and in which the sun of the Ossian poems was quoted.

When Malvina contemplates the British countryside she is at peace with her differences from society. In *Corinne*, instead of mirroring the situation and characteristics of the female misfit, Staël's portrayal of the northern British landscape heightens the protagonist's impression that she does not belong. Thus, whilst the landscape of Staël's novel certainly takes on a Romantic, melancholic aspect, like the landscape in *Malvina*, in this case the melancholy it provides is neither comforting nor cathartic. Instead, northern Britain provides a depressing melancholy for Corinne. To compound matters, the further north one travels, the more acute the effect of this melancholy gloom: 'Je m'avançais vers le nord; sensation triste et sombre que j'éprouvais, sans en concevoir bien clairement la cause' ['As I made my way north, I experienced a sad and gloomy sensation without clearly appreciating the cause of it'] (*C*, p. 362).

Most painful of all for Corinne is the fact that the more depressed she becomes because of this landscape, the more she begins to feel her talent dissipate: '[C]e qui m'affligeait davantage encore, je sentais mon talent se refroidir' ['[W]hat distressed me more was that I could feel my talent cooling'] (*C*, p. 371). Just as she is stifled by society, so too is her talent. Rather than echoing the female misfit's situation, by displaying wildness in the face of order, the northern natural landscape in *Corinne* exacerbates it. Nature surrounds her with a cold and unforgiving *milieu*, increases her state of depression, and thus illustrates more clearly for the reader the problems and emotions confronted by women writers of genius. The wilds of the North are as hostile as the people in their attack on her, as Corinne herself notes, 'il y avait dans la nature quelque chose d'hostile' ['there was something hostile in nature'] (*C*, p. 367).

On first reading, then, the northern landscapes in *Malvina* and *Corinne* appear to be employed to different ends. However, the full picture is not this simple, for two reasons. The negative presentation of Britain and the positive presentation of Italy in *Corinne* do not match Staël's original intentions when she first conceived the novel. Nor do they correspond to Staël's presentation of this landscape and its myths elsewhere in her works. Firstly, reconsidering Staël's original intentions for *Corinne* will help us to understand a closer link between the woman writer and the provision of assistance and asylum to the less fortunate, as we see in Cottin's *Malvina*. Secondly, reconsidering *Corinne* alongside Staël's philosophical writing will enable us to form more concrete conclusions about Staël's opinions on how true freedom for a nation can be achieved with the help of the wild northern landscape and Ossian. It will also help us to see how, in Staël's opinion, woman's voice and education is fundamental to the creation of true freedom. To achieve these aims, I will examine Karen de Bruin's reinterpretation of the novel alongside my own analysis of the novel's depiction of the Ossianic myths and landscape.[68] Bruin provides accurate analysis of Staël's argument that two types of liberty — political and social — are crucial for the foundation of true freedom, and states that it is with *Corinne* that Staël is able to present the success of this combination for the first time. Bruin argues ultimately that Corinne herself is the 'model of moral emulation for a nation seeking freedom'.[69] However, Bruin does not show how this model figure of freedom is permitted to become so because of her vital engagement with the Ossianic landscape, or how women writers in general might use that landscape (at the juncture of political and social freedom) as a platform for re-establishing their own voice. My analysis therefore adds to Bruin's own, by arguing that Staël employs the Ossianic cycle and its landscape in order to contribute to the contemporary debates over women's societal roles and the social or creative restrictions imposed on women.

On travelling to Italy, Staël noted it to be a country lacking political freedom, whose repressed people suffered under a corrupt and ineffectual government. She viewed the French situation similarly: suffering under the oppression of Napoleon. It was in fact Staël's intention with *Corinne* to compare this negative critique of Italy with the positive aspects that she admired about Britain. Indeed, these negative views creep into *Corinne* throughout the plot. When Oswald returns to Britain he admires the political freedom of his fellow Englishman and the consequent stability of his homeland, whereas he 'pensait à l'Italie pour la plaindre. [...] [E]n Italie les institutions et l'état social ne rappelaient, à beaucoup d'égards, que la confusion, la faiblesse et l'ignorance' ['thought of Italy to pity it. [...] [I]n Italy, institutions and the social conditions recalled, in many respects, only confusion, weakness and ignorance'] (*C*, p. 447). Staël's view of Britain corresponds largely with Oswald's: Staël 'creates a hierarchy of the freest and happiest nations and epochs. In this hierarchy, contemporary England, its regime of political liberty, and its melancholic people rank as superior'.[70] Staël, then, adheres to the views of the Enlightenment thinkers: that, in general, a society of greater political freedom existed in Britain than anywhere else in Europe.

Despite this, when *Corinne* appeared in 1807, the overall impression of Italy and its landscape was positive. This is because Staël's publisher, H. Nicolle, refused to print the book if the portrayal of Italy was critical. Staël asked her publisher to advance her 20,000 francs in return for the promise of a four-volume manuscript about Italy. Nicolle agreed on account of Staël's bestselling reputation, though later when he realized he knew nothing about the argument of Staël's intended book, he approached her to ask: 'Un mot encore, je vous prie, madame la baronne. J'ai omis de vous demander si le nouveau roman que vous allez me livrer est *pour* ou *contre* l'Italie?' ['One word more, please, Madam Baroness. I have forgotten to ask you whether the new novel that you are to present to me is *for* or *against* Italy'].[71] Staël's reply was clear:

> Contre, Monsieur, contre. Après avoir rendu au beau ciel de l'Italie la justice qui lui est due, après avoir parlé des belles collections de peinture et de sculpture qu'elle possède, indiqué les ruines majestueuses dont tout le monde a parlé, que voulez-vous qu'on dise *pour* l'Italie, ce pays sans mœurs, sans gouvernement, sans police, ce pays où il n'y a plus d'énergie que parmi les brigands qui infestent les grandes routes, où l'esprit de conversation est borné comme la loge au théâtre dans laquelle la société italienne fait et rend ses visites? [...] Oui, que dire *pour* un tel pays, Monsieur?

> [Against, Sir, against. After doing due justice to the beautiful Italian sky, after discussing the beautiful collections of paintings and sculptures that the country possesses, after pointing out the majestic ruins about which everyone has spoken, what would you like to be said *for* Italy — this country without morals, government or police, this county where there is no longer energy except that amongst the brigands who infest the highways, where the spirit of conversation is as limited as the box at a theatre in which Italian society pays and returns its calls? [...] Yes, what is there to be said *for* such a country, Sir?].[72]

Nicolle was horrified, and turned down Staël's manuscript: 'Mais alors, madame la baronne, si votre ouvrage est *contre*, j'ai le regret de vous avouer que je ne puis me charger de le publier' ['In that case, Madam Baronness, if your work is *against* Italy, I regret to inform you that I cannot take on its publication'].[73] He had only recently published Auguste Creuzé de Lessert's *Voyage en Italie et en Sicile* [*Journey through Italy and Sicily*], which also presented a negative view of Italy. Fearing that publishing a second criticism of the country so soon afterwards would affect his business, he informed Staël: 'Il faudrait, madame, que le vôtre fût pour' ['Yours, Madam, must be in favour [of Italy]'].[74]

Staël's desperate reaction — 'Mais, monsieur, j'ai besoin de mes 20 000 francs' ['But, sir, I need my 20,000 francs'] — is very revealing, for she had specific plans for the money: 'elle avait promis, pour un hôpital qu'on devait élever aux environs de Coppet, une somme de 20 000 francs' ['she had promised a sum of 20,000 francs to a hospital which was going to be constructed in the vicinity of Coppet'].[75] It is her intention to use the profits to provide financial assistance and physical shelter for those less fortunate which provokes the radical alteration in her manuscript. She finally agreed:

> En échange des 20 000 francs que vous me remettrez, je m'engage à vous livrer, dans les trois mois, le manuscrit de l'ouvrage en quatre volumes que je vais écrire... Et, *puisqu'il le faut*, l'ouvrage sera *pour* et s'appellera *Corinne*.

> [In exchange for the 20,000 francs that you will pay me, I agree to deliver to you, in three months, the manuscript of a work in four volumes that I will write... And, *since it must be so*, the work will be *for*, and will be called *Corinne*].[76]

Staël has more in common with Cottin, then, than it first appears. Cottin presents the woman writer as a provider of aid and shelter, and links her inextricably with the landscape and myths of northern Britain, which also provide Malvina with these much needed comforts. Staël sacrifices the argument she originally intended to make with her book in order that she might use the profits from her writing to provide that same assistance and asylum to those in need. It is somewhat ironic that, in order to do this, her depiction of a landscape which elsewhere is associated with the very provision of aid and shelter had to suffer. For Staël to present an even greater positive, warm atmosphere and landscape in Italy, her depiction of Britain had to provide contrast, and so we lose all sense of the wild North providing comfort to the female misfit, or being associated with her intellectual freedom. It is unsurprising to see British aristocratic society in *Corinne* (represented largely by Lady Edgermond, M. Maclinson and Oswald's father) arguing that women should not write; this is after all the same argument we see with Mistress Birton and Kitty Melmor in *Malvina*. However, it is surprising to see Staël presenting the landscape of northern Britain as a space which stifled artistic talent. She had certainly not presented it as such in *De la Littérature*. Knowing the story behind the publication, however, we might reasonably believe that, were we to see the work Staël originally intended, the British landscape might not be presented in this way at all. Analysis of *De la Littérature*, along with a crucial reconsideration of Ossianic passages from *Corinne*, indicates that Staël would have portrayed a landscape similar to that in Cottin's novel. Indeed, she has Corinne state (with regard to Britain): 'bien que je n'aimasse pas la petite ville que j'habitais, je respectais l'ensemble du pays dont elle faisait partie' ['although I did not like the small town in which I lived, I respected the larger country to which it belonged'] (*C*, p. 380).

In *De la Littérature*, northern Britain and the Ossianic cycle are connected with melancholy in the same positive, soothing way as in *Malvina*. Staël encourages melancholic emotion in her readers, arguing that the melancholy inspired by wild northern landscapes influences creativity: 'La mélancolie, ce sentiment fécond en ouvrages de génie, semble appartenir presque exclusivement aux climats du nord' ['Melancholy, that fertile sentiment in works of genius, seems to belong almost exclusively to northern climates'].[77] If melancholy does indeed, as Staël argues, inspire artistic production, and if *Corinne* had been permitted to echo *De la Littérature*, we might have seen the wild northern landscape mirroring the rebellious nature of Corinne, comforting her when society oppressed her, and allowing her to explore her literary talent further.

In *De la Littérature*, Staël also discusses how political liberty can be achieved for a nation, and, particularly, how emulating the North can promote this freedom in France. She believed three major aspects were required to attain political liberty: a melancholic disposition; virtuous, self-sacrificing duty towards civic service (the duty expected of you by and for society); and artistic and poetic talent. These three aspects, and their links to wild natural landscapes are vital to an analysis of Staël's presentation of Ossian in *Corinne*, and to the arguments she makes regarding women's writing and education.

Firstly, the melancholic disposition of the British leads to their political liberty:

> On se demande pourquoi les Anglais qui sont heureux par leur gouvernement et par leurs mœurs, ont une imagination beaucoup plus mélancolique que ne l'était celle des Français? C'est que la liberté et la vertu, ces deux grands résultats de la raison humaine, exigent de la méditation: et la méditation conduit nécessairement à des objets sérieux.

> [One wonders why the English, who are happy with their government and customs, should have a much more melancholic imagination than that of the French. It is because freedom and virtue, these two great results of human reason, require meditation, and meditation inevitably leads to serious things].[78]

The melancholy which begets this political liberty is rooted in the climate and landscape of the island in exactly the same way as is artistic production:

> Les peuples du nord sont moins occupés des plaisirs que de la douleur; et leur imagination n'en est que plus féconde. Le spectacle de la nature agit fortement sur eux; elle agit, comme elle se montre dans leurs climats, toujours sombre et nébuleuse. Sans doute les diverses circonstances de la vie peuvent varier cette disposition à la mélancolie; mais elle porte seule l'empreinte de l'esprit national.

> [Northern peoples are less occupied with pleasure than with pain, and their imagination is more fertile for it. The sight of nature has a strong effect on them; its effects on them are dark and cloudy, as it is in their climate. Undoubtedly the diverse circumstances of life can vary this disposition to melancholy, but that alone bears the mark of the national spirit].[79]

The second requirement for political liberty is the dedication of oneself to the duty of civil service. Staël argues: 'le pénible et continuel dévouement des emplois civils et des vertus législatives, le sacrifice désintéressé de toute sa vie à la chose publique, n'appartient qu'à la passion profonde de la liberté' ['the painful and continual devotion to civil employments and legislative virtues, the selfless sacrifice of their whole life to public affairs, belongs only to the profound passion for liberty'].[80] This, like reflection on serious subjects, is inspired by melancholy: 'civic melancholy [...] remov[es] the individual from vain aspirations and luxurious self-indulgence while simultaneously promoting civic ideals and public engagement'.[81] This argument is reiterated in *Corinne* by Oswald, who, in his descriptions of the origins of British political liberty, couples melancholy with the same virtue and duty towards society. According to Bruin:

> Suggesting that England has succeeded, at least politically, in founding its society upon the universal values of liberty and equality, Oswald cannot overcome his disdain for the lack of gravity and philosophy in Italy. He remains convinced that the English are more virtuous than the Italians because they are more attached to the 'cult of sorrow,' a cult that defines virtue as the resignation of the pain-filled soul to public service.[82]

Finally, because melancholic dispositions naturally beget both artistic talent and the civic duty required for political liberty, and because all three of these aspects flourish in a northern climate and landscape, according to Staël, '[l]a poésie du nord convient beaucoup plus que celle du midi à l'esprit d'un peuple libre' ['northern poetry is better suited to the minds of a free people than is the poetry of the South'].[83] Even northern poetry itself is therefore suited to the production of political liberty.

However, British liberty was not all-encompassing: Staël admired the political liberty while at the same time recognizing the significant lack of social liberty, particularly for women. This lack comes through strongly in *Corinne,* whose eponymous heroine is stifled by British society's objection to her work as a woman writer-performer. Bruin argues that in *Corinne* Staël brings two types of liberty together, therefore, in the two protagonists from their opposing countries: Oswald represents the political liberty and yet also the social rigidity of Britain, and Corinne represents the social freedom and political bondage of Italy. Corinne remarks upon this difference, stating that Italy 'n'est sûrement pas un pays où la liberté subsiste telle que vous l'entendez en Angleterre; mais on y jouit d'une parfaite indépendance sociale' ['is certainly not a country where liberty survives in the same way in which you understand it in England. Nonetheless, in Italy, people enjoy total social independence'] (*C*, p. 152). She sees this social independence as crucial for women's rights, since without it she could do neither the writing nor the performing she loves. As far as Oswald is concerned, however, duty and civic virtue is more important than social liberty. According to Bruin,

> any society that would give as much social independence to women would be antithetical to a society in which real political freedom can exist, and thus he dismisses the very notion of social independence. Instead, Oswald argues for a society that defines the individual as *he* who obeys all laws and who submits entirely to his duty toward convention and public opinion, even if this definition rejects women as both citizens and individuals (thus relegating them entirely to the domestic sphere). Corinne disagrees.[84]

By attributing the political liberty of Britain to Oswald and the social liberty of Italy to Corinne, Staël presents the discussion of true freedom in terms of gender as well as space. The political sphere is male dominant, and it is the male protagonist who argues for its importance. According to Oswald, *because* social liberty results in women's rights, it must be dismissed, for allowing women social freedom would undermine a country's political freedom. As we have seen, many believed that this had been the case in Ancien Régime France, and were keen to deny women this same freedom in post-revolutionary France.

Neither social nor political liberty is sufficient, by itself, for the creation of a truly free nation. As Bruin states:

> At this stage of the novel, Oswald and Corinne [...] do not yet recognize that it is at the conjuncture of personal freedom and political liberty that true freedom can exist. Consequently, neither Corinne nor Oswald yet embodies the liberal thinker that Staël believes should serve as moral compass for a future free French republic.[85]

It is, perhaps, no bad thing that Staël was forced to present Italy positively after all, for she turns it to her advantage. She shapes her new manuscript to discuss not only the political liberty of Britain but also the social liberty of women in Italy in order to promote both in her homeland. A true liberal thinker — or, as Bruin describes it, the moral compass that Staël believes is capable of leading France out of its oppression — will accept that a middle ground, shared between genders, must be sought between political and social independence.

According to Bruin, Staël clarifies in *De la Littérature* that a melancholy disposition must actively be sought in all nations desiring political liberty, but

> does not fully answer the question of how to harness melancholy's philosophical power in order to propagate a cult of freedom in France. It is through her novel *Corinne, or Italy* that Staël presents to her readers for the first time the solution.[86]

This is certainly true. However, I believe Bruin's arguments in fact form the stepping stone to further analysis and even deeper conclusions. The most interesting aspect of all can be found in the two points in this novel when Staël harmoniously conjoins the two contrasting definitions of liberty embodied by her protagonists. These two instances revolve around intertextual references to the Ossian cycle and its wild natural landscape, and they have, thus far, remained unexplored in three respects. Firstly, it is the very engagement with the Ossianic myths and their melancholy landscape that permits the success of the model of true liberty to be outlined. Secondly, when combined, these two instances illustrate the undeniable importance of women's writing and education for the 'cult of freedom in France' to which Staël aspires. Thirdly, these instances therefore ultimately allow Staël to contribute to the contemporary debate over women writers, and to do so in a manner very similar to that of Cottin.

The first instance in which Staël brings political and social liberty together takes place in front of a painting depicting the story of the son of Caïrbar, a tale from the Ossian cycle:

> [C]'est le fils de Caïrbar endormi sur la tombe de son père. Il attend depuis trois jours et trois nuits le barde qui doit rendre des honneurs à la mémoire des morts. Ce barde est aperçu dans le lointain, descendant de la montagne; l'ombre du père plane sur les nuages; la campagne est couverte de frimas; les arbres, quoique dépouillés, sont agités par les vents, et leurs branches mortes et leurs feuilles desséchées suivent encore la direction de l'orage. (*C*, pp. 237–38)

> [[I]t shows the son of Cairbar, sleeping on his father's tomb. For three days and three nights he has been waiting for the bard who is due to honour the memory of the dead. This bard can be seen in the distance, making his way down the mountain. The father's shadow hovers on the clouds. The countryside is covered with freezing fog. The trees, although bare, are stirred by the winds, and their dead branches and dried leaves still follow the direction of the storm.]

The gloomy, tempestuous atmosphere, wild landscape and withered vegetation, are reflected in the motifs of death, loss and sorrow in the story. This roots the painting clearly in the very imagery and melancholy of the myths of the wild Romantic North, which Staël, amongst others, believed inspired political liberty.

However, there is more to the presentation of the political liberty of the North in this painting. In 1955, Leo Spitzer coined the meaning of the term ekphrasis with which literary critics are now most familiar: 'the poetic description of a pictorial or sculptural work of art'.[87] Staël's use of ekphrasis is significant in allowing her reader to see her convey the three major components of British political liberty: melancholy; virtuous, self-sacrificing civic duty; and artistic and poetic talent.

By describing the story of Cairbar's son in a visual medium, Staël relates the painted art form to the poetic one, thus joining the two aesthetic genres of the plastic and the literary. Ekphrasis, from the Greek ἐκ: 'out', and φράζειν: 'speak', literally means to 'speak out' or 'explain'. Staël not only joins two arts forms together by using one to explain the other, she also uses these aesthetic media to join the present, past and future. In doing so, through one of the very techniques which ekphrasis permits, she connects each of the three aspects which combine to form British political liberty to one of these three time periods. Rather than describing the actions of the Ossianic tale through direct narrative, a medium which, by its very nature, requires movement through time, the subject-matter of Staël's description is in fact motionless: it is a painting. According to Ruth Webb:

> Instead of designating a dynamic mode of writing thought to have an immediate impact on its audience and whose range of subject-matter could include images of action and movement, *ekphrasis* came to be used of a work of literature in which the movement was found only in the flow of language, whose subject-matter was still, objectified.[88]

Describing a painting of the poem, rather than quoting the poem itself, allows the flow of time to be interrupted. Furthermore, inserting a tomb into a natural setting creates a deathscape at the heart of the wild natural scenery, and, as we have seen in previous chapters, the very essence of a deathscape allows time periods to be conflated in the same space. Thus, we do not see the events of the poem unfold in chronological time; rather we are able to visualize them all simultaneously.

In the painting, the present is associated with melancholy. The artist paints Cairbar's son in his present time grieving for his father, surrounded by a similarly grieving landscape. The son thus demonstrates the melancholy disposition necessary for the serious reflection and the 'resignation of the pain-filled soul to civil service' which allow for the creation of political liberty. Virtuous duty to the services expected by the public is connected in the painting with the past. Cairbar is deceased, and consequently belongs very much to the past. Nonetheless, his image is still represented in the painting — both by the presence of the tomb and by his ghostly shadow in the clouds — to remind the viewer of the expected, time-honoured duties that Cairbar's son must perform for his father according to society's rules. In this way, we see a depiction of the sacrifice of personal comfort necessary for the development of political liberty: the son has been waiting for three days and nights in a stormy landscape in order to properly 'rendre des honneurs à la mémoire des morts' ['honour the memory of the dead']. The future also appears in the painting, represented by the bard whose arrival Cairbar's son is anticipating and who is depicted in the background, making his way down the mountain towards the tomb. The bard represents '[l]a poésie du nord' ['[t]he poetry of the North'] itself, which 'convient [...] à l'esprit d'un peuple libre' ['is better suited to the minds of a free people'].[89] The creative spirit inspired in the northern people by their landscape, and which is the third component contributing to the creation of political liberty, is therefore linked with the future in this painting. We are reminded, here, of *Malvina*, where the Ossianic landscape was used to argue that writing and education belonged to the future.

Staël's ekphrasis is crucial to the reader's ability to appreciate the three major concepts which create the political liberty of Britain that Staël, through Oswald, desires to promote. Only by visualizing past, present and future at the same time, along with the notions of political liberty that Staël ties to each time period, are we able to understand precisely how each aspect must interact with the others in order for true political liberty to be achieved. The melancholy of the present in the painting is dependent upon the deaths of the past; the duty required by those who belong to the past rely on those who are still present to perform it; and both the past and the present must await the poetic visions of the future in order to come together. In the same way, in British society each factor is dependent upon the other for the creation of a free spirit. We must note, too, how past, present and future are each linked to an aspect of the landscape in Staël's ekphrasis, reminding us how the landscape itself contributes to the promotion of all those aspects which combine to form political liberty. Cairbar's son and the present are linked with the countryside and the trees, devastated by the storms just as the son himself is devastated by the power of his grief; the future, and the bard who represents it, are linked to the mountain which brings him closer, both in space and time, to Cairbar's son and the present; and the past is visualized as part of the clouds in the sky, looking down upon both present and future. Thus, the fusion of two types of Romantic nature — the untamed northern landscape and a natural deathscape — coupled with the use of ekphrasis, assist in the presentation of Staël's arguments.

Yet how is Staël's ekphrasis relevant for understanding the social liberty for women that she wishes to promote? Corinne's experience of the northern landscape has thus far caused her talent to wane. However, now, in front of this portrait which so vividly portrays the wild, Ossianic North, Corinne finds her artistic temperament kindled:

> Corinne prit sa harpe, et devant ce tableau elle se mit à chanter les romances écossaises dont les simples notes semblent accompagner le bruit du vent qui gémit dans les vallées. Elle chanta les adieux d'un guerrier en quittant sa patrie et sa maîtresse [...]. Oswald ne résista point à l'émotion qui l'oppressait, et l'un et l'autre s'abandonnèrent sans contrainte à leurs larmes. (*C*, p. 238)

> [Corinne took up her harp, and, in front of this picture, she began to sing the Scottish songs whose simple notes seem to accompany the sound of the wind which groans in the valleys. She sang of a warrior's farewells in leaving his homeland and his lover [...]. Oswald could not control the feeling that overwhelmed him, and both of them succumbed unrestrainedly to their tears.]

Corinne's artistic production is not stifled by the wild northern landscape now, but in fact sings its history. No longer threatened by the groaning winds in the valleys, Corinne now complements them. No longer bitter at the melancholy she previously felt in Britain, she now gives herself over to it, knowing that melancholy inspired by the views of a northern landscape does promote artistic talent. In front of a painting which portrays the very values of the political liberty which leads to the social oppression of the woman of genius, Corinne now finds that she is able to use that genius — born from her social independence — to enchant Oswald, the embodiment of political independence. The two forms of liberty are intertwined fully for the first time. Furthermore, in singing the myths of Ossian whilst accompanying herself on the harp, Corinne strongly echoes both Ossian himself and his daughter-in-law Malvina. As we have seen, 'Ossian calls to Malvina: "Bring me the harp, O maid, that I may touch it when the light of my soul shall arise — Be thou near, to learn the song; and future times shall hear of Ossian" '. Thus, just as in Cottin's *Malvina*, once again Ossian's legacy and future voice has been bequeathed to a woman writer: this time Staël's Corinne.

The woman writer's powerful legacy becomes even further apparent at the close of the novel, when Corinne is dying, and when the full significance of the conjoining of political and social liberty through Ossianic myth is realized. As Bruin argues, by this point, Corinne has sacrificed her love of Oswald to the knowledge that he must carry out his duty to society in marrying Lucile: 'L'innocence de Lucile, sa jeunesse, sa pureté exaltaient son imagination, et [Corinne] était, un moment du moins, fière de s'immoler pour qu'Oswald fût en paix avec son pays, avec sa famille, avec lui-même' ['Lucile's innocence, youth and purity exalted Corinne's imagination and she was, at least for a moment, proud to sacrifice herself in order for Oswald to be at peace with his homeland, his family and himself'] (*C*, p. 504). Through love, Corinne has finally learned the importance of the sacrifices which must be made for political liberty. She knows too, though, that her talent and work have been an important part of her life. In order to obtain true freedom before she dies, Corinne must therefore unite her acknowledgement of the importance of political liberty with a re-assertion of the importance of social liberty. She achieves this in two ways. She acknowledges in her last improvisation: 'Malheureuse! mon génie [...] se fait sentir seulement par la force de ma douleur [...]. [D]es muses fatales, l'amour et le malheur, ont inspiré mes derniers chants' ['Wretched woman! My genius [...] makes itself felt only by the force of my pain [...]. Fatal muses, love and unhappiness, have inspired my final songs'] (*C*, p. 583). Social liberty allows her to perform these songs, but they are now inspired by the melancholy of the politically free North, which she has fully experienced because of her sacrifice. Having acknowledged this, and knowing that she will soon die, Corinne then teaches the Scottish ballads she performed in front of the painting of Cairbar's son to Oswald's and Lucile's daughter Juliette, thus underlining her belief in the importance of women's right to social independence and to perform:

> Juliette alors exécuta sur sa harpe un air écossais, que Corinne avait fait
> entendre à lord Nelvil à Tivoli, en présence d'un tableau d'Ossian. [...] Quand
> Juliette eut fini, son père la prit sur ses genoux, et lui dit: 'La dame qui demeure

sur le bord de l'Arno vous a donc appris à jouer ainsi?' 'Oui', répondit Juliette
[...] '[E]lle m'a fait promettre de vous répéter cet air tous les ans, un certain jour,
le dix-sept de novembre, je crois'. (C, p. 576)

[Then Juliette played a Scottish air on her harp, which Corinne had played for
Lord Nelvil in Tivoli, in front of a picture of Ossian. [...] When Juliette had
finished, her father took her on his knees, and said to her: 'The lady who lives
on the banks of the Arno taught you to play like that, didn't she?' 'Yes', replied
Juliette [...] '[S]he made me promise to play that air to you every year, on a
certain day, the seventeenth of November, I think'.]

The same Scottish songs therefore appear at another moment which joins both
political and social liberty. According to Bruin, it is at this conjuncture of the
two opposing types of liberty that we find true liberty. Corinne has recognized
the importance of these songs (and of the landscape which inspired them) in the
creation of true freedom, and imparts this knowledge to Juliette. Furthermore,
by having Corinne teach these Scottish songs to Juliette and not to Oswald, Staël
underlines the importance of women's writing and education for the foundation of
true liberty, indeed for the future in general.

Firstly, let us examine Staël's arguments regarding the importance of women's
writing. Juliette, as a child, represents the future. In teaching Juliette, Corinne
passes her woman writer's voice on to the future generation. The future, Staël
continually tells us through her references to Ossianic myth (including the bard in
the painting of Cairbar's son), lies in poetry and creativity inspired by a melancholic
landscape. In the case of *Corinne*, it is in the *woman's* poetic voice and creativity that
the future lies: Juliette now possesses the harp passed down from Ossian to Malvina
to Corinne. Corinne requests that Juliette perform the Scottish songs that she has
taught her every year on the same date, and thus she acquires immortality for both
her own and Juliette's female voice.

Secondly, let us consider the arguments Staël makes about women's education.
The fact that Corinne teaches the songs which harmonize political and social liberty
to a girl, makes clear that Corinne (and, through her, Staël) believes the education
of women is necessary to the foundation of true liberty. Bruin confirms this
argument when she states that 'Corinne's new-found sense of sacrifice leads her to
devote herself to the moral education of future generations of women, represented
by the education that she provides to her niece Juliette'.[90] As Staël herself writes in
her chapter 'Des femmes qui cultivent les lettres' ['On Female Literature'] in *De la
Littérature,* the secret of establishing relationships which are both social and political
relies on equality in education between men and women:

Éclairer, instruire, perfectionner les femmes comme les hommes, les nations
comme les individus, c'est encore le meilleur secret pour tous les buts
raisonnables, pour toutes les relations sociales et politiques auxquelles on veut
assurer un fondement durable.

[To enlighten, to instruct, to improve women as well as men, and nations as
well as individuals: this remains the best secret for all reasonable goals, for
all social and political relations for which we would like to ensure a durable
foundation].[91]

According to *De la Littérature,* women's education is important to the creation of true liberty, and *Corinne* supports this by ensuring that the Scottish songs which conjoin the elements necessary for true liberty are passed on through the education of women.

It is important to note, here, that Staël's *Corinne* did indeed inspire a generation of future women writers, leaving a legacy of Romantic, literary power in their hands. Vincent discusses *Corinne's* influence on women writers across Europe, including on female translators and novelists such as Dorothea Schlegel (1764–1839) in Germany, on female improvisors in Italy 'such as Teresa Bandetti (1763–1837) and Massimina Fantastici (1788–1846)' whose works *Corinne* 'helped validate', and on poets such as Zinaïda Volkonskaya (1792–1862) in Russia who was 'herself known as the "Corinne of the North"', and Letitia Landon (1802–1838) in Britain who was 'the woman poet who "followed" Corinne most closely'.[92] Furthermore, these women writers, like Staël and her heroine Corinne, 'were not primarily concerned with expressing their own personal condition, but rather wished to voice their collective fear of cultural abandonment and to protest against social and political oppression'.[93] This was the same for later women poets in France, according to Vincent, who argues that Adélaïde Dufrénoy used an epistle entitled 'Corinne à Oswald' ['Corinne to Oswald'] to address the issue of having 'to conform herself to the First Empire's suffocating domestic ideology'.[94] It would seem, then, that Staël did indeed re-establish a platform for the female voice amid her written landscapes in *Corinne*, and bequeathed it to the future so that the next generation of Romantic women writers across Europe might use it to voice their own oppression as women.

Conclusion

The path was not smooth for women writers in late eighteenth- and early nineteenth-century France. Whilst some critics praised women's novels, many not only condemned women writers, but actually went so far as to argue that women should be banned from writing, or even from reading. As a result, we find female authors, in their correspondence and novels, justifying their decision to write. This highlights a key difference between the uses to which female writers put their income and those to which the famous male writers of the day put their income. Whilst male authors write in order to amass a fortune (later in the century Balzac and Dumas became very rich indeed) the woman writer publishes in order to provide financial assistance and physical shelter for others. Cottin justifies both her own and Mistress Clare's writing this way, and Staël actually reverses the original intentions of *Corinne* because of this. Presenting women's writing as a beneficial activity for society is therefore crucial to their work, and helps underline the argument that women should be allowed to write. But the arguments encoded within the landscape and intertextual references go deeper. Northern Britain is not an irrelevant backdrop, and description of the wild natural landscape is not gratuitous. Rather they articulate concerns which are crucial to the narrative, and arguments which are vital to understanding Staël and Cottin's opinions on the debate over women's social roles, and especially women's writing.

There is an obvious link between the woman writer, or female misfit, and the Scottish landscape in *Malvina,* due to the fact that wild, melancholy nature provides a metaphor for the woman's rebellion and melancholy. Similarly, the bleak landscape of Scotland in *Corinne* appropriately exacerbates the depressed woman's condition. In this way, Staël and Cottin use wild nature to highlight the issues faced by the woman writer of their day: her social exclusion and her consequent melancholic or rebellious reactions. However, neither novel stops here. *Malvina* and *Corinne* are both crafted in order to leave the reader with the image of the woman writer's voice remaining immortal, and with the image of the education of future generations lying in the hands of the woman writer. Staël even goes one step further, arguing with *Corinne* that educating women alongside men will bring about the foundation of a true liberty for all. All these arguments strongly challenge the prevailing patriarchal discourse of the society in which Cottin and Staël lived, for they not only promote women's writing and education, they also portray the woman writer in a very powerful light. Via *Corinne,* Staël in fact succeeds in bequeathing a future to women writers and in providing them with a platform to continue the rebellion, through authorship, against women's oppression.

This chapter has established previously untapped links between the works of Staël and Cottin, and has shown how they make similar arguments in favour of women's ability to transcend the sphere in which they have been pigeonholed. According to Bruin, for Staël, '[w]omen of superior mind must tread a new moral path for other women and for humanity', and this path must be 'superior to the only two paths open to women of superior mind: the masculine intellectual tradition or the subservient domestic role'.[95] This chapter has shown that both Staël and Cottin find this new path by turning to the very same intertexual landscapes. Each argument they make is encoded though their employment of references to Ossian and the Ossianic landscape, an appropriate intertextual choice because of the poems' gender egalitarianism. The above analysis of both novels contends that intertextual references establish a subtle dialogue between the writers and an implied reader. Understanding Cottin and Staël's defence of the woman writer relies on appreciation of the Ossianic myths, and consequently not all readers will perceive it. Indeed many scholars have, in dismissing the written landscape, missed some of the more subtle arguments. However, the proof of these arguments' importance is evident: Cottin ensures that the reader is aware of the significance of the Ossian references by stating as much when comparing Malvina's appreciation of the myths and landscape to others' dismissal of them. Similarly, in order to promote liberty from the repression of the Napoleonic regime in her homeland, Staël 'deemed it necessary to try to foster a culture of melancholy in France similar to that in England',[96] and she argues in *De la Littérature* that the melancholy emotions 'causées par les poésies ossianiques, peuvent se reproduire dans toutes les nations, parce que leurs moyens d'émouvoir sont tous pris dans la nature' ['provoked by the Ossianic poems, can be reproduced in all nations, because the elements within them that move us are all taken from nature'].[97] Staël makes it clear, therefore, that only when the public is aware of the Ossianic cycle and landscape will they be able to exhibit to the emotions necessary for the creation of a truly free nation. In the same way, in *Corinne*, it is only through appreciating the Ossianic landscape and its melancholia that the conjoining of political and social liberty are permitted, and only the conveying of the Ossianic songs of the wild North secure the future for the woman writer's voice and women's education, both so crucial in the foundation of true liberty. The descriptions of Ossianic landscapes are therefore crucial to the contributions Staël and Cottin make to the debate over women's writing and education. Furthermore, in exposing the power of these descriptions, we discover both the power bequeathed by the novels' heroines to the (intra-fictional) women of the future, and the consequent power of the writing and arguments left behind by Staël and Cottin themselves for posterity.

Notes to Chapter 5

1. Anon., 'Variétés', *Journal des Débats*, 24 ventose an VIII [15 mars 1800], De l'imprimerie de Le Normant, p. 3. (Original emphasis.)
2. Robert A. Nye, 'Forum: Biology, Sexuality and Morality in Eighteenth-Century France: Introduction', *Eighteenth-Century Studies*, 35:2 (2002), 235–38 (pp. 236–37).
3. Ibid., p. 237.
4. Foley, p. 4.
5. Mme de Staël, *De la Littérature considérée dans ses rapports avec les institutions sociales*, 2 vols (Paris: Maradan, 1800), II, p. 147.
6. Hesse, p. 132. (Original emphasis.)
7. Joseph de Maistre, *Lettres et opuscules inédits* (Paris: Vaton, 1851), Letter 42 (1808), p. 148.
8. Restif de la Bretonne, pp. 65–66.
9. Sylvain Maréchal, *Project d'une loi portant défense d'apprendre à lire aux femmes* (Paris: Massé, 1801).
10. Carpenter, p. 51.
11. Ibid.
12. Mme Cottin à Mme Jauge, April 1800. Sykes, p. 330. (Original ellipsis.)
13. Ibid.
14. Mme Cottin à (?) M. Devaines. Ibid., p. 350.
15. Marie-Joseph de Chénier, *Tableau historique de l'état et des progrès de la littérature française depuis 1789* (Paris: Ledentu, 1817), p. 244.
16. Hesse, p.40.
17. Foley, p. 9.
18. Béatrice Slama, 'Femmes écrivains', in *Misérable et glorieuse, la femme du XIXᵉ siècle*, ed. by Jean-Paul Aron (Paris: Fayard, 1980), pp. 213–43 (p. 217).
19. Josephine Grieder, *Anglomania in France 1740–1789: Fact, Fiction and Political Discourse* (Geneva: Librairie Droz, 1985), p. 4.
20. McManners, p. 336.
21. Pierre Carboni, 'Ossian and Belles Lettres: Scottish Influences on J.-B.-A. Suard and Late-Eighteenth-Century French Taste and Criticism', in *Scotland and France in the Enlightenment*, ed. by Deirdre Dawson and Pierre Morère (Lewisburg: Bucknell University Press, 2003), pp.74–89 (p. 75).
22. Ibid., p. 86. (Original parenthesis.) Jean-Baptiste-Antoine Suard was one of the translators and promoters of the Ossianic poems in France.
23. Andrew Hook, 'The French Taste for Scottish Literary Romanticism', in *Scotland and France in the Enlightenment*, ed. by Deirdre Dawson and Pierre Morère (Lewisburg: Bucknell University Press, 2004), pp. 90–107 (p. 103).

24. Carboni, pp. 74–89; Hook, pp. 90–107.
25. Charlton, *New Images*, p. 42.
26. Ibid., p. 43.
27. Mornet, p. 276.
28. Carboni; Fiona Stafford, *The Sublime Savage: A Study of James Macpherson and the Poems of Ossian* (Edinburgh: Edinburgh University Press, 1988); Paul Van Tieghem, 'Ossian en France', in *The French Quarterly*, I:2 & 3 (1919), 78–87.
29. Paul Van Tieghem, 'Ossian en France', p. 78.
30. Ibid., p. 79. (Original emphasis.)
31. Frank George Healey, *The Literary Culture of Napoleon* (Genève: Librairie Droz, 1959), pp. 127–30.
32. Carboni, p. 85.
33. Stafford, p. 76.
34. Paul Van Tieghem, 'Ossian en France', p. 83.
35. Minski, p. 82.
36. Paul Van Tieghem, 'Ossian en France', pp. 84–85.
37. Paul Van Tieghem, *Ossian en France*, 2 vols (Paris: Rieder & Cie, 1917), II, p. 25. Van Tieghem quotes from Mme de Berleps, '12 janvier 1811: Fragment de *Caledonia, ou voyage en Écosse*', in *Mercure de France*, trans. by A. M. Herdez.
38. Catherine Talbot, 'Imitations of Ossian,' in *The Works of the late Mrs. Catherine Talbot* (London: John Rivington, 1780).
39. JoEllen DeLucia, '"Far Other Times Are These": The Bluestockings in the Time of Ossian', *Tulsa Studies in Women's Literature*, 27:1 (2008), 39–62 (p. 39).
40. Ibid., pp. 39–40.
41. Leith Davis, 'Malvina's Daughters: Irish Women Poets and the Sign of the Bard', in *Ireland and Romanticism: Publics, Nations and Scenes of Cultural Production*, ed. by Jim Kelly (London: Palgrave MacMillan, 2011), pp. 141–60 (p. 142).
42. Carboni; Hook; Paul Van Tieghem, 'Ossian en France'; Paul Van Tieghem, *Ossian en France*; Colin Smethurst, 'Chateaubriand's Ossian', in *The Reception of Ossian in Europe*, ed. by Howard Gaskill (London: Thoemmes Continuum, 2004), pp. 126–42.
43. Staël, *De la Littérature*, I, pp. 296–97.
44. DeLucia, pp. 46–47.
45. Sykes, p. 401.
46. Bianciardi, p. 693.
47. Ibid.
48. Mme de Genlis, *La Femme auteur* (Paris: Gallimard, 2007), p. 76.
49. Sykes, pp. 33–34; Cf. Call, p. 47.
50. Sykes, pp. 128–29.
51. Paul Pelckmans, 'L'Écosse des Romancières', in *Locus in Fabula: La Topique de l'espace dans les fictions françaises d'Ancien Régime*, ed. by Nathalie Ferrand (Louvain: Editions Peeters, 2004), pp. 249–59 (p. 251).
52. Paul Van Tieghem, *Ossian en France*, p. 24.
53. Malvina is at first 'à peu près' in agreement with Mistress Birton, having been educated in a society which does not approve of women writers (M II, 77). However, upon meeting Mistress Clare, Malvina is persuaded by the reasons Mistress Clare gives for writing (M II, 85–86).
54. Women did not enjoy the same freedom, and in Britain, as in France, they were expected to remain in the domestic sphere.
55. Béat de Muralt, *Lettres sur les Anglais et les Français* (Berne: Steiger & Cie; Paris: Librairie Le Soudier, 1897), p. 2.
56. Voltaire, 'Lettres philosophiques', in Voltaire, *Œuvres complètes de Voltaire: avec des remarques et des notes historiques, scientifiques et littéraires* (Paris: Baudouin Frères, 1827), I, p. 71 (Lettre IX).
57. Eric Gidal, 'Civic Melancholy: English Gloom and French Enlightenment', *Eighteenth-Century Studies*, 37:1 (2003), 23–45 (p. 24).
58. Schama, p. 61.

59. Macpherson's Malvina is not the daughter of Ossian as Cottin states, but his daughter-in-law.

60. James Macpherson, *Ossian, Fils de Fingal, Barde du troisième siècle: Poésies galliques*, trans. by M. Le Tourneur, 2 vols (Paris: Musier, 1777), II, p. 155.

61. Ibid., I, pp. 303–06.

62. Marko Juvan, 'Spaces of Intertextuality / The Intertextuality of Space', *SDPK* (2004). Special Issue in English: 'Literature and Space. Spaces of Transgressiveness', <http://sdpk.zrc-sazu.si/PKrevija/2004-Literature&Space.htm#Marko%20Juvan> [accessed 28 August 2018].

63. Marko Juvan, 'Spaces, Transgressions and Intertextuality', in *Text and Reality*, ed. by Jeff Bernard, Jurij Fikfak and Peter Grzybek (Ljublijana: ZRC Publishing, 2005), pp. 43–54 (p. 43).

64. Davis, pp. 141–60 (142). Davis quotes from James Macpherson, *Works of Ossian, Son of Fingal*, 2 vols (London: T. Becket and P. A. DeHondt, 1765), I, p. 147.

65. Cresswell, p. 17.

66. Foley, p. 35.

67. Pelckmans, p. 255.

68. Karen de Bruin, 'Melancholy in the Pursuit of Happiness: Corinne and the Femme Supérieure', in *Staël's Philosophy of the Passions: Sensibility, Society and the Sister Arts*, ed. by Tili Boon Cuillé and Karyna Szmurlo (Lewisburg: Bucknell University Press, 2013), pp. 75–94.

69. Ibid., p. 76.

70. Ibid., p. 75.

71. Ferdinand de Cornot, *Baron de Cussy, Souvenirs du chevalier de Cussy, garde du corps, diplomate et consul général, 1795–1866*, publiés par Le Cte Marc de Germiny, 2 vols (Paris: Plon-Nourrit et Cie, 1909), II, p. 186. (Original emphasis.)

72. Ibid., p. 186. (Original emphasis.)

73. Ibid., p. 187. (Original emphasis.)

74. Ibid., p. 187.

75. Ibid., p. 186.

76. Ibid., p. 187. (Original ellipsis and emphasis.)

77. Staël, *De la Littérature*, I, p. 294.

78. Ibid., I, p. 368.

79. Ibid., I, p. 301.

80. Ibid., I, pp. 258–59.

81. Gidal, p. 25. (Original emphasis.)

82. Bruin, p. 82.

83. Staël, *De la Littérature*, I, p. 301.

84. Bruin., p. 82. (Original emphasis.)

85. Ibid., p. 87.

86. Ibid., p. 79.

87. Leo Spitzer, 'The "Ode on a Grecian Urn," or Content vs. Metagrammar', *Comparative Literature*, 7:3 (1955), 203–25 (p. 207). According to Webb, 'The revolutionary step of defining ekphrasis as an essentially *poetic* genre, totally divorced from the rhetorical form of ekphrasis, was taken by Leo Spitzer'. See: Ruth Webb, E*kphrasis, Imagination and Persuasion in Ancient Rhetorical Theory and Practice* (Burlington, VT: Ashgate, 2009), p. 33. (Original emphasis.)

88. Ruth Webb, '*Ekphrasis* ancient and modern: the invention of a genre', *Word and Image*, 15:1 (1999), 7–18 (p. 17).

89. Staël, *De la Littérature*, I, p. 301.

90. Bruin, p. 87.

91. Staël, *De la Littérature*, II, p. 152.

92. Vincent, p. 492.

93. Ibid., p. 493.

94. Ibid., p. 494.

95. Bruin, p. 88.

96. Ibid., p. 77.

97. Staël, *De la Littérature*, I, p. 303.

CONCLUSION

❖

Reclaiming a Space for Women's Writing

'Il est vrai', dit-elle, 'que la nature a tout fait, mais sous ma direction'.

['It is true', she said, 'that nature has done everything, but it was under my direction.]

ROUSSEAU, *Julie ou la Nouvelle Héloïse.*[1]

As Wolfgang argues, '[u]ntil recently, literary historians have ignored the scores of French women who played a vital role in the formation of their national literature'.[2] Situating itself within the slowly developing field which aims to re-examine French women's writing of the eighteenth and nineteenth centuries, this book sheds new light on the most popular authors of the First Republic and First Empire — Cottin, Genlis, Krüdener, Souza and Staël — who (with the exception of Staël) have since been almost completely forgotten. In so doing, it has revealed a key aspect of their work, the creation of a 'landscape of one's own', hitherto overlooked even by those scholars who have argued the case for studying women's writing of this period. Louichon, for example, has stated that, in all the works she analyses (by Cottin, Duras, Gay, Genlis, Staël and Souza), with the possible exception of Krüdener's *Valérie*, '[l]a place de la nature n'y est jamais signifiante' ['[t]he place of nature is never significant'].[3] Yet, an insight into female authors' written landscapes brings a new dimension to our appreciation of their engagement with the ongoing socio-political debates of the time concerning their sex.

This book has argued that Cottin, Genlis, Krüdener, Souza and Staël all employ images of the natural landscape strategically to re-establish a platform for the female voice, from which they might expose and comment on the preoccupations of women regarding marriage, motherhood, madness, death and authorship in the years following the Revolution. Via these 'landscapes of one's own', they also reveal their critical stance against the eighteenth and nineteenth centuries' separation of spheres according to gender, and thus challenge the prevalent contemporary argument that a woman's essence defines her existence. For Cottin, Genlis, Krüdener, Souza and Staël, nature is the lynchpin for constructing the complexities of their engagement with the ideas of the period relating to women and their place in society. The symbolic language of Mother Nature becomes their mother tongue, and the natural landscape the platform from which they speak. In this way, women writers of the First Republic and First Empire show that they look outwards in order to protest, and, in so doing, provoke society to look inwards.

There are three key conclusions to be drawn from the analysis conducted within this study of the written landscapes in the novels of the aforementioned women writers.

Firstly, the natural landscapes that become the podia for women's re-established voices are all landscapes for which there was a contemporary vogue. Because these sites were both recognizable and fascinating for the reading public, their pre-established characteristics can be used by Cottin, Genlis, Krüdener, Souza and Staël to expose problems more clearly and persuasively, and thereby to make their feelings speak to a wider community. However, these five women writers go further: they use the images and ideas associated with these fashionable spaces as foundation stones for building their own arguments.

The problems women faced with regard to marriage are addressed in Cottin's *Malvina*, Souza's *Émilie et Alphonse*, Staël's *Delphine* and Souza's *Adèle de Sénange,* as Chapter 1 has shown. In the first three of these novels the authors harness popular imagery of pastoral, utopian idylls in order to critique the real society with which these idylls are contrasted. In this way, Cottin, Souza and Staël engage with a tradition practised by earlier eighteenth-century male writers. However, these women do not portray the traditional qualities of fictional utopian or pastoral spaces. Rather, they sculpt a landscape which highlights the particular issue that they want to critique: the continued oppression of women in the face of a lack of marriage reform. In *Adèle de Sénange,* Souza engages with fashions for French- and English-style gardens. Yet, instead of portraying a clear dichotomy between those types, she portrays a linear progression through garden spaces, from one type of representation to another. Souza's sliding scale of restrictive-to-free gardens highlights, firstly, that old and new attitudes must work together if marital reform is to be successfully sought, and, secondly, that the ultimate level of freedom for a woman is to be found in establishing her autonomy outside of marriage.

In novels which deal with motherhood and maternal loss — *Valérie* and *Les Mères rivales* — Krüdener and Genlis employ as key settings, respectively, the newly fashionable image of a memorial garden deathscape and the pre-established image of a garden as a morally instructive space. When ordinary language does not suffice, the grieving or guilt-ridden heroines physically landscape the natural world in order to use the language of plants and gardens to convey their painful reactions to being unable to fulfil the ideal expected of them by society. The notion of a symbolic language of plants was not new; nonetheless, Chapter 2 has shown Krüdener and Genlis pushing boundaries with their written landscapes. In fact, Krüdener's heroine, in her attempt to recreate bonds with her deceased child, even begins to exhibit some of the bereavement behaviour which would later be modelled by twentieth-century grief theorists. Valérie's decision to create the memorial garden on an island engages retrospectively with Rousseau's gravesite, certainly. However, it is also significant in the bereavement tendencies it reveals, particularly given that a personal sense of grieving was only recently beginning to develop. Klaus and Kennell have identified the bereaved party as often experiencing 'a feeling of increased emotional distance from other people', and summarize this sentiment with the words of one grieving mother who states: 'I felt I was on an island by myself'.[4] Valérie's island physically embodies her feeling of emotional distance from those who have not experienced her pain, and transmits to others her feeling of emotional detachment. Furthermore, modern bereavement therapy has concluded that maintaining a sense of attachment with the deceased forms 'an integral part of successful adaptation to the death of a loved one'.[5] In the case of coming to terms with parental bereavement, '[t]he end of grief is not severing the bond with the dead child, but integrating the child into the parent's life [...] in a different way than when the child was alive'.[6] Vamik D. Volkan has noted that often a material object which the deceased owned, or which represents them in some way, is sought and used to establish this new bond:

> I have found that patients [...] typically select an inanimate object — a symbolic bridge (or link) to the representation of the dead person — to use in a magical way. I have called these objects 'linking objects' [...]. Such objects mainly provide a locus for externalized contact between aspects of the mourner's self-representation and aspects of the representation of the deceased. The mourner sees them as containing elements of himself and of the one he has lost. By using this linking object, the mourner can keep alive the illusion that he has the power [...] to return the dead person to life [...]; that is, he has the illusion of absolute control over the psychological meeting ground that is afforded by the linking object or linking phenomena.[7]

Valérie's painting of the memorial garden achieves both of the goals of the 'linking object'. Firstly, Valérie has herself physically placed within the garden next to her child's tomb, and thereby not only makes the linking object figuratively stand both for the representation of the dead child and for her representation of her 'self' as a bereaved mother, but actually ensures that the linking object includes a real, visual representation of both parties in the form of a painted image. Secondly, the painting also visually reproduces Volkan's 'psychological meeting ground': a middle space, which bridges the gap between the worlds of the living and the dead, permitting mother and child to meet in the natural space of the graveside garden. In *Les Mères rivales* Genlis also bridges gaps with her morally instructive garden, which cannot be concretely defined in terms of space or time. The garden incorporates elements both of rigidly tamed and winding, free nature. It also contains features which evoke multiple time periods. Finally, the garden is designed to bridge both public and private spheres, thus underlining how decisions regarding women's roles as mothers taken within the former can have devastating effects in the latter.

In her depiction of women rebelling against their oppression through madness in *Malvina* and *Mathilde*, Cottin engages with two spaces which received particular critical attention during her lifetime. Chapter 3 has revealed that, using the walled garden of *Malvina* to reflect the eighteenth-century theory of curing the mad *intra muros*, Cottin attenuates the success of the curative asylum by pointing out that it remains under man's dominion, therefore causing female protest to be continually repressed within it. The Palestinian desert of *Mathilde* reflects contemporary

Romantic and Orientalist discourse, both of which constructed the Middle East as a space of hostility, exoticism, timelessness, and oppression. Cottin turns to common descriptions of Eastern space in order to critique the West. In this respect, she echoes previous eighteenth-century male authors who also criticized the West by means of Eastern settings or characters. However, in order to critique the West's treatment of women and to restore a powerful voice to her sex, Cottin turns the desert into a 'landscape of one's own' which resists both restrictive definition and any attempts to contain it. Therefore, whilst Malvina loses control over her natural asylum to her husband and doctor, Agnès and Mathilde reclaim their desert asylum from the patriarchal figures who force them into this space. Meanwhile, Krüdener's *Valérie* reminds the reader that it is also possible for the men of post-revolutionary France to protest against the dominance of patriarchal society through madness. As Krüdener's hero rejects the patriarchal world, he resorts to the 'female malady' of hysteria as a means of protest, and seeks out Mother Nature to restore his silenced voice. Creating a landscape which permits the crossing of gender boundaries further reminds the reader that it is inappropriate to assign one gender permanently to one space.

Death provides another means of protest against oppressive and untenable situations, as is seen from the analysis of *Claire d'Albe, Amélie Mansfield, Corinne* and *Delphine* conducted in Chapter 4. Staël and Cottin engage with notions which already existed in Enlightenment and early Romantic thought that suicide could provide the individual with freedom and autonomy. They also engage with eighteenth-century fashions for contemplating death in natural spaces, and for giving nature pride of place in the descriptions of the deaths of literary heroines. However, the deathscape in *Claire d'Albe* is not just a memorial garden in which the heroine's father's tomb is located and loss is mourned, nor is it simply a natural space in which the heroine's almost lifeless body is found. In fact, it becomes the space that Claire reclaims from the patriarchal figure when, in her pursuit of freedom and autonomy, she decides to die. In *Amélie Mansfield, Corinne* and *Delphine,* the choice to employ waterscapes which carry pre-established woman-nature-death associations allows Cottin and Staël to invoke already-familiar images in the minds of their readers, and then to use these images as the foundations for a more complex argument. Ultimately, they do not portray a woman helpless in the face of the powers of nature; rather, they write a politicized landscape — a 'deathscape of one's own' — which harnesses the powers of waterfalls, wild seas and rivers to announce a woman's oppression, restore her autonomy and voice, and ensure her escape.

In order to add their voices to the contemporary debates over women's writing and education, Cottin and Staël draw on the late eighteenth- and early nineteenth-century fascination with the Scottish countryside in both *Malvina* and *Corinne,* as Chapter 5 has shown. The landscape of the Romantic North proves to be a perfect one in which to highlight the melancholy experienced by the woman writer and social misfit. Its untameable nature also provides a suitable metaphorical setting for the rebelliousness of the female figure who chooses to write, promote women's education, or take an interest in the work of local industry. However, there is more to the portrayal of the Scottish countryside than melancholy and allegory.

Through intertextual references to the Ossianic cycle, its landscape's provision of both voice and shelter, its combination of political and social liberty, and the gender egalitarianism that the poems allow for in an androcentric world, Cottin and Staël argue that women's writing and education have crucial roles to play in founding true liberty, and leave the reader with an image of the woman writer's voice as immortal.

Throughout the chapters of this book, it has been shown, then, that the natural world provides solace, escape, autonomy and a voice for the socially alienated or oppressed female protagonist. Yet the phenomenon we see here is not simply about passive women being given what they need. Just as Valérie, Rosalba and Adèle actively landscape their gardens to empower themselves, Cottin, Genlis, Krüdener, Souza and Staël craft natural story-worlds to give voice to the concerns which they were forbidden from announcing on the socio-political stage (indeed Staël was exiled for attempting to do so). They instrumentalize nature to expose, and ultimately challenge the unfairness that women face. Furthermore, just as Claire, Agnès and Mathilde reclaim the landscapes they inhabit from patriarchal figures, and just as Malvina and Corinne inherit the landscapes of Ossian for women writers, so too do Cottin, Genlis, Krüdener, Souza and Staël reclaim from previous male writers the spaces for which there was a contemporary fashion. In so doing, they situate themselves at the forefront of landscape presentation: not only do they continually engage with new or renewed landscape fascinations, but they take the expected images associated with these areas and build on them, pushing them forwards, moulding the landscapes to suit their argument. That is to say, they reclaim a fashionable landscape and shape it into a 'landscape of one's own'.

The second conclusion that can be drawn from our analysis of nature in these novels is the important recurrence of middle spaces and of diminished dichotomies. Souza develops a sliding scale of restricted-free garden space; Krüdener's landscape painting establishes a psychological meeting ground where mother and child are able to transcend the newly spatialized relationship between the living and dead; Cottin and Staël create liminal waterscapes which also allow transition between the worlds of the living and dead; Staël's Ossian painting, like Souza's and Krüdener's island deathscapes, conflates past, present and future in the same space; Genlis's morally instructive garden and Cottin's Palestinian desert combine images drawn from multiple historical periods; Cottin, Staël and Genlis use intertextual references (the first two to Ossian, the latter to Bunyan and Ovid) to bridge spatio-temporal gaps.

Furthermore, all the women writers analysed in this study bridge the gap between private and public within their landscapes. Often this involves conveying private emotions to a public audience, or using their landscapes in the same way as do Bending's gardeners, that is, 'as a private venture, as an image of their owner, and an opportunity to articulate one's identity', yet also 'as the opportunity for a self-fashioning engagement with cultural norms and narratives, a space in which the disparate agenda of eighteenth-century culture would inevitably have to be confronted'.[8] For Cottin, Genlis, Krüdener, Souza and Staël, as for their heroines, part of the process of determining their private identity involves confronting the problems created for women by the agenda of the public sphere.

By diminishing dichotomies and creating middle spaces with their written 'landscapes of one's own', women writers all emphasize the advantages of diminishing dichotomies within the very society that they use these landscapes to critique; that is, they criticize the practice of defining a social role according to a gender binary. Within their novels, rather than categorizing women according to a set of essentialist characteristics, post-revolutionary French women writers create heroines who seek intellectual, creative and social freedom. Through writing these novels, the same freedoms become available to the novelists.

There is a further reason that middle spaces are appropriate for making the voices of these women writers heard. The *OED* definitions of 'space' include, as we have seen, the notion of duration, or a 'lapse, extent, or passage of time between two definite points'.[9] These women themselves occupy a somewhat indeterminate middle space in literary scholarship between two extremely dominant periods: the Enlightenment and Romanticism. For many scholars of Romanticism, Staël epitomizes the occupation of this middle space. It is 'that heritage of Enlightenment and Revolution, which puts Staël among the last of the *philosophes*',[10] yet, 'Staël and her circle had strong liberal, progressive, and republican ideals [...] that would define 'le mouvement romantique' ['the Romantic movement'] when it finally emerged as late as in the 1820s'.[11] Perhaps John Claiborne Isbell summarizes Staël's stance between these two literary movements best when he remarks:

> Generations of critics have sought a mythic parent to link all Europe's Romantic movements, and the vast spread of Romantic civilisation: here, explicitly it stands. Janus-faced, Staël dominates the Romantic catastrophe. Behind lie France and the eighteenth century [...]. Ahead lie the Romantic and bourgeois nineteenth-century.[12]

The reference to the two-headed god of antiquity is a particularly relevant one, since Janus's name derives from the Latin word 'ianua' ['door']. Staël and her fellow women writers can be perceived as opening the door on to Romanticism, whilst not yet closing it on the Enlightenment. Like Staël, Cottin has also been noted by modern critics as occupying a middle space between these two periods. As a '[l]ectrice de Bernardin de Saint-Pierre et de Chateaubriand, des *Stürmer* allemands et des poètes anglais, Sophie Cottin représente toute la singularité de la période transitoire entre le déclin des Lumières et l'éclat du romantisme' ['[r]eader of Bernardin de Saint-Pierre and of Chateaubriand, of the German *Stürmer* and the English poets, Sophie Cottin represents the whole singularity of the transitional period between the decline of the Enlightenment and the explosion of Romanticism'].[13]

Paul Bénichou's *Le Sacre de l'écrivain* [*The Consecration of the Writer*] has argued that Romanticism is not simply a reaction to the Enlightenment, but is in fact a revision of it. He contends 'that the increasing secularization of culture and thought led to the creation of a new "priesthood" in the form of writers, beginning most notably with the *philosophes* of the Enlightenment, who, in turn, became the "mages et prophètes" ["magi and prophets"] of Romanticism'.[14] Analysing the novels of the women writing between the canonical works which epitomize these two movements upholds Bénichou's conclusions that 'l'Homme de Lettres du XVIIIe siècle a survécu et prospéré au XIXe moyennant une adaptation de sa foi à des circonstances nouvelles' [the eighteenth-century Man of Letters survived and prospered in the nineteenth century by adapting his faith to new circumstances'].[15]

This is what post-revolutionary French women's writing achieves. For Staël and Cottin are not alone in building on the socio-literary past to pave the way for its future; all the post-revolutionary French women writers analysed in this book do so. For the purposes of their own argument, they take the genre of utopian fiction used to critique French society by Enlightenment male authors, and adapt it for new circumstances, inserting images into it of melancholy wanderers and meditation at the heart of nature in order to highlight the issues women faced in the wake of the Revolution. They echo Rousseau's metaphor of the mother as landscape gardener and then rework it in order to bring to light the problems his influential thought later causes for mothers who do not fit his ideal. They revisit Enlightenment views that suicide was an essential human liberty and marry them to the Romantic notion of suicide as a heroic refusal to accept the world. They echo the views of Enlightenment *philosophes* such as Voltaire and Montesquieu on Britain's ordered society, and combine them with the Romantic wildness of British mountain landscapes (we should remember here Montesquieu's aversion to mountains) in order to craft their arguments about the struggle and success of the woman writer. They highlight how Enlightenment ideals failed women in the wake of the Revolution and led them to melancholy, depression, madness and suicide, all of which are common Romantic themes.

Ultimately, building on Rousseau's aesthetic portrayals of nature as a space of contemplation, freedom and happiness, women writers engage with these self-same images in order to challenge the revered philosopher's condemnation of their own sex. Throughout their novels, they revisit the supposed woman-nature link invoked by eighteenth-century Enlightenment *philosophes* and physicians in a clear feminine redeployment of that nature which allegedly confines and subordinates women in eighteenth-century thought. Howells argues that, '[i]n the eighteenth century [...] the source of the self becomes Nature',[16] and this is certainly true of women writers. Rather than allowing the position of their sex vis-à-vis nature to be defined for them, Cottin, Genlis, Krüdener, Souza and Staël move towards defining this relationship for themselves. Whilst their novels do offer a return to nature, it is a more polemical presentation of a return to nature than that of Rousseau, one which paves the way for arguments such as Hugo's, who 'proclaimed that the liberty of art had to go hand in hand with political liberty and that liberty of art was by definition directed against any despotism of systems, codes, and of rules. This progressive, revolutionary art Hugo called Romanticism'.[17]

The third key conclusion which can be drawn from our analysis is that, at the same time as they challenged the dominant patriarchal discourse and gender dichotomy of their day, Cottin, Genlis, Krüdener, Souza and Staël exerted an influence on the literary Romanticism which soon captured the French imagination. The approach undertaken by this study — rooting my reading of the written landscapes in the contemporary contexts of landscape theory and of socio-political debate — allows this conclusion to be drawn. These women write landscapes which were beginning to emerge in the early Romantic mind and which would later be taken up by French canonical Romantic writers. They use these landscapes to highlight the preoccupations of contemporary women, and we see frequently that these preoccupations correspond closely to several Romantic themes which are already beginning to emerge elsewhere in Europe and which would become increasingly common in French literature in the ensuing decades of the nineteenth century.

Nemoianu asks:

> Why must Van Tieghem bill 1760–1820 as preromanticism — a prologue twice as long as the main piece? [...] [I]s there at least a strong connection between the self-proclaimed young romantics of the 1820s and 1830s and this powerful, diverse preparatory movement? If there is, it has been strangely ignored by historians.[18]

There is indeed such a movement, and it has been ignored by scholars. It is to be found in women's writing. In 2015, Devoney Looser declared, with regard to British literary history, that '[t]he Romantic period [...] was a watershed moment for British women's writing. That statement now seems so self-evident and inarguable that it is difficult to believe that, just a few decades ago, it was neither'.[19] Yet, the impact of nascent Romantic thought on French women's writing, and, more specifically, the influence of French women's writing on what would become canonical Romantic writing, is still significantly understudied. It remains at the point where the scholarship of British Romantic women's writing found itself a few decades ago:

> The Romantic period has long been characterized as a time of innovation and change in both literary form and content, as well as a momentous era of new political thought and social upheaval. But for most of the twentieth century, the term "Romantic" did not serve to plumb the depths of that innovation and change. Instead, it focused on a small number of writers said to be the greatest ones. The Romantic period separated out the writings of what came to be called the Big Six male poets — William Blake, Samuel Taylor Coleridge, William Wordsworth, Percy Bysshe Shelley, John Keats, and Lord Byron — placing them at the center of a new tradition.[20]

This focus on canonical male writers still dominates studies of French Romanticism, as the introduction to this book revealed in its examination of compendia on European Romanticism and anthologies of Romantic writing. Still dominating the field are the works of Balzac, Baudelaire, Chateaubriand, Gautier, Lamartine, Musset, Nodier, Hugo, Stendhal, Senancour and Vigny; yet a study of women writers has much to add. With regard to British literature, Anthony Mandal argues that 'we should view the development of the novel during the Romantic period [...] as the result of the efforts of numerous women writers who drove many of its innovations'.[21] A study of women's writing is just as important for our understanding of the development of French Romantic writing; for, in France, as in Britain, women were driving many of Romanticism's innovations. For this reason, Anne K. Mellor's discussion of the ways in which British Romantic writers employed Romantic trends occasionally provides a useful lens through which to examine the ways post-revolutionary French women writers also engage with these trends and drive them forward.

Of all the themes associated with Romanticism, the most relevant to the present study is that of nature, and, particularly, the relations between humans and nature. This theme was a vital one in Romantic thought; indeed, 'Girardin held the romantic to be essentially a quality of the natural landscape'.[22] The landscapes women writers chose to write were, as we have seen, ones which featured prominently in the early Romantic imagination: untamed gardens, wild and sublime mountains, deathscapes and memorial gardens, landscapes which featured ruins, oriental deserts, tumultuous seas, and powerful waterfalls. Yet, whilst '[t]he male Romantic poet often positions himself [...] on top of a mountain, looking down on the natural world, a nature that he claims to understand and therefore speak for',[23] according to Mellor, British Romantic women writers displayed a very different relationship to the natural world. She argues that they suggested 'human beings should see Mother Nature as a friend and co-worker, one with needs of her own, a potentially powerful ally with whom we must cooperate'.[24] The works of Cottin, Genlis, Krüdener, Souza and Staël echo this latter relationship with nature very closely, and thus, in many respects, present nature in similar fashions to Mary Shelley, Charlotte Smith, or Ann Radcliffe. For the latter, sublime landscapes are invoked in order that they may 'open the possibility that her persecuted heroines can find solace in nature'.[25] This is precisely what is found in Cottin's *Malvina* and *Amélie Mansfield*, Staël's *Corinne* and Krüdener's *Valérie*.

Another common feature of Romantic literature is the social misfit or outcast. Frye characterizes the Romantic hero as 'placed outside the structure of civilization';[26] similarly, Betina L. Knapp argues that he exhibits 'feelings of isolation [and] alienation'.[27] Krüdener's Gustave is certainly an archetypal representative of the melancholy Romantic hero, solipsistic and self-isolating. Souza's Alphonse feels isolated from the world through his grief, and does indeed retreat to the mountains to cut himself off from the world. Staël's Oswald exhibits melancholy on account of loss and loneliness. Yet, the heroines penned by Cottin, Genlis, Krüdener, Souza and Staël also find themselves suffering from isolation and/or from being social outcasts. Corinne and Mistress Clare represent '[t]he theme of the talented person destined to remain an outsider [which] was to be central for writers of the Romantic movement';[28] Malvina finds herself outside the structure of social convention because she associates with women writers and advocates women's education; Amélie Mansfield is cast out for marrying beneath her social status; Valérie is isolated by her grief; Rosalba feels alone because no-one understands the pain she experiences on account of giving up her child; Souza's Adèle and Émilie, like Cottin's Claire d'Albe, feel isolated in their arranged marriages. In addition to characterizing the Romantic hero as isolated, Frye also proclaims that he 'represents the force of physical nature, [...] with a sense of power, and often leadership, that society has impoverished itself by rejecting'.[29] This description, too, matches post-revolutionary French heroines' situations. All have strong connections to nature, and many actively use the forces of nature to assist their protests. When we see the power and authority that Staël and Cottin attribute to the woman writer in *Corinne* and *Malvina,* we also understand the arguments that they make regarding the impoverishment of a society that rejects women's writing and education. The issue of whether the Romantic hero can indeed be female has been addressed by Susan Lanser and Margaret Homans, amongst others.[30] Lanser writes:

> By the turn of the nineteenth century, the association of Romantic subjectivity with the male voice had solidified so that constructing a female "Romantic hero" demanded a double overturning of Romantic norms: the displacement of male subjectivity from center to periphery, and the transformation of plot to allow the tropes of Romantic questioning a plausible female form.[31]

Despite these difficulties, Lanser identifies and analyses 'three novelists who do seem to have attempted, at separate moments across three decades, to create female counterparts to the Romantic hero's text': Staël, (Mary) Shelley, and Sand, who each 'wrote a novel in which a woman is a Romantic hero'.[32] In the first of the decades Lanser identifies (1800–1810), however, Staël is not alone writing a novel with a female Romantic hero, as this book has illustrated.

Building on the theme of the social misfit, is that of the exploration and expression of the self, which are also key Romantic notions. According to Mellor, '[t]he goal of the masculine Romantic self' in British literature, 'is nothing less than the construction of the individual who owns his own body, his own mind, his own labour, and who is free to use that body and labour as he chooses'.[33] Cottin, Genlis, Krüdener, Souza and Staël depict heroines who aim to establish themselves as autonomous individuals with rights to pursue their own talents, and to possess and control their own bodies and minds. Moreover, their heroines establish this autonomy at the heart of and with the aid of nature. Souza's Adèle seeks to explore her self-identity through landscaping her private island; Agnès seeks to establish autonomy by rejecting the domination of male religious, scientific and patriarchal figures and does so through her relationship with desert space; through identification with the northern landscape, Malvina discovers her true self, in contradiction to, rather than in harmony with societal norms; Claire d'Albe, Amélie Mansfield, Corinne, Delphine and Malvina all seek autonomy through a self-willed death enabled by a natural land- or waterscape.

The *mal du siècle,* the melancholy malady provoked by a disillusionment with life and society and by 'cycles of nostalgia and expectations, elation and horror, hope and disappointment',[34] is also prevalent in women's writing. Throughout late eighteenth- and early nineteenth-century France, the topics considered in each chapter of this book — marriage, motherhood, madness, death, and female authorship — all come under scrutiny. As society discussed and debated these issues in the wake of the Revolution, glimpses of new possibilities gradually emerged. Yet, all too often these glimmers of hope were thwarted, and women found that the problems they faced remained unresolved. Demands for marital reform went unheeded; society refused to alter its traditional views on arranged and forbidden marriages, leaving women's marital fate still subject to the decisions of the family. Although the new ideal of motherhood accorded a crucial role to women in the development of society's education and morals, emotional difficulties arose for those women who were unable to live up to the new expectations. Despite new attempts to cure rather than punish the insane, women still found themselves the victims of male authority within institutions. Unattainable ideals were still imposed on women, expected both to embody angelic virtue and to inspire sexual desire. Despite the increasing popularity of women writers' works, women also continued to confront difficulties in publishing and, in the face of continued gender bias, still felt the need to justify themselves for entering the public sphere in this way.

The Revolution's calls for liberty therefore achieved little for the freedom of women, who continued to be subordinated. Bertrand-Jennings argues that, at certain periods in history — and the 1789 Revolution and its aftermath constitutes a perfect example — men acquired rights whilst women's rights declined.[35] Throughout their works, the female novelists writing in this period portray the problems and consequent melancholy faced by women as a result of such thwarted possibilities. However, they also show women rebelling against the status quo which restricted their social and creative activity based on their biological essence, and it is Romantic themes which enable this rebellion: madness, suicide (or self-willed death), and the extolling of the writer-poet. The rebellions in literature can be said to have reflected those in life: in late eighteenth- and early nineteenth-century France women were more likely to be pathologized and incarcerated on account of insanity than men; those who committed suicide frequently did so as a reaction to their oppression and victimization; and those who took up their pen found that 'l'écriture est protestation, témoignage contre l'enfermement féminin, cri de révolte contre la condition féminine' ['writing is a protest, a testimony against female confinement, a cry of revolt against the condition of women'].[36]

Finally, Romantic writers often expressed political opinions in their works. As this book has argued, the works of post-revolutionary French women writers certainly engage with contemporary socio-political debates and issues. Again, we can employ scholarship on British Romanticism to reflect on what these French women writers achieve. While, as Mellor has noted, British male Romantic writers exhort 'the overthrow of the British monarchy and the creation of a democratic republic, founded on the rights of man'[37] (in much the same manner as the French Revolution), British female Romantic writers argued instead 'that social reform is a process, not of revolution but of gradual evolution, a process that is furthered by educating the populace'.[38] In this description there are uncanny echoes of Souza's *Adèle de Sénange,* which argues for gradual reform and not the uprooting of the past, and of Staël's *Corinne* (and, to a slightly lesser extent, Cottin's *Malvina*), which argues strongly in favour of educating women as well as men in order for a nation to establish true liberty (incorporating both political and social liberty).

Therefore, just as the works of British Romantic women writers have been uncovered and analysed in recent decades, we also need to pay closer attention to the works of French women writers of the period 1789–1815, and to their engagement with a nascent Romanticism. As we have seen, Cottin, Genlis, Krüdener, Souza and

Staël highlight self-expression and the need to establish autonomy; they celebrate the figure of the melancholic wanderer, the social misfit, the grieving, the mad and the suicidal; they call on the cult of Ossian; they evoke the timelessness and danger of the Orient;[39] they engage with the sublime; they extol the figure of the writer-poet. Moreover, they continually achieve all this through their portrayal of nature and through the evocation of their protagonists' personal relationships to nature. Other, more specific, images which feature in the works of the later Romantic writers had also already appeared in the novels of Cottin, Genlis, Krüdener, Souza and Staël. Later in the nineteenth century, both Hugo and Balzac would take up the notion of the garden playing an instructive role in 'Poème du jardin des plantes' and *La Peau de chagrin*, respectively.[40] Echoing the island gravesite of Krüdener's *Valérie,* there is also a 'Loire burial island for Mme de Valentin in *La Peau de chagrin*', which 'represent[s] the imminence and the omnipresence of death', because of 'the envelopment offered by [...] its waters'.[41] Finally, Staël draws on images created by the German Romantic writer Goethe when she depicts gondolas as coffins on the Venetian canals, and later it is the English Romantic Byron who inherits the same image, though from Staël's *Corinne*. The written landscapes of post-revolutionary French female novelists therefore strongly tap into the themes and images which would later become increasingly associated with the Romantic movement.

Having drawn these three major conclusions, we might well ask whether the themes and arguments prevalent throughout the works of Cottin, Genlis, Krüdener, Souza and Staël were noted by the reading public, and, in particular, by those who would go on to dominate the Romantic canon.

Firstly, as Wolfgang notes, '[t]he growing literary public responded enthusiastically to prose fiction produced by women writers'.[42] Cottin's work had a profound effect on an admiring readership, particularly on account of her ability to elicit a reader's emotions. The *Journal des Débats* wrote of *Amélie Mansfield*: 'l'auteur possède à un degré éminent le don d'émouvoir, de disposer de l'âme du lecteur et de lui laisser une impression profonde' ['the author possesses, to an eminent degree, the gift of moving and manipulating the heart of the reader and of leaving a profound impression on it'].[43] Similarly, Fiévée, in the *Mercure de France*, praised *Mathilde* for its ability to draw the tears of the reader.[44] For Krüdener's *Valérie*, too, 'la critique fut très favorable' ['the reviews were very favourable'].[45] Genlis's readers praised her for her ability to present society as it was, including its problems: 'Genlis [...] a quelquefois excellé à rendre les tracasseries [...] de la société' ['Genlis [...] has sometimes excelled in painting the frustrations [...] of society'].[46] Her readers were also aware of the arguments she made about women writers suffering at the hands of a disparaging patriarchal society: 'Genlis prétend [...] que tous les hommes, sans exception, conspirent contre la gloire littéraire des femmes' ['Genlis claims [...] that all men, without exception, conspire against the literary glory of women'].[47]

The natural landscape settings were also appreciated by critics. In the *Mercure de France*, Michaud noted that, in *Valérie,* 'l'auteur, placé entre le climat de l'Italie et celui de Suède, oppose avec beaucoup d'art le ciel poétique de Venise et de Rome, avec la nature sauvage et quelquefois sublime des rivages de la Baltique' ['the author, situated between the climates of Italy and Sweden, very skilfully contrasts the poetic sky of Venice and Rome with the wild and sometimes sublime nature of the shores of the Baltic'].[48] Links were noted between the characters and settings in *Corinne*. Constant states in *Le Publiciste* that, '[l]'Italie est empreinte dans Corinne. Corinne [...] est la fille de ce ciel, de ce climat, de cette nature' [Italy is impressed within Corinne. Corinne [...] is the daughter of these skies, of this clime, of this nature'].[49] Cottin's knowledge and use of the northern British Ossianic myths and landscape was remarked upon by contemporary readers, who loved these settings.[50] Genlis expressly drew her readers' attention to the significance she attributed to nature. She writes: 'pour faire parler l'amour maternel [...] il n'existe qu'un seul langage; c'est celui de la nature [...]; et nul lecteur ne peut le méconnaître' ['to make maternal love speak [...] only one language exists; that is the language of nature [...], and no reader can mistake it'].[51] Genlis states this argument in *Les Mères rivales,* a novel which uses the language of nature to discuss motherhood, thereby ensuring that her readers will bear it in mind throughout. This quotation clearly made a great impression, for, although originally from the novel itself, it was later included in a separately printed book of the most poignant maxims and *pensées* drawn from throughout Genlis's work.

Staël's *Corinne* directly influenced the works of future women Romantic writers across Europe, including Teresa Bandetti, Massimina Fantastici, Zinaïda Volkonskaya, and Letitia Landon, as we have seen in Chapter 5. Staël also influenced the work of Marceline Desbordes-Valmore, whose *Elégies, Marie et romances* (1819) 'helped inaugurate the Romantic movement in France alongside Alphonse de Lamartine's *Méditations* (1820)'.[52] *Corinne* was highly praised by male Romantics and members of the Coppet group, too, such as Schlegel, Constant, Sismondi, and Meister, who wrote for the French journal *Le Publiciste.*[53] In fact, Staël's influence on French (and indeed on European) Romanticism has been well documented, particularly with regard to *De l'Allemagne, De la Littérature* and *Corinne*, and it is therefore unnecessary to reiterate these arguments here.[54] However, to these studies we can add conclusive remarks about Staël's celebration of the female writer-poet. The suffering the poet endures as an outsider is well documented in studies of Romanticism, as is the glory and prestige conferred on the figure of the poet by the Romantic movement. However, Staël's *Corinne*, like Cottin's *Malvina*, builds on these images, extending them to women. She not only documents the female writer-poet's own brand of suffering, she also confers immortal glory and power on the female writer-poet, bequeathing to her both the future of writing itself and a platform from which she might express her suffering.

However, Staël was not alone in influencing later Romantics with the themes and arguments she employed. Sykes reminds us, for example, that the Romantic generation knew Mme Cottin well. He cites several canonical Romantic names who praised her writing, including Musset, Hugo and Lamartine:

> Musset, en 1831, évoque le temps, 'il y a trente ou quarante ans... où *Malvina* faisait couler les larmes et répandait l'insomnie dans les pensionnats'. En 1817, écrit Hugo dans *Les Misérables*, '*Claire d'Albe* et *Malek-Adhel* étaient des chefs-d'œuvre; Mme Cottin était déclarée le premier auteur du jour'. Parmi les écrivains de prédilection de ses *Muses romantiques,* M. Bouteron cite, en lui

donnant 'une place d'honneur', Mme Cottin, 'auteur de l'ossianique *Malvina*'. Certes, elle fut très goûtée par le jeune Lamartine qui, le 28 novembre 1808, écrit à son ami Guichard de Bienassis: 'Je lis pendant ces longues soirées du mois de novembre quelque bons romans [...]. J'en suis à présent à un ouvrage de Mme Cottin, *Malvina*; c'est fort bien écrit'.

[In 1831, Musset evokes a time 'thirty or forty years ago... when *Malvina* caused tears to flow and spread insomnia in girls' boarding schools'. In 1817, Hugo writes in *Les Misérables*, '*Claire d'Albe* and *Malek-Adhel* were masterpieces; Mme Cottin was declared to be the foremost author of her day'. Amongst his favourite writers mentioned in his *Romantic Muses*, M. Bouteron cites Mme Cottin, 'the author of the Ossianic *Malvina*', granting her 'a place of honour'. Certainly, she was greatly enjoyed by the young Lamartine, who, on 28th November 1808, writes to his friend Guichard de Bienassis: 'During these long November evenings, I am reading some good novels [...]. At present I am reading one of Mme Cottin's works, *Malvina*. It is very well written'].[55]

Several factors become obvious from reading Sykes's list of Cottin's admirers. Firstly (although writing in 1926, over a hundred years after the publication of Cottin's novels) Marcel Bouteron actually employs the adjective 'ossianique' ['Ossianic'] to describe the whole of *Malvina*, evidencing the fact that her readers certainly did not see the landscape setting or intertextual references in this novel as irrelevant or rare, as Pelckmans (and indeed Sykes himself)[56] have done.[57] Secondly, the argument in Chapter 3 of this book, that Cottin prefigured the famous Romantic names who portrayed the Orient and the early Romantic themes associated with desert spaces, is in fact a little understated. She did more than prefigure, she inspired. Hugo, it transpires, was not only familiar with Cottin's *Mathilde* (which he refers to by the name of its hero Malek-Adhel), but considered it a masterpiece. He would later take up the same Romantic-Orientalist discourse as Cottin in his *Les Orientales*. So, too, would Lamartine, who we see here praising *Malvina*. Despite reserving some criticism for *Mathilde* twenty years later, nonetheless, 'Lamartine reprit, consciemment ou non, certains décors, personnages et thèmes de Mme Cottin, dans les *Visions* et dans *Jocelyn*, et [...] en 1836 il s'inspira un peu de *Mathilde* pour écrire son plan de la *Chute d'un ange*' ['consciously or not Lamartine used certain of Mme Cottin's settings, characters and themes in his *Visions* and *Jocelyn*, and [...] in 1836 he drew a little inspiration from *Mathilde* in order to write his plan for the *Fall of an Angel*'].[58]

Cottin, like Staël, also had a profound effect on the women writers who came after her. Marceline Desbordes-Valmore, in particular, expressed her admiration through one of her poems which refers to both *Malvina* and *Mathilde*. Certain lines of the poem reveal her understanding of what Cottin had succeeded in conveying:

> Mais quelle voix plus tendre
> S'exhale au fond des bois:
> Cotin [sic], je crois entendre
> Ta gémissante voix.
> Non, c'est la tourterelle,
> Qui pleure ses amours:

> Tu fus triste comme elle,
> On te plaindra toujours...
>
> [Yet what softer voice
> Emanates from the depths of the woods:
> Cotin [sic], I think I hear
> Your sorrowful voice.
> No, it is the turtledove,
> Who laments her loves:
> You were sad like her,
> You will be pitied forever...].[59]

This stanza links Cottin with nature. Like the voices of her heroines Claire d'Albe and Malvina, Cottin's own voice emanates from the depths of the woods, thus indicating that the woman writer's voice has been re-established in a natural space. The simile which compares Cottin to the turtledove also highlights Cottin's melancholy (or perhaps that in her works), which was clearly evident to Desbordes-Valmore. The final words of the poem are also highly revealing:

> Il est doux de connaître
> Un cœur comme le tien:
> Il est cruel, peut-être,
> De l'entendre trop bien.
>
> [It is sweet to know
> A heart like yours:
> It is cruel, perhaps,
> To understand it all too well.][60]

The fact that Desbordes-Valmore has been deeply touched by Cottin's work is clear throughout the poem, but nevertheless the final lines emphasize something new: that Desbordes-Valmore appreciates the depth and feeling of Cottin's work on a personal level. For, she too, is a female writer who feels the continued oppression of women that Cottin has evoked throughout her novels.

Krüdener was also admired by her fellow women Romantic writers, and inspired them with her novel *Valérie*. Francis Ley declares that

> La romancière allemande, Sophie Laroche, disciple de Richardson et amie de Goethe, écrivait à l'un de ses proches, après avoir lu *Valérie*: 'jamais, jamais il n'a existé quelque chose de plus beau!" et "deux petits volumes, les plus purs que j'aie jamais lus!'
>
> [The German novelist Sophie Laroche, a disciple of Richardson and friend of Goethe, wrote to a close acquaintance after reading *Valérie*: 'Never, never has there existed anything more beautiful!' and 'two little volumes, the purest I have ever read!'][61]

Krüdener even anticipated some of the arguments with regard to landscape that Staël herself would make famous several years later:

> Le poste diplomatique de Venise, en 1784–1786, allait révéler à Julie [de Krüdener] l'opposition du Nord et du Midi. Son roman, *Valérie*, écrit en 1802, sera le reflet de ce violent contraste que Madame de Staël reprit, quatre ans plus tard, dans *Corinne*.

[The diplomatic post in Venice, between 1784 and 1786, would reveal to Julie [de Krüdener] the opposition between North and South. Her novel, *Valérie*, written in 1802, would reflect the same violent contrast that Staël would describe, four years later, in *Corinne*].[62]

The Romantic tendencies of Souza were noted by Sainte-Beuve, who thought that the 'types de beaux jeunes gens mélancoliques, comme le marquis de Fargy, comme ailleurs l'Espagnol Alphonse, comme dans *Eugénie et Mathilde* le Polonais Ladislas, tombent volontiers dans le romanesque'.[63] Despite Sainte-Beuve's use of the word 'romanesque' (usually meaning 'fictional'), this comment was translated into English in 1868 as 'specimens of handsome, melancholy, young persons, like the Marquis de Fargy, and, elsewhere, the Spaniard Alphonse and Ladislas the Pole, in *Eugénie et Mathilde*, easily fall into [...] romanticism'.[64]

Despite her concern over the 'unknown, incomprehension, boredom, confusion, and disorder' of Romanticism, Genlis nonetheless, 'announces romanticism by the characterisation of [her] heroes, by [her] particular treatment of love, death, and religion', and 'was already romantic without knowing it'.[65] Therefore, even though 'Genlis did not like the new romantic school',[66] this does not prevent her work from incorporating some of its themes or, moreover, from being admired by later Romantic writers: 'M. de Lamartine prie madame la Comtesse de Genlis d'agréer ce trop faible hommage de son respect pour sa personne et de son admiration pour son génie' ['M. de Lamartine begs Madame de Genlis to accept this all too feeble expression of his homage and respect for her person and of his admiration for her talent'].[67]

However, despite commonalities between some of their works, despite their shared influence on later Romantic writers, and despite the fact that Cottin, Genlis, Krüdener, Souza and Staël were aware of each other's works, it is important to remember that these women were not always in harmony one with the other. Whilst Genlis praised Krüdener in her memoirs,[68] she was much less kind in both her words and her actions towards Cottin and Staël. Genlis in fact conspired against Staël, about whom Michel Winock states: 'les malveillances de ses ennemis, parmi lesquels se distingue Mme de Genlis, sa rivale, trouvent aisément l'oreille de Bonaparte' ['the malice of her enemies, including particularly her rival, Mme de Genlis, had no difficulty in gaining Bonaparte's ear'].[69] Genlis heavily criticized Cottin's *Malvina* and *Claire d'Albe* in *De l'influence des femmes*.[70] Similarly, 'Souza intensely disliked Genlis whom she accused of lies and ingratitude'.[71] The similar uses to which these women writers put nature in their novels was not the result, therefore, of the collective decision of a sisterhood of solidarity. Instead, it was the result of several women working independently and finding they had similar recourse to the natural landscape in order to convey their controversial messages in a subtle and nuanced way. This makes their re-appropriation of natural space all the more intriguing.

Mornet remarks that, in the eighteenth century, 'le sentiment de la nature [...] a mérité d'entrer dans l'histoire sociale comme dans l'histoire littéraire' ['the feeling for nature [...] has justly found a place in both social and literary history'].[72] However, it is not enough to say, certainly with regard to women's writing, that in the period 1789–1815 nature simply enters into social and literary history. In entering literary history, it critiques social history. The historical and socio-political approach undertaken throughout this book in its analysis of written landscapes has demonstrated this clearly. Reading these novels through the lens of eighteenth- and early nineteenth-century French theories of natural spaces and in light of eighteenth- and early nineteenth-century socio-political debate around issues which concerned women has allowed us to conclude that, for Cottin, Genlis, Krüdener, Souza and Staël, representation of the natural world becomes a method of producing subtle critical commentary. This fact is somewhat paradoxical in itself; for an *escape* into nature on the part of female protagonists becomes a means by which their creators *confront* the everyday reality faced by women in the turbulent socio-historical era following the Revolution.

In the final analysis, then, when the title of this conclusion speaks of 'reclaiming a space for women's writing', it refers not only to the fact that it has highlighted how women writers reclaim a space for their own voice by writing a 'landscape of one's own'. It also refers to the fact that it is wrong to say that 'the revolutionary years in France are marked by a conspicuous dearth of innovative, original works of literature'.[73] Similarly, it is wrong to dismiss the sentimental novel of the First Republic and First Empire as apolitical; it is wrong simply to argue that Cottin, Krüdener, Genlis, Souza and Staël negotiate the same critical territories as those of their male contemporaries such as Bernardin de Saint-Pierre or Chateaubriand; and it is wrong to leave the works of the prominent writers of this period un(der) studied. Their works must be examined in their own right, for, clearly, they still have much to reveal.

Notes to the Conclusion

1. Rousseau, *Julie ou la Nouvelle Héloïse*, p. 354.
2. Wolfgang, p. 12.
3. Louichon, p. 292.
4. Marshall H. Klaus and John H. Kennell, *Maternal-Infant Bonding* (Saint Louis: The C.V. Mosby Company, 1976), pp. 211–12.
5. Nigel P. Field, 'Whether to Relinquish or Maintain a Bond with the Deceased', in *Handbook of Bereavement Research and Practice,* ed. by Margaret S. Stroebe, Robert O. Hansson, Henk Schut, and Wolfgang Stroebe (Washington, DC: American Psychological Association, 2008), pp. 113–32 (p. 113).
6. Dennis Klass, *The Spiritual Lives of Bereaved Parents* (Philadelphia: Taylor & Francis, 1999), p. 87.
7. Vamik D. Volkan, *Linking Objects and Linking Phenomena: A Study of the Forms, Symptoms, Metapsychology, and Therapy of Complicated Mourning* (New York: International Universities Press, Inc., 1981), p. 20.
8. Bending, *Green Retreats,* pp. 3–5.
9. *Oxford English Dictionary,* 'space, n.1. I.4.a', online <http://www.oed.com> [accessed 11 August 2018].
10. John Claiborne Isbell, *The Birth of European Romanticism: Truth and Propaganda in Staël's* De l'Allemagne, *1810–1813* (Cambridge: Cambridge University Press, 1994), p. 5.
11. Christoph Bode, 'Europe', in *Romanticism: An Oxford Guide,* ed. by Nicholas Roe (Oxford: Oxford University Press, 2005), pp. 126–36 (p. 130).
12. Isbell, p. 9.
13. Geneviève Goubier-Robert, 'Sophie Ristaud-Cottin: Un *Sturm-und-Drang* à la française?', in *Études sur le XVIIIe siècle: Portraits de Femmes,* ed. by Roland Mortier and Hervé Hasquin (Bruxelles: Éditions de l'Université de Bruxelles, 2000), pp. 53–60 (p. 59).

14. Ann Jefferson, *Biography and the Question of Literature in France* (Oxford: Oxford University Press, 2007), p. 39. Jefferson quotes from Paul Bénichou, *Les Mages romantiques* (Paris: Gallimard, 1988), p. 25.
15. Paul Bénichou, *Le Sacre de l'écrivain, 1750–1830* (Paris: José Corti, 1973), p. 471.
16. Howells, *Regressive Fictions*, p. 1.
17. Bode, p. 131.
18. Nemoianu, p. 79, referring here to Philippe Van Tiegham, *Histoire de la littérature française* (Paris: Fayard, 1949), pp. 287–373.
19. Devoney Looser, 'Preface', in *The Cambridge Companion to Women's Writing in the Romantic Period*, ed. by Devoney Looser (Cambridge: CUP, 2015), p. xiii–xvi (p. xiii).
20. Ibid.
21. Anthony Mandal, 'Fiction', in *The Cambridge Companion to Women's Writing in the Romantic Period*, ed. by Devoney Looser (Cambridge: CUP, 2015), pp. 16–31 (p. 30).
22. Raymond Immerwahr, '"Romantic" and its Cognates in England, Germany, and France before 1790', in *'Romantic' and its Cognates: The European History of a Word*, ed. by Hans Eichner (Manchester: Manchester University Press, 1972), pp. 17–97 (p. 87).
23. Mellor, p. 187.
24. Ibid.
25. Ibid.
26. Northrop Frye, *A Study of English Romanticism* (New York: Random House, 1968), p. 41.
27. Bettina L. Knapp, review of Lloyd Bishop, *The Romantic hero and his heirs in French literature* (1984), *The French Review*, 59:5 (1986), 787–88.
28. Fairweather, p. 327.
29. Frye, *A Study of English Romanticism*, p. 41.
30. Lanser; Margaret Homans, *Women Writers and Poetic Identity: Dorothy Wordsworth, Emily Brontë, and Emily Dickinson* (Princeton: Princeton University Press, 1980).
31. Lanser, p.161. C.f. Homans, pp. 3–5.
32. Lanser, p.162.
33. Mellor, pp. 185–86.
34. Moore, p. 178.
35. Bertrand-Jennings, p. 11.
36. Slama, p. 222.
37. Mellor, p. 188.
38. Ibid.
39. Schlegel argued in 1800 that 'We must seek the highest Romanticism in the Orient', F. Schlegel, *Gespräch über die Poesie*, in *Kritische-Friedrich-Schlegel-Ausgabe*, ed. by H. Eichner, vols 2–3 (München, Paderborn, Wien: Verlag Ferdinand Schöning, 1967 [1800]), II, p. 320. Translation of Schlegel's quotation by Saglia, in: Diego Saglia, 'Orientalism', in *A Companion to European Romanticism*, ed. by Michael Ferber (Oxford: Blackwell, 2005), pp. 467–85 (p. 484). In 1805, Cottin's *Mathilde* certainly contains detailed focus on Romantic Orientalism, which would be taken up later by writers such as Hugo and Lamartine.
40. In *La Peau de chagrin*, it is in the garden that Vautrin seduces Rastignac, leading him astray. See: Michael Scott, *Struggle for the Soul of the French Novel* (Basingstoke: Macmillan, 1989), p. 8.
41. Owen Heathcote, *Balzac and Violence: Representing History, Space, Sexuality and Death in La Comédie humaine* (New York: Peter Lang, 2009), p. 130.
42. Wolfgang, p. 5.
43. Sykes, p. 247.
44. Mme Cottin to Mme Verdier, August 1805. Ibid., p. 395.
45. Francis Ley, *Madame de Krüdener et son temps 1764–1824* (Paris: Plon, 1962), p. 167.
46. Louis-Simon Auger, *Ma Brochure en réponse aux deux brochures de Mme de Genlis* (Paris: Colnet; Delaunay, 1811), p. 22.
47. Ibid., p. 26.
48. Michaud, *Mercure de France*, 10 décembre 1803. See: Francis Ley and Jean Gaulmier, *Madame de Krüdener, 1764–1824: romantisme et Sainte-Alliance* (Paris: Champion, 1994), p. 172.

49. *Le Publiciste.* See: Simone Balayé, *Madame de Staël: Écrire, lutter, vivre* (Genève: Droz, 1994), p. 255.

50. Colette Cazenobe, 'Une préromantique méconnue, Madame Cottin', *Travaux de littérature,* 1 (1988), 175–202 (p. 185).

51. Fortia de Piles and Genlis, p. 289.

52. Vincent, p. 495.

53. *Le Publiciste,* 12 mai 1807, in Benjamin Constant, *Recueil d'articles, 1795–1817* (Genève: Droz, 1978), pp. 84–88; C.f. Michel Winock, *Mme de Staël* (Paris: Fayard, 2010), p. 302.

54. Isbell; Vincent; Moore; Bode; Fairweather; Bénichou; Charlton, *The French Romantics*; Biancamaria Fontana, 'Literary History and Political Theory in Germaine de Staël's Idea of Europe', in *The Oxford Handbook of European Romanticism,* ed. by Paul Hamilton (Oxford: OUP, 2016), pp. 33–51.

55. Sykes, p. 256; C.f. A. de Musset, *Œuvres complètes,* 10 vols (Paris: Charpentier, 1865), IX, p. 87; V. Hugo, *Les Misérables,* ed. by Maurice Allem (Paris: Gallimard, 1952), pp. 123–24; M. Bouteron, *Muses romantiques* (Paris: Le Goupy, 1926), p. 10; A. de Lamartine, *Correspondance,* publiée par Mme V. de Lamartine, 4 vols (Paris: Hachette, 1873–1874), I, pp. 69–70.

56. Sykes, pp. 128–29.

57. Pelckmans, p. 251.

58. Sykes, pp. 256–57.

59. Ibid., p. 258.

60. Ibid.

61. Francis Ley, 'Madame de Krüdener (1764–1824), in *Études sur le XVIIIe siècle: Portrais de Femmes,* ed. by Roland Mortier and Hervé Hasquin (Bruxelles: Éditions de l'Université de Bruxelles, 2000), pp. 61–74 (p. 66).

62. Ibid., p. 63.

63. Sainte-Beuve, *Portraits de femmes,* p. 34.

64. C. A. Sainte-Beuve, *Portraits of Celebrated Women,* trans, by H. W. Preston (Boston: Roberts Brothers, 1868), p. 84. This translation is fitting, since, as Immerwahr notes, 'the term romantique was introduced to France somewhat later than its cognate in Germany [...]. It remained, however, largely a concept of criticism, never completely supplanting the earlier *romanesque* in general usage'. Immerwahr, p. 84.

65. Poortere, pp. 66; 82; 47.

66. Ibid., p. 66.

67. Maurice Souriau, *Histoire du romantisme en France,* 3 vols (Genève: Slatkine, 1973), I, p. 85.

68. Mme de Genlis, 'Mémoires de madame la comtesse de Genlis', in Mme de Genlis, *Œuvres complètes de madame la comtesse de Genlis; Histoire, mémoires et romans historiques,* 12 vols (Bruxelles: P.J. de Mat, 1828), VIII, p. 30.

69. Winock, p. 213.

70. Mme de Genlis, *De l'influence des femmes sur la littérature française, comme protectrices des lettres et comme auteurs, ou Précis de l'histoire des femmes françaises les plus célèbres* (Paris: Maradan, 1811), p.346; C.f. Stewart, pp. 187–98; Sykes, p.225.

71. Stewart, p. 200.

72. Mornet, p. 217.

73. Bode, p. 130.

BIBLIOGRAPHY

❖

Primary Texts

COTTIN, MADAME SOPHIE, *Amélie Mansfield,* 4 vols (Paris: Maradan, 1802)

——*Claire d'Albe,* ed. Margaret Cohen (The Modern Language Association of America: New York, 2002)

——*Malvina,* 4 vols (Paris: Maradan, an IX [1800])

——*Mathilde, ou mémoires tirés de l'histoire des croisades,* 4 vols (Paris: Ménard et Desenne, 1824)

GENLIS, MADAME DE, *Les Mères Rivales, ou la Calomnie,* 4 vols (Paris: Librairie de Du Pont, an IX [1800])

KRÜDENER, MADAME DE, *Valérie* (Paris: Éditions Klincksiek, 1974)

SOUZA, MADAME ADÉLAÏDE DE, *Adèle de Sénange,* in Madame de Souza, *Œuvres complètes de Madame de Souza,* 6 vols (Paris: Alexis Eymery, 1821–1822), I

——*Émilie et Alphonse,* in Madame de Souza, *Oeuvres complètes de Mme Adélaïde de Souza,* 6 vols (Paris: Alexis Eymery, 1822), V

STAËL, MADAME DE, *Corinne ou l'Italie* (France: Gallimard, 1985)

——*Delphine,* 2 vols (Paris: Flammarion, 2000)

Secondary Texts Pre-1900

ANON, *Letters to Honoria and Marianne, on Various Subjects,* 3 vols (London: J. Dodsley, 1784)

ANON., 'Variétés', *Journal des Débats,* 24 ventose an VIII [15 mars 1800], De l'imprimerie de Le Normant

AUGER, LOUIS-SIMON, *Ma Brochure en réponse aux deux brochures de Mme de Genlis* (Paris: Colnet; Delaunay, 1811)

BADÍA Y LEBLICH, DOMINGO (Ali Bey), *Voyages d'Ali Bey el Abbassi en Afrique et en Asie pendant les années 1803, 1804, 1805, 1806 et 1807* (Paris: P. Didot, 1814)

BERLEPS, MME DE, '12 janvier 1811: Fragment de *Caledonia, ou voyage en Écosse',* in *Mercure de France,* trans. A. M. Herdez

BOIGNE, COMTESSE DE, *Mémoires,* 5 vols (Paris: Émile-Paul Frères, 1921)

BONAPARTE, NAPOLÉON, *Napoléon: Ses opinions et jugements sur les hommes et sur les choses,* ed. M. Damas Hinard (Paris: Duféy, 1838)

BOSSUET, JACQUES-BÉNIGNE, 'Fragment sur la brièveté de la vie et le néant de l'homme', in Jacques-Bénigne Bossuet, *Œuvres,* 43 vols (Versailles: J.A. Lebel, 1816)

BOUTERON, M., *Muses romantiques* (Paris: Le Goupy, 1926)

BRACHET, JEAN-LOUIS, *Traité de l'hystérie* (Paris: J.-B. Baillière, 1847)

BRIQUET, P., *Traité Clinique et thérapeutique de l'hystérie* (Paris: J.-B. Baillière et fils, 1859)

BRISSOT DE WARVILLE, J.-P, A. BRISSOT DE WARVILLE, and F. MONTROL, *Mémoires de Brissot sur ses contemporains et la Révolution française,* 2 vols (Paris: Ladvocat, 1830)

BUFFON, GEORGES LOUIS LECLERC, COMTE DE, *Les Époques de la nature,* 2 vols (Paris: L'Imprimerie royale, 1780)

BUNYAN, JOHN, *The Pilgrim's Progress* (London: Penguin, 1987)

——*Le Pélerinage d'un nommé Chrétien, écrit sous l'allégorie d'un songe,* trans. anon (Paris: Frères Estienne, 1772)

BURKE, EDMUND, *A Philosophical Inquiry into the Origin of Our Ideas of the Sublime and Beautiful; with an Introductory Discourse Concerning Taste* (New York: Harper and Brothers, 1844)

BYRON, GEORGE GORDON, *Beppo: A Venetian Story* (London: John Murray, 1818)

CABANIS, PIERRE J. G., *Rapports du physique et du moral de l'homme* (Paris: Crapart, Caille et Ravier, 1805)

CHATEAUBRIAND, FRANÇOIS-RENÉ DE, *Atala* (Paris: Lordereau, 1831).

——*Itinéraire de Paris à Jérusalem* (Paris: Furne et Cie, 1865)

——*Mémoires d'outre- tombe,* 6 vols (Paris: Dulfour, Mulat and Boulanger, 1860)

CHÉNIER, MARIE-JOSEPH DE, *Tableau historique de l'état et des progrès de la littérature française depuis 1789* (Paris: Ledentu, 1817)

Code civil des Français (Paris: Imp. de la République, an XII [1804])

COLOMBIER, JEAN, ET FRANÇOIS DOUBLET, *Instruction sur la manière de gouverner les Insensés, et de travailler à leur guérison dans les Asyles qui leur sont destinés* (Paris: L'Imprimerie Royale, 1785)

CONSTANT, BENJAMIN, *Recueil d'articles, 1795–1817* (Genève: Droz, 1978)

CORNOT, FERDINAND DE, BARON DE CUSSY, *Souvenirs du chevalier de Cussy, garde du corps, diplomate et consul général, 1795–1866,* 2 vols (Paris: Plon-Nourrit et Cie, 1909)

COTTIN, MME, *Claire D'Albe* (Paris: Hiard, 1831)

DAQUIN, JOSEPH, *La philosophie de la folie, ou Essai philosophique sur le traitement des personnes attaquées de folie* (Paris: Libraire Née de la Rochelle, 1792)

DENON, DOMINIQUE-VIVANT, *Voyage dans la basse et la haute-Égypte pendant les campagnes du général Bonaparte* (Paris: P. Didot, 1802)

DEZALLIER D'ARGENVILLE, ANTOINE-JOSEPH, *Théorie et pratique du jardinage* (Paris: Mariette, 1747)

Dictionnaire de L'Académie française, 4th Edition (1762) <http://portail.atilf.fr/cgi-bin/dico1look.pl?strippedhw=nature&headword=&docyear=ALL&dicoid=ALL&articletype=1#ACAD1762>

Dictionnaire de L'Académie française, 5th Edition (1798) <http://portail.atilf.fr/cgi-bin/dico1look.pl?strippedhw=travestir&dicoid=ACAD1798&headword=&dicoid=ACAD1798>

Dictionnaire de l'Académie française, 5e édition, 2 vols (Paris: J.J. Smits, L'An VI de la République [1798])

DIDEROT, DENIS, *De l'interprétation de la nature* in *Textes Choisis,* ed. by Jean Varloot, 7 vols (Paris: Éditions sociales, 1953)

——*Sur les femmes,* in *Œuvres complètes de Denis Diderot* (Paris: Deterville, An VIII [1799–1800])

DUCHESNE, ANTOINE NICOLAS, *Sur la formation des jardins* (Paris: Pissot, 1779)

Encyclopédie ou Dictionnaire raisonné des sciences, des arts et des métiers, 21 vols (Stuttgart; Bad Cannstatt: F. Frommann, 1988 [1751–1772])

FORTIA DE PILES, ALPHONSE COMTE DE, and STÉPHANIE FÉLICITÉ COMTESSE DE GENLIS, *Esprit de Madame de Genlis, ou, portraits, caractères, maxims et pensées, extraits de tous ses ouvrages publiés jusqu'à ce jour* (Paris: Porthmann, 1814)

GENLIS, MME DE, *Adèle et Théodore, ou Lettres sur l'éducation, contenant tous les principes relatifs aux trois differents plans d'éducation, des princes, des jeunes personnes, et des hommes,* 3 vols (Paris: Chez M. Lambert et F. J. Baudouin, 1782)

——*Adelaide and Théodore, or Letters on Education,* ed. and trans. Gillian Dow (London: Pickering and Chatto, 2007)

———*De l'influence des femmes sur la littérature française, comme protectrices des lettres et comme auteurs, ou Précis de l'histoire des femmes françaises les plus célèbres* (Paris: Maradan, 1811)

———*Herbier moral, ou receuil de fables nouvelles et autres poésies fugitives* (Hamburg: Pierre Chateauneuf, 1799)

———*La Botanique historique et littéraire: suivie d'une nouvelle intitulée* Les fleurs, ou les artistes (Paris: Maradan, 1810)

———*La Femme Auteur* (Paris: Gallimard, 2007)

———'Mémoires de madame la comtesse de Genlis', in Mme de Genlis, *Œuvres complètes de madame la comtesse de Genlis; Histoire, mémoires et romans historiques*, 12 vols (Bruxelles: P.J. de Mat, 1828)

HARDY, SIMÉON-PROSPER, and OTHERS, *Siméon-Prosper Hardy: Mes Loisirs, ou journal d'événements tels qu'ils parviennent à ma connaissance (1753–1789)* (Québec: Presses de l'Université Laval, 2008).

H.D. 'Introduction' to Mme Cottin, *Claire D'Albe* (Paris: Hiard, 1831)

HOUDRY, VINCENT, 'Sermon 24: Du soin des enfants' (1696), in Élisabeth Badinter, *L'Amour en plus: Histoire de l'amour maternel (XVIIe–XXe siècle)* (Paris: Flammarion, 1980)

HUGO, V., *Les Misérables*, ed. by Maurice Allem (Paris: Gallimard, 1952)

KANT, IMMANUEL, *Observations on the Feeling of the Beautiful and Sublime*, trans. by John T. Goldthwait (London: University of California Press, 1991 [1764])

KRÜDENER, FRAU [MRS] BARBARA JULIANE VON, BARONESS VON KRÜDENER, 'Frau [Mrs] Barbara Juliane von Krüdener, baroness von Krüdener to Jacques Henri Bernardin de Saint-Pierre: Tuesday, 7 September 1790 — [letter]', in *Electronic Enlightenment*, ed. by Robert McNamee et al.
<HTTP://WWW.E-ENLIGHTENMENT.COM/ITEM/SAINJAVF0031161_1key001cor/>

LA METTRIE, J. O. DE, *L'Homme-machine* (Paris: Henry, 1865 [1747])

LA TOUR, CHARLOTTE DE, *Le Langage des fleurs* (Paris: Garnier Frères, 1858)

LABORDE, ALEXANDRE DE, *Description des nouveaux jardins de la France et de ses anciens châteaux, mêlée d'observations sur la vie de la campagne et la composition des jardins* (Paris: Delance, 1808)

———*Discours sur la vie de la campagne et la composition des jardins* (Paris: Delance, 1808)

LACLOS, CHODERLOS DE, 'Des Femmes et de leur éducation', in *Œuvres complètes*, ed. by Laurent Versini (Paris: Gallimard, 1979)

———*Œuvres complètes*, ed. by Laurent Versini (Paris: Gallimard, 1979)

LAMARTINE, A. DE, *Correspondance*, publiée par Mme V. de Lamartine, 4 vols (Paris: Hachette, 1873–1874)

LE COMTE D'ANTRAIGUES, *Observations sur le Divorce* (Paris: Imprimerie nationale, 1789)

LE PÈRE DUCHESNE, *L'Indignation du Père Duchesne contre l'indissolubricité du mariage, et sa motion pour le Divorce* (Paris: Tremblay, c.1790)

LINGUET, SIMON-NICOLAS-HENRI, *Voyage au labyrinthe du jardin du roi* (La Haye: Libraires Associés, 1755)

LOUIS XIV, *Manière de montrer les jardins de Versailles* (Paris: Catherine Szántó Publication, 2013)

LOUYER-VILLERMAY, JEAN-BAPTISTE, *Traité des maladies nerveuses, ou vapeurs et particulièrement de l'hystérie et de l'hypocondrie* (Paris: Méquignon, 1816)

MACPHERSON, JAMES, *Works of Ossian, Son of Fingal* (London: T. Becket and P. A. DeHondt, 1765)

———*Ossian, Fils de Fingal, Barde du troisième siècle: Poésies galliques*, trans. M. Le Tourneur, 2 vols (Paris: Musier, 1777)

MAISTRE, JOSEPH DE, *Lettres et opuscules inédits* (Paris: Vaton, 1851)

MARÉCHAL, SYLVAIN, *Project d'une loi portant défense d'apprendre à lire aux femmes* (Paris: Massé, 1801)

MERCIER, LOUIS-SÉBASTIEN, *Néologie, ou vocabulaire de mots nouveaux, à renouveler, ou pris dans des acceptions nouvelles*, 2 vols (Paris: Moussard; Maradan, 1801)

MICHAUD, JOSEPH F., and BAPTISTIN POUJOULAT, *Correspondance D'orient 1830–1831*, 8 vols (Brussels: Gegoir, Wouters and Co., 1841)

MILLOT, JACQUES ANDRÉ, *L'art d'améliorer et de perfectionner les hommes, au moral comme au physique*, 2 vols (Paris: Migneret, 1801)

MOLLET, ANDRÉ, *Le Jardin de Plaisir* (Moniteur : Paris, 1981 [1651])

MONTESQUIEU, CHARLES DE SECONDAT, BARON DE, *Voyages de Montesquieu*, 2 vols (Bordeaux: G. Gounouilhou, 1894)

MOREAU, JACQUES-LOUIS, *Histoire naturelle de la femme*, 3 vols (Paris: Duprat; Letellier, 1803)

MURALT, BÉAT DE, *Lettres sur les Anglais et les Français* (Berne: Steiger & Cie; Paris: Librairie Le Soudier, 1897)

MUSSET, A. DE, *Œuvres complètes*, 10 vols (Paris: Charpentier, 1865)

OSSIAN, BARDE DU IIIème siècle, *Poésies galliques en vers français*, trans. by P. M. L. Baour Lormian (Paris: Giguet et Michaud, 1809)

OVID, *Metamorphoses XI*, ed. G. M. H. Murphy (Bristol: Bristol Classical Press, 1979)

POPE, ALEXANDER, *Essay on Man*, ed. by Mark Pattison (Oxford: Clarendon Press, 1871)

RESTIF DE LA BRETONNE, *Les Gynographes, ou idées de deux honnêtes-femmes sur un projet de reglement proposé à toute l'Europe: pour mettre les femmes à leur place, et opérer le Bonheur des deux sexes; avec des notes historiques et justificatives, suivies des noms des femmes célèbres* (Paris: Gosse & Pinet; Humblot, 1777)

ROUSSEAU, JEAN-JACQUES, *Émile ou de l'Éducation*, in Jean-Jacques Rousseau, *Œuvres complètes de J. J. Rousseau* (Paris: Furne, 1835), II

——*Julie ou La Nouvelle Héloïse* (Paris: Garnier Flammarion, 1967).

——*Les Confessions* (Paris: Charpentier, 1862)

——*On Women, Love, and Family*, ed. by Christopher Kelly and Eve Grace (Hanover, N.H: Dartmouth College Press, 2009)

ROUSSEL, PIERRE, *Système physique et moral de la femme* (Paris: Masson, 1869 [1775])

SAINTE-BEUVE, CHARLES-AUGUSTIN, *Causeries du Lundi* (Paris: Garnier Frères, n.d.)

——*Portraits de femmes* (Paris: Didier, 1844)

——*Portraits of Celebrated Women*, trans, by H. W. Preston (Boston: Roberts Brothers, 1868)

SCHLEGEL, F., *Gespräch über die Poesie*, in *Kritische-Friedrich-Schlegel-Ausgabe*, ed. by H. Eichner, vols 2–3 (München, Paderborn, Wien: Verlag Ferdinand Schöning, 1967 [1800])

SHAKESPEARE, WILLIAM, *Hamlet*, in *The Library of Shakespeare* (London: Midpoint Press, 2005)

STAËL, MADAME DE, *De l'influence des passions sur le bonheur des individus et des nations* (Lausanne: J. Mourer, 1796)

——*De la Littérature considérée dans ses rapports avec les institutions sociales*, 2 vols (Paris: Maradan, 1800)

——*Réflexions sur le suicide* (London: Schulze and Dean, 1813)

STROHL, ÉDOUARD, *Recherches statistiques sur la relation qui peut exister entre la périodicité de la menstruation et les phases de la lune* (Strasbourg: Silbermann, 1861)

TALBOT, CATHERINE, 'Imitations of Ossian,' in Catherine Talbot, *The Works of the late Mrs. Catherine Talbot* (London: John Rivington, 1780)

TENON, JACQUES-RENÉ, *Mémoires dur les hôpitaux de Paris* (Paris: L'Imprimerie de PH.-D. Pierres, 1788)

THOMAS, ANTOINE LÉONARD, *Essai sur le caractère, les mœurs et l'esprit des femmes dans les différents siècles* (Paris: Moutard, 1772)

THOMAS, A. L., DIDEROT, MADAME D'EPINAY, *Qu'est-ce qu'une femme*, ed. Élisabeth Badinter (Paris: P.O.L., 1989)

VAN DE SPIEGEL, ADRIAAN, *De formato foetu liber singularis, aenis figuris exornatus* (Padua: Patavii, 1626)

VIARDEL, COSME, *Observations sur la pratique des accouchements* (Paris: Chez l'Autheur, 1674)

VIREY, JULIEN-JOSEPH, *De la femme, sous ses rapports physiologique, moral et littéraire* (Paris: Crochard, 1825)

VOLNEY, C-F., *Voyage en Syrie et en Egypte pendant les années 1783, 1784, et 1785*, 2 vols (Paris: Volland, 1787)

VOLTAIRE, *Œuvres complètes de Voltaire: avec des remarques et des notes historiques, scientifiques et littéraires* (Paris: Baudouin Frères, 1827)

——*Lettres philosophiques* (Amsterdam: E. Lucas, 1734)

Secondary Texts Post-1900

ABENSOUR, LÉON, *La femme et le féminisme avant la révolution* (Paris: Éditions Ernest Leroux, 1923)

AGHION, IRÈNE, *Héros et dieux de l'Antiquité: guide iconographique* (Paris: Flammarion, 1994)

AGNEW, JOHN, 'Space and Place', in *Handbook of Geographical Knowledge,* ed. by J. Agnew and D. Livingstone (London: Sage, 2011), pp. 316–30

AGNEW, J. and D. LIVINGSTONE, eds., *Handbook of Geographical Knowledge* (London: Sage, 2011)

ALEXANDROVA EKATERINA, R., ' "This salutary remedy": Female suicide and the novel as Pharmakon in Riccoboni's *Histoire de M. Le Marquis de Cressy* and Rousseau's *La Nouvelle Héloïse*' in Adriana Teodorescu, ed., *Death Representations in Literature: Forms and Theories* (Newcastle: Cambridge Scholars Publishing, 2015), pp. 97–116

AMEND-SÖCHTING, ANNE, 'La Mélancolie dans *Corinne*', in José-Luis Diaz, ed., *Madame de Staël, Corinne ou l'Italie, 'l'âme se mêle à tout'* (Paris: Sedes, 1999), pp. 101–10

ANDERSON, SARAH, *Readings of Trauma, Madness and the Body* (New York: Palgrave Macmillan, 2012)

ARNELLE, *Une Oubliée: Mme Cottin d'après sa correspondance* (Paris: Librairie Plon, Plon-Nourrit et Cie, 1914)

ARON, JEAN-PAUL, ed., *Misérable et glorieuse, la femme du XIXe siècle* (Paris: Fayard, 1980)

ASTBURY, KATHERINE, *Narrative Responses to the Trauma of the French Revolution* (London: Legenda, 2012)

AUSLANDER, LEORA, *Taste and Power: Furnishing Modern France* (Berkeley: University of California Press, 1996)

BACHELARD, GASTON, *La poétique de l'espace* (Paris: Presses universitaires de France, 1961)

——*L'Eau et les rêves* (Paris: Librairie José Corti, 1942)

BADINTER, ÉLISABETH, *L'Amour en plus: Histoire de l'amour maternel (XVIIe–XXe siècle)* (Paris: Flammarion, 1980)

——'Préface', in Élisabeth Badinter, ed., A. L. Thomas, Diderot, Madame d'Epinay, *Qu'est-ce qu'une femme?* (Paris: P.O.L., 1989), pp. 7–47

BAKER, GEORGE M., 'Madame de Staël's Attitude toward Nature', in *The Sewanee Review,* 20:1 (1912), 45–64

BAKHTIN, MIKHAIL, *The Dialogic Imagination: Four Essays,* ed. Michael Holquist, trans. Caryl Emerson and Michael Holquist (Austin, University of Texas Press, 1981)

BAL, MIEKE, *Narratology: Introduction to the Theory of Narrative* (Toronto; Buffalo; London: University of Toronto Press, 1997)

BALAYÉ, SIMONE, *Les Carnets de Voyage de Madame de Staël: Contribution à la genèse de ses œuvres* (Genève: Librairie Droz, 1971)

——*Madame de Staël: écrire, lutter, vivre* (Genève: Droz, 1994)

BARIDON, MICHEL, 'Understanding nature and the aesthetics of the landscape garden', in Martin Calder, ed., *Experiencing the Gardens in the Eighteenth Century* (Oxford: Peter Lang, 2006), pp. 65–85

BARRE, NICOLE, *Le Désert et la littérature de voyage européenne du XIXe siècle* (Doctoral Thesis, Università di Bologna, 2014)

BEAUVOIR, SIMONE DE, *Le Deuxième Sexe*, 2 vols (Paris: Gallimard, 1976 [1949])

BEHBAHANI, NOUCHINE, *Paysages dans* La Nouvelle Héloïse (Oxford: Voltaire Foundation at the Taylor Institution, 1989)

BEIZER, JANET, *Ventriloquized Bodies: Narratives of Hysteria in Nineteenth-Century France* (New York: Cornell University Press, 1994)

BENDING, STEPHEN, *A cultural history of gardens in the age of enlightenment* (London: Bloomsbury, 2013)

——*Green Retreats: Women, gardens and eighteenth-century culture* (Cambridge: Cambridge University Press, 2013)

BÉNICHOU, PAUL, *Le Sacre de l'écrivain, 1750–1830* (Paris: José Corti, 1973)

——*Les Mages romantiques* (Paris: Gallimard, 1988)

BERNARD-GRIFFITHS, S., F. LE BORGNE, and DANIEL MADELÉNAT, eds., *Jardins Et Intimité Dans La Littérature Européenne (1750–1920): Actes Du Colloque Du Centre De Recherches Révolutionnaires Et Romantiques, Université Blaise-Pascal (Clermont-Ferrand, 22–24 Mars 2006)* (Clermont-Ferrand: Presses Universitaires Blaise-Pascal, 2008)

BERTRAND-JENNINGS, CHANTAL, *Un Autre mal du siècle: Le Romantisme des romancières, 1800–1846* (Toulouse: Presses Universitaires du Mirail, 2005)

BIANCIARDI, DAVID, *Sophie Cottin, une romancière oubliée à l'orée du romantisme, (contribution à l'étude de la réception)* (Doctoral Thesis, Université de Metz, 1995)

BIEDERMANN, ALFRED, ed., *Romantisme européen*, 2 vols (Paris: Larousse, 1972)

BLAYO, YVES, 'La mortalité en France de 1740 à 1829', *Population*, 1 (1975), 123–42

BLOCH, JEAN, 'The eighteenth century: women writing, women learning' in Sonya Stephens, ed., *A History of Women's Writing in France* (Cambridge: Cambridge University Press, 2000), pp. 84–101

BLOCH, MAURICE and JEAN H. BLOCH, 'Women and the Dialectics of Nature in Eighteenth-Century French Thought', in Carol P. MacCormack, and Marilyn Strathern, eds., *Nature, Culture, and Gender* (Cambridge: Cambridge University Press, 1980), pp. 25–41

BODE, CHRISTOPH, 'Europe', in *Romanticism: An Oxford Guide*, ed. by Nicholas Roe (Oxford: Oxford University Press, 2005), pp. 126–36

BOURDIEU, PIERRE, *Language and Symbolic Power*, trans. by Gino Raymond and Matthew Adamson, ed. by John B. Thompson (Cambridge, MA: Harvard University Press, 1991)

BRANNIGAN, MICHAEL C., *The Pulse of Wisdom: The Philosophies of India, China, and Japan* (Belmont, CA: Wadsworth, 1995)

BRONFEN, ELISABETH, *Over Her Dead Body: Death, Femininity and the Aesthetics* (Manchester: Manchester University Press, 1992)

BROUARD-ARENDS, ISABELLE, *Vies et images maternelles dans la littérature française du 18e siècle* (Oxford: The Voltaire Foundation, 1991)

BRUIN, KAREN DE, 'Melancholy in the Pursuit of Happiness: *Corinne* and the *Femme Supérieure*', in Tili Boon Cuillé and Karyna Szmurlo, eds., *Staël's Philosophy of the Passions: Sensibility, Society and the Sister Arts* (Lewisburg: Bucknell University Press, 2013), pp. 75–94

BRUNEL, PIERRE, ed., *Romantismes européens et Romantisme français* (Montpellier: Éditions espaces, 2000)

BUELL, LAWRENCE, *The Environmental Imagination: Thoreau, Nature Writing, and the Formation of American Culture* (Cambridge, MA; London: Belknap Press of Harvard University Press, 1996)

BURROWS, SIMON, 'The Innocence of Jacques-Pierre Brissot', *The Historical Journal*, 46:4 (2003), 843–71

BUTLER, JUDITH, *Gender Trouble* (New York: Routledge, 2007)

CALDER, MARTIN, ed., *Experiencing the Gardens in the Eighteenth Century* (Oxford: Peter Lang, 2006)

——'Foreward' to *Experiencing the Gardens in the Eighteenth Century*, ed. by Martin Calder (Oxford: Peter Lang, 2006), pp. 7–11

——'The Experience of Space in the Eighteenth-Century French Garden: From Axis to Circuit to Closed Circuit', in Emma Gilby and Katja Hautsein, eds., *Space: New Dimensions in French Studies* (Oxford: Peter Lang, 2005), pp. 41–58

CALL, MICHAEL J., *Infertility and the Novels of Sophie Cottin* (Newark: University of Delaware Press; London: Associated University Presses, 2002)

CAPITAN, COLETTE, *La Nature à l'ordre du jour, 1789–1973* (Paris: Kimé, 1993)

CARBONI, PIERRE, 'Ossian and Belles Lettres: Scottish Influences on J.-B.-A. Suard and Late-Eighteenth-Century French Taste and Criticism', in Deirdre Dawson and Pierre Morère, eds., *Scotland and France in the Enlightenment* (Lewisburg: Bucknell University Press, 2003)

CARLASSARE, ELIZABETH, 'Destabilizing the Criticism of Essentialism in Ecofeminist Discourse', *Capitalism Nature Socialism*, 5:3 (1994), 50–66

CARPENTER, KIRSTY, *The Novels of Madame de Souza in Social and Political Perspective* (Oxford: Peter Lang, 2007)

CARRABINO, VICTOR, 'The Nouveau Roman and the Neo-Romantic Hero', in *The Comparatist*, 7 (1983), 29–35

CARROLL, ROBERT, and STEPHEN PRICKETT, eds., *The Bible*, Authorized King James Version with Apocrypha (Oxford: Oxford University Press, 1997)

CAZENOBE, COLETTE, *Au Malheur des dames: Le roman féminine au XVIIIe siècle* (Paris: Honoré Champion, 2006)

——'Une préromantique méconnue, Madame Cottin', *Travaux de littérature*, 1 (1988), 175–202

CHARLTON, D. G., *New Images of the Natural in France: A Study in European Cultural History, 1750–1800* (Cambridge: Cambridge University Press, 1984)

——'Prose Fiction', in D. G. Charlton, ed., *The French Romantics*, 2 vols (Cambridge: CUP, 1984), I, pp. 163–203

——, ed., *The French Romantics*, 2 vols (Cambridge: CUP, 1984)

CHARVET, P. E., *A Literary History of France: The Nineteenth Century* (London: Benn, 1967)

CHASE, DANA, *Mother Nature and the Nature of Woman: Rousseau's* Nouvelle Héloïse *and the Novels of Sophie Cottin and Adélaïde de Souza* (Electronically published doctoral thesis, Columbia University, 2001) <http://search.proquest.com/docview/275807092/fulltextPDF?accountid=8312>

CHEVALIER, JEAN and ALAIN GHEERBRANT, *A Dictionary of Symbols* (Oxford; Cambridge, MA: Blackwell, 1994)

CIORANESCU, ALEXANDRE, *L'Avenir du passé: utopie et littérature* (Paris: Gallimard, 1972)

CIXOUS, HÉLÈNE, and CATHERINE CLÉMENT, *La Jeune Née*, trans. Betsy Wing (London: I. B. Tauris, 1996)

CLADIS, MARK SYDNEY, *Public Vision, Private Lives: Rousseau, Religion, and 21st-century Democracy* (New York: Columbia University Press, 2003)

COHEN, MARGARET, 'Introduction', Sophie Cottin, *Claire d'Albe,* ed. Margaret Cohen (The Modern Language Association of America: New York, 2002), pp. vii–xxii

——*The Sentimental Education of the Novel* (Princeton: Princeton University Press, 1999)

——'Women and fiction in the nineteenth century', in Timothy Unwin, ed., *The Cambridge Companion to the French Novel* (Cambridge: Cambridge University Press, 1997), pp. 54–72

COLT, GEORGE HOWE, *November of the Soul: The Enigma of Suicide* (New York: Scribner, 2006)

COOK, MALCOLM, 'Politics in the Fiction of the French Revolution, 1789–1794', *Studies on Voltaire and the Eighteenth Century,* 201 (1982), 233–340

——'Utopian Fiction of the French Revolution', *Nottingham French Studies,* 45 (2006), 104–13

COURBAGE, YOUSSEF and MANFRED KROPP, *Penser l'Orient: Traditions et actualité des orientalismes français et allemands* (Beirut: Presses de l'Ifpo, 2004)

CRANSTON, MAURICE, *The Romantic Movement* (Oxford: Blackwell, 1994)

CRESSWELL, TIM, *Place: A Short Introduction* (Chichester: Wiley-Blackwell, 2015)

CRONNON, WILLIAM, 'Forward', in Marjorie Hope Nicholson, *Mountain Gloom and Mountain Glory, the development of the aesthetics of the Infinite* (Cornell: Cornell University Press, 1997), pp. vii–xii

CUILLÉ, TILI BOON, *Narrative Interludes: Musical Tableaux in Eighteenth-century France* (Toronto: University of Toronto Press, 2006)

CUILLÉ, TILI BOON and KARYNA SZMURLO, eds., *Staël's Philosophy of the Passions: Sensibility, Society and the Sister Arts* (Lewisburg: Bucknell University Press, 2013)

CUSSET, CATHERINE, 'Sophie Cottin ou l'écriture du déni', *Romantisme,* 77 (1992), 25–31

DARNTON, ROBERT, 'The Grub Street Style of Revolution: J.-P. Brissot, police spy', *Journal of Modern History,* 40:3 (1968) 301–27

DARROW, MARGARET H., 'French Noblewomen and the New Domesticity, 1750–1850', *Feminist Studies,* 5:1 (1979), 41–65

DAVIS, LEITH, 'Malvina's Daughters: Irish Women Poets and the Sign of the Bard', in Jim Kelly, ed., *Ireland and Romanticism. Publics, Nations and Scenes of Cultural Production* (London: Palgrave MacMillan, 2011), pp. 141–60

DAWSON, DEIRDRE and PIERRE MORÈRE, eds., *Scotland and France in the Enlightenment* (Lewisburg: Bucknell University Press, 2003)

DEITZ, PAULA, *Of Gardens: Selected Essays* (Pennsylvania: University of Pennsylvania Press, 2011)

DELASSELLE, CLAUDE, 'Les enfants abandonées de l'Hôtel-Dieu de Paris: l'année 1793', in *Enfance abandonnée et société en Europe, XIVe–XXe siècle. Actes du colloque international de Rome (30 et 31 janvier 1987)* (Publications de l'École française de Rome), 140:1 (1991), 503–12

DELUCIA, JOELLEN, '"Far Other Times Are These": The Bluestockings in the Time of Ossian', *Tulsa Studies in Women's Literature,* 27:1 (2008), 39–62

DEMBOWSKI, PETER F., ed., *La Vie de Sainte Marie l'Égyptienne: versions en ancien et en moyen français* (Geneva: Droz, 1977)

DENBY, DAVID J., *Sentimental Narrative and the Social Order in France, 1760–1820* (Cambridge: Cambridge University Press, 1994)

DESAN, SUZANNE, *The Family on Trial in Revolutionary France* (California: University of California Press, 2006)

DEVINE, MAUREEN, *Woman and Nature: Literary Reconceptualizations* (Metuchen, NJ: Scarecrow Press, 1992)

DIAZ, JOSÉ-LUIS, ed., *Madame de Staël, Corinne ou l'Italie, 'l'âme se mêle à tout'* (Paris: Sedes, 1999)

DÍAZ-DIOCARETZ, MYRIAM and MARTA SEGARRA, eds., *Joyful Babel: Translating Hélène Cixous* (Amsterdam: Rodopi, 2004)

Dictionnaire de L'Académie française, 4th Edition (1762)
<http://portail.atilf.fr/cgi-bin/dico1look.pl?strippedhw=nature&headword=&docyear=AL L&dicoid=ALL&articletype=1#ACAD1762>

Dictionnaire de L'Académie française, 5th Edition (1798)
<http://portail.atilf.fr/cgi-bin/dico1look.pl?strippedhw=travestir&dicoid=ACAD1798&he adword=&dicoid=ACAD1798>

Dictionnaire de l'Académie française, 5e édition, 2 vols (Paris: J.J. Smits, L'an VI de la République [1798])

DOCK, TERRY SMILEY, *Woman in the* Encyclopédie: *A Compendium* (Potomac, MD: Studia Humanitatis, 1983)

DOW, GILLIAN, 'The British Reception of Madame de Genlis's Writings for Children: Plays and Tales of Instruction and Delight', *Journal for Eighteenth-Century Studies*, 29:3 (2006), 367–81

DUNCAN, CAROL, 'Happy Mothers and Other New Ideas in French Art', *The Art Bulletin*, 55:4 (1973), 570–83

EICHNER, HANS, ed., *'Romantic' and its Cognates: The European History of a Word* (Manchester: Manchester University Press, 1972)

EL DIWANI, RACHIDA, *Le Discours Orientaliste de Volney* (Morrisville, NC: Lulu Press Inc., 2008)

ELDEN, STUART, and JEREMY W. CRAMPTON, *Space, Knowledge and Power: Foucault and Geography* (Brookfield: Taylor and Francis, 2016)

ESTOK, SIMON C., 'Shakespeare and Ecocriticism: An Analysis of "Home" and "Power" in *King Lear*', *Journal of the Australasian Universities Language and Literature Association*, 103 (2005), 13–36

FAGUET, ÉMILE, *A Literary History of France* (London: T.F. Unwin, 1907)

FAIRWEATHER, MARIA, *Mme de Staël* (London: Constable and Robinson, 2006)

FELLOWS, OTIS and DIANA GUIRAGOSSIAN CARR, eds., *Diderot Studies XX* (Genève: Droz: 1981)

FELMAN, SHOSHANA, 'Women and Madness: The Critical Phallacy', *Diacritics*, 5 (1975), 2–12

FERBER, MICHAEL, ed., *A Companion to European Romanticism* (Oxford: Blackwell, 2005)

FERMON, NICOLE, *Domesticating Passions: Rousseau, Woman, and Nation* (Hanover, NH: Wesleyan University Press, 1997)

FERRAND, NATHALIE, ed., *Locus in Fabula: La Topique de l'espace dans les fictions françaises d'Ancien Régime* (Louvain: Editions Peeters, 2004)

FIELD, NIGEL P., 'Whether to Relinquish or Maintain a Bond with the Deceased', in Margaret S. Stroebe, Robert O. Hansson, Henk Schut, and Wolfgang Stroebe, eds., *Handbook of Bereavement Research and Practice* (Washington, DC: American Psychological Association, 2008), pp. 113–32

FINCH, ALISON, *Women's Writing in Nineteenth-Century France* (Cambridge: Cambridge University Press, 2000)

FINNEY, GAIL, 'Garden Paradigms in Nineteenth-Century Fiction', *Comparative Literature*, 36:1 (1984), 20–33

FOLEY, SUSAN K., *Women in France since 1789: The Meaning of Difference* (Basingstoke: Palgrave Macmillan, 2004)

FONTANA, BIANCAMARIA 'Literary History and Political Theory in Germaine de Staël's Idea of Europe', in *The Oxford Handbook of European Romanticism*, ed. Paul Hamilton (Oxford: OUP, 2016)

FONTENAY, ÉLISABETH DE, *Diderot ou le matérialisme enchanté* (Paris: Grasset, 1981)

FOUCAULT, MICHEL, *Histoire de la folie à l'âge classique* (Paris: Gallimard, 1972)

——*History of Madness*, trans. Jonathan Murphy and Jean Khalfa (Oxford and New York: Routledge, 2009)

——*Naissance de la clinique* (Paris: Presses Universitaires de France, 1963)

——'Of Other Spaces', trans. by Jay Miskowiec, *Diacritics*, 16:1 (1986), 22–27

FRYE, NORTHROP, *Anatomy of Criticism: Four Essays* (Princeton, NJ: Princeton University Press, 1957)

——*A Study of English Romanticism* (New York: Random House, 1968)

FURST, LILIAN R., 'Romanticism in Historical Perspective', *Comparative Literature Studies*, 5:2 (1968), 115–43

——'The "Imprisoning Self": Goethe's Werther and Rousseau's Solitary Walker', in Gerhart Hoffmeister, ed., *European Romanticism: Literary Cross-Currents, Modes, and Models* (Detroit: Wayne State University Press, 1990), pp. 145–61

GALEWSKY, J., and others, 'Climate Over Landscapes', *Eos*, 89:16 (2008), 151

GASKILL, HOWARD, ed., *The Reception of Ossian in Europe* (London: Thoemmes Continuum, 2004)

GAULMIER, JEAN, 'Sophie et ses malheurs ou le romantisme du pathétique', *Romantisme*, 3 (1971), 3–16

GENGEMBRE, GÉRARD, 'Introduction to French Romanticism', in *European Romanticism: A Reader,* ed. by Stephen Pricket and Simon Haines (London: Continuum, 2010), pp. 33–37

——*Le Romantisme* (Paris: Ellipses, 1995)

GIDAL, ERIC, 'Civic Melancholy: English Gloom and French Enlightenment', *Eighteenth-Century Studies,* 37:1 (2003), 23–45

GILBERT, SANDRA M., and SUSAN GUBAR, *The Madwoman in the Attic: The Woman Writer and the Nineteenth-Century Literary Imagination* (New Haven & London: Yale University Press, 1979)

GILMAN, SANDER L., ed., *Hysteria Before Freud* (California: University of California Press, 1993)

GODERNE, RENÉ, 'Les Nouvellistes des Années 1780–1820', in Paul Viallaneix, ed., *Préromantisme: Hypothèque ou hypothèse?* (Paris: Klincksieck, 1975)

GOLDMAN, JANE, 'The Feminist Criticism of Virginia Woolf', in *A History of Feminist Literary Criticism,* ed. by Gill Plain and Susan Sellers (Cambridge: Cambridge University Press, 2007), pp. 66–84

GOODDEN, ANGELICA, *Madame de Staël: The Dangerous Exile* (Oxford: Oxford University Press, 2008)

GOUBIER-ROBERT, GENEVIÈVE, 'Sophie Ristaud-Cottin: Un *Sturm-und-Drang* à la française?', in *Études sur le XVIIIᵉ siècle: Portraits de Femmes,* ed. by Roland Mortier and Hervé Hasquin (Bruxelles: Éditions de l'Université de Bruxelles, 2000), pp. 53–60

GOULBOURNE, RUSSELL, and DAVID HIGGINS, eds., *Jean-Jacques Rousseau and British Romanticism: Gender and Selfhood, Politics and Nation* (London: Bloomsbury, 2017)

GREEN, F. C., *French Novelists From the Revolution to Proust* (London & Toronto: J. M. Dent & Sons Ltd., 1931)

GRIEDER, JOSEPHINE, *Anglomania in France 1740–1789: Fact, Fiction and Political Discourse* (Geneva: Librairie Droz, 1985)

GUIGNERY, VANESSA, CATHERINE, PESSO-MIQUEL, and FRANÇOIS SPECQ, eds., *Hybridity: Forms and Figures in Literature and the Visual Arts* (Newcastle: Cambridge Scholars Publishing, 2011)

GUTWIRTH, MADELYN, AVRIEL H. GOLDBERGER and KARYNA SZMURLO, eds., *Germaine de Staël: Crossing the Borders* (New Brunswick, NJ: Rutgers University Press, 1991)

HAAS, LYNDA, 'Of Waters and Women: The Philosophy of Luce Irigaray', *Hypatia* 8:4 (1993), 150–59

HABERMAS, JÜRGEN, *The Structural Transformation of the Public Sphere: An Inquiry into a Category of Bourgeois Society*, trans. by Thomas Burger with the assistance of Frederick Lawrence (Cambridge, MA: The MIT Press, 1991)

HADDAD, EMILY, *Orientalist Poetics: The Islamic Middle East in Nineteenth-Century English and French Poetry* (London; New York: Routledge, 2017)

HAGENENDER, FRED, *The Meaning of Trees: Botany, History, Healing, Lore* (San Francisco: Chronicle Books, 2005)

HALL, MARTIN, 'Eighteenth-century women novelists: genre and gender', in Sonya Stephens, ed., *A History of Women's Writing in France* (Cambridge: Cambridge University Press, 2000), pp. 102–19

HAMILTON, PAUL, ed., *The Oxford Handbook of European Romanticism* (Oxford: OUP, 2016)

HARKNESS, NIGEL, LISA DOWNING, SONYA STEPHENS, and TIMOTHY UNWIN, 'Introduction', in Nigel Harkness, Lisa Downing, Sonya Stephens, and Timothy Unwin, eds., *Birth and Death in Nineteenth-Century French Culture* (Amsterdam; New York: Rodopi, 2007), pp. 9–16

——*Birth and Death in Nineteenth-Century French Culture* (Amsterdam; New York: Rodopi, 2007)

HARSIN, JILL, 'Gender, Class, and Madness in Nineteenth Century France', *French Historical Studies*, 17:4 (1992), 1048–1070

HARTIG, K.V. and K.M. DUNN, 'Roadside Memorials: Interpreting New Deathscapes in Newcastle, New South Wales', *Australian Geographical Studies*, 36 (1998), 5–20

HEALEY, FRANK GEORGE, *The Literary Culture of Napoleon* (Genève: Librairie Droz, 1959)

HEATHCOTE, OWEN, *Balzac and Violence: Representing History, Space, Sexuality and Death in La Comédie humaine* (New York: Peter Lang, 2009)

HERMAN, DAVID, *Story Logic: Problems and Possibilities of Narrative* (Lincoln; London: University of Nebraska Press, 2002)

HESSE, CARLA, *The Other Enlightenment: How French Women became Modern* (Princeton: Princeton University Press, 2003)

HIGONNET, MARGARET, 'Suicide as Self-Construction', in *Germaine de Staël: Crossing the Borders*, ed. by Madelyn Gutwirth, Avriel Goldberger, and Karyna Szmurlo (New Brunswick, NJ: Rutgers, 1991), pp. 69–81

HILGER, STEPHANIE M., *Women Write Back: Strategies of Response and the Dynamics of European Literary Culture, 1790–1805* (Amsterdam; New York: Rodopi, 2009)

HOFFMANN, PAUL, *La Femme dans la pensée des Lumières* (Paris: Ophrys, 1977)

HOFFMEISTER, GERHART, ed., *European Romanticism: Literary Cross-Currents, Modes, and Models* (Detroit: Wayne State University Press, 1990)

HOMANS, MARGARET, *Women Writers and Poetic Identity: Dorothy Wordsworth, Emily Brontë, and Emily Dickinson* (Princeton: Princeton University Press, 1980)

HOOK, ANDREW, 'The French Taste for Scottish Literary Romanticism', in Deirdre Dawson and Pierre Morère, eds., *Scotland and France in the Enlightenment* (Lewisburg: Bucknell University Press, 2004), pp. 90–107

HOSFORD, DESMOND, and CHONG J. WOJTKOWSKI, eds., *French Orientalism: Culture, Poltics, and the Imagined Other* (Newcastle: Cambridge Scholars Publishing, 2010)

HOUSTON, R. A., 'Madness and Gender in the Long Eighteenth Century', *Social History*, 27:3 (2002), 309–26

HOWELLS, ROBIN, *Regressive Fictions: Graffigny, Rousseau, Bernardin* (London: Legenda, 2007)

HUNT, JOHN DIXON, *The Picturesque Garden in Europe* (London: Thames and Hudson, 2003)

HUOT, SYLVIA, *Madness in Medieval French Literature: Identities Found and Lost* (Oxford: Oxford University Press, 2003)

IMMERWAHR, RAYMOND, ' "Romantic" and its Cognates in England, Germany, and France before 1790', in Hans Eichner, ed., *'Romantic' and its Cognates: The European History of a Word* (Manchester: Manchester University Press, 1972), pp. 17–97

IRIGARAY, LUCE, *Ce sexe qui n'en est pas un* (Paris: Éditions de minuit, 1977)

ISBELL, JOHN CLAIBORNE, *The Birth of European Romanticism: Truth and Propaganda in Staël's De l'Allemagne, 1810–1813* (Cambridge: Cambridge University Press, 1994)

IZENBERG, GERALD N., 'Seduced and abandoned: The rise and fall of Freud's seduction theory', in Jerome Neu, ed., *The Cambridge Companion to Freud* (Cambridge: Cambridge University Press, 1991), pp. 25–43

JACOBSEN, ERIC O., *The Space Between: A Christian Engagement with the Built Environment* (Grand Rapids, MI: Baker Academic, 2012)

JACQUIER, CLAIRE, *L'Erreur des désirs: Romans sensibles au XVIIIe siècle* (Lausanne; Payot, 1998)

JATON, ANNE-MARIE, 'La Définition de la femininité dans 'Les Raports du physique et du moral, de Cabanis et dans *"La Loi naturelle de Volney"*,' ' in *Volney et les idéologues: Actes du colloque d'Angers,* ed. by Jean Roussel (Angers: Presses Universitaires d'Angers, 1988), pp. 183–91

JEFFERSON, ANN, *Biography and the Question of Literature in France* (Oxford: Oxford University Press, 2007)

JENNAWAY, MEGAN, *Sisters and Lovers: Women and Desire in Bali* (Lanham, MD: Rowman & Littlefield, 2002)

JENSEN, HEATHER BELNAP, *Portraitistes à la plume: Women Art Critics in Revolutionary and Napoleonic France* (University of Kansas: ProQuest, 2007)

JENSON, DEBORAH, "Hélène Cixous, Translator of History and Legend: *'Ce transport vertigineux'*", in Myriam Díaz-Diocaretz and Marta Segarra, eds., *Joyful Babel: Translating Hélène Cixous* (Amsterdam: Rodopi, 2004) pp. 197–204

JONES, JAMES FLEMING, *La Nouvelle Héloïse: Rousseau and Utopia* (Genève: Droz, 1977)

JORDANOVA, LUDMILLA, *Nature Displayed: Gender, Science and Medicine, 1760–1820* (London; New York, NY: Longman, 1999)

JUNG, HWA YOL, *Transversal Rationality and Intercultural Texts: Essays in Phenomenology and Comparative Philosophy* (Athens, OH: Ohio University Press, 2011)

JUVAN, MARKO, 'Spaces of Intertextuality / The Intertextuality of Space', *SDPK* (2004) Special Issue in English: 'Literature and Space. Spaces of Transgressiveness', <http://sdpk.zrc-sazu.si/PKrevija/2004-Literature&Space.htm#Marko%20Juvan>

——'Spaces, Transgressions and Intertextuality', in Jeff Bernard, Jurij Fikfak and Peter Grzybek, eds., *Text and Reality* (Ljubljana: ZRC Publishing, 2005), pp. 43–54

KADISH, DORIS Y., *The Literature of Images: Narrative Landscape from* Julie *to* Jane Eyre (New Brunswick and London: Rutgers University Press, 1987)

KALE, STEVEN, *French Salons: High Society and Political Sociability from the Old Regime to the revolution of 1848* (Baltimore: The Johns Hopkins University Press, 2004)

KATIBOGLU, MONICA, 'Constructing the Orient: Pierre Loti's Re-interpretations in *Aziyadé*', in Desmond Hosford and Chong J. Wojtkowski, eds., *French Orientalism: Culture, Poltics, and the Imagined Other* (Newcastle: Cambridge Scholars Publishing, 2010), pp. 135–36

KAY, SARAH, and MIRI RUBIN, eds., *Framing Medieval Bodies* (Manchester: Manchester University Press, 1994),

KELLY, JIM, ed., *Ireland and Romanticism: Publics, Nations and Scenes of Cultural Production* (London: Palgrave MacMillan, 2011)

KHALFA, JEAN, 'Introduction', in Michel Foucault, *History of Madness* (Oxford and New York: Routledge, 2009), pp. xv–xvi

KIEFER, CAROL SOLOMON, *The Empress Josephine: Art and Royal Identity* (Amherst: Amherst College, 2005)

KLASS, DENNIS, *The Spiritual Lives of Bereaved Parents* (Philadelphia: Taylor & Francis, 1999)

KLAUS, MARSHALL H., and JOHN H. KENNELL, *Maternal-Infant Bonding* (Saint Louis: The C.V. Mosby Company, 1976)

KLUCKERT, EHRENFRIED, *Parcs et jardins en Europe de l'antiquité à nos jours* (Potsdam: h.f.ullmann, 2005)

KNAPP, BETTINA L., review of Lloyd Bishop, *The Romantic Hero and his Heirs in French Literature* (1984), *The French Review*, 59:5 (1986), 787–88

KOLIG, ERICH, *Conservative Islam: A Cultural Anthropology* (Lanham, MD: Lexington Books, 2012)

KONG, L., 'Cemeteries and Columbaria, Memorials and Mausoleums: Narrative and Interpretation in the Study of Deathscapes in Geography', *Australian Geographical Studies*, 37:1, 1–10

KRISTEVA, JULIA, *The Impudence of Uttering: The Mother Tongue*, trans. by Anne Marsella, <http://www.kristeva.fr/impudence.html>

KROMM, JANE E., 'The Feminization of Madness in Visual Representation', *Feminist Studies*, 20:3 (1994), 507–35

LANDES, JOAN B., *Women and the Public Sphere in the Age of the French Revolution* (Ithaca, NY: Cornell University Press, 1988)

LANSER, SUSAN SNIADER, *Fictions of Authority: Women Writers and Narrative Voice* (Ithaca: Cornell University Press, 1992)

LAPLANCHE, JEAN, and J.-B. PONTALIS, *Vocabulaire de la psychanalyse* (Paris: Presses Universitaires de France, 1971)

LAQUEUR, THOMAS, *Making Sex: Body and Gender from the Greeks to Freud* (Cambridge, MA: Harvard University Press, 1990)

LARNAC, JEAN, *Histoire de la littérature féminine en France* (Poitiers: Impr. Nicolas, Renault et Cie; Paris, éditions Kra, 1929)

LASSERRE, PIERRE, *Le Romantisme français: essai sur la Révolution dans les sentiments et dans les idées au XIXe siècle* (Genève: Slatkine, 2000)

LAURENS, HENRY, 'L'orientalisme des Lumières', in *Penser l'Orient: Traditions et actualité des orientalismes français et allemands,* ed. by Youssef Courbage et Manfred Kropp (Beirut: Presses de l'Ifpo, 2004), pp. 103–28

LE BORGNE, FRANÇOISE, 'Idylle et intimité dans *Les Jardins* de Delille' in S. Bernard-Griffiths, F. Le Borgne and Daniel Madelénat, *Jardins Et Intimité Dans La Littérature Européenne (1750–1920): Actes Du Colloque Du Centre De Recherches Révolutionnaires Et Romantiques, Université Blaise-Pascal (Clermont-Ferrand, 22–24 Mars 2006)* (Clermont-Ferrand: Presses universitaires Blaise-Pascal, 2008), pp. 67–79

LE MÉNAHÈZE, SOPHIE, 'Le jardin pittoresque entre ouverture et exclusion: les paradoxes de l'intimité', in S. Bernard-Griffiths, F. Le Borgne and Daniel Madelénat, eds., *Jardins Et Intimité Dans La Littérature Européenne (1750–1920): Actes Du Colloque Du Centre De Recherches Révolutionnaires Et Romantiques, Université Blaise-Pascal (Clermont-Ferrand, 22–24 Mars 2006)* (Clermont-Ferrand: Presses Universitaires Blaise-Pascal, 2008), pp. 42–53

LEASK, NIGEL, *British Romantic Writers and the East: Anxieties of Empire* (Cambridge: Cambridge University Press, 2000)

LECERLE, JEAN-LOUIS, 'La femme selon Jean-Jacques', in *Jean-Jacques Rousseau: Quatre études* (Neuchâtel: Editions de la Baconnière, 1978)

LEFEBVRE, H., *The Production of Space* (Oxford; Cambridge, MA: Blackwell, 1991)

LEVY, GAYLE A., 'A Genius for the Modern Era: Madame De Staël's *Corinne*', *Nineteenth-Century French Studies*, 30:3/4, 2002, 242–53

LEY, FRANCIS, 'Madame de Krüdener (1764–1824), in *Études sur le XVIIIe siècle: Portrais de Femmes,* ed. by Roland Mortier and Hervé Hasquin (Bruxelles: Éditions de l'Université de Bruxelles, 2000), pp. 61–74

——*Madame de Krüdener et son temps* (Paris: Plon, 1962)

LEY, FRANCIS and JEAN GAULMIER, *Madame de Krüdener, 1764–1824: romantisme et Sainte-Alliance* (Paris: Champion, 1994)

LIDDLE, JOANNA and SHIRIN RAI, 'Feminism, Imperialism and Orientalism: the challenge of the "Indian Woman"', in *Women's History Review*, 7:4 (1998), pp. 495–520

LLOYD, GENEVIEVE, *The Man of Reason: 'Male' and 'Female' in Western Philosophy* (Minnea-polis: University of Minnesota Press, 1984)

LOGAN, CAROLYN, *Counterbalance: Gendered Perspectives on Writing and Language* (Peterborough, Ontario: Braodview Press, 1997)

LOOSER, DEVONEY, 'Preface', in *The Cambridge Companion to Women's Writing in the Romantic Period* , ed. by Devoney Looser (Cambridge: CUP, 2015), p. xiii–xvi

——, ed., *The Cambridge Companion to Women's Writing in the Romantic Period* (Cambridge: CUP, 2015)

LOUGEE, CAROLYN C., *Le Paradis des Femmes: Women, Salons and Social Stratification in Seventeenth-Century France* (Princeton, NJ: Princeton University Press, 1976)

LOUICHON, BRIGITTE, *Romancières sentimentales, 1789–1825* (Saint-Denis: Presses Universitaires de Vincennes, 2009)

MACARTHUR, ELIZABETH, 'The Tomb in the Garden in Late Eighteenth-Century France', *Dalhousie French Studies*, 29 (1994), 97–111

MACCORMACK, CAROL P., and MARILYN STRATHERN, *Nature, culture, and gender* (Cambridge: Cambridge University Press, 1980)

MADDRELL, AVRIL, and JAMES D. SIDAWAY, eds., *Deathscapes: Spaces for Death, Dying, Mourning and Remembrance* (Surrey, UK; Burlington VT: Ashgate, 2010)

MAKSUD, MONIQUE and ALFRED NIZARD, 'Enfants trouvés, reconnus, légitimés: Les Statistiques de la filiation en France, aux XIXe et XXe siècles', *Population*, 6 (1977), 1159–1220

MANDAL, ANTHONY, 'Fiction', in *The Cambridge Companion to Women's Writing in the Romantic Period* , ed. by Devoney Looser (Cambridge: CUP, 2015), pp. 16–31

MANN, MARIA, *La Mère dans la littérature française 1678–1831* (New York: Peter Lang, 1989)

MARGRAVE, CHRISTIE, 'Early Developments of Ecofeminist Thought in French Women's Early Romantic Fiction', *Essays in French Literature and Culture*, 55 (2018) 43–62

MARONGIU-PERRIA, OMERO, *En finir avec les idées fausses sur l'islam et les musulmans* (Ivry-sur-Seine: Éditions de l'Atelier, 2017)

MARTIN, PHILIP W., *Mad Women in Romantic Writing* (Sussex: The Harvester Press; New York: St. Martin's Press, 1987)

MARTINET, MARIE-MADELEINE, *Le Voyage d'Italie dans les littératures européennes* (Paris: Presses Universitaires de France, 1996)

MASSEY, DOREEN, *Space, Place and Gender* (Cambridge: Polity Press, 1994)

MASUY-STROOBANT, GENEVIÈVE, ET MICHEL POULAIN, 'La variation spatiale et temporelle du déclin de la mortalité infantile dans nos régions', *Espace, populations, sociétés*, 1 (1983), 67–73

MATLOCK, JANN, 'Novels of testimony and the 'invention' of the modern French novel', in T. Unwin, ed., *The Cambridge Companion to the French Novel: From 1800 to the Present* (Cambridge: Cambridge University Press, 1997), pp. 16–35

McCALLAM, DAVID, 'The Volcano: From Enlightenment to Revolution', *Nottingham French Studies*, 45:1 (2006), 52–68

McCARTHY, CONOR, *The Cambridge Introduction to Edward Said* (Cambridge: Cambridge University Press, 2010)

McCLELLAND, J.S., *A History of Western Political Thought* (London; New York: Routledge, 2005)

McINTOSH, CHRISTOPHER, *Gardens of the Gods: Myth, Magic and Meaning* (London: I.B. Tauris & Co Ltd., 2005)

McKUSICK, JAMES C., 'Nature', in Michael Ferber, ed., *A Companion to European Romanticism* (Oxford: Blackwell, 2005), pp. 413–32

McMANNERS, JOHN, *Death and the Enlightenment: Changing Attitudes to Death among Christians and Unbelievers in Eighteenth-Century France* (New York: Oxford University Press, 1981)

McMILLAN, JAMES F., *France and Women: 1789–1914* (London: Routledge, 2000)

MELLOR, ANNE K., 'Feminism', in *Romanticism: An Oxford Guide*, ed. by Nicholas Roe (Oxford: Oxford University Press, 2005), pp. 182–98

MERCHANT, CAROLYN, *Earthcare: Women and the Environment* (New York: Routledge, 1995)

——*Radical Ecology: The Search for a Livable World* (New York: Routledge, 2005)

MERCIER, ROGER, *L'Enfant dans la Société du XVIIIe siècle (Avant Émile)* (Dakar: Université Faculté des Lettres et Sciences Humaines, 1961)

MERCKEN-SPAAS, GODELIEVE, 'Death and the Romantic Heroine: Chateaubriand and de Staël', in Robert L. Mitchell, ed., *Pre-text, Text, Context: Essays on Nineteenth-Century French Literature* (Columbus, OH: Ohio State University Press, 1980), pp. 79–86

MERRICK, JEFFREY, 'Patterns and Prosecution of Suicide in Eighteenth-Century Paris', *Historical Reflections*, 16:1 (1989), 1–53

——'Rescued from the River: Attempted Suicide in Late Eighteenth-Century Paris', *Social History*, 49:98 (2016), 27–47

MILLER, MARGARET, 'Géricault's Paintings of the Insane', *Journal of the Warburg and Courtauld Institutes*, 4:3–4 (1941–1942), 151–63

MINSKI, ALEXANDER, *Le Préromantisme* (Paris: Armand Colin, 1998)

MITCHELL, ROBERT L., ed., *Pre-text, Text, Context: Essays on Nineteenth-Century French Literature* (Columbus, OH: Ohio State University Press, 1980)

MONGLOND, ANDRÉ, *Le Préromantisme français*, 2 vols (Rennes: Presses des Imprimeries réunies, 1965)

MONLEÓN, JOSÉ, *A Specter is Haunting Europe: A Sociohistorical Approach to the Fantastic* (Princeton: Princeton University Press, 1990)

MONNIER, PHILIPPE, *Venice in the Eighteenth Century* (London: Chatto & Windus, 1910)

MOORE, FABIENNE, 'Early French Romanticism', in *A Companion to European Romanticism*, ed. by Michael Ferber (Oxford: Blackwell, 2005), pp. 172–91

MORNET, DANIEL, *Le Sentiment de la nature en France de J.-J. Rousseau à Bernardin de Saint-Pierre* (Genève: Slatkine, 1980)

MORTIER, ROLAND, and HERVÉ HASQUIN, eds., *Études sur le XVIIIe siècle: Portrais de Femmes* (Bruxelles: Éditions de l'Université de Bruxelles, 2000)

MOSSER, MONIQUE and GEORGES TEYSSOT, 'Introduction: The Architecture of the Garden and Architecture in the Garden', in Mosser, Monique and Georges Teyssot, eds., *The History of Garden Design. The Western Tradition from the Renaissance to the Present Day* (London: Thames and Hudson Ltd., 1991), pp. 11–23

——*The History of Garden Design. The Western Tradition from the Renaissance to the Present Day* (London: Thames and Hudson Ltd., 1991)

MOUSSA, SARGA, 'Imaginary Hybridities: Geographic, Religious and Poetic Crossovers in Victor Hugo's "Les Orientales"', in Vanessa Guignery, Catherine Pesso-Miquel and François Specq, eds., *Hybridity: Forms and Figures in Literature and the Visual Arts* (Newcastle: Cambridge Scholars Publishing, 2011), pp. 280–90

MURRAY, CHRISTOPHER JOHN, ed., *Encyclopedia of the Romantic Era, 1760–1850*, 2 vols (New York: Fitzroy Dearborn, 2004)

MURRAY, MARY, 'Laying Lazarus to Rest: The Place and the Space of the Dead in Explanations of Near Death Experiences', in Avril Maddrell and James D. Sidaway, eds., *Deathscapes: Spaces for Death, Dying, Mourning and Remembrance* (Surrey, UK; Burlington VT: Ashgate, 2010), pp. 37–54

NAPIER, SUSAN, *The Fantastic in Modern Japanese Literature: The Subversion of Modernity* (London; New York: Routledge, 1996)

NEMOIANU, VIRGIL, *The Taming of Romanticism: European Literature and the Age of Biedermeier* (Cambridge, MA: Harvard University Press, 1984)

NEU, JEROME, ed., *The Cambridge Companion to Freud* (Cambridge: Cambridge University Press, 1991)

NHANENGE, J., *Ecofeminism: Towards Integrating the Concerns of Women, Poor People, and Nature into Development* (Lanham: University Press of America, 2011)

NICHOLS, ROSE STANDISH, *English Pleasure Gardens* (Jaffrey, NH: David R. Godine, 2003)

NICHOLSON, MARJORIE HOPE, *Mountain Gloom and Mountain Glory, the development of the aesthetics of the Infinite* (Cornell: Cornell University Press, 1997)

NOAKES, SUSAN, 'The Rhetoric of Travel: The French Romantic Myth of Naples', *Ethnohistory*, 33:2 (1986), 139–48

NYE, ROBERT A., 'Forum: Biology, Sexuality and Morality in Eighteenth-Century France: Introduction', *Eighteenth-Century Studies*, 35:2 (2002), 235–38

O'NEILL, MICHAEL, MARK SANDY, and SARAH WOOTTON, eds., *Venice and the Cultural Imagination: 'This Strange Dream Upon the Water'* (Oxford: Routledge, 2016)

ORTNER, SHERRY B., 'Is Female to Male as Nature is to Culture?', *Feminist Studies*, 1:2 (1972), 5–31

O'SHEA-MEDDOUR, WENDY, 'Gaston Bachelard's *L'Eau et les rêves:* conquering the feminine element', *French Cultural Studies* 14:1 (2003), 81–99

Oxford English Dictionary, <http://www.oed.com>

PACINI, GIULIA, 'A Culture of Trees: The Politics of Pruning and Felling in Late Eighteenth-Century France', *Eighteenth-Century Studies*, 41:1 (2007), 1–15

PASCO, ALLAN H., *Sick Heroes: French Society and Literature in the Romantic Age, 1750–1850* (Exeter: University of Exeter Press, 1997)

PELCKMANS, PAUL, 'L'Écosse des Romancières', in Nathalie Ferrand, ed., *Locus in Fabula: La Topique de l'espace dans les fictions françaises d'Ancien Régime* (Louvain: Editions Peeters, 2004), pp. 249–59

PLAIN, GILL and SUSAN SELLERS, *A History of Feminist Literary Criticism* (Cambridge: Cambridge University Press, 2007)

POORTERE, MACHTELD DE, *The Philosophical and literary Ideas of Mme de Staël and of Mme de Genlis* (New York: Peter Lang, 2007)

POPIEL, JENNIFER J., *Rousseau's Daughters: Domesticity, Education, and Autonomy in Modern France* (Durham, New Hampshire: University of New Hampshire Press, 2008)

PRICKETT, STEPHEN, 'General Introduction', in *European Romanticism: A Reader*, ed. by Stephen Pricket and Simon Haines (London: Continuum, 2010), pp. 1–20

PRICKET, STEPHEN and SIMON HAINES, eds., *European Romanticism: A Reader* (London: Continuum, 2010)

RACAULT, JEAN-MICHEL, *L'Utopie narrative en France et en Angleterre 1675–1761* (Oxford: Voltaire Foundation, 1991)

RILEY, DENISE, 'Does Sex Have a History? 'Women' and Feminism', *New Formations*, 1 (1987), 35–45

RIPA, YANNICK, *Women and Madness: The Incarceration of Women in Nineteenth-Century France* (Cambridge: Polity Press, 1990)

ROBB, BONNIE ARDEN, *Félicité de Genlis: Motherhood in the Margins* (Newark: University of Delaware Press, 2008)

ROBERTS, HELENE E., *Encyclopedia of Comparative Iconography: Themes Depicted in Works of Art* (Chicago; London: Fitzroy Dearborn, 1998)

ROGERS, NANCY, 'The Wasting Away of Romantic Heroines', *Nineteenth-Century French Studies*, 11:3–4 (1983), 246–56

ROUSSEL, JEAN, ed., *Volney et les idéologues: Actes du colloque d'Angers* (Angers: Presses Universitaires d'Angers, 1988)

SAAR, MAARJA and HANNES PALANG, 'The Dimensions of Place Meanings', *Living Reviews in Landscape Research*, 3 (2009), 1–24

SAGLIA, DIEGO, 'Orientalism', in *A Companion to European Romanticism,* ed. by Michael Ferber (Oxford: Blackwell, 2005), pp. 467–85

SAID, EDWARD W., *Orientalism* (London: Penguin, 2003)

SANDY, MARK, 'Reimagining Venice and Visions of Decay in Wordsworth, The Shelleys and Thomas Mann', in Michael O'Neill, Mark Sandy and Sarah Wootton, eds., *Venice and the Cultural Imagination: 'This Strange Dream Upon the Water'* (Oxford: Routledge, 2016), pp. 27–42

SANTARCANGELI, P., *Le Livre des labyrinthes* (Paris: Gallimard, 1974 [1967])

SCHAMA, SIMON, *Landscape and Memory* (London: Harper Perennial, 2004)

SCHRODER, ANNE L., 'Going Public Against the Academy in 1784: Mme de Genlis Speaks out on Gender Bias', *Eighteenth-Century Studies*, 32:3 (1999), 376–82

SCHWARTZ, JOEL, *The Sexual Politics of Jean-Jacques Rousseau* (Chicago: The University of Chicago Press, 1985)

SCOTT, JOHN T., *Jean-Jacques Rousseau: Critical Assessments of Leading Political Philosophers* (London; New York: Routledge, 2006)

SCOTT, MICHAEL, *Struggle for the Soul of the French Novel* (Basingstoke: Macmillan, 1989)

SHERIDAN, GERALDINE, *Louder than Words: Ways of Seeing Women Workers in Eighteenth-Century France* (Lubbock, TX: Texas Tech University Press, 2009)

——'Women in the Book Trade in Eighteenth-Century France', *British Journal for Eighteenth-Century Studies*, 15 (1992), 51–70

SHERMAN, CAROL L., *The Family Crucible in Eighteenth-Century Literature* (Burlington, VT; Aldershot, UK: Ashgate, 2005)

SHOWALTER, ELAINE, 'Hysteria, Feminism, and Gender', in Sander L. Gilman, ed., *Hysteria Before Freud* (California: University of California Press, 1993)

——*The Female Malady: Women, Madness and English Culture, 1830–1980* (London: Virago, 1987)

SIMON, BENNETT and RACHEL B. BLASS, 'The Development and Vicissitudes of Freud's Ideas on the Oedipus Complex', in *The Cambridge Companion to Freud,* ed. by in Jerome Neu (Cambridge: Cambridge University Press, 1991), pp. 161–74

SLAMA, BÉATRICE, 'Femmes écrivains', in Jean-Paul Aron, ed., *Misérable et glorieuse, la femme du XIXe siècle* (Paris: Fayard, 1980), pp. 213–43

SMALL, HELEN, *Love's Madness: Medicine, the Novel, and Female Insanity, 1800–1865* (Oxford: Clarendon Press, 1996)

SMETHURST, COLIN, 'Chateaubriand's Ossian', in Howard Gaskill, ed., *The Reception of Ossian in Europe* (London: Thoemmes Continuum, 2004), pp. 126–42

SNAITH, A., *Virginia Woolf: Public and Private Negotiations* (New York: Palgrave Macmillan, 2003)

SOURIAU, MAURICE, *Histoire du romantisme en France,* 3 vols (Genève: Slatkine, 1973)

SPENCER, SAMIA I., ed., *French Women and the Age of Enlightenment* (Bloomington: Indiana University Press, 1984)

SPITZER, LEO, 'The "Ode on a Grecian Urn," or Content vs. Metagrammar', *Comparative Literature,* 7:3 (1955), 203–25

STAFFORD, FIONA, *The Sublime Savage: A Study of James Macpherson and the Poems of Ossian* (Edinburgh, 1988)

STEPHENS, SONYA, ed., *A History of Women's Writing in France* (Cambridge: Cambridge University Press, 2000)

STEWART, JOAN HINDE, *Gynographs: French Novels by Women of the Late Eighteenth Century* (Lincoln and London: University of Nebraska Press, 1993)

STOOKEY, LORENA, *Thematic Guide to World Mythology* (Westport, CT; London, UK: Greenwood Press, 2004)

STROEBE, MARGARET S., ROBERT O HANSSON, HENK SCHUT, and WOLFGANG STROEBE, eds., *Handbook of Bereavement Research and Practice* (Washington, DC: American Psychological Association, 2008)

STUART, ANDREA, *Josephine: The Rose of Martinique* (London: Pan Macmillan, 2011)

SWENSEN, ANDREW, 'Theology and Religious Thought', in Christopher John Murray, ed., *Encyclopedia of the Romantic Era, 1760–1850,* 2 vols (New York: Fitzroy Dearborn, 2004), II, pp. 1128–1130

SYKES, LESLIE, *Madame Cottin* (Oxford: Basil Blackwell, 1949)

SZMURLO, KARYNA, ed., *The Novel's Seductions, Staël's* Corinne *in Critical Inquiry* (Cranbury, NJ; London, England; Mississauga, Ontario: Associated University Presses, 1999)

TANNER, TONY, *Venice Desired* (Cambridge, MA: Harvard University Press, 1992)

TEO, HSU-MING, *Desert Passions: Orientalism and Romance Novels* (Austin: University of Texas Press, 2012)

TEODORESCU, ADRIANA, ed., *Death Representations in Literature: Forms and Theories* (Newcastle: Cambridge Scholars Publishing, 2015)

THOMAS, RUTH P., 'The Death of an Ideal: Female Suicides in the Eighteenth-Century French Novel', in Samia I. Spencer, ed., *French Women and the Age of Enlightenment* (Bloomington: Indiana University Press, 1984), pp. 321–31

TOUBIN-MALINAS, CATHERINE, *Heurs et malheurs de la femme au XIXe siècle: 'Fécondité' D'Émile Zola* (Paris: Méridiens Klincksieck, 1986)

TRAER, JAMES F., *Marriage and the Family in Eighteenth-Century France* (Ithaca; London: Cornell University Press, 1980)

TRAHARD, PIERRE, *Les Maîtres de la sensibilité française au XVIIIe siècle (1715–1789),* 4 vols (Paris: Boivin, 1931–33)

TROUILLE, MARY SEIDMAN, *Sexual Politics in the Enlightnment: Women Writers Read Rousseau* (Albany, NY: State University of New York Press, 1997)

TUAN, YI-FU, *Space and Place: The Perspective of Experience* (Minneapolis, MN: University of Minnesota Press, 1977)

TURNER, TOM, *Garden History: Philosophy and Design 2000 BC–2000 AD* (London and New York: Spon Press, 2005)

UNWIN, TIMOTHY, ed., *The Cambridge Companion to the French Novel* (Cambridge: Cambridge University Press, 1997)

USSHER, JANE M., *The Madness of Women* (London and New York: Routledge, 2011)

VAILLANT, ALAIN, ed., *Dictionnaire du Romantisme* (Paris: CNRS Editions, 2012)

VAN TIEGHEM, PAUL, *Le Préromantisme: études d'histoire littéraire européenne,* 3 vols (Paris: Felix Alcan, 1924–1947)

——*Le Sentiment de la nature dans le préromantisme européen* (Paris: A. G. Nizet, 1960)

——'Ossian en France', in *The French Quarterly*, I: 2 & 3 (1919), 78–87

——*Ossian en France* (Paris: Rieder & Cie, 1917)

VAN TIEGHEM, PHILIPPE, *Histoire de la littérature française* (Paris: Fayard, 1949)

——*Le Romantisme français* (Paris: Presses Universitaires de France, 1999)

VENKATARAMAN, PRABHU, 'Romanticism, Nature, and Self-Reflection in Rousseau's *Reveries of a Solitary Walker*', in *Cosmos and History: The Journal of Natural and Social Philosophy*, 11:1 (2015), 327–41

VIALLANEIX, PAUL, ed., *Préromantisme: Hypothèque ou hypothèse?* (Paris: Klincksieck, 1975)

VICENS-PUJOL, CARLOTA, 'Du jardin à l'île, de l'île au jardin: un parcours (1760–1875)', in S. Bernard-Griffiths, F. Le Borgne and Daniel Madelénat, *Jardins Et Intimité Dans La Littérature Européenne (1750–1920): Actes Du Colloque Du Centre De Recherches Révolutionnaires Et Romantiques, Université Blaise-Pascal (Clermont-Ferrand, 22–24 Mars 2006)* (Clermont-Ferrand: Presses universitaires Blaise-Pascal, 2008), pp. 117–28

VINCENT, PATRICK, 'A Continent of Corinnes: The Romantic Poetess and the Diffusion of Liberal Culture in Europe, 1815–1850', in *A Companion to European Romanticism*, ed. by Michael Ferber (Oxford: Blackwell, 2005), pp. 486–504

VOLKAN, VAMIK D., *Linking Objects and Linking Phenomena: A Study of the Forms, Symptoms, Metapsychology, and Therapy of Complicated Mourning* (New York: International Universities Press, Inc., 1981)

VOVELLE, MICHEL, *La Mort et l'Occident de 1300 à nos jours* (Paris: Gallimard, 1983)

WALLER, MARGARET, *The Male Malady: Fictions of Impotence in the French Romantic Novel* (New Brunswick, NJ: Rutgers University Press, 1993)

WALKER, LESLEY H., *A Mother's Love: Crafting Feminine Virtue in Enlightenment France* (Lewisburg: Bucknell University Press, 2008)

WARMAN, CAROLINE, 'Pre-Romantic French Thought,' in *The Oxford Handbook of European Romanticism*, ed. Paul Hamilton (Oxford: OUP, 2016), pp. 17–32

WEBB, RUTH, '*Ekphrasis* ancient and modern: the invention of a genre', *Word and Image*, 15:1 (1999), 7–18

——*Ekphrasis, Imagination and Persuasion in Ancient Rhetorical Theory and Practice* (Burlington, VT: Ashgate, 2009)

WEISGERBER, JEAN, *L'Espace romanesque* (Lausanne: Editions L'Age d'Homme, 1978)

WEISS, PENNY A., 'Rousseau, Antifeminism, and Woman's Nature', *Political Theory* 15:1 (1987), 81–98

WELLMAN, KATHLEEN, 'Physicians and Philosophes: Physiology and Sexual Morality in the French Enlightenment', in *Eighteenth-Century Studies*, 35:2 (2002), 267–77

WHITE, NICHOLAS, *French Divorce Fiction from the Revolution to the First World War* (Oxford: Legenda, 2013)

WILLIAMS, DAVID, *Rousseau: Les Rêveries du Promeneur Solitaire* (London: Grant & Cutler, 1984)

WINEGARTEN, RENEE, *Accursed Politics: Some French Women Writers and Political Life, 1715–1850* (Chicago: Ivan R. Dee, 2003)

——*Mme de Staël* (Leamington Spa: Berg, 1985)

WINN, SHAN M. M., *Heaven, Heroes and Happiness: The Indo-European Roots of Western Ideology* (Lanham, MD: University Press of America, 1995)

WINOCK, MICHEL, *Mme de Staël* (Paris: Fayard, 2010)

WOGAN-BROWNE, JOCELYN, 'Chaste Bodies: Frames and Experiences', in Sarah Kay and Miri Rubin, eds., *Framing Medieval Bodies* (Manchester: Manchester University Press, 1994), pp. 24–42

WOLFGANG, AURORA, *Gender and Voice in the French Novel, 1730–1782* (Burlington, VT: Ashgate, 2004)

YEGENOGLU, MEYDA, *Colonial Fantasies: Towards a Feminist Reading of Orientalism* (Cambridge: Cambridge University Press, 1998)

ZONANA, JOYCE, 'The Sultan and the Slave: Feminist Orientalism and the Structure of *Jane Eyre*', in *Signs,* 18:3 (1993), pp. 592–617

INDEX

❖